CW00827982

David Zeisberger

David Zeisberger, 1721–1808.

Courtesy of the Moravian Church Archives.

David Zeisberger

A Life among the Indians

Earl P. Olmstead

Foreword by George W. Knepper

The Kent State University Press

KENT, OHIO, & LONDON, ENGLAND

Library of Congress Catalog Card Number 96-30833
ISBN 0-87338-568-3
Manufactured in the United States of America

04 03 02 01 00 99 98 97 5 4 3 2 1

Library of Congress Cataloging-in-Publication Data
Olmstead, Earl P., 1920–
David Zeisberger : a life among the Indians / Earl P. Olmstead ;
foreword by George W. Knepper.
p. cm.
Includes bibliographical references (p.) and index.
ISBN 0-87338-568-3 (cloth : alk. paper) ∞
1. Zeisberger, David, 1721–1808. 2. Delaware Indians—Missions.
3. Delaware Indians—History—Sources. 4. Missionaries—Ohio—
Tuscarawas River Valley—Biography. 5. Moravian Church—Missions—
Ohio—Tuscarawas River Valley. 6. Tuscarawas River Valley (Ohio)—
History—Sources. I. Zeisberger, David, 1721–1808. II. Title.
E99.D2Z457 1991
977.1'03'092—dc20
[B] 96-30833

British Library Cataloging-in-Publication data are available.

To my father

Earl Gilmore Olmstead

who taught me

the love of history

Contents

APPENDIXES

Illustrations

Foreword

THE WRITING of history is subject to fashions as new social attitudes direct attention to formerly neglected or "misunderstood" aspects of American life. And so it is with the history of the American Indians. Their story has long fascinated scholars and the inspired amateurs who have created a vast literature on the subject. Perhaps too much of this effort was directed at describing Indian peoples largely through their interaction with Euro-Americans. Familiar stereotypes resulted—the courageous frontiersmen defending their lonely forest plots from savage attack; the idle Indian failing to develop the rich lands he inhabited and standing in the way of those who would. Some writers made romantic figures of tribal life and leaders. Few, however, showed Indians as real people subject to the full range of human virtues and vices, people who had their own legitimate views about the significance of white intrusion and how best to counteract or adapt to it.

The raising of social consciousness in the post–World War II era led to a plethora of studies directed at formerly neglected or underplayed segments of American society—women, minorities, immigrants. In like manner, a new generation of scholars reevaluated American Indian history. In this process historians expanded their reach by borrowing techniques from anthropology, linguistics, demography, and other specialties. Thus as "ethnohistorians" they recast American Indian history. Their special virtue was to enhance the Indian voice and viewpoint.

They also demonstrated what the Indian peoples had contributed to the adaptation of Euro-American culture in the New World. In the recent past, much has been written about the "middle ground" resulting from prolonged interaction between Indian and Euro-American cultures.

When used with proper caution, the ethnohistorical approach has added to our understanding of Indian cultures and has provided a more evenhanded description of their interaction with whites. But just as many early histories gave excessive credit to white frontiersmen and echoed their self-righteous accounts of the "invasion" of Indian lands, so some revisionist studies come close to reestablishing the myth of the "noble savage." Indians are pictured as superior to whites in matters of personal honor, environmental responsibility, and purity of motive.

Earl Olmstead has done us a service in these pages by retelling the dramatic story of one of the more successful efforts to reconcile Indian and Euro-American cultures. David Zeisberger and his fellow Moravian missionaries came to America with the best of motives. They wanted to convert the Indian peoples to their vision of the Christian faith and the uplifting lifestyles that they believed accompanied it. In the process, they would preserve the constructive features of native life. The Christian Indian would be taught how to improve his lot in life without, in the process, destroying his self-esteem and self-identity.

Some may argue that *any* trifling with native custom was presumptuous and demonstrated a lamentable European arrogance. Such persons overlook the hard realities of history, for the human record is replete with an unbroken succession of cultural modifications imposed by one group upon another. Pure, undisturbed cultural isolation in times of geographical expansion is a will-o-the-wisp.

Cultural clash is inevitable when one people confront another in a contest for territory and status. It is interesting and instructive to read how David Zeisberger and his fellow Moravians handled that situation in an effort to minimize the social trauma. Zeisberger was indeed "indomitable" in this effort, and he led one of history's most successful efforts at reconciling Indian and white interests. One can only wonder how the course of our nation might have differed if his model had endured and prevailed.

This volume's overarching contribution is that it reveals the Indian peoples in all their humanity. Some are the good citizens that one finds in every culture. A few exhibit extraordinary talents. A few are social misfits, mean-spirited people disliked by their own people and a threat to Zeisberger's work. We find instances when ordinarily reliable leaders dissimulate: they speak with the "forked tongue" so often attributed to whites. Some Indian converts make a lifetime commitment to the new Christian faith to which they hold through thick and thin. Some join the mission villages only to serve their short-term interests.

These observations were made by consecrated and dedicated friends of the Indians. The Moravians got no satisfaction from reporting incidents of misconduct or abandonment. There is no hint of the attitude, "well, what can you expect of a Indian?" Instead, each loss is sincerely regretted and becomes a catalyst for self-examination: "What might we have done to prevent this?"

David Zeisberger emerges in this volume as a man of substance whose accomplishments deserve to be better known. He believed in his cause: to bring enlightenment to the Indian peoples. He learned their languages and their customs. On their behalf, he made arduous and dangerous journeys that would have deterred all but the most committed. His preaching and teaching were enhanced by his organizational abilities. He kept his courage and supported his converts through one disaster after another. He earned the trust of those who followed him and the respect of most who did not.

This volume should be read in conjunction with Earl Olmstead's earlier work, *Blackcoats among the Delaware* (Kent: Kent State University Press, 1991), which concludes the story of Zeisberger and his converts. Together these books provide the scholar with invaluable source material and the interested reader with an instructive and exciting story. These books will now stand along with the physical properties at Schoenbrunn, Gnadenhutten, and Goshen in Ohio's Tuscarawas River Valley as memorials to a brave people and their experiment in cultural reconciliation

George W. Knepper

Preface

DAVID ZEISBERGER is a relatively unknown historical character. Yet he has been judged "A Candle of Hope," lighting the way to a better way of life for a substantial number of Native Americans whose lives he touched.

David Zeisberger was a zealot, like many other missionaries of his time. James Axtell, in *The Invasion Within: The Contest of Cultures in Colonial North America*, explains that, "Christianity, from its inception, has been an evangelical and proselytizing religion. Jesus Christ preached the spiritual conquest of the world and both the Old and New Testament relate the epic story ending in the Last Day of Judgment. Conversion is essential to its very nature and missionaries are the life blood of its survival."

In 1732, the Moravian Church became the first Protestant church to dedicate itself to mission work, and Zeisberger was one of its most distinguished evangelists. For sixty-three years he lived and worked among Native Americans. None of his contemporaries approached this record. He loved the Indians, and they returned his affection; otherwise he would have been forced to leave their villages long before his death in 1808.

Zeisberger's approach was distinctly different from that of most missionaries who lived among the Indians during the eighteenth and nineteenth centuries. He loved the Indians, spoke their language fluently, and admired many of their cultural traits. He also understood their desperate attempt to fight the ever-encroaching Euro-American efforts to dislodge them from their lands. He did not attempt to convert the natives to the white man's world but desperately tried to reach an accommodation between the native culture and mission life.

He did not insist that the mission Indians adopt all of the white man's cultural traits, as was standard practice among nineteenth-century missionaries, notably at the Carlisle School for Indian Children. Rather, he took a halfway approach, borrowing from native culture characteristics that did not conflict with his Christian teachings. He did not attempt to remove his converts from their native environment but to find an accommodation near to their friends and neighbors.

Zeisberger's mission had strict rules, but those who violated them were always shown compassion and were usually forgiven and permitted to remain at the mission, providing they agreed to mend their ways and abide by the rules. Little attempt was made to restrict the wandering nature of the native lifestyle. Mission Indians were permitted to travel and visit their relatives providing they notified the native helper in the village. This rule was primarily designed to keep track of all village residences. Their native friends' or relatives' visits to the missions were not restricted, and the mission villagers entertained numerous native and white visitors.

The village residents had great respect for the peace and orderliness of the mission village and the security from hunger that constantly threatened native villages. This sense of security was one of Zeisberger's most important contributions. Most native life was a continuous cycle of feast and famine. Mission Indians did not depart for weeks in April and May fighting with their enemies, but instead planted the corn crop for food for the cold winter season. The introduction of hogs and cattle and the growing of vegetables provided the Indians meat, milk, and wholesome food. All visitors to a Moravian mission were fed immediately—an old Indian custom that Zeisberger adopted during his early training as a missionary. Friend or foe would be in a more amenable mood with a full stomach.

None of the Moravian missions, including Zeisberger's, was a communal settlement. Each convert built his own home, fenced and planted his own "plantation," and was responsible for the care and feeding of his family. Tending the orchards, however, was a community project, and the crop was shared by all the villagers. Corn was the main product, but pumpkins, turnips, beans, cabbage, and squash were also grown.

It is convenient, with our twentieth-century hindsight, to criticize Zeisberger's approach. The missionary movement, especially among the American Indians, has met intense criticism from some historians in the last few years. It is true that the loss of many of the most intelligent men and women, who left the native tribes and joined the Moravians as Christian converts, weakened the tribes' ability to govern. But Zeisberger had a genuine concern for that problem. On numerous occasions, he recommended that the person remain with the native tribe but continue to be friend of the mission.

Many of the greatest benefits from Zeisberger's work were nonreligious. The thousands of pages of his and other Moravian missionaries' diaries are available to historians. They are valuable sources for scholars in history, linguistics, anthropology, and sociology and for those interested in descriptions of plants and animals.

Zeisberger kept hundreds of Delaware, Wyandot, Shawnee, and other Indian warriors neutral during the early years of the American Revolution. It is impossible to say how many lives were thus saved. The Moravian Brethren also brought traditional education and culture to the wilderness. They taught crafts and skills to their people and brought comfort and confidence and a more orderly way of living for their converts.

This book provides a brief glimpse into the life of certain Indians in the eighteenth century. It is based on the thousands of pages of diaries written by David Zeisberger and preserved in the Moravian Church Archives at Bethlehem, Pennsylvania. Zeisberger's diaries were written in old German script, but they have been carefully translated into English. These translations and microfilms of the originals are housed in the Tusc-Kent Archives at the Tuscarawas Branch of Kent State University, New Philadelphia, Ohio.

The book is divided into four parts. Part 1 covers the first thirty-two years of Zeisberger's life, the beginnings of the Moravian Church in America, and the years of turmoil immediately before the French and Indian War. Part 2 deals with the French and Indian War and the struggle to keep the Indian mission movement alive during the war. Zeisberger was on the close periphery of the efforts to reach a peaceful settlement with the native Indian tribes during and immediately following the war. Part 3 covers the ten years between the close of the French and Indian War, the reorganization of the missionary movement, the beginning of the western missions on the Allegheny River in western Pennsylvania, and the Dunmore War with the Shawnee Indians in the Ohio Country. It reveals a hitherto unknown effort by the Delaware chief White Eyes to reach a settlement with the Shawnees that protected them from destruction by the colonial army. The final part deals with the founding of the five missions in the

Muskingum River valley and Zeisberger's role in keeping the Delaware Nation neutral during the Revolutionary War. It ends with the disbursement of the Indian congregations, the massacre of the Indians at the Gnadenhutten mission, and Zeisberger's first effort to reorganize the mission movement.

The final period of Zeisberger's life has been recorded in my book, *Blackcoats among the Delaware: David Zeisberger on the Ohio Frontier*, published by The Kent State University Press in 1991.

Acknowledgments

THE ORIGINS of this book go back to a brisk, windswept November day in 1929, when, in my ninth year, I accompanied my father on a visit to the lonely Indian cemetery at the small village of Goshen near New Philadelphia, Ohio. It was the seventeenth day of the month and the 121st anniversary of the death of the missionary David Zeisberger. My father knew the basic Zeisberger story, as did most Tuscarawas Countians of his day. I was enchanted as he related the history of this fascinating man and his many Indian friends who lay buried at our feet in this lonely little cemetery. The cemetery is still there, just as it was those many years ago, a testament to the Moravian Church, which owns the land, and the Tuscarawas County Historical Society members, who care for and maintain the cemetery.

For the next fifty years I gave little thought to David Zeisberger and his friends. I was too busy providing for a wife and four children though I lived all this time only several miles from the Goshen cemetery.

By 1980, I was semiretired, and it was time to give some thought to David Zeisberger. In the meantime, much had been done in Tuscarawas County to perpetuate his story. In 1921, the Tuscarawas County Historical Society was formed specifically to find the exact location of, and partially to rebuild, Zeisberger's Schoenbrunn mission. Ten years later the project was completed, and today the little village, operated by the Ohio Historical Society, entertains well over twenty-five thousand visitors annually. It is capably managed by Susan Goehring and Linda Beal, the director and assistant director.

In 1970, Ohio's first outdoor drama was organized. Called "Trumpet in the Land," it is capably managed by Margaret Bonamico. It plays every summer to over thirty thousand guests and relates the fascinating story of David Zeisberger's life. But little had been written about Zeisberger since Edmund De Schweinitz's 1870 biography. His book is definitive but is entirely from a religious perspective. The story needed to be told from a secular viewpoint. Over the last fifty years, almost all of Zeisberger's diaries have been translated into English, with the exception of five years between 1775 and 1781. These years were crucial because they covered the Revolutionary War period. I commissioned Margaret Wilde, an assistant at the Bethlehem Archives, to translate those three hundred pages in the original manuscript. They proved to be a treasure trove of firsthand, never-before-published information concerning events on the western frontier during this period.

In the summer of 1980, I began my research. Over the next twelve years, David Zeisberger would take me many thousands of miles into the states of New York, New Jersey, Maryland, Virginia, Pennsylvania, Ohio, Indiana, and Michigan and to Upper Canada (almost all sites of his missions or areas that contained parts of his life story) in a total of thirty research trips.

Writing a historical biography requires the assistance of hundreds of people: librarians, academic historians, lay people, historical researchers, archaeologists, anthropologists, ethnologists, and other interested persons. Many people in each field have contributed to this work.

The first contacts were made at the Moravian Church Archives in Bethlehem, Pennsylvania. The archivist, Vernon Nelson, is now my dear friend. I shall never forget my first visit. I told Rev. Nelson I planned to do a biography of David Zeisberger. I can recall his eyes rolling as he thought, "Oh my God, not another one." But after several visits, I think he came to the conclusion that I was for real. Rev. Nelson introduced me to the Fliegel Index of the Moravian Archives. Fortunately for a Zeisberger researcher, in 1970 most of the Moravian Archives were microfilmed by Research Publications, Inc., of New Haven, Connecticut. There are forty reels of Moravian material, thirteen of which cover the Zeisberger years. With my microfilm reader, I was able to read and study the original records in the comfort of my home. I wish to thank Vernon for answering so many questions over the years. In the early years, my daughter Barbara, who was the ombudsman at the *Christian Science Monitor,* helped refine my writing skills. She read and corrected many pages of my manuscript. Also in those early years, Bishop Edwin Sawyer spent time showing me the interesting Zeisberger site around Bethlehem, and Rev. Arthur Nehring and his wife, Rose, provided, at Bethlehem, my home away from home. To all I extend my thanks.

I am especially grateful to Helen Wilson, former head reference librarian of the Western Historical Society of Pittsburgh, Pennsylvania, who on very short notice mailed me copies of the *Colonial Records* and the *Pennsylvania Archives,* 1st series. (Today both of these valuable sets of books are in the Tusc-Kent Archives.) My old friend Jack Hetrick, past president of the Northumberland Historical Society at Sunbury, Pennsylvania, led the archaeological excavation of the Zeisberger mission at Shamokin in Sunbury, discovering an incredible group of artifacts from the 1745 period. Throughout my research trips I have visited many libraries located near the sites of Zeisberger's former missions, especially in New York, Pennsylvania, and Ohio. To all of these local librarians I offer my grateful thanks. Special among this group was Ann Sindler of the Western Reserve Historical Society, who introduced me to the Draper Manuscripts microfilms, where I discovered the original letters of Zeisberger and John Heckewelder, written between 1777 and 1781. These letters gave a totally new dimension to the Zeisberger saga during the Revolutionary War. And finally, I am indebted to Dan Cooley, the head librarian at the Dover Public Library, and his capable reference librarian, Jacqueline Metzger, who located more than 150 out-of-print books valuable for the Zeisberger story. All of these books were photocopied and are now in the Tusc-Kent Archives collection.

Four special friends are directly responsible for this narrative. Without their assistance this book would never have been written. First is Albert Frank, minister at the Dover Moravian Church in Dover, Ohio, who read all of the many versions of the manuscript. Frank is a knowledgeable Zeisberger scholar and kept all things Moravian historically accurate. Philip Weeks, a professor of history at the Stark Campus, Kent State University, read numerous revisions and helped make many critical and necessary suggestions. My old and dear friend ninety-year-old Hazel Lightel served as my copy editor. Hazel taught most of the Olmstead children and is a dear friend of our family, a mortal enemy of misspelled words, split infinitives, and jumbled syntax. She roots them out with a vengeance. Finally, George Knepper, a retired distinguished professor of history, from the University of Akron, Akron, Ohio, is considered by his peers to be the leading scholar in

Ohio history. His recent book, *Ohio and Its People*, is used for Ohio history courses. He has been my mentor throughout this fifteen-year process, offering encouragement and constructive criticism. He read all the many drafts, and he helped shape the final form that made this publication possible. I owe him a deep debt of gratitude, more than I shall ever be able to repay.

· PART 1 ·

Unitas Fratrum: From the European Underground to the New World, 1721–1753

· 1 ·

That Dusty Road, 1721–1736

HE LAID the quill pen on the table beside the large stack of manuscripts and quietly sighed, "It's finished."

From his chair he could see that the sun had almost set, but the wind continued to blow snow into small drifts against one side of the windowpane. Rising slowly, he stood beside the crude desk, the only piece of furniture, except a bed, in the small cabin that had been his home these past several months. A cold chill shook his body. He walked to the corner of the room, selected several hickory logs from the pile, and placed them on the fire. Within a few moments the fire was burning briskly. The rising flames quickly warmed the cabin and drove the chill from his body.

Through the window, the soft blue of the coming evening covered the landscape before him, yet the faint glow of the sun behind the clouds gave the valley a warm glow. For hundreds of years, perhaps millennia, the ancestors of the people who lived in the twenty bark and log huts surrounding the chapel behind his cabin had roamed this land where he now lived. These Native Americans called it the "Black Forest." The Muskingum River (now the Tuscarawas) slowly winds through the floor of the valley.[1]

The missionary had selected this location some ten years before, and for the past nine years the valley had been his home. This was the Moravian Indian mission of New Schoenbrunn. The year was 1780.

Turning back to the desk, David Zeisberger began to arrange the papers in neat piles. An old friend, George Henry Loskiel, who planned to write a history of the Moravian missions in America, asked him to record some of his experiences and observations. For almost two years Zeisberger had labored at this task, writing more than eighty thousand words. It was a calm, straightforward, well-founded narrative of the eastern American Indians, whom he knew intimately.[2]

Zeisberger would be fifty-nine in one month, and for the past thirty-seven years he had lived among the Indians, first with the Onondaga Iroquois of the Six Nations in New York, then among the Delawares and Mahicans of Pennsylvania.[3] He had constantly moved westward, with his little band of converted Christian Indians, attempting to escape the onrushing wave of the hostile white pioneers. In 1772 his converts settled in the Ohio Country, on the banks of the Muskingum River.[4]

The solitude of the little cabin and the warmth of the fire provided an environment for reflection. His mind wandered back many years to a similar valley in Moravia. There in the small village of Zauchtenthal, nestled within the Carpathian Mountains, he was born on Good Friday morning April 11, 1721, the first of four children born to David and Rosina Zeisberger.[5]

David's father and grandfather, both named David, had lived in Zauchtenthal for many years and were freeholders who had accumulated considerable wealth. They were also clandestine members of the Unity of the Brethren Church.

He would never forget the early morning in July of his sixth year, when his mother awakened him from a sound sleep. With her fingers to her lips indicating he should be silent, she told him to dress and hurry downstairs for breakfast. Moments later he entered the kitchen where his mother was feeding his little sister, Anna, a healthy, robust child born the year before. David's father was briskly arranging several backpacks on the kitchen floor, and his young son remembered vividly the worried expression on his father's face as he urged his wife to hurry.

Within an hour, as the sun began to cross the top of the mountains, they were on the dusty road leaving the village. With the packs strapped to their backs and Anna in her mother's arms, the father held his son's hand and urged him along. Only later did he understand that they were fleeing the persecution of the Catholic king against the followers of the Bohemian church—sacrificing all material possessions for the sake of religious freedom.

This was not the first time the Moravian Brethren felt the lash of the pope and the Catholic king. For three hundred years the followers of John Huss had been tracked down, captured, imprisoned, tortured, and killed for their beliefs.

The Bohemian church, which originated in the early part of the fifteenth century following the martyrdom of John Huss, based its doctrine on his teachings. Huss had been the pastor of the Bethlehem Chapel, a large Catholic church in Prague.

In 1412 he mounted a scathing attack against the pope's attempt to sell indulgences, a well-known practice of the Catholic Church. Indulgences were sold to the faithful who believed they could reduce or erase time in purgatory, thus making amends for their sins and transgressions. Huss prohibited this selling in his church even though it was done in every Catholic church in the city. As a result, he was excommunicated. Two years later, he was seized, held in prison, condemned, and finally burned at the stake on July 6, 1415.

Following Huss's death came the explosive growth of the Hussite movement and the beginning of the Protestant revolution one hundred years before Martin Luther nailed his famous ninety-five theses on the door of the Catholic church in Wittenberg. The Hussite movement gave birth to the Unity of Brethren (Unitas Fratrum) in 1457.

The spark lit by the controversial Hussite movement burst into a flame that burned its way over half of Europe, defying all efforts to extinguish it.[6] Cities, towns, and villages were destroyed in battles between Catholics and Hussites, killing tens of thousands of men and women, including some in the Moravian Brotherhood. By 1721 only a small remnant of Hussites remained. They had no formal church administration to coalesce the members and to keep their faith alive; rather they met in their homes, constantly on guard against the king's soldiers. Among the remaining faithful was a carpenter living in the kingdom of Saxony, thirty-two-year-old Christian David.

In 1717 he crossed the border into Austria to visit the Moravian Brethren, sharing his faith and experience and developing his own newfound talents as a speaker.[7] The following year he returned to Austria, visiting Sehlen, where he met the five Neisser brothers, all members of the clandestine brotherhood, who longed to live in a land free from oppression. David promised the Neissers that he would search for a place of refuge across the border in Saxony.[8] Returning to Gorlitz, he made their wishes known to his friends John Andrew Rothe and Pastor Johann Schwedler.

During his theological studies Rothe had met and developed a close personal friendship with the wealthy and pietistic twenty-two-year-old Count Nicholas Lewis von Zinzendorf. The count was employed by the elector of Saxony as a judicial counselor in the city of Dresden.

In April 1722, Zinzendorf purchased from his grandmother a large tract of land, which included the small village of Berthelsdorf. The village, a separate parish since 1346, formed part of the diocese of Lobau and had been Protestant since 1538.[9] About the time of the purchase, Pastor Schwedler died, and Zinzendorf appointed Rothe to take his place.

As the new pastor, Rothe made frequent trips to Dresden to visit Zinzendorf. In May 1722, during one of these visits, he mentioned the plight of Christian David's Moravians. The young count suggested that David should come to Dresden and discuss the situation; perhaps he would find a way to accommodate the Moravians. David immediately visited Zinzendorf and explained the plight of his friends. After a short discussion, the count agreed to provide asylum for the Moravians and to shelter them temporarily on his own estates.

Christian David was elated; for four years he had hoped for this opportunity. He crossed the border and arrived in Sehlen on May 23 and informed his friends Augustine and Jacob Neisser of his conversation with the count. Four days later, leaving everything behind, the Neissers, their wives and children, and two close relatives were on their way on foot to Saxony. Christian David led the party of ten—six adults and four very young children.[10]

The journey was well over two hundred miles. The refugees, scrambling up the menacing Carpathian Mountains, crossed the border and descended the tortuously narrow roads, arriving almost empty-handed at Bethelsdorf. Lady Gersdorf, the count's grandmother, was not pleased by their arrival and gave them a cool reception. She finally relented and permitted the Moravians to remain on her estate. A temporary dwelling was provided for them and a cow was given to supply milk for their children.

The first order of business for the new settlers was to build permanent homes. On June 17, Christian David felled the first tree and helped build the first log home.[11] They had been assigned a location on the estate at the base of a hill known as Hutberg, and in a few days they would call the new village Herrnhut (the Lord's Watch).

Christian David led additional Brethren from Moravia to Herrnhut, making ten trips to escort groups to freedom. It was during one of these trips in July 1726, that he led five-year-old David Zeisberger, his sister Anna, and their parents into the village at the base of the Hutberg.[12] It is little wonder that fifty-four years later, the man who sat before the blazing fire on the banks of the Muskingum River would retain vivid recollections of that exciting journey.

Count Nicholas Ludwig (Lewis) von Zinzendorf

For the next twenty-six years, David Zeisberger's life would be influenced by Count Zinzendorf. The burgeoning little village of Herrnhut continued to grow as additional families joined the Neissers and Zeisbergers at the base of the Hutberg. Count Zinzendorf watched over the expanding community with increasing interest.

Zinzendorf's ancestry dated back to the Catholic Duchy of Austria in the eleventh century. Because of his adherence to the Protestant faith, Nicholas's grandfather, seeking greater freedom, fled Austria and settled in the kingdom of Saxony.[13] Here Nicholas was born on May 26, 1700. The tragic death of his father two months later brought the young count under the direct care of his grandmother, the Baroness Henriette Catherine von Gersdorf.[14]

Like all young men of noble blood, he was privately tutored as a young child. When he was ten years old, he entered Halle Academy.[15] At sixteen, after completing his work at Halle, he matriculated at Wittenberg University. Following graduation from the university, he took his uncle's advice and entered government service. In October 1721 he settled at Dresden and became a judicial counselor in the electoral government of Saxony. The following May, his chance meeting with Christian David occurred.

In September 1722, he married the Countess Erdmuth Dorothea von Reuss, and by the next summer they had moved into a new home at Berthelsdorf. By the spring of 1727, a year after the Zeisbergers arrived at Herrnhut, he requested and was granted release from service to the government of Saxony, which permitted him to devote full time and effort to his religious activities. The balance of his life would be spent among the Brethren and in the service of the Moravian Church. Zinzendorf was the first of several men who recognized the talents of young David Zeisberger and contributed to his early education.

Count Nicholas Ludwig (Lewis) von Zinzendorf, 1700–1760. Courtesy of the Moravian Church Archives.

The Herrnhut community to which the Zeisbergers came in 1726 was in transition. It had grown to a village of thirty-four dwellings and approximately three hundred souls. As with any growing community of widely divergent nationalities and languages, there were problems. The sheer size of the community began to demand an expanded formal organization with more complex rules and regulations.

By July 1727, despite the count's autocratic position as "Lord of the Manor," the community held town meetings at which citizens could express their opinions, a church council that regulated secular and religious affairs, and a court of justice that directed all agricultural, commercial, and industrial activities—a strikingly democratic organization for the eighteenth century.

During 1727, the Herrnhutters began to divide into small groups based on age, gender, and marital status. They met daily for worship and informal discussion. From these informal groups sprang the first development toward the "Choir" system.[16] In February 1728, the first of these choir associations, the unmarried men or single brethren, were separated and housed in their own dormitory. The men were initially assigned the task of spinning wool, but their duties quickly expanded to include numerous other handicrafts such as making shoes and items of clothing. Some of the younger men learned a trade; others were trained for work in the mission field. By 1737 this household contributed fifty-six recruits to the foreign mission undertaking. In 1730, a similar choir was established for the eighteen unmarried women under the supervision of fifteen-year-old Anna Nitschmann.

The young children also were housed in a separate facility, which led to the famous Moravian boarding schools that were to prove popular in America in the eighteenth and nineteenth centuries among non-Moravian families. Eventually the choir system initiated Moravian Church rituals such as the Easter sunrise service, the cup of covenant, love feast, foot washing, song services, and festival days.

A new procedure was introduced about this time. When the Moravians were in doubt regarding any matter of importance, they immediately put the question in the hands of the Lord, asking for his assistance through a practice called the lot. Alternatives were written on slips of paper, then placed in a container. One of the brethren was requested to draw one slip from the container, and it was believed to be the Lord's answer to the problem. The procedure was treated with great solemnity and prayer.[17] The Moravians were not the first to use the lot, nor was it unique to them. It had been used frequently by pietist groups. Rothe first used the lot as early as 1725 to assign duties to villagers. Three years later it became the standard practice for making decisions throughout the Moravian Church, including the selection of marriage partners. The practice continued for the next 150 years, but as time passed, it came under increasing criticism, especially among those clergy who believed it was an escape from a more intelligent and realistic method for solving problems. After many long and contentious debates, the practice was abandoned in 1850.

It was perhaps inevitable that the brand of Christianity practiced at Herrnhut would spread. The atmosphere pervading the village seemed contagious, and religious exiles from all over Europe began to descend on the little settlement. Many came from Moravia and Bohemia, others from Poland, Switzerland, Holland, and the northern provinces of Germany. Among those immigrants were the Zeisbergers seeking to build a new life.

Although Zinzendorf was pleased with the burgeoning and successful community, he dreamed of more than just the revival and extension of another church. His great hope was that these inspired Christians could become a body for missionary and evangelistic service. This particular kind of evangelism was called diaspora, or dispersion (from 1 Peter, verse 1): Brethren ministering among the "scattered" in all churches regardless of their denominations.[18] Ecumenically, he was two hundred years ahead of his time.

One of these journeys, which began on September 27, 1727, had far-reaching effects on the history of the Moravian Church and its mission work. Several of the Brethren visited Jena and spoke with Jena University professor John Francis Buddeus, a friend of the Moravians. Among the professor's students was a young man named Augustus Gottlieb Spangenberg. The visitors made a deep impression on this twenty-five-year-old student. Several months later, Zinzendorf stopped at Jena and met the young man. They began a voluminous correspondence. The next year Zinzendorf again returned to the university and founded a diaspora group of the Herrnhut type. Spangenberg became the group leader. It was a short step from the diaspora to the mission field. The Moravians were ready to make this step, and Spangenberg would lead the vanguard.

Augustus Gottlieb Spangenberg

No man was more beloved by, or had a more dramatic influence on, David Zeisberger than Augustus Gottlieb Spangenberg. Spangenberg has been described as courageous, conciliatory, intelligent, self-sacrificing, and temperate. He was born July 25, 1704, at Klettenberg in Prussia, near the Hartz Mountains, the youngest of four sons of the Lutheran pastor George Spangenberg and his wife, Elizabeth. By the time Augustus was ten, both parents had died. Only through the tireless energy of his older brothers,

Augustus Gottlieb Spangenberg, 1704–1792. Courtesy of the Moravian Church Archives.

who recognized the lad's talents, was Augustus given the traditional Gymnasium education and entered the University of Jena in 1720, at the age of sixteen. Here he fell under the paternal guidance of Professor Buddeus, a well-respected member of the faculty and a leader of the pietist movement at the university. Augustus lived with the Buddeus family for the next ten years and was increasingly influenced by the distinguished professor, whom he considered his foster father. During this period he abandoned the study of law for theology, receiving his master's degree in 1726. After graduating, he accepted an assistant professorship in theology at the university. The following year, he met the itinerant missionaries from Herrnhut and began his friendship with Zinzendorf.

In 1732, with Zinzendorf's recommendation, he accepted an assistant professorship in the theological school and the superintendency of the orphanage at the University of Halle, Zinzendorf's alma mater.[19] Initially his work was well received, but after several months he came under severe attack from the pietists at the university. Most of this criticism was the result of his friendship with Zinzendorf, who was becoming anathema to Halle, although there were more specific complaints, principally over theological interpretations involving the confession and the administration of communion.[20] On February 27, 1733, Spangenberg was stripped of his duties as superintendent and on April 2 was dismissed by royal mandate from the university. When the king's message arrived, he calmly replied, "All the earth is the Lord's," packed up his meager possessions, and left for Herrnhut, where Zinzendorf was waiting.[21] He quickly became a major influence in the Moravian missionary movement.

Almost simultaneously with Spangenberg's arrival, the followers of Kasper Schwenkfeld, recently banished from Silesia, were granted asylum on the count's estates. Approximately 180 of them were living near Berthelsdorf and in the area of Gorlitz. The previous year, halfway around the world, James Oglethorpe, English general and philanthropist, landed a small colony of refugees on the coast of Georgia with the intend of providing asylum for insolvents in England and oppressed Protestants from the Continent.

Zinzendorf, aware of Oglethorpe's plan, obtained from the Georgia trustees the promise of a grant of land and free passage for the Schwenkfelders to Savannah. Led by Christopher Wiegner, the Schwenkfelders left Berthelsdorf on May 26, 1734. At their request, a Moravian evangelist, George Boehnisch, accompanied them. After arriving in Holland, they changed their plans and sailed for Pennsylvania. The Moravians would later meet them again.

Meanwhile, during the count's negotiations, the Georgia trustees had suggested that the Moravians might wish to secure land in Georgia. The idea appealed to the leaders at Herrnhut and conformed with their plans to evacuate should they be forced out of Saxony. Also, the Georgia colony's location would permit the Brethren to found a mission among the Creek and Cherokee Indians, who lived nearby. Missions among the American Indians fit well with Zinzendorf's diaspora philosophy.

Near the end of the year Spangenberg was dispatched to London, where he had numerous interviews with General Oglethorpe and the secretary of the trustees, James Vernon. Great negotiating skill and patience were required to complete the arrangements because the English court preacher Ziegenhagen, who represented the Hallensian party, opposed the Moravians.[22] This was another of the many obstructionist tactics used by the count's enemies at Halle, who objected to anything connected with Herrnhut. But Ziegenhagen had a formidable competitor in Spangenberg. Nine Brethren, led by David Nitschmann, the syndic, arrived at London on January 14, 1735, a few days before the trustees were to make their formal decision.[23] Here was a ready-made, albeit small, colony prepared to leave immediately for the new settlement. The trustees were favorably impressed, and the request was granted despite the court preacher's objection. Spangenberg's adroitness as mediator was becoming evident.

The ship *Two Brothers* was chartered by the trustees. Nine of the party embarked from London on February 3, 1736; Spangenberg boarded at Gravesend three days later.

If the mission was to be a success, reinforcements had to come as quickly as possible. The leaders in Herrnhut recognized this and planned to send more Brethren immediately after the departure of the first contingent. By the end of July 1736, the second group was ready: seventeen men and eight women led by the new bishop, David Nitschmann.[24] Among the twenty-five were several prominent Moravians who will appear again in this book, the leader David Nitschmann, Martin Mack, and George Neisser. There were three married couples, among them David and Rosina Zeisberger, the parents of David.

The Zeisbergers had lived in Herrnhut for nine happy, exciting, work-filled years, building the village and raising their young son and daughter. During this time another son, George, was born. They planned to leave the children in Herrnhut in care of the Brethren so they could continue their education. David was now fourteen, small for his age, fine-featured, and bright and was doing well in the Brethren's school. He displayed unusual talent for learning languages, a skill that would later be useful in understanding and interpreting the complicated Indian dialects. He was also beginning to form the personality of his adult life: reticent, somewhat introverted, highly sensitive, and pacifistic.

When leaving, his father warmly embraced the boy, and his mother kissed his cheek and tenderly wiped the tears from his face. Words were not necessary. Their love for each other and the sorrow of the parting were in their eyes. David followed the carts down the road out of the village. Just before they passed from sight, his mother turned and waved her handkerchief. Many times in David's later life he experienced similar emotions of loneliness and sorrow, but the pain of that moment would never be erased from his heart. On one of those later occasions he mused about this incident: "And my friends wonder at my reticence and my search for solitude, perhaps it was God's way to begin my education for the life I have led."

· 2 ·

Branded as a Thief, 1736–1742

COUNT ZINZENDORF's diaspora efforts involved numerous trips to England and the European continent. These sojourns were primarily focused on expanding the successful work of the brotherhood begun at Herrnhut. Several similar communities were founded at Heernhaag and Marienborn in Germany as well as a new community in Holland called Heerendyk. The initial concept called for a community to be devoted to the training and preparation of future missionaries.

Early in 1736 Zinzendorf, his wife, daughter Benigna, and twelve other Brethren left Herrnhut for the new settlement located in the Barony of Ysselstein to check on the progress of construction. Among the twelve Brethren accompanying the Zinzendorf party was young David Zeisberger. At fifteen, David was an intelligent boy whose gift for languages had attracted the count's attention. He was fond of David and believed that if his talents were developed, he could play a prominent role in the building of the brotherhood. But he needed more education than the schools of Herrnhut could provide. The count believed the educational facilities in Heerendyk would do. Therefore, David was invited to join the new community.[1]

On arrival at Heerendyk, Zeisberger found the Brethren developing the commercial shops and manufacturing trade centers that they were particularly skilled at organizing. The village was rapidly becoming a popular shopping center visited by gentry from the surrounding countryside. David was employed as an errand boy to several of the village merchants, delivering packages and messages to stores. He easily mastered Dutch, and, being personable, active, and punctual, he became a favorite among the customers and merchants. At the same time he attended school and completed his formal education. But he was not content. Separated from his parents and in a foreign village without his Herrnhut friends, he felt isolated and homeless.

The Dutch school he attended was similar to those described one hundred years later by Charles Dickens, who vividly and realistically pictured the conditions and the treatment of students in European schools. The narrow curriculum and the harsh discipline were severe to a fault. The rigidly enforced rules left little room to consider the temper, previous training, or personality of students.

David Zeisberger's sensitive nature and warm heart rebelled against these conditions. Wrongly accused of minor infractions, he was mercilessly beaten on numerous occasions, leaving permanent scars on his back and an intense hatred of violence. Most of this punishment he accepted philosophically, but a decisive incident occurred a few months after his arrival.[2]

A wealthy stranger arrived one day requesting a guide to Ysselstein, some miles from Heerendyk. David was appointed to guide him. After arriving at their destination, the man offered him an unusually large fee. The Moravian code for doing favors forbade him to accept fees from visitors. The boy rejected the offer, but the man insisted and thrust several gold coins into his hand, then departed.

David faced a dilemma. If he concealed the gift, it would be an act of dishonesty, but if he revealed the coins, he would be punished. The sixteen-year-old finally arrived at a solution. He would keep half of the money and deliver the other half to his employer.

When he returned and explained the incident, his employer did not believe him, saying: "No stranger would give such a large gift to a mere errand boy, you have come by this money dishonestly, and we will expose your deceitfulness." Two persons accompanied David back to Ysselstein to confirm the story, but the man had departed without revealing his destination. Instead of establishing his innocence, David returned to Heerendyk branded a liar and a thief. He had reached the breaking point. David had made friends with a fellow student, John Michael Schober, also sixteen years old, who, upon learning of his experience, shared his indignation. They agreed to run away.[3]

The boys heard stories about General Oglethorpe, who had returned to London from his Georgia colony. Since his mother and father were in Georgia, David knew of the new settlement. The boys decided to go to London, search out the general, and attempt to secure passage to Georgia.

Fortunately, David still had half the money the stranger had given him, which assured the boys' passage to London. Arriving in the city, they were befriended by a German innkeeper who arranged an interview with General Oglethorpe. He was so impressed with the boys and their story that he immediately gave each of them money to purchase shoes, trousers, shirts, and warm coats, and arranged free passage on a ship ready to weigh anchor for Georgia. After an uneventful ten-week voyage, the boys arrived in Savannah on January 28, 1738.[4]

During the eighteen months of separation from his parents, David had grown from a boy to a young man. His mother and father were overwhelmed by the change and hardly recognized him, but they were grateful to be reunited.

Reflecting back on his experience in Heerendyk, Zeisberger wrote later, "From the day I left the Brethren in Holland, to the day of my arrival in Georgia, the Lord graciously preserved me from all harm in body and soul. . . . Upon the whole, I see the finger of God in all that occurred; since I can the more readily forgive the Brethren in Holland the injustice which I suffered at their hands. Indeed I have forgiven them from my heart."[5]

When David joined his parents, the village of Savannah was almost six years old.[6] It became the seat of the new government of Georgia and remained so until 1786. The Moravian mission and the Zeisberger home were in the village.

The adult Zeisbergers were ill equipped for the rigors of frontier life. Although the Spangenberg and Nitschmann parties had completed some of the buildings and cleared part of the land, fields had to be prepared and the stumps of virgin white oak, water hickory, loblolly pine, and slash pine timber had to be removed. All this was backbreaking work for people unaccustomed to such activity, but for sixteen-year-old David Zeisberger it was sheer ecstasy. Away from his Heerendyk tormentors, rejoined with his parents, he was building a new home in a new world.

Shortly after he arrived in Georgia, his inexperience almost cost him his life. One evening David overheard his parents discussing a village problem with their neighbors. Deer were breaking through the enclosures surrounding their rice fields and destroying the crops. Determined to correct the situation, David took his musket, climbed a tree, and fired at the first deer to approach. He was unaccustomed to the weapon's recoil, and it flew from his hands and struck his forehead, inflicting a serious wound and knocking him from the tree. For several hours he lay on the ground unconscious and bleeding. Finally regaining consciousness, he dragged himself to the nearest neighbor's cabin, where he received assistance. Only after several months of painful convalescence did he fully recover. Thus began the training for the life he eventually led as a pioneer and backwoodsman. He later became proficient with weapons and an expert canoeist.[7]

The Seed Is Planted

For the first two years the Georgia mission prospered, finding favor with the government and the local inhabitants.[8] Shortly after young Zeisberger and Schober arrived in January 1738, however, a series of events radically altered the Brethren's fortunes. In March 1736, one month after the Nitschmann party's arrival, Spangenberg left the colony and went to Pennsylvania to develop the American agenda which Zinzendorf had assigned to him in Europe.

Shortly thereafter, Nitschmann also left the colony, bound for Europe. Anton Seiffert, one of the original settlers in the Spangenberg party and recently ordained by Nitschmann, was appointed superintendent.[9] Under his direction, some progress was made toward the mission's main objective, preaching the Gospel to the Indians. An Indian schoolhouse was constructed five miles from Savannah on an island called Irene. Several of the Brethren lived near the school, teaching and preaching to the Indians.[10]

Nine months after Zeisberger and Schober arrived in Georgia, two other men joined the congregation, Peter Boehler and his assistant George Schulius. They were sent by Count Zinzendorf to establish a mission among the Negroes at Purysburg, a small German settlement twenty miles from Savannah. Boehler, a recent graduate of the University of Jena, was an exceptional scholar, a skilled linguist, and a thoroughly trained theologian who spoke and wrote fluent German, French, Latin, and English.[11]

From its inception, the projected mission in Purysburg was a disappointment. Both Boehler and Schulius became violently ill with fever. David Zeisberger nursed the pair during their sickness, but Schulius died on August 4, 1739.

During his long convalescence, Boehler appointed David, then seventeen, as his new assistant. They spent their days taking long, leisurely walks through the pine forest near the village and their evenings in lengthy conversations in front of the fire in their comfortable little cabin. For the next few years Zeisberger remained at Boehler's side. This close, personal relationship profoundly affected David, added substantially to his education, and provided his first exposure to missionary work. Later in his life he wrote of this experience "as a highly profitable and pleasant time."[12]

Meanwhile, the Spanish government in Florida began to make threatening gestures toward the English colony of Georgia. Ostensibly, the controversy arose over a question concerning trade in Negroes. (Spain had enjoyed a thirty-year monopoly on the slave trade.) In the winter of 1730–31, the Spaniards began to restrict the passage of English ships and prohibit landings in ports along the Florida coast. One reason for founding the Georgia colony was to protect the English against such threats. Finally, in the spring of 1737, Oglethorpe issued a call for muster of a local militia, including the Brethren. They flatly refused. Their contract with the trustees stated that "they neither could, nor would bear arms under any conditions."[13]

Some of the Brethren wanted to leave Georgia immediately, but cooler heads prevailed. They sent for Spangenberg, who made a quick trip from Pennsylvania. He suggested that they refer the problem to the trustees in London, and several of the Brethren were dispatched to do so. On August 3, 1737, they received their answer: the colony was bound to furnish two men or purchase substitutes, one for each of their city lots, but the Moravians would not be compelled to bear arms. But the colonial government prohibited all trips into the interior, making it impossible for them to have contact with the Indians. This directive effectively canceled the principal objective of the mission.

With the prohibition against contact with the Cherokee and Creek Indians and the floundering of Boehler's Negro mission, there was little reason for the Brethren to remain in Georgia. The controversy with Oglethorpe and the Savannah authorities had taken its toll on their numbers. By the time Boehler arrived in late September 1738, the original colony of thirty-seven Brethren had been reduced to nine men and women and three boys. Seven of the original group had died during the three-year period, succumbing to the harsh conditions of the frontier, and a substantial number had become disenchanted with conditions in Georgia and moved to Pennsylvania.[14]

The final incident that tore the mission apart was the receipt of news from London that England had declared war on Spain.[15] The British government ordered General Oglethorpe to muster his militia and attack the

Spanish coastal forts, especially the fortress at St. Augustine. Again the summons went out to all able-bodied men, including the Moravians, and again they refused. But it was a hollow effort. By then there were only six men and one woman remaining at the mission: Peter Boehler, Anton Seiffert, John Boehner, Martin Mack, David Zeisberger, Sr., his wife, Rosina, and their son David.[16] The death knell had been sounded for the Georgia project. Peter Boehler and his fellow Brethren began to make plans to leave.

On New Year's Day 1740, a ship docked at the wharf in Savannah. Aboard were the famous Protestant evangelist George Whitefield and his business manager and financial benefactor, William Seward. Whitefield and Peter Boehler were friends. They had never met but had corresponded voluminously. Whitefield, learning that Boehler was in Savannah, arranged a meeting. Whitefield quickly succumbed to the engaging personality and deep sincerity of the warm and hospitable Boehler.

Whitefield was a spellbinder, capable of holding thousands of people entranced for hours with his message of salvation. He was twenty-six years old when he arrived in Savannah and held a bachelor's degree from Oxford.[17] He planned to start a school for Negroes on five thousand acres of land purchased in Pennsylvania near the "Forks of the Delaware" (the junction of the Lehigh and Delaware Rivers) called the Barony of Nazareth (now Northampton County). Whitefield was on his way to Pennsylvania and allowed Boehler and his associates to accompany him.

The seven Brethren boarded the Whitefield sloop the *Savannah* on April 13, 1740, and arrived at Philadelphia twelve days later. The Georgia mission was finished, but the Moravians had learned a lesson. In the future, personnel must be more carefully screened and greater discipline demanded of the leadership. Harmony and compatibility were essential to success.

Events moved rapidly for the Boehler party. They spent the night in Germantown, just west of Philadelphia, as guests of the former members of the Georgia colony. Early the next morning they were on the road to Christopher Wiegner's farm at Skippack, some thirty miles west of Philadelphia, arriving that afternoon. Wiegner was the leader of the Schwenkfelders who immigrated to America from Herrnhut in 1734.

At Wiegner's home on May 5 Whitefield visited Boehler and suggested a possible solution to their need to find a home. Recognizing that some of the Brethren were carpenters and masons, he offered to employ the party to construct his new schoolhouse on the Nazareth Tract and proposed that Boehler be the general superintendent.[18]

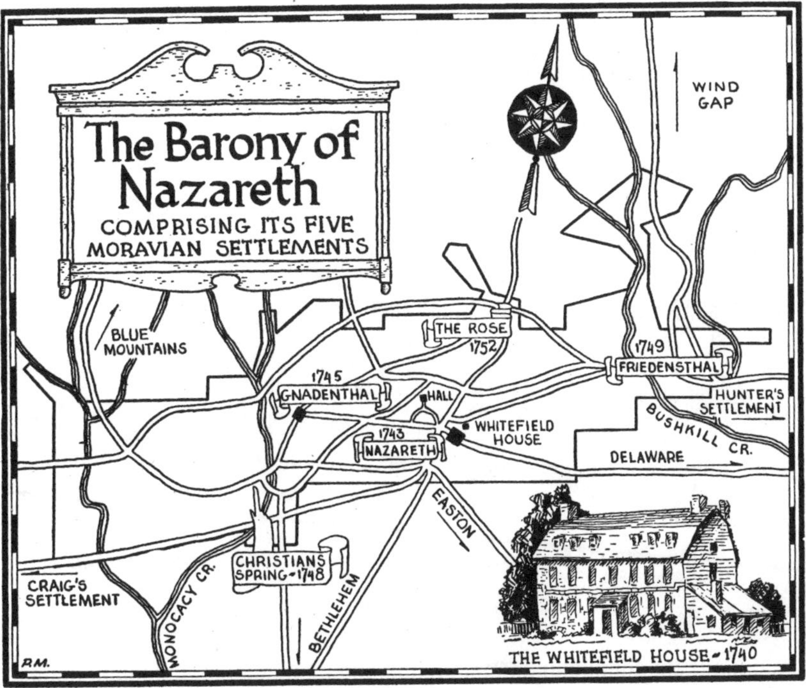

The Barony of Nazareth. Courtesy of the Moravian Church Archives.

The next day Boehler, Anton Seiffert, and Henry Antes set out for the proposed site. Antes, a former German count, was a Reformed lay preacher and became an intimate friend of the Moravians. Two days later, they arrived at the village of the Delaware Indian chief Tatamy, which was located at the edge of the Whitefield tract. Tatamy was the first of many Delaware chiefs to have a close personal relationship with the Moravians, especially David Zeisberger, over the next sixty-five years. After inspecting the proposed site, the men returned to Skippack. A serious discussion was held, and finally the question was submitted to the will of the Lord. The lot responded affirmatively, and Boehler accepted Whitefield's proposition.

Returning to Germantown for supplies, Boehler's party, including David Zeisberger and his family, was back on the road again on May 24, accompanied by two other Brethren and two indentured boys. They arrived in Nazareth three days later.[19]

As the sun rose the next morning, the first tree came crashing down and the workers began to build a crude temporary shelter of branches and

The Whitefield House. Courtesy of the Moravian Church Archives.

limbs. Whitefield's men arrived shortly after and staked out the site of "the stone house," which is still known as the Whitefield House. While Boehler returned to Skippack and adjacent communities to engage masons, lime burners, and other skilled craftsmen, the Brethren began to erect a log dwelling a few yards west of the northwest corner of the big house. It was ready for occupancy by the end of June.

All through the late spring and summer they gathered and cut stone for the building. The season was unusually wet, which, coupled with the critical shortage of material and the inexperience of some of the Brethren, caused the work to go slowly.

By September the building was constructed only up to the doorsills. Boehler realized he could not face the winter without adequate shelter and wisely constructed a larger cabin with one and one-half stories. This building became known as the Grey Cottage. It still stands at the rear of the Whitefield House.

It was mid-autumn before Boehler returned to Philadelphia to give his employer a progress report on the construction. Whitefield, like most zealots, was opinionated and doctrinaire, especially in his religious principles. During the presentation of his report, a controversy developed and then escalated until, in a fit of temper and bristling with anger, Whitefield ordered Boehler and the Brethren to leave his property.[20]

In fairness to Whitefield, the doctrinal differences were probably not the root cause of his actions. The Moravians' Scotch-Irish neighbors living near the forks had complained to Whitefield that the presence of the Moravians was a serious menace to their religious beliefs and way of life, and they wanted the Brethren driven from the area. With winter approaching, the situation was critical, but Whitefield was finally persuaded to allow the Moravians to spend the winter at Nazareth.[21]

In October, they received heartening news when Brother Andrew Eschenbach arrived from Europe. A party led by Bishop David Nitschmann was on its way to join them with instructions to purchase land in Pennsylvania.[22] Boehler's problem was solved. Within a few weeks, his party could remove to a new site and build their own settlement.

Sealed with a Handshake

Spangenberg arrived in Pennsylvania during the spring of 1736, just one year after he led the first contingent to the Georgia mission. For fifty years before his arrival, thousands of his countrymen had left Europe and settled along the banks of the Schuylkill River, west of Philadelphia. The large population growth of the English colonies, especially in Pennsylvania, was one of the most striking developments in America during the first half of the eighteenth century. An accurate census was not taken until 1790, but estimates indicate that William Penn's colony entered the 1700s with approximately 18,000 people. By 1780 it had grown 550 percent to 327,000. Over one-third of these were German immigrants. Their numbers were slightly exceeded by the English, but by only a few percentage points.[23]

With the Mennonites settled in Germantown and most of the Palatines in New York, hundreds, perhaps thousands of the immigrants settled farther west in Pennsylvania in small communities such as Skippack, Frederickstown, Oley, and Trappe. The majority of these immigrants, especially the Lutherans and German Reformed, came for economic reasons. Others, like the Mennonites (1683), Dunkards (1719), Siebentagers (1720), and Schwenkfelters (1734), were fleeing religious persecution.

It was a long and trying trip, usually beginning in April or May and ending in October or November: four to six weeks on the Rhine, another month or two in Holland, followed by a week to a month's voyage to England, then, if luck was with the captain, two to three months before the ship reached Philadelphia. At each stop the cost mounted until the sum consumed most of the immigrants' available cash. "Pitiful signs of distress" were everywhere, "smells, fumes, horrors, vomiting, various kinds of seasickness, fever, dysentery, headaches, heat, constipation, boils, scurvy, cancer, mouth-rot . . . caused by the age and highly salted state of the food, especially the meat, as well as the very bad and filthy water . . . hunger, thirst, frost, heat, dampness, fear, misery, vexation, and lamentation. . . . So many lice, especially on the sick people, that they had to be scraped off the body."[24] All these miseries were compounded if the ship encountered a storm. Even in good weather, the close confinement turned people against one another. But still they came by the thousands. Most families had limited resources, having spent what little money they had for passage, and were almost destitute by the time they reached America.

Spangenberg arrived in Pennsylvania during the spring of 1736. A big, broad-shouldered man, he projected an image of strength and stability. He was friendly with a sense of humor and an engaging smile, a natural leader. Unlike Zinzendorf, he had a conciliatory nature and seldom created controversy among the many different religious groups he encountered during his four-year stay. During most of his visit he traveled extensively, calling on small communities and outlying farms, making friends and discussing the problems of frontier life.

During his four years of travel through the Pennsylvania countryside, Spangenberg met Conrad Weiser, who resided on the Tulpehocken Creek, some seventy miles west of Philadelphia. They became instant friends. Both men were sincere, forthright, and unpretentious, and their friendship endured over the years, despite several strong disagreements. Weiser was the Indian interpreter for the Penn proprietors and the most knowledgeable man in the province on Indian affairs. He provided Spangenberg with valuable information about the Indians.

In 1739 Spangenberg returned to Europe and delivered his report to Zinzendorf. While Zinzendorf and Spangenberg were developing the Indian mission program, Bishop David Nitschmann, who had just returned to Europe from the unsuccessful Georgia experiment, was commissioned to return to America and purchase land for a permanent settlement in Pennsylvania. After arriving in Philadelphia on December 15, 1740, he joined the Peter Boehler party at Nazareth. He was carrying instructions that reassigned Boehler to England. It was with a heavy heart that Boehler's associates, especially the young David Zeisberger, parted from their friend. For more than two years David had listened to his wise counsel, receiving invaluable advice he would later use in his missionary endeavors. On January 29, Boehler sailed for Bristol and Nitschmann returned to Nazareth.

Bishop Nitschmann's first priority was to find a suitable location for the new Moravian village. The areas considered included a site several miles

Conrad Weiser, 1696–1760. From Charles Hanna, *The Wilderness Trail* (New York: G. P. Putnam and Sons, 1911).

south of Nazareth, between the Monocacy Creek and the Lehigh River in the forks of the Delaware. The selection of the site was resolved in the usual manner, by resorting to the lot, and the forks area was chosen. The land was owned by William Allen, a rich merchant and land speculator in Philadelphia. Fortunately for the Moravians, Allen's agent was their old friend Nathaniel Irish, a merchant who had sold Boehler supplies during the past summer and had gained a healthy respect for the persistent Germans.[25]

With the location of the site resolved, Bishop Nitschmann entered into negotiations to purchase five hundred acres of William Allen's land. The acreage lay on both sides of the Monocacy Creek and on the north side of the Lehigh River. Except for steep banks along the Lehigh, the land sloped gradually to the north from the river, was well forested, free from floods, and provided an ideal location for the projected village. Since the Moravians were not naturalized and the church was not a legal corporation in America, it was necessary for some friendly naturalized citizen to act on their behalf. Spangenberg's friend Henry Antes agreed to sponsor the purchase.[26] On April 2, 1741, Henry Antes and the bishop completed the formal transaction.

Later that year, Whitefield's business manager suddenly died, and Whitefield discovered that he was in a shaky financial condition. When he was forced to sell the Nazareth tract, the Moravians were the logical buyers. The transaction was concluded on July 16, 1741, and the Brethren now possessed two valuable tracts of land fifty miles north of Philadelphia.

The Nazareth party did not wait for the legal formalities to be concluded. By the beginning of March, the Monocacy and the Lehigh resounded with the sounds of the ax and falling trees as the group began a flurry of activity. There were eight in the working party, including David and Rosina Zeisberger and nineteen-year-old David.[27]

The site selected for the first building was several hundred yards from the Monocacy Creek on a lovely hill overlooking the valley, just above a spring that provided abundant water for the village. Despite the bitter cold and ankle-deep snow, they began to fell trees and shape the logs for the first cabin. It was a single-story combination dwelling and stable, twenty feet by forty feet, with a large projecting gable roof.[28] They called it the Rubal House.

Slightly more than half of the structure was devoted to living quarters and the rest set aside for future storage of crops and sheltering the cattle. Here seven men and one woman, with little privacy and no amenities, began their primitive village, cooking, eating, sleeping, planning, and dreaming of the future.

These were exciting days for David Zeisberger. He loved the broad forests of Pennsylvania and the robust, invigorating life, felling trees, cutting stone, and constructing buildings. Despite the urgency of the work, he sometimes took long walks in the woods with his musket and fishing rod. The clear blue water of the Monocacy provided excellent bass and trout fishing, and the forest yielded an abundant supply of wild game.[29] During these walks, he frequently visited the small Delaware village of Chief Tatamy several miles east of Nazareth. The chief had become a friend of the Moravians and often visited both Nazareth and the Monocacy locations. Young Zeisberger took every opportunity to return these visits to Tatamy's warm and hospitable people and within a few months could carry on fragmentary conversations in their tongue.

By fall, with the harvest completed, they began to excavate the basement of the second building. This was a much larger structure, also of hewn logs, chinked with clay and straw, two stories, forty-five by thirty feet, with a truncated gable roof. A later addition lengthened the building to ninety feet. On September 28, the first stone was laid in the southwest corner of the foundation. A small pewter box in the cornerstone contained a list of fifteen people present at the ceremony. The seventh name was "David Zeisberger, Junior of Moravia."[30] Work continued on the building for the rest of the year. When completed, it became the first official house of worship in the village and was soon known as the Gemeinhaus (Community House). It is still standing, a testament to Father Nitschmann's and the Moravians' superior craftsmanship.

The Count in America

In November the Moravians received exciting news. Count Zinzendorf, their benefactor and leader, was on his way to pay them a visit. No simple reason can be ascribed to Zinzendorf's coming to America in 1741, and it would be a mistake to attribute it to some grand design or master strategy. He frequently acted on impulse, motivated by his massive ego.[31] The party departed from England on August 7 and arrived in New York on November 30, 1741, only to find that the Reformed clergy had circulated the story that the Moravians were secretly Crypto-Papists and emissaries of the French. The clergy considered the Moravians dangerous to both the colony and other Protestants and proposed that they be expelled. Zinzendorf deftly parried these accusations, but they would haunt the Moravians and later bring disaster to the missionary programs in New York, creating endless problems, even for David Zeisberger. This antagonism cut short

Rubel House *(top)*, the first dwelling in Bethlehem, and Gemeinhaus, or the Community House *(bottom)*, also in Bethlehem. Courtesy of the Moravian Church Archives.

Zinzendorf's New York visit, and his party left for Philadelphia, where they found the tolerant religious climate much more to their liking.

Eager to visit his fellow Moravians on the banks of the Monocacy, Zinzendorf left Philadelphia on December 18. After days of hard riding the party approached the Monocacy. In the distance were the flickering lights of Isaac Ysselstein's family home near the river. The Ysselstein children lit torches and guided the party to the old Indian ford where they were to cross the river. Other torches appeared on the opposite bank as the settlement was alerted to their arrival. The hardy, deep-throated, guttural voices of the German men and the shrill sounds of the women floated down the river as they greeted each other along the banks and climbed the hill to the Gemeinhaus. Among the welcoming party were twenty-year-old David Zeisberger and his family.

Sunday, December 24, was a memorable day for the more than thirty people assembled at the new village. That evening they gathered before the roaring fire in the lonely little combination log cabin and stable to celebrate the birth of their Savior. Few there would forget that night.

Following the Christmas Eve celebration at the newly named village of Bethlehem, Zinzendorf returned to Philadelphia. He remained in America for one year. During that period he made three missionary trips among the Indians and attempted to organize the Pennsylvania Germans into elaborate religious groups collectively called the Pennsylvania synod. But by far his most important contribution was the organization of the Bethlehem congregation.

The three-day session of religious and administrative meetings began at Bethlehem on Saturday, June 23, 1742. On the surface, the proceedings appeared to be democratic, but one did not have to be an astute observer to see that the new organization sprang from the imaginative mind of the count. The village was divided into two "companies": the Pilgrim and home congregations. The first was assigned to man the missionary outpost and the second to operate the home base while supporting the mission work. Each brother was assigned to one of the two groups, either by appointment or by the lot. This selection applied not only to the eighty residents of Bethlehem but also the forty members of the church living in other areas. In those early days, there were frequent reassignments from one group to the other. In Neisser's journal David Zeisberger's name appeared as a member of the home congregation but for only a few days. He soon joined the members of the Pilgrim group as a missionary apprentice.

On Monday evening, June 25, the final announcement of the count's new plan of organization was given to the congregation, following an inspired service in the newly dedicated chapel of the Community House. June 25 is still observed as the anniversary of the Bethlehem congregation.[32]

Zinzendorf's visit to America contained both successes and failures, and the count would be the first to admit he was partially to blame for the latter. The count was a good man with a dream, and he had both vision and talent. Unfortunately, he had no tact and easily offended those who disagreed with him. His great asset was the ability to organize and plan, but it took another man, Augustus Spangenberg, to implement those plans, visions, and dreams.

Zinzendorf's departure deeply affected David Zeisberger. He was twenty-one at the time, and the elders of the church appointed him to accompany the count to Europe. No record survives to tell us why he was sent, although his parents were consulted, and they approved. He, however, was not anxious to leave. Frontier life agreed with the young man, and he thoroughly enjoyed working and living in Bethlehem. But David was placed in charge of one of the two wagons containing luggage, and he left Bethlehem January 2 and drove directly to New York.

It was a melancholy and depressed young man who leaned against the rail of the ship *James*, Nicholas Garrison at the helm, in the harbor at New York the morning of January 20, 1743. The ship bustled with activity, but the unnoticed and lonely David gazed mournfully toward the land that had been his home for the last six years. Zinzendorf and a large party of his friends were bidding their last farewell in the stern of the ship as Captain Garrison shouted, "Cast off the cables." Bishop Nitschmann, who was the last to embrace the count, quickly turned and headed for the shore. As he passed the young man standing near the gangplank, he noticed his sad expression and stopped abruptly:

"David," he said, "do you not return to Europe willingly?"

"No indeed," Zeisberger responded, "I would rather remain in America."

"For what reason?"

"I long to be truly converted to God, and serve him in this country."

Nitschmann was both surprised and pleased by the young man's response, and, seizing him by the shoulders, he answered:

"Then in God's name boy, if I were in your place, I would leave this ship immediately and return to Bethlehem, with me."

David did not have to be told a second time, and he seized his luggage, followed the bishop down the gangplank, and returned to Bethlehem.[33]

There was no pretense or hypocrisy in the young man's comments to the bishop, and he later wrote of this experience, "At the time my heart was not yet converted to God, but I longed to enjoy his grace and fully."[34] For several months after he returned, he spent long hours of serious conversation with Gottlob Buettner, a close personal friend, who was five years his senior. Buettner made a deep impression on the young man.

He and his friends were gathered around the dinner table one evening, singing a German hymn written by Zinzendorf, whose subject touched upon the love of Christ. The words thrust into his heart like a sword, and as the final verse was sung, he burst from the room and spent the night weeping and praying until he found the peace of God. That evening he resolved to devote his life to serving God, spreading his Gospel among the American Indians.

· 3 ·

Preventing Mischief, 1743–1745

THE SNOW-LADEN clouds of January 1743 hung heavy in the northern skies as David Zeisberger and Bishop Nitschmann left New York City. They were well on their way to Bethlehem when the ship carrying the Zinzendorf party cleared New York Harbor and headed to the open sea. Zeisberger's aborted trip to Europe marked a turning point in the twenty-one-year-old's life. Although the reason for sending him to Europe is not revealed in Moravian archives, it is clear he preferred to work in America. Within a few months he was assigned to the new language school. Classes began early in February 1744.

Moravian Church elders, both in Europe and America, were aware of the many and varied dialects of the American aborigines and the inherent linguistic difficulties in communicating with them. Most of the earlier Protestant missionary efforts collapsed because of their inability to master the Indian dialects. They knew that conducting social discourse required the use of a mutually understandable language. They could not expect the Indians to learn German or English. Thus missionaries must be trained as quickly as possible to master the Indian tongues. The task could take months, possibly years.

John Christopher Pyrlaeus, the prospective instructor of the new language school, had arrived in America with Gottlob Buettner on October 26, 1741. He was a university-educated Latin scholar, well liked, a brilliant student. He was adapt at teaching both children and adults. Being multilingual, he was especially good at teaching languages and thus was the ideal instructor for the Indian language school.[1]

On February 4, 1744, Pyrlaeus opened his language school at Bethlehem in the newly completed Brethren House (now the Moravian Theological Seminar Music Building across the street from the Gemeinhaus). There were seven students in the first class. Only three besides Zeisberger play a role in this book. John and Margaret Hagen will appear briefly, but Joseph Bull (later known as Schebosh), who had recently joined the Moravians, would later walk by the side of David Zeisberger and share many of his hardships.

Throughout 1744 the seven students faithfully attended Pyrlaeus's classes. It must have been a pleasant and agreeable experience for all. The Bethlehem Diary contains many entries kept by George Neisser referring to their activities: love feasts, night watches, birthday parties. But as the year progressed, Zeisberger emerged as the most promising student and was the first one given the opportunity to apply his training practically.

Shortly after the beginning of 1745, a plan was devised to send Christian Frederick Post and Zeisberger into the Mohawk country to develop their skills with the Iroquois language. This was Zeisberger's initial visit to Indian territory, except for his occasional visits to old Chief Tatamy, east of Nazareth.

Traveling north along the Roeliff Jasen Kill, they arrived at the Hudson River, then continued north down the Schoharie Creek valley to Fort Hunter. From its beginning, Fort Hunter was a marginal operation. Built by English traders from Albany, it lay on the south side of the Mohawk River at the mouth of Schoharie Creek. It was the last white outpost between the Mohawks at Canajoharie and the whites at Schenectady. The fort was a commercial rather than a military operation, and it provided a convenient location for the Iroquois traders to exchange their furs for English products treasured by the Indians.

The arrival of the young strangers without passports from the governor of the colony triggered suspicion among the soldiers, especially since the visitors were sent by a church widely accused of sympathy with the French. Some of the soldiers unofficially examined the young men, but their answers seemed innocuous and they were permitted to proceed to

Canajoharie, some twenty-five miles upriver from Fort Hunter. When they arrived at the Mohawk Castle, the trio received a warm reception from Tiyanoga (pronounced Tie-an-No-gah), whose English name was Hendricks.[2] He was the head chief among the Mohawks and also one of the so-called kings who had visited Queen Anne in the embassy of 1710.

Post and Zeisberger brought greetings from Pyrlaeus and his wife who had spent several months earlier in the year among the Mohawks in preparation for beginning the language school. Hendricks, grateful, bowed low in appreciation. After a short conference with the tribe, he agreed to receive the two missionaries into his village and instruct them in the language. Their visit to Fort Hunter was dutifully reported to the fort's superiors at Albany.

Ten days after they arrived at Mohawk Castle, as they were leaving their cabin to gather wood for the fireplace, there was a knock at the door. As the door opened, the two strangers outside took one look at the men, axes in hand, and beat a hasty retreat. After a good laugh, Christian and David went about their work and returned to the cabin with an ample supply of wood. Waiting for them was a neighbor who invited them to come to his cabin. When they arrived, the same two men who had fled from their cabin were waiting with a summons to appear immediately at Albany. When Hendricks heard of the arrest he was livid with anger at the soldiers. "Your people," he said, "have just settled your disputes with us, and now you begin a new quarrel! You deserve to be killed!" Without waiting for further discussion, the soldiers loaded their prisoners into the sleigh and headed for Albany.

In Albany they were taken to Mayor Peter Schuyler, who immediately sent them to the courthouse to be examined by his council. Zeisberger said in the course of the inquest, the magistrates "asked many filthy and insolent questions, laughing among themselves," until he, with calm self-possession, suggested, "We hope the honorable Magistrates will behave more discreetly and avoid asking similar questions." This seemed to end the offensive and vulgar language, and "they appeared to be ashamed."[3] After declaring that they were loyal subjects of King George, Zeisberger and Post were released.

The next morning a corporal and four heavily armed soldiers appeared at their lodgings and marched them to police headquarters, placing the two under the jurisdiction of a Captain Rutherford, who appointed a guard to take them to New York. When questioned, Post and Zeisberger were advised that their offense was failing to swear the oath to the king, a requirement of all New York colonial citizens. Before departing, the mayor took one final verbal shot: "If you or any of your Brethren come here again without a pass from the Governor I will have you whipped out of town." When they reached New York City, they were confined to the jail in city hall but were permitted to write a short note to Thomas Noble, a friend and successful merchant in the city. Peter Boehler and Anton Seiffert, who were in New York awaiting a ship to England, wrote a heartening letter to the missionaries. Noble sent his clerk, Henry Van Vleck, to notify the Mission Board in Bethlehem of their arrest.

The following day, February 23, the pair was taken before Governor George Clinton and his council. Probably because he was the youngest, Zeisberger was the first to be examined.[4] When they were finished with Post, Zeisberger was recalled, and the secretary read to him the new statute prohibiting the activities of the Moravians. The questioning hit upon a most delicate subject to Zeisberger. The councilman asked him, "Do you understand this?" Zeisberger responded, "Most of it, but not all." "Will you take the oath?" "I hope," Zeisberger said, "the Honorable Council will not force me to do it." The councilman replied, "We will not constrain you; you may let it alone if it is against your conscience; but you will have to go to prison again." Proudly, Zeisberger responded, "I am content."[5]

Before leaving the council chambers Zeisberger asked what crime they had committed. One of the council members, after making several ponderously trite statements, concluded by saying, "We must prevent mischief before it is brought about." Such was justice in New York in 1745. They were promptly sent back to jail. The next morning Boehler and Seiffert visited the prisoners and assured them that people in Bethlehem were working on their problem.

In the meantime, both seemed to be enjoying their confinement. "We count it an honor," wrote Zeisberger, "to suffer for the Saviour's sake." With Post's assistance, he used the time to continue studying the Mohawk language. It was over a month before the prisoners received any information about their fate. On March 20, a paragraph was inserted into the council's minutes:

> The petition of David Zeisberger & Christian Frederick Post having been Presented to his Excellency & read, desiring to be free'd from their confinement & to have leave to return home, & certificate of Conrad Weiser Esquire one of his Majesty's Justices of the Peace for County of Lancaster to the said Petition annexed being also read:

> Ordered that the said David Zeisberger & Christian Frederick Post be released from their confinement Paying their fees.[6]

But it was April 8 before the council, at last, ordered their release.

Two days later, after they had paid "their fees," the sheriff turned the key of their cells for the last time. After fifty-one days of confinement, they repaired to the home of their principal benefactor, Thomas Noble, collected their mental faculties, and were off to Bethlehem, arriving there on April 16.

David Zeisberger spent his twenty-fourth birthday in that New York City jail cell suffering, as he later wrote, "For the Saviour's sake." The experience left a profound impression on him, and though his life was never in danger during the incarceration, it hardened his resolve to make that sacrifice willingly if the occasion demanded. This was the first of many occasions that shaped his cool, calm, serene personality, and he soothed others' hysteria in moments of crisis, eliciting in them the same innocent faith he possessed. The experience helped to develop in him an equanimity that later served him well.

One month before Zeisberger and Post's return, the Brethren had the joy of baptizing the "first fruits" of their gospel among the Delaware Nation. For the last four years Anton Seiffert, Martin Mack, Nathaniel Seidel, John Hagen, and others had made numerous trips into the Delaware country north of Bethlehem. Each journey lasted several days. During one visit, they invited a chief of the Turtle Clan and his wife to Bethlehem. So impressed were they with the Moravians that they asked to be baptized. The ceremony was performed in March 1745, and the two were given the names "Gottlieb" and "Mary."

This event caused great consternation in their Delaware village. Tribal members concluded that the chief and his wife had been kidnapped and would become slaves of the Brethren. A messenger was sent to Bethlehem to invite them to return to their village for a visit, but the converts refused to leave Bethlehem.

The Delawares then decided to take the couple from the Moravians by force if necessary and sent a delegation of thirty-six warriors to Bethlehem. They arrived in a rowdy and boisterous mood, but Spangenberg called upon the Indian custom to "feed them before you talk." He led the party into a large room while the women of the village set out a bountiful table of meat, vegetables, and drink. After they finished eating and received Gottlieb and Spangenberg's explanation, they departed in peace, expressing satisfaction and amazement at the sincerity and hospitality of the

Brethren. Five months later, in September, Gottlieb enjoyed the pleasure of seeing his brother baptized and named Joachim.[7]

Meanwhile, Spangenberg and the Mission Board continued to wrestle with the problem of what to do with the Shekomeko Indian mission founded in 1740 by missionary Christian Heinrich Rauch (see Appendix A, number 1). A recent law passed by the New York Colonial legislature prohibited the religious teaching in other than approved denominations. Since the Moravians did not come under the protection of this law, they were forced to close the Shekomeko mission. Four months had passed since the sheriff closed the chapel and all preaching and teaching were ceased. Several plans had been suggested, including one to bring those who wished to Bethlehem. But the favored plan was to move the entire village into the Wyoming Valley. Most of the Shawnees living there had moved to the Ohio Country, leaving only a remnant that should not create problems. Except for a scattering of Delawares under Chief Nutimus and a small village of Nanticokes, the valley was deserted.[8] But such a move required permission from the Iroquois League, which controlled all of the land in and around the valley, and authorization could come only from the general council at Onondaga. As president of the Mission Board, Spangenberg was responsible for securing that permission.

Choosing two of his best men, Zeisberger and Joseph Bull (Schebosh, his Indian name), to go with him, Spangenberg departed from Bethlehem on May 24, 1745, for the journey to Onondaga. Fortuitously, Conrad Weiser was also making the same trip on behalf of Pennsylvania's Governor George Thomas to discuss several important questions with the Iroquois. This opportunity to travel with Weiser may have been the principal reason for Spangenberg's decision because he had little previous experience negotiating with the Iroquois.

They arrived at Shamokin on June 21. The village was to be the rendezvous point for the other members of the party, Shickellamy, a Cayuga chief, and his two sons. Unfortunately, Shickellamy had gone to Chamber's Mill some forty miles from Shamokin. Spangenberg and his two assistants, however, preached at every opportunity and also visited the famous Indian chief Madame Montour, who lived in the area near Shamokin. They also visited Chief Allummapees (Sassoonan), head chief of the Delawares), whom they found confined to his cot, blind and poverty-stricken.[9] Driven from the Delaware River after the Walking Purchase Treaty, most of his tribesmen had gone further west, but he and a scattering of his clan settled at Shamokin. Several years after this meeting, Weiser wrote to Richard Peters, the provincial secretary: "Allummapees would

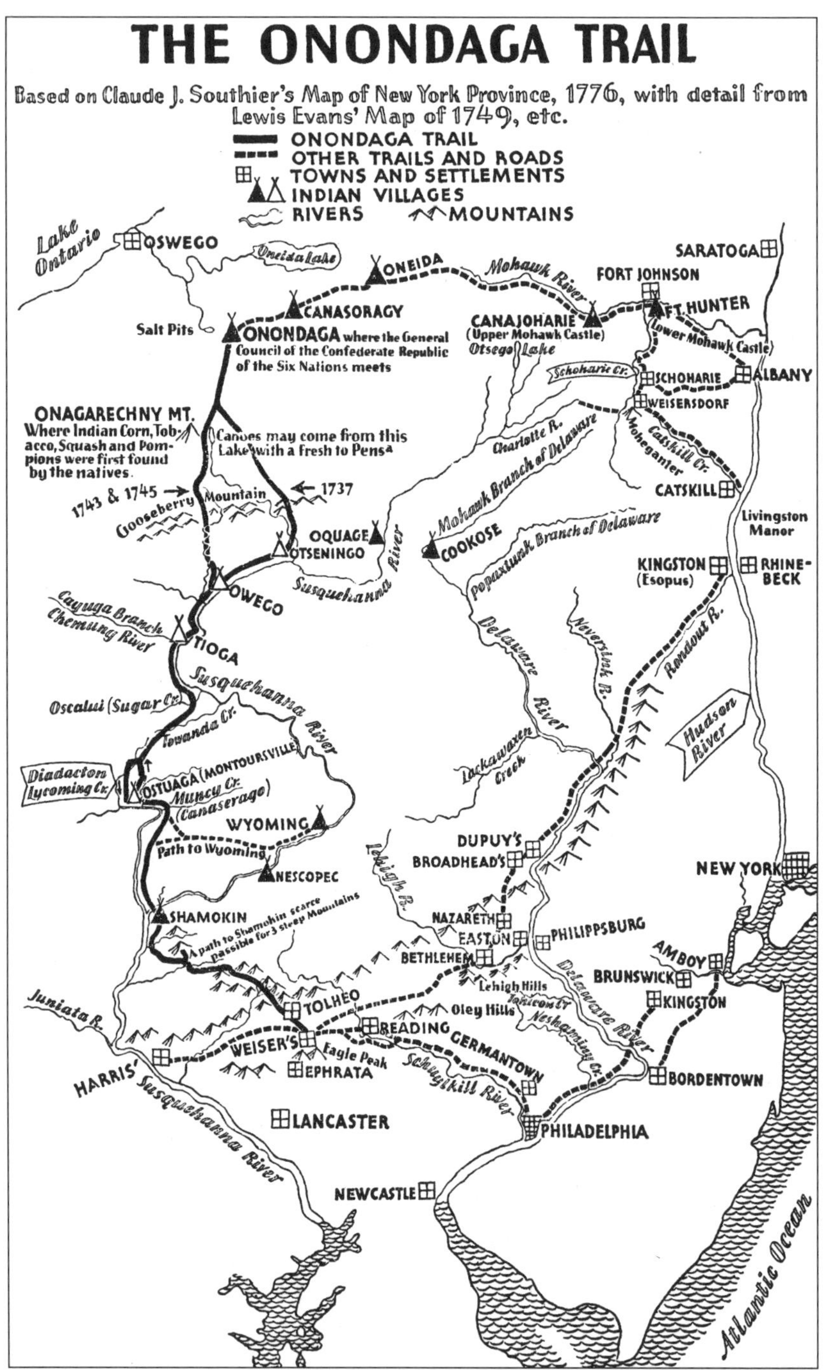

Onondaga Trail Map

have resigned his crown before now, but as he had the keeping of the public treasure, consisting of belts of Wampum, for which he buys Liquor, and has been drunk for this two or three years almost constantly, it is thought he won't die, so long as there is one single Wampum left in the bagg."[10] Three months after he wrote these lines, Allummapees was dead. The bag was empty.

Shickellamy returned on May 25 and consented to guide the party to Onondaga. They left Shamokin two days later on horseback. The group now consisted of the chief, his lame son, James Logan, Andrew Montour, Weiser, and the three missionaries.[11] They traveled up the west branch of the Susquehanna and stopped the first night at the mouth of Warriors' Run.

As they sat around the campfire discussing the day's events, a lone, footsore Iroquois warrior silently entered the circle. Wearing no shoes, stockings, or shirt, having no gun, hatchet, fire flint, or knife, he wore only a few tattered rags and a torn blanket thrown over his back. He was the sole survivor of a party of warriors returning from an expedition against the Catawbas. Weiser, recognizing him as one of the Onondaga braves he had met on a previous trip, described the conversation that followed:

> I knew him, and asked, how he could undertake to go on a journey of Three Hundred Miles so naked and unprovided, having no provisions, nor any arms to kill Creatures for his Substance? . . . He told me very cheerfully, that God fed everything which had life, even the Rattlesnake itself, though it was a bad creature; and that God would provide in such a Manner, that he should arrive at Onondaga; . . . that a visible God was with the Indians in the Wilderness, because they always cast their care upon him; but that, contrary to this, the Europeans always carried Bread with them.[12]

Spangenberg called him the "Limping Messenger." He remained with the party for two days to regain strength. Then, equipped with moccasins, flint, tinder, knife, and hatchet, he was dispatched to Onondaga to announce their coming.

One evening they bivouacked on the banks of Lycoming Creek where it cuts through the Laurel and Tiadaghton Hills, near the present village of Roaring Branch. After supper, Andrew Montour and James Logan gathered an immense quantity of wood and fed it into the fire until the flames rose to an impressive height. It was well after dark and the red light of the flames cast mysterious shadows against the dense forest. Shickellamy quietly rose and folded his arms across his chest. Slowly he raised his arms high over his head and, in the traditional salute to his God, turned to the north and south, then to the east and west, pausing in each direction momentarily to offer a prayer. Thus began the ceremony to adopt the three missionaries into the Iroquois confederacy. Spangenberg became Tgirhitontie, or "A Row of Trees," adopted into the Oneidas and the Clan of the Bear. Zeisberger's new name was Ganousseracheri, or "On the Pumpkin," and he entered the tribe of the Onondagas, the Turtle Clan. Schebosh became Hajingonia, or "One Who Twists Tobacco, the Clan of the Bear." The mystical magic of that brief moment remained with Zeisberger and Schebosh (both twenty-four at the time) until their dying days. Perhaps it was this impressive forest ceremony that cemented their forty-three-year friendship.

On January 6, they arrived at the "castle" of the Onondaga.[13] The journey had taken eighteen days. The "Limping Messenger" had also made good time, arriving three days ahead of the main party—just in time to delay the chiefs from departing on a visit to the French Canadian governor at Montreal. Runners were sent to the outlying nations to summon the members of the council to hear what Tarachiawagon and Tgirhitontie (Weiser and Spangenberg) had to say. The arrival of the party was celebrated with a parade of villagers playing violins, flutes, and drums, followed by the customary feast.[14]

The council met three days later. Weiser was the first speaker. He presented his business, then turned the meeting over to Spangenberg, who proposed that the Iroquois renew their bond of friendship established by Zinzendorf and the Six Nations in 1742. He also requested permission to begin a settlement for the Christian Indians at Wyoming (present Wilkes-Barre). Belts of wampum were laid before the chiefs and the hall resounded with "Jo-ha," the familiar term to indicate approval.

The next day Weiser and Spangenberg received their answer. The speaker was the "Black Prince" (Tocanunite), no stranger to Weiser. They had met on September 16, 1736, at the beginning of Weiser's career as the proprietor's interpreter, and on numerous occasions since. He was usually the spokesman at Iroquois conferences during this period. The French held him in such esteem that they refused to conduct any treaty negotiations without him present.[15]

Tocanunite first responded to Weiser's requests, then directed his remarks to Spangenberg. The Prince replied that the Onodagas would be delighted to renew the compact made with Zinzendorf in 1742 and, furthermore, had no objection to the settlement of the Mahicans from New York in the Wyoming Valley. In fact, they welcomed the move. With this, the conference closed. Following their deliberations, the guests were entertained with food, drink, music, and dancing. Two days later, they began the return journey and arrived back in Bethlehem during the third week in July.[16]

· 4 ·

Shamokin: The Stronghold of the Prince of Darkness, 1746–1749

WHEN SPANGENBERG returned to America in 1744, he brought with him an elaborate and comprehensive communal plan of organization for Bethlehem. It was the result of many months of intensive planning and became known as the "General Economy." The new concept influenced church activities not only in Bethlehem but also in other Moravian settlements, including villages later built on the Nazareth lands. New names such as Friedensthal, Christianbrunn, and Gnadenthal would be added to the lexicon of Moravian interests. The Economy brought under one manager, the vicar general, all personnel required to operate the religious, agricultural, commercial, industrial, and mission activities of the church.

Spangenberg and the men who surrounded him were not academic theorists, religious doctrinarians, or starry-eyed dreamers. They were sober-minded, hardworking men of affairs who had lived in the wilderness long enough to know how to cope with the problems they faced.

The Bethlehem plan was unique among the communal experiments of the time. The residents volunteered to join the Brethren for an indefinite period and gave their time and labor for the common cause. In return they received food, shelter, and spiritual guidance. No personal liberty was surrendered. There were no written contracts stipulating a period of time the

Brethren must serve, and members could leave any time they wished, as some did. Never was there the slightest interference with the right to hold private property. The immigrants were brought to Pennsylvania without charge and were not required to reimburse the church if they decided to leave. Spangenberg once said, "Any dissatisfied person is at liberty to leave at any time for there are no walls around Bethlehem."[1] The leaders did reserve the right to expel persons for cause, and all members were required to conform to the regulations of the Economy.

Spangenberg had most of the plan for the Economy in place before he departed on his trip to Onondaga in May 1745. His party arrived back in Bethlehem on July 21. Zeisberger, a member of the party, returned to the language school, and Spangenberg directed his attention to other important matters, principally the removal of the Shekomeko converts to the Wyoming Valley, now that permission had been granted by the Iroquois confederacy. With the Mission Board's approval, a messenger was dispatched to the Indian village inviting the converts to make the move, but, much to everyone's embarrassment, the Indians refused to accept their invitation. Abraham (Shabosh), one of the "first fruits," led the opposition. He correctly reasoned that the area lay directly on the path of the Iroquois warriors' war route to the Catawbas, and any village in that location would be subject to constant interruption from the most undesirable element of war-minded Indians. He also noted that the area abounded with "wanton women" who would seduce all respectable men who might live there.

The Mission Board then suggested they move to Bethlehem. Delighted with that option, the converts made the move over the next year. The mission was located on the north bank of the Monocacy, behind the present Widow's House and Clewell Hall. They began to construct a cluster of cabins which became known as Friedenshutten. It received its first converts when the migration from Shekomeko began in the spring of 1746. But a more permanent location was required.[2]

During the year 1745 the church had purchased 197 acres on the north side of the Blue Mountains in the Mahoning Valley.[3] The original tract lay on the west bank of Mahoning Creek, near the junction with the Lehigh River (present Lehighton, Carbon County, Pennsylvania). It became the site of the first of five missions to carry the name Gnadenhutten (Tents of Grace).

Early in the spring of 1746, Martin Mack, David Zeisberger, and several other young men from Bethlehem, along with a party of Indians, traveled to the area to begin clearing the land and laying out the new village. Two months later they had completed the first buildings. After an impressive love feast on June 13, the first contingent of converts left Friedenshutten, some by canoe and others on foot, bound for their new homes. Mack was appointed as the first missionary, and Christian Rauch, the former head missionary at Shekomeko, acted temporarily as his assistant.

Under Martin and Jeanette Mack's care, Gnadenhutten would grow to be an Indian town such as Pennsylvania had never seen. It prospered both materially and spiritually until 1755. Sadly, Jeanette would not be with her husband the full nine years. The little black-eyed, Palatine girl he met on the banks of Wapinger's Creek near the Shekomeko mission died on December 15, 1749.

Within a year after the Spangenbergs came back to America, the enormous responsibility and the vast complexity of their assignment began to affect the physical and emotional health of both Spangenberg and his wife, Eva Maria. He wrote to Zinzendorf asking for an assistant. Early in January 1747 the snow, *John Galley*, arrived off the Delaware coast at Cape Henlopen and put in at the port of Lewes.[4] Aboard was John Christopher Frederick Cammerhoff, Spangenberg's new assistant, and his wife, Anna. They arrived at Bethlehem on January 12.

Spangenberg's new assistant was a gifted young man full of piety, fire, and determination.[5] Cammerhoff would blaze across the Bethlehem sky like a comet, but in only four years he would be gone, his health broken from a prodigious display of energy unmatched by any of his contemporaries.[6]

While the activity at the two missions of Friedenshutten and Gnadenhutten was progressing, Spangenberg and the Mission Board were also directing their attention to another location. Since Zinzendorf's 1742 visit, the Indian village of Shamokin (now Sunbury, Pennsylvania, where the north and west branches of the Susquehanna join), the Brethren had been intrigued with the idea of developing the land located at the forks of the Susquehanna. Since then, they had been receiving encouraging signals from both Shickellamy, the Iroquois vicegerent of the region, who lived at the village, and their friend Conrad Weiser, who frequently visited the chief. Shamokin was reasoned to be a strategic location, but the site had several inherent problems. It lay on the warriors' path to the Catawbas. Iroquoian war parties regularly passed through the village, creating confusion and tension. It was also the rendezvous point for many different tribes, Delaware, Tuteloe, Nanticoke, remnants of the Susquahannock, and others. Such a polyglot of dialects and a warlike atmosphere added to the foreboding nature of the location as a mission site.

In the autumn of 1745, the board sent a couple experienced in mission work, Martin and Jeanette Mack, to the village to test the waters. So arduous and difficult was their visit that Martin, on leaving, called the village "The Stronghold of the Prince of Darkness." Warriors from throughout the Indian country met there regularly and engaged in the most "abominable orgies." To escape sure death on many nights the pair fled into the forest. They remained at Shamokin for three months, returning to Bethlehem on November 10. Their experience made any prospect of success there seem doubtful.[7]

At the beginning of 1747, Spangenberg turned his attention again to the prospect of developing the Shamokin mission. Several positive events had occurred in the year since the Macks' unfortunate experience in the autumn of 1745. Their old friend Conrad Weiser was encouraging Bethlehem to establish a mission at Shamokin.

In addition to Weiser's favorable comments, Spangenberg was aware that Shickellamy, the head chief at the village, had requested the governor of Pennsylvania to place a blacksmith at the village. The governor assented, and the Moravians agreed to furnish the building, equipment, and smithy, providing they could build and staff a mission.

Before the end of May all arrangements were completed and the construction crew was on the trail back to Shamokin. John Hagen, Joseph Powell, and David Bruce carried the final instructions written in Mohawk, along with a supply of wampum to be given to Shickellamy.[8]

When the party arrived at the village, Shickellamy was jubilant. To indicate his pleasure, he gathered each of the men in his arms in a gesture of friendliness and affection. They pitched their tent under a spreading beech tree near the chief's home and were taken inside, where bearskin rugs and seats were spread on the floor. When the chief's councillors were called, Hagen explained the objective of the visit by reading his Mohawk instructions followed with the presentation of the wampum. The next day Shickellamy pointed out the proposed location of the new mission house, some twelve paces from his own home, then provided horses to drag the logs to the construction site. The building, at least temporarily, would be a combination structure, housing both the mission quarters and the smithy. When it was completed, they would send for the blacksmith and his wife. In the interim, Hagen would remain as the missionary.[9]

The building was completed by the middle of July, and word was sent to Bethlehem that they were ready for the blacksmith. By the end of the month Christian Rauch escorted blacksmith Anton Schmidt and his wife, Anna Catharine, to their new home; Hagen's wife, Margaret, also accompanied the party. They arrived on August 3, and fifteen days later a formal reception was held by the Indian council and the villagers welcomed the new blacksmith to their town. They named Schmidt "Rachustone."

It was an auspicious beginning. But they had hardly settled into the routine of their daily lives when disaster struck. With no warning, on September 16 John Hagen died. He was buried in a rude coffin in the turnip patch near the mission. When the melancholy news reached Bethlehem, the people reacted in the stoic fashion typical of the eighteenth century. Martin Mack was appointed to succeed Hagen, and life went on.

The new year, 1748, was full of contradictions, mystery, sadness, and joy. In April, Zeisberger was appointed to be Martin Mack's assistant at the new mission. He was delighted and plunged into his work with enthusiasm and determination, beginning a project that engaged his attention for over ten years. Both Pyrlaeus and Spangenberg had been encouraging him to compile Iroquois-to-German and Iroquois-to-English dictionaries. Such volumes would be invaluable for training future missionary candidates. Shickellamy proved to be a treasured asset in helping with the project. By now Zeisberger had become fluent, especially in the Mohawk-Iroquois dialect.[10]

Near the first of July, Zeisberger and Mack began an extensive tour along both branches of the Susquehanna River north of Shamokin to explore the potential for additional converts and to proselytize among the various tribes they might encounter. What they found was sickness, famine, and death.

Traveling up the west branch of the Susquehanna River on the Great Shamokin Path, which ran from Shamokin to Kittanning Village on the Allegheny River, they stopped at Madame Montour's old village, which lay deserted and in ruins. Continuing west as far as the Great Island (Lock Haven, Pennsylvania), the pair stopped at the Delaware village. The island, covered with rank grass, seemed almost deserted. Only a few gaunt old men, emaciated women, and cadaverous children gathered around the two missionaries. Zeisberger asked, "Where are all our brothers who used to hunt along the river?" One of the old men pointed to the nearby hut. As Zeisberger pulled back the dirty cloth that covered the door, he was almost overcome by the stench. In the gloom of the hut he could see half-dead bodies lying on cots, covered with pus-filled sores. Again smallpox, the white man's curse, was taking its toll. The scene was the same everywhere they visited. Most of the able-bodied men were on their summer hunt. Those who remained were slowly starving or dying of smallpox. Gaunt figures huddled around the fire, and a kettle of boiled grass was a luxury.[11]

Retracing the trail to Ostonwakin, they left the river and cut southeast across country, probably taking the Muncy-Mahoning Path to present Danville, where they struck the north branch of the Susquehanna. They

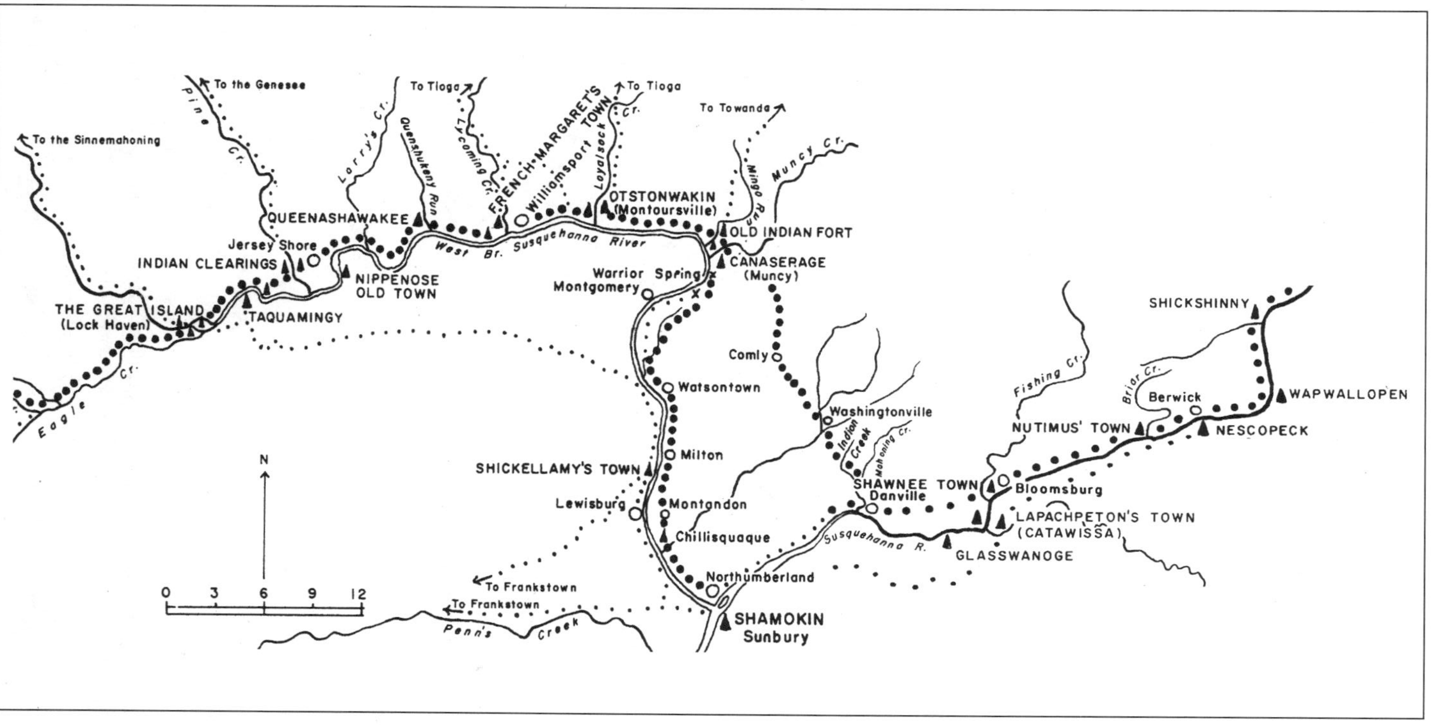

Exploratory Journey among the Delaware, 1748. From Paul A. W. Wallace, *Indian Paths of Pennsylvania*, Pennsylvania Historical and Museum Commission, 1965.

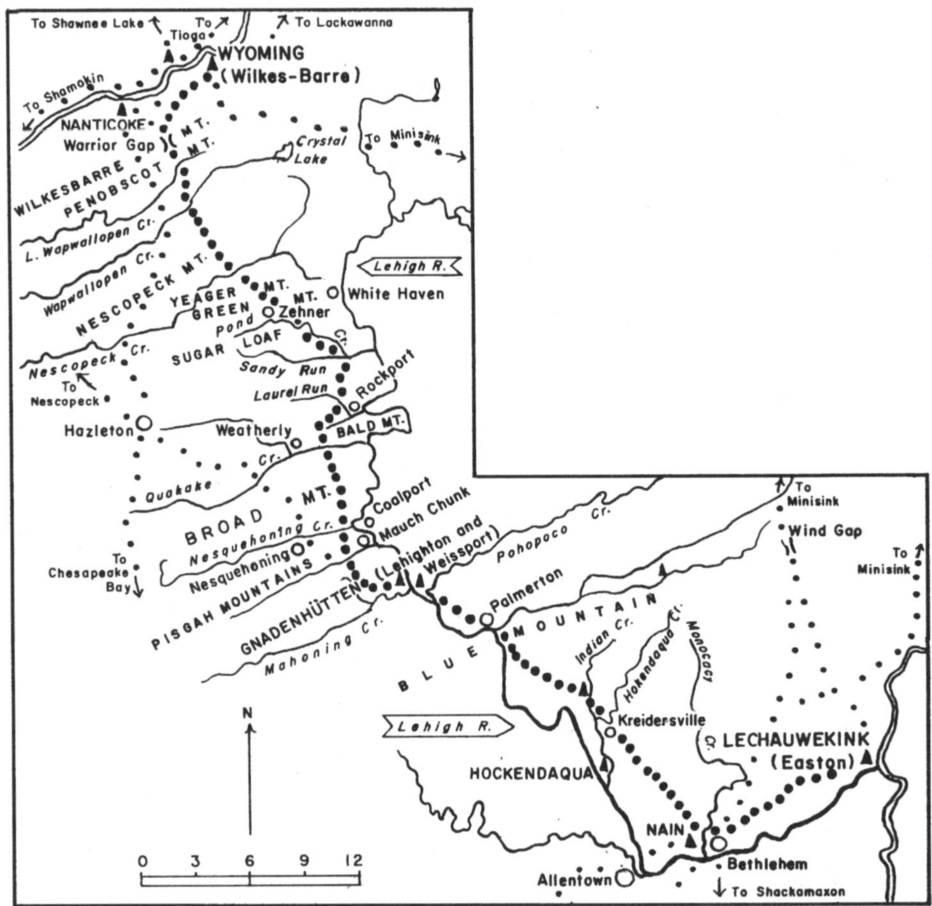

Lehigh Path. From Paul A. W. Wallace, *Indian Paths of Pennsylvania*, Pennsylvania Historical and Museum Commission, 1965.

then turned north along the Great Warriors' Path to the Nanticoke village and the Wyoming Valley and again found small groups crouched around the fires, eating boiled tree bark, unripe grapes, and roots. It was a depressing scene as the sorrowful pair left the village. They reached Bethlehem on August 1, 1748, and reported to the Mission Board.[12]

After his Susquehanna River trip, Zeisberger did not return to his missionary post at Shamokin but remained at Bethlehem for two months.

Word had been received in Bethlehem that Baron John de Watteville, accompanied by his wife, Benigna, who was Zinzendorf's oldest daughter, would be visiting Bethlehem.[13]

Soon after the de Watteville party arrived at Bethlehem on September 19, 1748, he inspected the new mission at Gnadenhutten and the Indian territory north of the Blue Mountains. Cammerhoff and Martin Mack accompanied him; Zeisberger acted as their interpreter. On October 1, they arrived at the new mission. The whole village was there to meet them. The afternoon and evening were spent greeting and preaching while Zeisberger interpreted.

Time was precious because the weather was uncertain, so the next day they proceeded north into the wilderness up the Lehigh Path. The trail, the shortest way from Bethlehem to the Wyoming Valley, was also the most difficult because it climbs the Mauch Chunk, Pisgah, Broad, Yeager, Nescopek, and Wilkes-Barre Mountains. But it had certain advantages for the unencumbered travelers, for it was a dry and direct route.[14]

Three days later, they overcame the final barrier, Wilkes-Barre Mountain at Warriors' Gap, and looked down into the beautiful Wyoming Valley. On the evening of October 7, the baron gathered his companions around the bright flames of the campfire to hold the first Lord's Supper in the Wyoming Valley. Their hymns reverberated across the valley as the Indians stood in silent awe and viewed the strange white man's ceremony.

Within a few days they were welcomed by Powell and Schmidt at Shamokin. Shickellamy was particularly pleased to meet the bishop, who made a deep impression on the dying chief. The baron had brought several pieces of expensive silverware, mounted in a beautiful morocco case, as a gift from Zinzendorf.[15] The old chief was overcome with gratitude. He promised de Watteville he would visit Bethlehem. Faithful to his promise, several weeks after de Watteville's departure from Shamokin, Shickellamy, eager to learn more about Jesus, arrived in Bethlehem, accompanied by Zeisberger.

Even though the horses had walked at a "crab's pace," it had been a tiring journey for the old man. When he arrived at Bethlehem, it was obvious that he was "sick unto death." The trials of the past year, the responsibility of his office, and the sickness and death that had destroyed eight members of his immediate family were almost more than his frail constitution could bear.[16] In his sorrow, he sought the quiet comfort, peace, and love of the Shamokin mission. He welcomed the change from the thieving white traders and carousing drunkards among his own people.

Perhaps, he thought, among the Brethren at Bethlehem, who traded only in "God's love," he might find peace and tranquillity during his final years. He remained at Bethlehem for several weeks, enjoying the Brethren's hospitality. On the return journey he fell seriously ill at Tulpehocken and only with Zeisberger's help mustered enough strength to return to his village, where he lay down on his mat for the last time. David ministered to his needs until December 6, when, with a bright smile on his face, as Zeisberger stroked his brow, Shickellamy joined his great Manitou in heaven.[17]

Zeisberger immediately passed word of the chief's death to Conrad Weiser, who notified Governor James Hamilton. The governor sent messages of condolence and the usual presents to the chief's sons and requested one of his sons, John Shickellamy, to act as the Iroquois deputy until a permanent appointment could be made.[18] Zeisberger, not trusting an express messenger, delivered news of the chief's death to Bethlehem in person.

David had intended to return to Shamokin, but de Watteville delayed him for several months visiting churches in Pennsylvania. After the bishop's party returned from its visitations, de Watteville ordained the young missionary into the ministry on February 16, 1749. He then released Zeisberger, who returned to Shamokin accompanied by his new assistant, Jonathan, the young son of John (Tschoop), their first convert. Zeisberger was now in charge of the Shamokin mission.

The next six months were vexing times for David and his new assistant because the village and its native people continued in their "heathenish" life despite the Christian influence of the mission. If anything, the village's condition seemed to be deteriorating. Many of the native tribes within miles of Shamokin were bringing their hatchets, knives, guns, and other paraphernalia to be repaired by the blacksmith. Adding to the confusion were the usual comings and goings of Iroquois war parties on the way to fight the southern Catawbas. Situated approximately halfway between Onondaga and the Catawbas capitals, the Shamokin village became an ideal location for relaxation and entertainment, particularly when war parties were carrying captured prisoners, who were cruelly forced to amuse the village.

Throughout the spring and summer of 1749, Zeisberger continued his hapless work at the mission. Meanwhile, the Penn proprietors called a council meeting with the chiefs of the Six Nations confederacy, to be held at Philadelphia. The occasion provided the Brethren with an opportunity to advance their cause of a mission among the Iroquois. The governor, concerned about the movement of white settlers into the Indian lands north of the Blue Mountains, found an excuse to negotiate for the purchase of this land. A small delegation, representing each of the Six Nations, was expected. But on August 13, to everyone's surprise, Onondaga, Seneca, Mohawk, Cayuga, Oneida, Tuscarora, Shawnee, Nanticoke, Delaware, Mahican, and Tuteloe tribesmen arrived in Philadelphia. In all, the contingent, led by Onondago chief Canassatego, totaled 260 people. Weiser, whose home they had visited on the way to Philadelphia, was disgusted and offended by the whole lot, since it was his responsibility to feed the hungry mob as they passed through Tulpehocken.[19]

It took eleven days to complete the negotiations. Happily for everyone in Philadelphia, on August 25, the Indian delegation was sent, half-drunk and grumbling, on its way home. The proceeding had not been one of the proprietors' shining moments. Beginning with Weiser, no one seemed to be in good humor. Canassatego, the leader of the Indians, had let the delegation become too large, and the proprietors badly handled the food problem. They missed Shickellamy.

The treaty called for the sale of most of the land north of the Blue Mountains, beginning at a point on the Susquehanna River near the mouth of Mahanoy Creek, which was a few miles south of Shamokin, running in a straight line northeast to the mouth of the Lackawaken Creek, on the Delaware. At the insistence of the Iroquois chiefs, it did not include any of the Wyoming Valley. That sacred region would remain under the control of the Six Nations.

The treaty did provide an opportunity for the Brethren to talk to the Six Nations chiefs. They met at the parsonage on Race Street during a lull in the negotiations. De Watteville, Cammerhoff, Pyrlaeus, Seidel, and Spangenberg, who was greatly loved by the chiefs, attended. Canassatago led the Indian delegation. The chiefs granted permission for an embassy to visit Onondaga in the spring of 1750. Cammerhoff was to be the official envoy, and Zeisberger was to act as interpreter.[20] A messenger was sent to Shamokin to give Zeisberger the good news. He had long desired to begin his work among the Iroquois.

In the meantime, a mission station was begun twenty-five miles north of Bethlehem at the Delaware Indian village of Meniologameka (Men-io-la-go-ME-ka). Located in the narrow Smith Valley on the Aquashicola Creek, it lay just north of the Blue Mountains from Bethlehem. (The Zinzendorf party had visited there in 1742.) The chief of the village, George Rex, and his wife had made several visits to Bethlehem and Gnadenhutten and were impressed with the progress the Brethren were making among their fellow tribesmen. On April 20, 1749, after frequent requests, they

Indian Treaty Map, 1682–1795

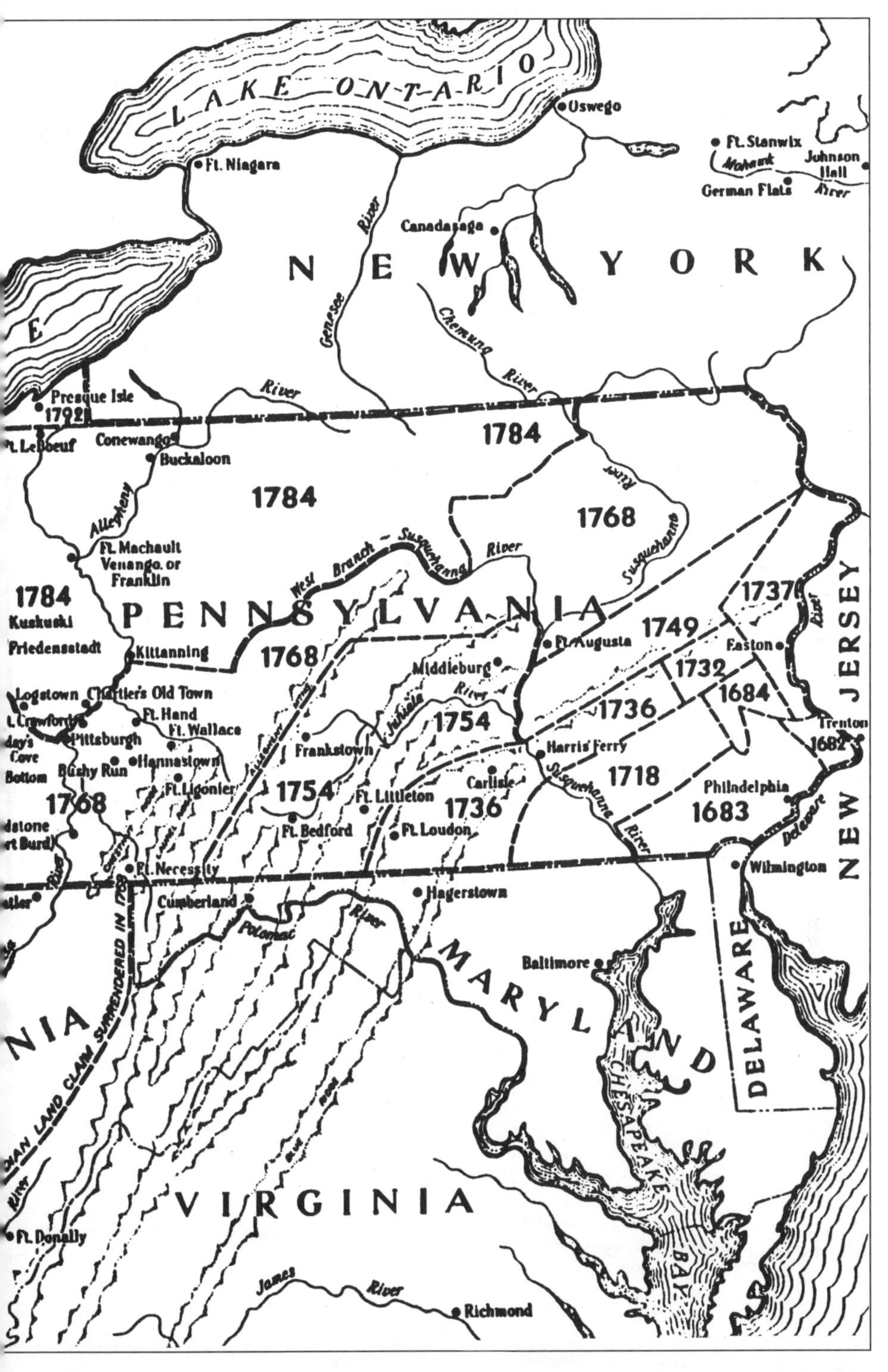

LAKE ONTARIO
Oswego
Ft. Niagara
Ft. Stanwix
Mohawk River
Johnson Hall
German Flats
Canadasaga
Genesee River
NEW YORK
Chemung River
Presque Isle 1792
Ft. LeBoeuf
Conewango
Buckaloon
1784
1784
1768
Allegheny
Ft. Machault Venango or Franklin
West Branch Susquehanna River
Susquehanna River
1784
Kuskuski
Friedensstadt
PENNSYLVANIA
Kittanning
1768
Ft. Augusta
1749
1737
Easton
Middleburg
Juniata River
1732
1684
Logstown
Chartier's Old Town
Ft. Hand
Ft. Wallace
Pittsburgh
1754
1736
Trenton
1682
Frankstown
Harris Ferry
Bushy Run
Hannastown
Ft. Ligonier
Carlisle
1718
Philadelphia
1768
1754
Ft. Littleton
1736
1683
Ft. Bedford
Ft. Loudon
Ft. Necessity
Wilmington
Cumberland
Hagerstown
Potomac River
NEW JERSEY
Baltimore
MARYLAND
DELAWARE
CHESAPEAKE BAY
VIRGINIA
Ft. Donally
James River
Richmond

were baptized as Brother Augustus and Sister Esther. Shortly following his conversion, Brother Augustus convinced many of his fellow tribe members that they too should embrace the word of Jesus and become Christians.[21] Augustus's efforts were soon successful so the Brethren decided to assign him as a national assistant in charge of the village station. The Bethlehem officials often visited the new station throughout the next months, and in January 1752 it became a full-fledged mission with Bernard Grube serving as the first missionary.[22]

By far the most successful of the five existing missions was Gnadenhutten, whose population had grown to well over one hundred converts. In July a new chapel was constructed to accommodate the increasing numbers of members. De Watteville, who sailed for Europe on October 15, 1749, carried the gratifying news of the Brethren's progress to his father-in law, Count Zinzendorf, back in Germany.

· 5 ·

A Journey into Hell, 1750

By January 1750, when four missions and one mission station were functioning (Pachgatgoch, Wechquadnach, Gnadenhutten, Shamokin, and Meniologameka), the Brethren were about to begin their missionary activities among the Six Nations confederacy. In August 1749, after the meeting of the chiefs in Philadelphia, John Frederick Cammerhoff and Zeisberger were assigned to make the preliminary contact with the Onondagas.

By 1750 the Moravian missionaries had been successful mainly among scattered groups of Delawares and remnants of lesser tribes, such as the Mahican, Nanticoke, and Wampanoag. It was quite another matter to attempt such activities among the highly organized, proud, and powerful Iroquois, who seemed indifferent, if not hostile, toward all men of the cloth. "Blackcoats," they called them, to differentiate them from the black-robed Jesuits from French Canada. The Iroquoian experience with the Catholic Jesuits and some Protestant missionaries over the previous one hundred years had taught them to be wary of black-coated white men.

The journey for Zeisberger and Cammerhoff began from Bethlehem. Zeisberger departed on Monday, May 10, 1750, bound for Shamokin to pick up their guide. Cammerhoff left the following Friday, traveling a different route over the Lehigh Pass, through Gnadenhutten, directly north to their rendezvous point, the Wyoming Valley. It took Cammerhoff six days to reach Wyoming, and Zeisberger arrived the following day, but without the guide, who was to follow several days later.

They waited seven days for the guide, but when he failed to arrive, they prepared to embark without him. Just before their departure on the morning of May 28, they were loading their canoes when the guide, Hahotschaunquas, arrived with his wife, Gejehne, and their two children, a boy of fourteen named Tagita and his four-year-old sister. The father was a member of the Gajuka (Cayuga) nation (hereafter referred to as the Gajuka).[1]

Their route ran along the Susquehanna to the junction of the Chemung River, then up the Chemung for a short distance to the site of the present city of Waverly, New York. Here they would disembark from the canoes, secure horses, and travel overland through the present counties of Chemung, Schuyler, Tompkins, and Cayuga to Onondaga, their destination.

One incident during their trip is worthy of note. As they approached the Cayuga Lake inlet, Six-Mile and Fall Creeks rush and tumble almost perpendicularly from a height of ninety feet, passing through the present campus of Cornell University and falling into Cayuga Lake at the present city of Ithaca, New York.[2] Cammerhoff recorded the following as they proceeded up the eastern shores of Cayuga Lake:

> Today we crossed at least 200 creeks which enter into the lake (Cayuga). . . . After we had continued on our way we reached a creek called by the Indians Gientachne [Salmon Creek] where their warriors usually encamped. Here we saw the whole chancery court on archives of the Cayugas painted or hanging in the trees. Our Gajuka gave us a lengthy explanation of it all. When the great warriors go to war against the Catawbas, they make a painting of themselves. We saw several of these fine work of arts, done in Indian style. On their return they added their deeds in a painting, showing what scalps they have taken, what they bring with them in the shape of treasures, bracelets, wampum and the like. . . . Toward evening we reached the first farm of the Cayuga, which is still some distance from the town. It is situated on the lake, and on a creek by the name of Gaheskao [Great Gully Brook]. . . . A great crowd at once assembled around us, in which were many fine, brave looking fellows.[3]

On June 18, they turned east and plunged again into the wilderness, crossing the northern tip of Lakes Owasco and Skaneateles. That evening they camped a few miles from the council fires of the Onondagas.[4]

Arriving at the village the next morning, they learned that Canassatego was attending a meeting of the grand council. A messenger was sent announcing the Moravians' arrival. He returned promptly with a summons requesting their presence. Within minutes they entered the council longhouse and observed at least thirty chiefs gathered in a circle surrounding Canassatego, who with outstreched arms strode to meet them. They were introduced and shook hands with the chiefs. Cammerhoff addressed the group, thanking the chiefs for their warm reception. He hoped to meet again after several days of rest and discuss the object of their visit. Strings of wampum were presented along with a pipe and some tobacco. Zeisberger translated the remarks into Mohawk. After the translation there was great applause and the usual exclamations of affirmation, "Jahuh! Jahuh!"

Although this beginning was auspicious, it was followed by the delay typically encountered in Indian diplomacy, which frequently frustrated white and Indian negotiations. Clock and calendar were never important factors with the Indians, and successful mediations required the ultimate in timing and patience.

Over the next two days the missionaries consulted among themselves to determine the best way to approach the council. Their greatest concern was Zeisberger's ability to interpret their conversations correctly into the Iroquois dialects. Although he had had considerable experience at Shamokin and had been tutored in the Mohawk dialect by Pyrlaeus, the language spoken at Onondaga was far more sophisticated than that spoken at Shamokin. Because of their fears about David's inability to translate, they decided to submit their request to Canassatego and have him make the presentation to the council. Finally, on the afternoon of June 21, they were granted a private audience with the chief. Several members of the council were meeting at the same time in Canassatego's home, but he left them to meet with the missionaries "in the bush."

The missionaries wished to make four requests to the council:

1. They wanted a renewal of the Moravians' covenant negotiated in 1742 at Conrad Weiser's home in Tulpehocken and later renewed at Onondaga by Spangenberg in 1745.
2. By far the most important, they entreated the council to permit several of the Brethren to visit Onondaga and learn the dialects of the Six Nations.
3. On behalf of the Nanticokes, they requested a resident blacksmith in the Wyoming Valley.
4. They asked permission to visit the Senecas' castle at Chenussio in response to the invitation made in Philadelphia the previous year.

These petitions were first relayed by Cammerhoff to Zeisberger, then Zeisberger translated them into Mohawk for Canassatego. Each point was confirmed with a fathom of wampum.

Little progress was made toward convening the entire council, despite Canassatego's best efforts. Cammerhoff's journal attributes the cause to the drunken condition of some of its members. On June 23 the missionaries decided to request permission to visit the Senecas, hoping to save time and provide Canassatego with more time to convene the council. At this meeting Canassatego gave the missionaries permission to visit the Senecas.

The Seneca Visit

Two days were required to cover the forty miles to the Cayuga village of Ganatarage. The first night was spent at their old French camp near the lower end of Lake Skaneateles, now St. John's Beach.[5] By Thursday evening they were comfortably installed in their old quarters at the village, again attended by the Gajuka's mother, who hovered over them like a mother hen. They arose late the next morning and in the afternoon walked the few miles to the Cayuga village, where they found their guide. The next morning, after affectionate farewells, they packed and went down to the lakeshore, where the ferryman waited. He was a fine-looking, broad-shouldered Indian named Gannekachtacheri.

The next fourteen days were like a journey into hell, and on many occasions both men wondered if they would ever return. Since coming to America in early 1748, Cammerhoff had committed himself to an incredibly strenuous schedule. A frail man, small in stature, though twenty-nine, he looked more like a boy of sixteen. He could carry no more than twenty to thirty pounds, which forced Zeisberger to carry the additional weight. A man of "excitable feelings," Cammerhoff poured his energy into every project assigned to him. Their erratic diet, the inhospitable terrain, and the unseasonably hot weather were beginning to take a toll on his frail constitution. But there was never a word of complaint in his journal of the fatigue suffered by himself or Zeisberger.[6]

The friendly and hospitable treatment they had received from the Cayugas and Onondagas contrasted sharply with what they were about to experience from the Senecas. As keepers of the western door of the confederacy, the Senecas had for years been forced to fight off the encroachment of hostile enemy tribes who were leagued with the French. Either through diplomacy or actual conflict, they successfully maintained their suzerainty over these tribes, but the cost in lives had been great.

Debarking on the western shore of Lake Cayuga, the missionaries traveled almost due west until they reached the northern end of Lake Seneca (near the present site of Geneva, New York). This was the location of the small Indian village of Nuquiage. Here they found a French trader, dressed in Indian clothes, doing a land office business and, according to Cammerhoff, "filling the whole neighborhood with rum." He invited them into his quarters and offered roasted eel and punch. His merchandise consisted chiefly of liquor, of which little remained. Business had been good, and Indians from as far away as the Seneca Castle of Chenussio had been here to make purchases. During their short stay, the Gajuka took advantage of the opportunity to join his Indian brothers in a few rounds. After considerable persuasion, David managed to lure him away from the village, half intoxicated. They borrowed their host's canoe, crossed the rapid and deep Seneca outlet, and camped the night of June 27 on the northern shore of the lake.

The next day they headed west into Seneca country. The Gajuka forewarned that they would pass over a bad road. Cammerhoff explains:

> We went through swamps and marshes, where the flies troubled us greatly. For miles (6) we were obliged to walk on trees and branches, as on both sides were deep marshes, brushes and thorns, which make an inconvenient bridge, for we sometimes slipped from the trees and branches, and fell into the swamp, and could scarcely get up again with our heavy bundles. We called the road the Long Bridge. It would have been quite impassable with horses, and the Indians say that no one can travel this road except on foot.[7]

They stopped just a few miles east of the present Canandaigua, New York, and spent the evening in a hut they called the "Seneka Mail Station." The shortage of food was becoming a serious concern. Cittamun, the Indian name for dried ground corn and nut meats, made into a paste with hot water and drunk as a tea, was a traditional Indian breakfast. For the Moravian travelers it was breakfast, dinner, and supper.

Several miles beyond the previous evening's camp they crossed a bridge spanning Lake Canandaigua outlet, built on stakes driven into the ground and bound together by bark precariously overlaid with small trees and poles. While they were resting along the shore of the lake, an Indian crossed the bridge carrying a deer that he had shot. He stopped to converse, in a friendly manner, and suggested the party accompany him to his home in the nearby Seneca village of Canandaigua.[8]

They followed their Indian friend to the village and were invited to spend the day with him. He promised to serve venison for supper, and the half-starved visitors accepted the invitation without hesitation. The village huts were ornamented with paintings of deer, turtle, and bears, designating the owner's clan. Assigning a couch to each of the men, he took two guns, went outside, and fired four shots to indicate that a distinguished man had come under his roof. After the Indian furnished his guests with corn and beans, they laid down to rest, quickly falling asleep to the aromatic smell of venison broiling over the fire.

Cammerhoff's journal gives us the first indication of his deteriorating condition. He noted, "I did not feel well." Throughout the day he continued to weaken and was racked with chills and fever accompanied with a severe headache and exhaustion.

By nightfall a drinking party at the village began in earnest with the Gajuka at the center of attention. Round after round, it continued throughout the night. Before dawn, the missionaries decided to leave the village. Quietly moving about the dark gloom of the hut, they packed their bags, hoping to depart without being detected. As they left, they noticed the inert form of the Gajuka in the corner of the hut, dead drunk. They proceeded without his assistance. The cloak of darkness proved useless, as they were discovered and surrounded by a mob of shrieking and brawling Indians, who pulled at their clothes and pushed them toward the edge of the village. Moving quickly, they escaped their tormentors, sped on their way by shots fired overhead by the laughing and screaming villagers.

Fortunately, the day proved to be pleasant but warm. Despite Cammerhoff's condition, he noted in his journal that they traveled thirty miles (actually the distance was less than fifteen miles).[9] Near evening they arrived at the north end of Honeoye Lake, where they found a small Seneca village.[10] The old chief, Tschokagaas, after listening to an account of their past evening's experience, showed great pity, plied the pair with good Indian food, and provided two comfortable beds. During the night a remorseful and contrite Gajuka quietly joined the missionaries in their hut.

The morning of July 1 broke warm and humid. With a sobered Gajuka, they were ready to leave by sunup. They hoped to make the final leg of their journey to Chenussio by nightfall. Despite the early morning hour, most of the village children gathered around the departing party. Their gaiety and laughter sharply contrasted with the parting of the previous day. Babbling like early morning birds, the children pulled the missionaries by the hand far beyond the village and pointed the way to Chenussio.

By noon, the intense July sun was depleting their strength. It was soon evident they would have to modify their plan if they were to reach the Seneca Castle by evening. Cammerhoff's steadily deteriorating physical condition further complicated the situation. In spite of these handicaps, they made good time, rounding the north end of Hemlock Lake, continuing west until they reached Conesus Lake, then traveling north along its eastern shore until they passed the northern end and crossed the outlet. Here they found a small hunting lodge where they decided to spend the night. David had shot a large turkey during the day, and they roasted and ate the bird with great relish. The exertion caused by the trip and crossing of the rapid waters of the lake outlet completely exhausted Cammerhoff. He wrote that evening, "I was feverish, with much pain in my head and heaviness in my limbs." Zeisberger was becoming concerned and remarked that his companion "looked very sick and miserable."[11]

They were now within five miles of the village and reached it early the next morning. Chenussio (present Geneseo, New York) lies in a beautiful valley several miles long and drained by the Genesee River. The village on the river consisted of forty or more well-constructed large huts and a population of two to four hundred souls, depending upon when one took the census. When the village came in view, Zeisberger and Cammerhoff could hear great shouting and quarreling. This could mean only one thing: the whole population was intoxicated, men, women, and children. Their hearts sank. They knew what to expect when they arrived. Cammerhoff gives us his version:

> On entering the town we saw many drunken Indians, who all looked mad with drink. We inquired for the lodge of Chief Garontianechqui, and were obliged to pass through the whole village in order to reach it. On our way we were everywhere surrounded by drunken savages. The sachem was not at home, but his wife, an aged, good little woman, stood outside of the hut and gave us a kindly welcome, urging us, to enter as a great drunken crowd surrounded the dwelling and wanted to approach us. We went in and sat down, but were immediately followed by the drunken savages . . . showing that they had been in this frightful state of intoxication for some days.

It took the Gajuka only a few minutes to evaluate the situation. He pushed past the drunken Indians, ran out the door, and disappeared beyond the eastern hills. He had fulfilled his contract, having brought them to the Senecas. Now safety for his life became his paramount concern. It would be seven days before the missionaries would see him again.

The sachem's wife sent for her husband. After considerable delay, he appeared, drunk like his fellow villagers. Their hostess was becoming concerned for the safety of her guests as the house was filled with yelling and threatening savages. She suggested that they retire to a nearby hut. They quickly accepted the invitation. It was a small structure, which Cammerhoff described as "having only enough space for six to seven standing persons." The move did little to alleviate the dangerous situation. As evening approached, their hostess suggested that they return to her quarters and occupy a small garret in the gable end of the house. She assigned her brother-in-law to guard the ladder that gave access to the area.

The loft, directly under the roof, was a veritable prison. It was so small they had to lie side by side, and it was intensely hot, day or night, during the summer. The only outside access was by ladder to the inside floor or through a small window. Only a small person could crawl through the opening. They spent the evening, frightened and concerned, trying to eat some of the half-cooked beans and corn the old wife had prepared.

Later in the evening the clatter and chaos moved from the house into the village streets, and most of the two hundred or more residents caroused all night long. The new location did little to improve the missionaries' situation. Both men spent a restless night. The hours were not wasted, however, as they began to lay plans for an escape from the village. In the morning they would make one more attempt to speak with the chiefs. If that proved unsatisfactory, they would leave.

The morning meeting with Chiefs Garontianech and Hagastaes proved frustrating. Both men were still intoxicated. They seemed to be obsessed with one question: Were the missionaries commissioned by Onas, or Conrad Weiser, to invite the chiefs to Philadelphia this year? Despite David's insistence that that was not the reason for their visit, the question kept recurring, until, in desperation, Zeisberger gave up trying to continue the meeting. He advised the chiefs that he and Cammerhoff would leave the next day. This displeased them, and they tried to persuade the missionaries to remain for at least two more days. By that time the liquor would have been consumed, and they would then call all the chiefs together to speak with both men. Patiently, David explained that they must leave the next day to return to Onondaga to await the decision of the Six Nations council.

That afternoon they asked the sachem's wife, who had cared for them so faithfully, to prepare some Indian meal for their journey. Meanwhile, Cammerhoff remained in the hut resting and trying to regain strength for the return trip. Both men had eaten little in the last several days, and David tried to make tea for his companion. It was an ambitious undertaking, as the spring was half a mile from their quarters. To get the water, he would pass most of the village houses. As he returned with the filled kettle, several drunken Indians caught him and roughly forced him into their hut, took the kettle, and drank the water. He finally regained the container and returned to the spring. He was pursued by other Indians but outran his assailants by using a circuitous route through long grass around the edge of the village and eventually returned to the hut. It was well worth the effort despite his harrowing experience. That evening Cammerhoff wrote, "It was the first nourishment I had taken in two days."

But David was not through with the carousing inhabitants of the village. Toward evening he went for a short walk. As he was returning, a group of naked women and others almost naked gathered around him, tearing at his clothes and making obscene gestures, suggesting sensuous designs on his person. He began to reign blows with his fists in every direction, in an effort to drive them away. He eventually reached the hut and climbed the ladder to the garret just before they tore it from under his feet. This incident only reinforced their decision to leave in the morning.

Later that evening, the chief's wife brought the Indian meal she had at last prepared, "without which," Cammerhoff wrote, "we would not have started."

The night was a repetition of the orgies of the preceding evening, with continual yelling throughout the village.

Early the next morning, as the light began to filter through the cracks of the bark house, they completed preparations to leave. Cammerhoff describes their attempt to wake the sleeping Indian on the floor below:

> At first we did not venture to leave without giving notice, and as we could not go down into the hut from within, David did his utmost to awake our protector by repeated calls. We also rapped vigorously to arouse him, but all to no purpose; and we looked upon it as a special providence of the Lord that the Indians did not awake. David was obliged to jump out of the opening and search for the ladder, which the savages had removed. We then wished to throw out our packs, but David's was so large that he found it necessary to open it, and cast down its contents singly. All this was done amid great fear of being seen by the drunken savages. The Lord watched over us in such a manner that all the savages were in their huts, not a creature to be seen. Even the dogs, numbering nearly 100 in the whole village, were all quiet, wonderful to relate, and not a sound was heard.[12]

Fortunately, a dense fog covered the village, and as they quietly crept pasted the last hut, a woman stood at the door, but she was sober and smiled, silently waving a friendly greeting. Time was now of the essence, and they rapidly crossed over the eastern hill just beyond the village. If their escape were to succeed, they had to cover many miles. Feeling euphoric after leaving the village undetected, both men, adrenaline flowing, travelled at a brisk pace as they placed mile after mile between themselves and the village.

Late in the afternoon they reached the friendly village of Chief Tschokagaas at the northern end of Hemlock Lake, where they had spent the pleasant evening of June 30. Any danger of pursuit had passed.

The Last Few Days in Onondaga

During the afternoon of July 10 they descended the last of the Prince's Peaks and arrived in Onondaga. The old Oneida chief who befriended them during their first visit welcomed them with bad news. The day before, Canassatego and a party of Onondaga chiefs had gone to Oswego, the English trading post on Lake Ontario. They were not planning to return to the village for five to six days. Zeisberger and Cammerhoff inquired if their offer had been considered; the chief replied that it had not.

Canassatego, along with his wife and daughter, returned to the village the morning of July 19, bringing an ominous letter for the missionaries from Arend Stevens, the New York Indian interpreter at Oswego. Stevens wanted to know why they were in Onondaga, what business they had with the Onondagas, and whether they had secured a passport from the governor of New York. The inquisitive and slightly hostile tone of the letter gave both men cause for concern. True, they did not have a passport from the New York governor, but neither did they have a formal passport from Governor Hamilton of Pennsylvania. They did, however, have his verbal approval.

In the early afternoon of the same day, the council was called to the longhouse for another meeting, but not before Cammerhoff appealed to the chief to bring their questions before the group. Following the lengthy council meeting, Canassatego returned to his quarters and informed the missionaries that other important business had used up all of the meeting time.

The council was called again the next morning, and in a few hours, Canassatego, instead of sending a messenger, came himself and invited the missionaries to come to the meeting to learn the results of their deliberations. Zeisberger was seated in the center of the large room, Cammerhoff immediately behind him, and the Indians in a circle surrounding the two men.

Canassatego delivered the Indians' response, acknowledging and renewing their bond of friendship with the Moravians. Spangenberg, Zinzendorf, and Mack, called by their adopted Indian names, were mentioned, and a string of wampum was presented to Zeisberger. The chief then said they agreed to permit several Brethren to come and live with them for a few years, or more if necessary, to learn the language, then presented another string of wampum. The third request, regarding a blacksmith for the Nanticokes, was rejected with the suggestion that these tribes could use the existing blacksmith at Shamokin. Zeisberger accepted the string of wampum and interpreted these remarks to Cammerhoff. Almost as an afterthought, the fourth point confirmed permission for the missionaries to visit the Senecas. The final string of wampum was a token that the journey was undertaken with their consent. The meeting was concluded with the customary Indian greetings.

Before they departed, the usual amenities were exchanged and Canassatego wished the missionaries a safe journey. They left Onondaga with a clear conscience. Despite the hardships and delays, the mission was accomplished. They had renewed old friendships, made new friends, and secured permission to return with two missionaries who would study the Iroquoian dialect. The happy but tired travelers arrived in Bethlehem one hour after midnight on August 17, 1750.

Within twenty days, Canassatego would writhe in the pains of death, poisoned by his own people or those in league with the French interest. Cammerhoff would join him within nine months, probably a victim of tuberculosis.

· 6 ·

You Need Never Fear among Us,
1750–1753

The years between 1749 and the outbreak of open hostilities in 1754 between England and France brought major changes in the Moravian mission program, and David Zeisberger played an ever-increasing role in these events.

Late in the fall of 1749 or early in the spring of 1750, a new Delaware Indian couple moved into Gnadenhutten. For several months Teedyuscung (TEE-dee-US-shung) and his wife loitered about the mission requesting permission to join the converts, but their reception was put off because of his "wavering disposition." Sometimes called "Honest John," Teedyuscung was reputed to be "unstable as water and like a reed shaken before the wind." On March 19, 1750, during one of Cammerhoff's quick visits to the village, he impulsively baptized the couple and gave them the Christian names of Gideon and Elizabeth.[1]

Born near Trenton, New Jersey, about 1700, Teedyuscung was one of five "high-spirited sons" of a Captain Harris. He was relatively unknown until he became a convert. Because of Cammerhoff's impulsive baptism, the Moravians now had in their midst one of the most controversial characters in eighteenth-century Indian history. Anthony Wallace, in his biography of the Delaware, says, "In Teedyuscung that strange mixture of love and hatred for Europeans which he learned in New Jersey made him notorious as both the enemy and the friend of the white man; and the conflict in his nature between this love and his hatred was the leading motive of his political career."[2]

Two months following Cammerhoff and Zeisberger's return from Onondaga, David was on the road again. Carrying instructions from the Mission Board, Nathaniel Seidel and Zeisberger sailed from New York harbor, bound for Europe. They were to report to Count Zinzendorf on the progress of the Indian mission work in America and explain their future plans. Captain Nicholas Garrison was at the helm of the *Irene*, a snow built in New York and commissioned on September 8, 1748.[3] The vessel was owned by the Moravians and had sailed on numerous trips. This rough voyage demanded the best of Garrison's sailing skills to bring his battered ship into the harbor at Plymouth, England.[4]

Zeisberger and Seidel proceeded by way of London and Holland on to Herrnhut, arriving on December 19, 1750. "We reached Herrnhut safely and in a happy frame of mind," wrote Zeisberger. The two missionaries remained in Germany for almost six months, spending most of the time in Herrnhut. They had frequent conversations with Zinzendorf and other members and officials of the church. The count was especially pleased with the work Zeisberger was doing and developed a high regard for him. In an unusual ceremony, he appointed him "a perpetual missionary to these people." The presentation was concluded with a special blessing, the imposition of hands. He was never to be employed in any other work of the church except as a missionary among the Indians.[5]

The two men left Herrnhut on June 5, 1751, retracing their trip to London, where they found the *Irene* completely repaired. The return voyage was made without incident, and the pair arrived in New York on September 24. Four days later they were back in Bethlehem.

By the beginning of 1752 Zeisberger was back at his mission station in Shamokin, but his heart was with the Aquanoschioni (Iroquois) at Onondaga. He brought to Shamokin a belt of wampum and greetings from Bishop Spangenberg, who had also recently returned from Europe.[6] The bishop was most anxious to renew his friendship with the Indians and expand the mission work. He and a party of Moravians, including Nathaniel Seidel and Johann Schmick, visited the Wyoming Valley distributing fifty bushels of wheat to the famished Delawares, Nanticokes, and Shawnees living there.[7] It was rare for white men to show such interest in Indian welfare. This act of consideration would be remembered by the Shawnees when in 1782 they came to the help of starving Moravian converts on the banks of the Sandusky River in the Ohio Country.

But Spangenberg's mind was also on the Aquanoschioni, specifically the Onondagas. It was now time to follow up on Cammerhoff and Zeisberger's journey of 1750 among the Iroquois. Zeisberger, who previously had been adopted into the Six Nations, was to be officially accepted among them so that he might eventually preach the Gospel as a brother both in name and in fact.[8] But Zeisberger was instructed by Spangenburg not to reveal to the Onondagas that he planned to began a mission program, only to say that he was there to learn the language. The reasons behind this charade have been lost in antiquity. Why Spangenberg and the Mission Board chose not to be forthright and inform the Onondagas that their ultimate objective was to establish missions, rather than just learn their language, has never been adequately explained. It was a spurious arrangement that confused the Onondagas and placed the missionaries in a false and misleading position.

Spangenberg sent Martin Mack, his most experienced missionary, with Zeisberger. Godfrey Rundt, who had come to America the year before, also accompanied the Brethren.[9] The three left Bethlehem on July 21, bound for New York, where they embarked on a sloop for Albany. Leaving Albany with one packhorse, they proceeded by foot along the Mohawk River to Fort Hunter, then continued west along the Mohawk until they reached the last frontier cabin of a German settler named Kash (present Little Falls, New York).

The party arrived at Onondaga on August 20 and was welcomed into the lodge of Chief Ganatschiagaje. It was two years and one month to the day since Zeisberger and Cammerhoff had left the village in 1750. They were welcomed hospitably.

Three days after the missionaries arrived, the chiefs were ready to receive them in combined council. There were thirty present: four Seneca, four Cayuga, and the balance Onondaga.[10]

Since Zeisberger was the most proficient in speaking the Cayuga dialect, he was seated next to an old Cayuga chief. In the Indian half chant and half lyrical song, he made the Moravians' presentation. After presenting the salutation from their friends in Bethlehem and overseas, then mentioning Cammerhoff's death, he requested permission to live among them for as long as a year. He then proffered the gifts they had brought: twenty-two yards of excellent linen, some thread, and tobacco. The gifts were then divided into thirds, one part for each tribe represented. Later in the afternoon the missionaries received an affirmative answer to their request. Ganachgagregat of the Onondagas gave his permission for the missionaries to attend council any time one was in session and further suggested that they visit any house in the village so as to enhance their opportunity to converse with the Indians. The plan was to remain in Onondaga until late fall, spend the winter months with the Cayugas, then return in the spring to Onondaga.[11] With formal negotiations completed, Martin Mack left the village on August 26 and returned to Bethlehem, leaving his two companions on their own. Zeisberger was now in charge.

The Brethren remained in Onondaga until the first week in November. The missionaries spent their time visiting both the upper and lower villages of the Onondagas, attending council meetings, and digging gentian roots in the woods. Sir William Johnson's agents occasionally visited, giving them opportunities to trade the roots for blankets, corn, and other items necessary for their survival. They were showered with Indian hospitality and seldom went hungry. If the villagers had food, they shared it generously with their guests.

On November 5, Zeisberger decided to leave Onondaga and move on to the Cayuga country. After the appropriate consultations with their host, they received his blessing and assurances of a welcome back in Onondaga anytime in the future. Early the next morning, the missionaries left the village. Two days later they arrived at Ganatarage, the first of the Cayuga towns, where they received two pieces of unwelcome news: most of the men were out on the winter hunt, and French traders had just arrived with large quantities of rum for sale. This was an ominous portent for the future. They spent the night at Ganatarage and the next day were on the road to the Cayuga village. As they neared the town they met two chiefs, Onochsagerat and T'gaaju, the former a friend of David's, the latter a chief in the Cayuga delegation during the recent council at Onondaga. The chiefs were on their way to meet the traders but would return in the evening. In the meantime they directed the missionaries to the home of T'gaaju, who agreed to be their host.

Later the two chiefs returned, and they all spent the evening in conversation. Just before retiring, they were joined by one of the traders, who from the moment he arrived appeared in an irritable humor, sullenly sitting before the fire in brooding silence. The man, an ugly, ill-looking, intemperate Dutchman, whose name remains happily in oblivion, spoke no words of welcome to the missionaries. After sitting near the fire for some time, he suddenly turned and gruffly asked Zeisberger, "What are you doing in Iroquois country?" David interrupted his conversation with one of the chiefs, turned to the trader, and quietly replied, "We are here to learn their language by permission of the Grand Council and the Colonial government." "Produce your passports," the trader shouted. Without changing the level of his voice David responded, "You have no authority to demand of us to present our passport."[12] Uttering a string of oaths, the trader jumped to his feet, grabbed an Indian war club, and struck David across the side of the head, knocking him to the ground. Then, snatching a brand from the fire, he began to beat and kick the prostrate form with his heavy boots. The attack was unexpected, and only the intercession of the chiefs saved Zeisberger's life. But the Dutchman was defiant. He drew his knife and again tried to approach the disabled missionary but was finally overpowered and dragged from the cabin by the chiefs. David was in pain, but he was not seriously wounded. He did, however, spend the night in great discomfort.

The next morning, the missionaries decided to return to Onondaga. Since the traders would probably winter in Cayuga, the wisest course seemed to be to leave the area. Despite the protestations of their host and his assurances of future protection, they packed their bags and passed from the village as the early morning revelry began. By noon on November 11, they were back in Onondaga, just five days after their departure.

Daily life in an Indian village was normally calm and peaceful. The head chief and his council did their best to maintain stability, but the fiercely independent Indian personality, especially that of the young members of a tribe, sometimes interfered with these efforts. Liquor was a most disruptive influence. Men, women, and even children became intoxicated for long periods, sometimes days, and, on rare occasions, weeks at a time. For visitors during the summer months these infrequent interruptions were never a serious problem. If life in the village became too dangerous, they simply retired to the woods a safe distance from the village. But during the winter, such escape was impossible.

Toward evening on November 20, the missionaries heard disturbing news. One of the women Indian traders had just brought twenty kegs of rum to the village. Since most of the younger men were on the winter hunt and there were only a few people in town, the presence of this much liquor posed a serious problem for the missionaries. David decided it would be prudent to return to Bethlehem before winter set in to prevent their departure.

The next morning the Brethren discussed their departure plans with their host, Otschinachiatha. At first, the chief seemed startled and had nothing to say, but when David explained that they intended to return in the spring, he was reconciled. The chief was also concerned about how they intended to return to the settlements. When assured by Zeisberger that they planned to travel down the Mohawk River through Schenectady, he was relieved. This was by far the safest route. After only three to four days in the woods, they would reach white settlements. On the cool, crisp morning of November 25, surrounded by many friendly villagers, they left Onondaga with a promise to return in the spring. Luckily, there was little snow on the ground, and they were back in Bethlehem by December 15, 1752.

Problems at the Gnadenhutten Mission, and Another Year among the Onondagas, 1753

In early March the Brethren at Bethlehem received a dispatch from their Indian friends in the Wyoming Valley. Agreeable to their promise of the previous year and looking for food, a delegation of twenty-two hungry Nanticokes, Delawares, and Mahicans arrived at Bethlehem. To give them official status, the party was led by three Iroquois chiefs, all friends of Zeisberger. One, Ganatschiagaje, had been his host at Onondaga the previous year. David was proud and overjoyed to welcome him to Bethlehem.

But as the Brethren soon discovered, the Indians brought more than their hunger. The Gnadenhutten converts were about to become the victims of intricate eighteenth-century Indian diplomacy, some of it unwittingly the result of Moravian actions. First, the Indians wanted to thank the Brethren for their hospitality and generosity during the famine of the previous autumn. Had it not been for their kindheartedness, many would have suffered hunger and possibly starvation. Second, they wished to inform the Brethren that the Iroquoian grand council had ordered the Nanticokes to move north of the Wyoming Valley to territory next to the Tuscaroras. As the speaker introduced the third item on the agenda, his countenance changed. He began to tremble, well aware that his next proposal would probably be unacceptable to the Brethren and the converts at Gnadenhutten. The grand council proposed that the Gnadenhutten Indian congregation move to the Wyoming Valley. The reasons were obvious. Once again, the Iroquois were trying to strengthen their hold on the valley. Since the Shawnees had left and moved to the Ohio Country, there were few Indians living in Wyoming.

Although the initial reaction to this proposal was shock and concern, the Brethren responded only by saying "that they would not determine anything, but must insist upon this point, that no means of constraint should be used on either side." The Moravians needed time. The deputation remained in Bethlehem for one more week, then returned to the Wyoming Valley. The decision to stay or leave Gnadenhutten would now be entirely in the hands of the mission residents. The incident sobered the converts at Gnadenhutten. They argued and speculated over what course of action to take. Some left the village, while others "lost their cheerfulness and serenity, became gloomy and shy."[13] It was some time before order was restored and another year before the question was unhappily resolved.

Meanwhile, in Bethlehem, the warm April sun was expanding the green buds on the oak and hickory trees and melting the snow in the deep mountain passes. The trail to Onondaga was now open. Zeisberger, accompanied by Henry Frey, left the settlement on April 23 to resume his studies among the Six Nations. They left Bethlehem on April 23 and took the Tulpehocken Trail, arriving at Shamokin on April 26. Again they canoed up the Susquehanna, but at Tioga, rather than taking the Chemung, they followed the Susquehanna northeast. As they camped on the banks of the river at Tioga, Frey celebrated his thirtieth birthday. He was one of the rare missionaries during this period to be born in America.[14] As they passed through the Wyoming Valley they encountered the Nanticokes busily preparing to leave the area for their new location. Rather than join them, which would slow their progress, the two pushed ahead, only to become hopelessly lost while attempting to travel cross-country without a guide. With their food supply exhausted, they retraced the trail and found the Nanticokes coming upstream on the Susquehanna. Taking no further chances, they stayed with the dispossessed Indians until they reached Zeniinge, the location of their new homes at the branch of the Chenango and Tioughnioga Rivers (Chenango Forks, New York).[15]

Fortunately, a hunting party passed through the area and one of the hunters was a friend of David's from Shamokin. He told Zeisberger, "When I was in great trouble in Shamokin you showed me great kindness, therefore I cannot refuse to assist you."[16] Four days later, they entered the Tioughnioga River traveling north toward their destination, finally arriving at Onondaga on June 8, where they were warmly greeted by Chief Otschinachiatha.

The chief was delighted to see his friends but looked worried. He produced an ominous looking belt of wampum the Indians had just received from Onontio (the governor of New France). The belt was designed to inform the Iroquois that "he was on the way to Ohio with his men, and held the tomahawk firmly in his hand, and would destroy all who opposed him." He assured them, however, "that he would do no harm to the Six Nations, but only meant to attack the English." Some of the Onondaga chiefs had been at Oswego (the English trading post on Lake Ontario) when the French expedition passed the fort and observed, "They had never seen so many people together, and they feared evil results from all of this." Otschinachiatha warned Zeisberger that if the war cry came from the Cayugas and the situation looked dangerous, he would say to them: "Brethren, depart now; it is time; go and tell our Brethren the state of things here." It was a time to be cautious and not an auspicious beginning for a visit.[17]

Zeisberger observed that famine was rampant throughout the area. Most of the residents were spending their time in the woods digging roots and herbs. The lack of food in the village had become critical. David decided to travel east to the white settlements, hoping to purchase corn and flour from the colonists. He and Frey departed on July 17, but not before the Onondaga gave Frey his adopted Indian name of Ochschugore, the name of one of their former chiefs.[18]

After several days on the trail, sick and exhausted, they arrived at Kash's cabin on the Mohawk River. Kash, their host the year before, was a crusty old German. He took them in but uttered invectives laced with profanity and plain speech which only the German language can express so elegantly: "Idiots, wasting your lives and destroying your health on such miserable pieces of thankless human baggage." The love the missionaries felt for their fellow humans, regardless of color, was beyond the understanding of this poor, plain German settler. They spent several days with the cranky old man, helping him with his harvest. He asked Frey to teach him the Pennsylvania method of harvesting, which he much preferred to his own.[19]

In the evenings they went to the woods to gather bark for a canoe so they could return to Onondaga by water. While they were working on the canoe and making little progress, an Oneida brave and several of his comrades passed by and observed them. Modestly, they asked if they might assist, an offer the missionaries could not refuse. The braves immediately dismantled the canoe and began from scratch. Within two hours they had assembled a stout little craft. The next morning Kash and his son brought their baggage down to the riverbank on their horse and helped with the loading. The seven days spent with the old man had mellowed his attitude, and it was obvious that he secretly admired their devotion. From the bank of the river he called a warm farewell and cordially invited them to return if they came that way again.[20]

Loaded with supplies, the missionaries were now traveling one of the most famous and historic water trails in early America. For centuries the Indians had traveled from the Atlantic Ocean at New York up the Hudson to the mouth of the Mohawk, then up the Mohawk to its headwaters near present Rome, New York. Here they portaged four miles to Woods Creek (the Great Crossing Place), then passed down this stream to Oneida Lake, crossed the lake, and took the Oneida River to where it joins the Seneca. (The Seneca drains some of the Finger Lakes.) The two rivers join to become the Oswego River, which flows into Lake Ontario. The route provided access from the Atlantic Ocean to the Great Lakes. By using this historic route, the missionaries, after entering the Oneida River and reaching the Seneca, turned down this river to the Onondaga outlet and entered Onondaga Lake, reaching the village on the evening of August 8, ten days after they departed from the Kash farm.

There is a strange entry in Zeisberger's journal for Saturday, August 25. The men had been assisting Chief Otschinachiatha in inspecting his fish weirs and making a canoe at Lake Tionctong (Cross Lake). They had just finished and launched the canoe in the lake. "Preparations were made to return to the town. Otschinachiatha asked Brother David if the report, circulated among the Indians, that Ganousseracheri (Zeisberger) was a minister, was correct. Brother David told him that he was no minister."[21] Zeisberger had been ordained a deacon on February 16, 1749, by Bishop John de Watteville. Why did he answer in the negative? No explanation is available.

On August 6, Sir William Johnson arrived at Onondaga. His three boats, in regal splendor, entered the lake and were welcomed by a flotilla of Indian canoes. Johnson, a thirty-eight-year-old immensely wealthy Irishman, was just reaching the height of his political career. He spoke fluent Mohawk and was a trusted friend of the Iroquois, especially the Mohawks and their head chief, Hendricks. In 1750, the king of England had appointed him a life member of the governor's council. Over the next twenty-one years no man in all the colonies exerted more influence among the Indians, especially the Iroquois, than he did, and he was directly responsible for keeping them neutral throughout most of this period. Johnson's greatest attribute was his ability to think and sometimes act like an Indian. He was perfectly at home living among them, so much so that he is humorously credited with fathering more than three hundred Indian children, a historical rumor no one can prove or disprove. One of his wives was the sister of the famous Mohawk Joseph Brant (Thay-en-dan-e-ge-a). Zeisberger and Frey stayed at the lake until the late afternoon before returning to the village.

Near the end of September, in a casual conversation, Chief Gaschwechtioni told the missionaries that the council had recently received a communication from Onontio. The governor at Montreal expressed his displeasure that the Moravians were living at Onondaga. By October 4 they were convinced that they should accept the advice of their friend Chief Otschinachiatha and return to Bethlehem for the winter. Nine days later, they retraced their spring route to Bethlehem, arriving home on November 12.

Zeisberger had little time for rest and reflection. In the middle of October, while he and the Onondagas were contemplating the results of the council meeting with William Johnson, his old friend and mentor Peter Boehler arrived in Bethlehem as the temporary replacement for Spangenberg. He was among the first to greet the two missionaries as they walked into the village on the cold, crisp afternoon of November 12, 1753. No man except Spangenberg meant more to Zeisberger than Peter Boehler.

In the next few days Zeisberger, with Boehler's approval, set forth new procedures to be used with the Six Nations. Recognizing the incongruity of their current policy, he recommended that they put aside caution and advise the Onondagas of their true objective: to convert the entire league to the living God. Further, on any future visit, they should send one of the students of the Iroquoian language school along with an accredited minister of the Gospel to Onondaga. The proposal, along with a letter, was sent to Spangenberg and Zinzendorf in Germany. For Zeisberger, the year 1753 had ended on a happy note, full of pleasant memories and with great anticipation for the coming year.

· PART 2 ·

What Shall It Be: The Fleur-de-Lis or Saint George's Cross? 1754–1764

· 7 ·

Prelude to Tragedy, Then Defeat and Disaster, 1754–1755

DAVID ZEISBERGER greeted the new year of 1754 optimistically. His long-cherished dream of beginning a mission among the Iroquois was about to become reality. Within four months he would celebrate his thirty-third birthday. Church officials at Herrnhut, including Zinzendorf and Spangenberg, agreed with his plan to begin the mission this year. David planned to leave Bethlehem for Onondaga near the first of June, when the moderate weather and spring runoff permitted rapid travel. Karl Friedrich, a new Moravian missionary to the colonies, would accompany him.[1] But there were menacing clouds on the horizon. Neither he nor any other colonial resident could ignore the growing tension between England and France for possession of the North American continent.

Critical events were taking place in Bethlehem, too. It had been a year since the Nanticoke, Delaware, and Mahican Indian delegation from the Wyoming Valley had appeared at the village demanding that their brothers at Gnadenhutten leave the mission and rejoin the tribes in the Wyoming Valley. At the heart of the Gnadenhutten converts' removal was the diplomatic maneuvering by the Six Nations council and, unfortunately, a previous action of the Mission Board at Bethlehem. In 1745, when Spangenberg, Weiser, Zeisberger, and others appeared before the Six

Nations council and secured permission for the Shekomeko Indians to move to the valley, the Mahicans refused to move. But that had not put an end to the matter for the Iroquois. The geopolitics of the proposed move fit too neatly into the Iroquois's overall diplomatic strategy. Since the valley provided a buffer zone between white encroachment and Iroquois lands on the Mohawk River, it was critical that friendly Indian tribes occupy the Wyoming area. If the "Praying Mahican" did not prefer to live there, perhaps the Gnadenhutten Delaware converts would.[2] Christian Frederick Post succinctly described for the Pennsylvania governor the Iroquoian strategy: "Be watchful that nobody of the White People may come to settle near you [in the Wyoming Valley]. You must appear to them as frightful Men, & if notwithstanding they come too near, give them a Push. We will secure and defend you against them."[3]

The Six Nations had waited two years for the "Praying Indians" at Gnadenhutten to relocate. Now the council expected compliance.[4] Gideon (Teedyuscung) and Abraham (Shabash), at Gnadenhutten, while playing their own game, fit neatly into the Iroquois strategy. During the ensuing year a serious schism had developed among the converts, led by Gideon and Abraham.

Abraham's motives were obvious. Since his conversion and baptism in 1742, he had lived with the Moravians, becoming one of the most trusted elders. But additional Indian accolades had come his way in the last few months of 1753. He had just been nominated captain by a small non-Christian tribe of Mahican Indians living at Captain Harris's old village of Wechquetank, on the north side of Wire Creek, one of the tributaries of the Pocopoco (Monroe County, Pennsylvania).[5] He now longed for the tributes and honor paid to such an office under the old native culture.

Gideon was a far more complicated and complex person. After being baptized by Cammerhoff in 1750, this "reed shaken like in the wind" seems to have made an honest effort to accept Moravian ways. But upon hearing, in 1753, that his Delaware tribesmen in the Wyoming Valley had elected him their chief, he began to side with Abraham, and the two organized a group of dissidents at Gnadenhutten who decided to break with their fellow converts and abandon the mission village.

During the previous year the two had been successfully propagandizing the mission congregation, which caused much contention among wives, husbands, and children. Their efforts convinced a sizable number to make the move. In April, fifty-six converts, led by Abraham and Gideon, left Gnadenhutten. Then, without invitation, fifteen more left shortly thereafter to settle at the old village of Nanticoke, also in the valley.[6] Within a few days, the Moravian mission village had lost seventy-six Indian converts. Through Teedyuscung and Shabash's efforts, Iroquoian diplomacy succeeded where all other efforts had failed. It was not the last time a conspiracy within the converts' own ranks caused such a defection.

Meanwhile, the Brethren began to bring order out of the chaos at Gnadenhutten. Nestled deep in the narrow Aquashicola Creek Valley was the growing mission of Meniologameka, formerly an Indian village settled by a Delaware chief called Captain George Rex.[7] Bernard Grube became the first missionary, succeeded six months later by John Schebosch (John Bull). In February 1753, after a serious gun accident wounded Schebosch, Abraham Bueninger was assigned to continue the work. By the end of the year Bueninger recorded a list of fifty-six mission members. With adequate housing now available at the Mahoning Creek mission, the Brethren could combine the two villages. By the end of April the Mission Board adopted Bueninger's request to move his people to Gnadenhutten.

With the two missions combined and Spangenberg back from Europe, activities at Bethlehem began to increase. One project involved developing the 130 acres just across the Lehigh River from the Gnadenhutten mission, a part of the 1750 purchase.[8] This plantation acreage of rich, flat bottomland was well suited for residential buildings and farming. In early spring of 1754 they began to move the existing cabins across the river, reassemble them, and build additional structures.[9]

They called their new village New Gnadenhutten. The dwellings were arranged with the Mahicans on one side of the street and the Delawares on the other. The old chapel remained across the river and became the dwelling of the missionaries and a place where visiting Brethren could stay. Those who helped to care for the mills and plantations also lived there. All of the farm buildings and the flour and planing mill remained on the west bank of the Mahoning Creek. Within four months they had recovered from the almost fatal blow of the previous April, and the future looked promising. David Zeisberger, like so many of his fellow Bethlehem Brethren, helped move the Gnadenhutten converts to the east side of the Lehigh River.

Zeisberger was back in Bethlehem in time to complete plans for a return to Onondaga. Accompanied by Karl Friedrich, he departed on June 9, 1754, for Albany, New York.[10] Three days later, they arrived in New York City, booked passage on a Hudson River ship, and reached Albany on June 9. They left Albany on the morning of June 27, traveling by canoe up the Mohawk River, the same route Zeisberger and Frey had taken the previous year, and arrived at Onondaga on the afternoon of Sunday, July 21.

Safely stored within Zeisberger's pack was the detailed plan of his new missionary program among the Iroquois, approved by Spangenberg and Zinzendorf. The Moravians had agreed to shed the disguise of merely "learning the language" and to proceed with the missionary program.

The two Brethren remained in Onondaga for approximately ten months. What took place in those 308 days still remains a mystery. Their journals are silent about any attempt to begin the missionary program. Oblique and evasive conversations are recorded, but there was no direct attempt or open effort to preach or proselytize to even one person, nor was there any attempt to gather groups for religious discussions.

On arrival, they were met by nine chiefs who desired to know "what we had to say." Again Zeisberger carefully explained, "It is not land we are after," repeating the all too familiar strain, "We came to learn the language, and as soon as we are sufficiently advanced we wish to bring you the words of the Creator."[11] Although this was an open admission of their true intentions, the proposed missionary program never developed.

Since the visitors planned to remain in Onondaga for the winter, they were granted permission to build a permanent log cabin, which was completed by the middle of November, before the severe weather set in. The building, 13 1/2 feet by 12 1/2 feet, was constructed of hewn logs and roofed with shingles. Although the smallest structure in the village, it was generally considered the "best house in Onondaga." Because the cabin was so secure, the missionaries granted the council's request to store its entire collection of wampum belts and other valuable documents in their new home. Contrary to De Schweinitz's claim in his *Life and Times*, Zeisberger did not become the "keeper of the wampum," an official office usually held by the head chief or a similarly responsible sachem but one never entrusted to a nonnative.[12]

The Year of Disaster, 1755

Although the Brethren were plagued with the usual annoyances—drinking and loud, boisterous parties—the greatest challenge was finding enough food to eat. They made at least one trip to the white settlements to secure supplies. By now, however, Zeisberger was beginning to understand and reconcile himself to the hardships and vagaries of Indian life. This was the beginning of a slow process that ultimately brought him to prefer life among the Indians to that at the white settlements.

One incident demonstrates the respect and esteem the Indians came to feel for this dedicated man. Some children were calling to him on the street one day, "That is an Assaroni" (a white man). The parents sharply corrected them by saying: "No, No, he is an Aquanouschioni (an Onondagian), not an Assaroni!"[13]

Two days later, the speaker of the council, Chief Gaschwechtioni (the Belt of Wampum, or Red Head), visited the Brethren's quarters with disturbing news. Karl Friedrich recorded the conversation: "He told us the Governor of Virginia had fought a battle, and intended to give another." That evening the journal entry read, "It seems the Indians are displeased."[14] Experience had taught the Indians that any clash of arms between the English and French would involve them in war. The war that shook the world had begun in 1754 in southwestern Pennsylvania. The youthful Major George Washington and a militia contingent from Virginia met and defeated a small scouting party led by the French commander Coulon de Jumonville. The battle lasted only fifteen minutes, but it would alter the course of events in both the North American and European continents. In America the hostility that followed became the French and Indian War; in Europe, the Seven Years' War.

The clouds of the Anglo-French war hung heavily over the Bethlehem settlement. Spangenberg and other church officials were aware that the outbreak of fighting could interrupt the tenuous relationship between the Indians and the white settlers. For fifteen years the Moravians had struggled to establish their community and build the missionary organization. War between France and England and their Indian allies could destroy all their assiduous labor. The mission at Shamokin, on the forks of the Susquehanna, continued to function, but its position deep within Indian territory made the site vulnerable. Pachgatgoch, an Indian settlement on the Connecticut–New York border, was again experiencing hostility from its fearful white neighbors. Gnadenhutten's position on the north side of the Blue Mountains left it unprotected and exposed to Indian attack.

There was some consolation that with Post now in the Wyoming Valley, they would receive accurate intelligence from the heart of the Indian community. Of the numerous men the Moravians trained for the missionary field, none would serve with more skill in this situation than Christian Frederick Post. He had married and lost in untimely death two Indian wives. He was fluent in Delaware, Mahican, and Mohawk dialects and was respected and trusted by both friendly and hostile Indians.

Two months before Zeisberger's return from Onondaga, Nathaniel Seidel and Henry Frey spent several weeks visiting Post and various villages in the Wyoming Valley. Except for a shortage of food, they found the residents living in relative peace. During this visit they had conversations with Paxinosa, Teedyuscung, and old Abraham, who were now the head chiefs

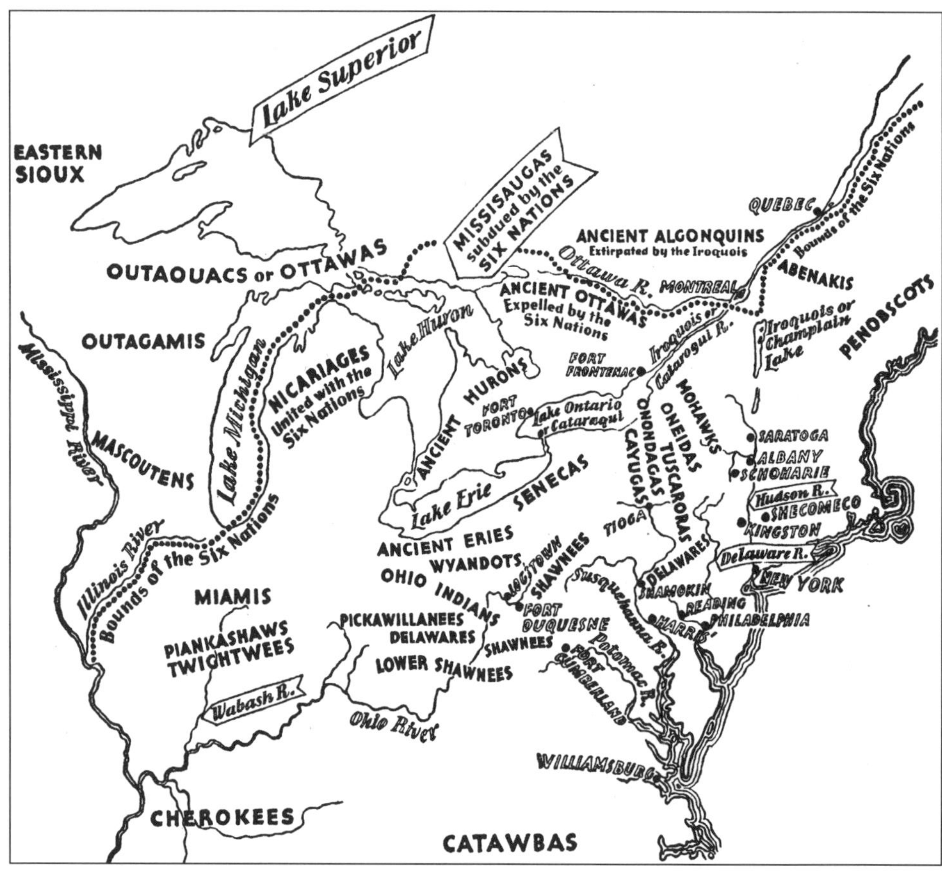

The Indian Country: Bounds of the Six Nations, 1755

of all the valley Indians. Throughout the winter and early spring, the trio had attempted to remain loyal to their English friends. But now they were concerned about a threat of hostile actions from the French Indians to the west (which also interrupted normal trading activity) and a possible invasion from the white Connecticut settlers on the east. The loss of their new crop because of a late spring frost and the absence of white traders on which their economy desperately depended made their survival tenuous. Unless they received immediate food and other assistance from Brother Onas, they would have no alternative but to join the French, who could provide traders to meet their needs. Paxinosa advised Seidel that they planned to visit Philadelphia within a few days to discuss the problem with the Pennsylvania governor.[15]

The two parties traveled together, arriving in Gnadenhutten on April 5. Paxinosa and his men proceeded on to Philadelphia. The Indian party arrived in the colony's capital on the fourteenth, only to find Governor Robert Hunter Morris absent from the city, visiting General Edward Braddock, the newly arrived British commander. Braddock had been appointed by the king to lead his English regulars against the French at Fort Duquesne and reclaim the western land recently seized by the French. In the meantime, Paxinosa and his party were entertained by the governor's council; Teedyuscung, their speaker, eloquently explained that they came to renew the covenant of friendship and seek the advice of Brother Onas.[16] The Pennsylvania governor returned to Philadelphia on April 22, accompanied by Governor William Shirley of Massachusetts. Both joined the council, and the honored guest was introduced to the Paxinosa party. On behalf of Shirley and William Johnson, the newly appointed superintendent of Indian affairs for the northern colonies, Morris presented several handsome wampum belts, which, in effect, instructed the Wyoming Indians to go home and wait for orders from Johnson and the Six Nations. Paxinosa, Teedyuscung, and their party obediently returned to the valley to wait for the answer. At the end of the year they were still waiting.

While Paxinosa and Teedyuscung were conducting their affairs with the Pennsylvania governor, Zeisberger and Friedrich were returning from their year at Onondaga. They stopped in the Wyoming Valley at the end of May and inquired about the former Gnadenhutten converts. Zeisberger was pleased to discover that Christian Frederick Post was living in the neighborhood. Post briefed the pair on the fragile nature of his position in the valley, and Zeisberger promised to return and assist within a few days.

Shortly after he returned to Bethlehem on June 4, 1755, Zeisberger and Nathaniel Seidel were back in Wyoming and Post was giving both men an appraisal of his dismal position. For three weeks Zeisberger and Seidel ranged up and down the valley searching for food to feed Post's small, huddled flock, who were trying to remain loyal to their Christian teachings. With only modest success, they left the small village and returned to Bethlehem with the hope of bringing additional food in the next several weeks. They arrived back in the settlement on Saturday afternoon, July 19, only to receive appalling and disastrous news.

Just that morning, as the Brethren were gathering for morning worship, a lone courier rode into the village. He was carrying an urgent dispatch from Governor Morris at Philadelphia, to be delivered to Governor Shirley at Albany.[17] The rider reported that on July 9, Braddock's army of fifteen hundred British regulars and American colonials had been attacked on the banks of the Yogiougheny, less than eight miles from Fort Duquesne. From the cover of dense woods, two hundred French soldiers and six hundred of their Indians allies drove into three sides of the strung-out Braddock column. In less than three hours the English and the Americans had been completely routed, leaving almost one-half of their men killed or seriously wounded, including the mortally wounded Braddock, who died the following day.[18] The ignominious Anglo-American retreat did not stop until arriving back in Philadelphia.

Though Braddock's defeat had enormous consequences throughout the English colonies, it was particularly serious for the people along the frontier of Pennsylvania and among the western Indian tribes generally loyal to the British. The Delaware tribe was in the most critical position. They had preferred to await the results before declaring their loyalties. The destruction of Braddock's army left the Pennsylvania frontier defenseless. The Delawares and their Munsee cousins, the Mingoes and Shawnees, saw no option but to join the French.[19]

News of Braddock's catastrophe spread throughout the West like a forest fire. Fort Duquesne's new commander, Captain Jean-Daniel Dumas, the architect of Braddock's defeat, immediately dispatched runners among the Delawares, Shawnees, and Mingoes, all former friends of the English, bearing the message that he intended to drive the English into the sea.[20] The Indians reluctantly responded. By the first of October, the commander had no less than six to eight hostile Indian parties roaming the forest west of the Susquehanna River looking for isolated white settlements to destroy. Most were led by French partisan soldiers dressed as Indians. Each group consisted of from twenty to one hundred Indian warriors. Despite Dumas's attempts to control the savagery of these troops, continually counseling them to refrain from killing women and children or torturing prisoners, they were guilty of depredations that were brutal to an extreme. The first of the Pennsylvania incidents occurred near the Susquehanna River, some sixty miles north of present Harrisburg.

Flowing down from the Penn Creek Mountain runs a small stream by the same name, which empties into the west side of the Susquehanna, at present Selinsgrove, Pennsylvania (just six miles below the Moravian Shamokin mission). Numerous German settlers lived along the stream. On October 16, 1755, the small community of twenty-five men, women, and children was attacked by a party of Delaware Indians, led by Chief Kechenepaulin, an envoy of Shingas. Thirteen men, an elderly woman, and a small child were killed and scalped. The remaining settlers were carried away to Kittanning. Two days later, another settlement of twenty-five pioneers, at the mouth of Mahoney Creek just five miles south of Shamokin, was attacked. All were killed or carried into captivity, and every building in the village was burned.[21]

Within several days the news of the two massacres reached the settlement at Harris' Ferry. On October 23, John Harris, Captain Alexander McKee, and Thomas Forster led a party of forty men up the Susquehanna to bury the dead. John Shickellamy (the son of the famous chief) met Harris at the site and encouraged him to come to Shamokin to assess conditions at the village rather than return to Paxtang as originally planned. They stayed at Shamokin during the night of the twenty-fourth and heard alarming talk from their few loyal Delaware friends.[22] The next day, Scaroyady, a friendly Indian chief, advised the party to travel along the east side of the Susquehanna on their return to Paxtang. They left on the morning of the twenty-fifth but, suspecting this advice to be wrong, passed over to the west side of the river. When arriving at the mouth of Penn Creek, they were ambushed by a party of more than 120 Delawares, led by Shingas's brother Pisquetomen. Three of the party were killed in a gunfight in the woods and another five drowned while trying to escape across the river.[23]

When news of this disaster reached Shamokin a few days later, the friendly Indians understood why the English, particularly Brother Onas, refused to supply them with arms and ammunition to fight the French. These few remaining Delawares no longer held the white man's trust. It was obvious Onas now must believe they were in liaison with Shingas and his brother the Beaver, or Harris would have gone down the east side of the river. To these remaining loyal Delawares with their sensitive Indian psyche, this loss of faith was the final devastating blow.

The Indians became panic-stricken. With white blood shed on three occasions, they correctly concluded that the English, in revenge, would massacre any Indians they could find. The entire Shamokin group vacated the village, fled up the Susquehanna to Nescopek, forcing John Shickellamy, the Iroquois vicegerent, to join them, despite his objection. (He and his two brothers, James Peters and James Logan, wanted to go down and live among the whites.) Shickellamy's presence might provide some protection against attack by the French-led western tribes. The Moravian missionaries were now alone at Shamokin.[24]

At the end of October, rumors were coming out of Philadelphia that the French had promised to restore all of the Delawares' ancestral land and to release them from their obligations with the Iroquois. By November, houses, barns, and fields were burning in a vast semicircular arc from Maryland, up the Susquehanna, along the Blue Mountains, and east to the Delaware Water Gap; men, women and children were either being killed and scalped or led into captivity.[25]

The same day that John Harris and his party left Paxtang to bury the Penn Creek dead, David Zeisberger and Nathaniel Seidel again left Bethlehem for the Wyoming, unaware of the disastrous events of the previous week. Several days later, they came down into the valley, carrying a few bags of corn for the beleaguered flock with Post at his small mission station. Tension and intrigue hung heavy over the area, and even the laconic Post seemed to believe he was no longer safe.

Before leaving the valley, Zeisberger and Seidel visited Paxinosa, who had just been to Shamokin. He was waiting for them with a letter from three Shamokin village missionaries, Godfrey Roessler, Peter Wesa, and Marcus Kiefer, detailing the news of the Penn Creek massacre and warning Zeisberger and Seidel to leave the valley immediately. They remained two more days conversing with Paxinosa, Teedyuscung, and Abraham, who continued to wait for news from William Johnson or Brother Onas. The chiefs told the two men that their people were "in great fear of the French Indians & are also under a great Concern lest the White People Should think that they have a Hand in the late Disturbances."[26]

On the last day of the month the missionaries turned homeward, reaching Bethlehem on the night of November 2. At once they reported to Justice Timothy Horsfield, briefing him about the beginning of hostilities and the conditions in the valley. Their statement was forwarded to the governor and the assembly by a special express. Through special arrangements made by Spangenberg and Horsfield, the Moravians were now the only source of information covering this area for the Pennsylvania authorities.

Two days before Zeisberger and Seidel arrived in Bethlehem, Godfrey Roessler and Peter Wesa escaped from the Shamokin mission and reached Bethlehem.[27] The news they brought was frightening. For several weeks two white scalps hung in the village square, brought by envoys of Shingas, the symbol of an invitation for all the valley Indians to join his forces and fight the English.

Marcus Kiefer, the master smith, remained in Shamokin. The Bethlehem Archives contain Kiefer's terse comments on his last few days in the village, which demonstrate his fearlessness and bravery. He wrote on October 11: "The warning of danger is brushed off and not taken seriously; October 23, I do not believe I am in any danger; October 24, I do not believe the end of the mission is in sight; October 26, I am entirely alone at the mission."

On Saturday, November 15, John Shickellamy, keeping his father's promise to remain a friend of the Moravians, escorted Marcus Kiefer into the Gnadenhutten mission. The details of Shickellamy's rescue of Kiefer were amazing. Late in October, Paxinosa and Abraham, concerned for Kiefer's safety, sent their two sons to find the blacksmith at Shamokin and escort him to the Wyoming Valley. Here he was joined by Shickellamy, who escorted him through the hostile territory to Gnadenhutten.

Near the end of November, much anxiety began to develop in Bethlehem about Christian Post. It had been two weeks since any news of his whereabouts had been received. Wyoming was now known to be entirely in control of the French element and any white man could meet instant death. Post, sensitive to Indian culture, knew their methods and movements so when two strange Indians with "questionable motives" inquired about him, he disappeared without a word to anyone as to where he was going. On November 22, he surfaced at the mission church at Dansbury (now Stroudsburg). Two days later, he was in Bethlehem safe from his enemies.[28]

November 24 was an exciting day in Bethlehem. The village streets were filled with marching militiamen, their drums rolling and bugles blaring. Excited children and barking dogs followed the soldiers through the confusion-filled streets. All day soldiers came from New Jersey and the lower neighborhoods of Pennsylvania to scour the woods north of the village, searching for marauding Indians. David Zeisberger, with the permission of the militia captains, was ordered to deliver a message from Justice Horsfield to Martin Mack, the head missionary at Gnadenhutten. Since the militia would be reconnoitering in the area of the mission, the Indians were instructed to stay in the village so they would not be mistaken for hostiles.

That afternoon Zeisberger mounted his horse and left the village. Somewhere along the way he was stopped by an excited contingent of Irish militia, who suspected him of carrying intelligence to the hostile camp to warn the "French Indians." Once again Zeisberger would demonstrate the coolness and tact required in such an emergency. His quiet, modulated voice possessed a conscious innocence that immediately instilled confidence. He was permitted to ride on.

Darkness was approaching as he rode into the Gnadenhutten mission on the east side of the Lehigh and delivered his message to Mack. Despite the head missionary's plea, David refused to remain in the village. He mounted his horse and passed down to the ford, intending to deliver the message to the white mission helpers who lived across the river at the old mission site and possibly spend the night with them. Mack and a small party followed him to the river. Just before the horse reached the stream they heard gunshots coming from the other side. The sound of gunfire was not unusual because the militia sometimes signaled in such a fashion to communicate among their contingents. Reaching the ford, he splashed into the stream and began to cross.

Just moments after Zeisberger began his passage across the river, Mack, Schebosch, and the converts on the east bank noticed two men on the west bank, Joachim Sensemann and George Partsch, shouting and waving their arms frantically. Schebosch pushed a canoe into the stream and in a few minutes returned with the two men. In the meantime, Mack, screaming at the top of his voice, tried to get Zeisberger's attention, but the splashing of the water and crack of the stones as his horse passed through the river prevented Zeisberger from hearing his cries. Just as he reached the other side, young Joseph Sturgis, with blood streaming down his face, came rushing down the bank toward Zeisberger and blurted out that the Indians were massacring the Brethren on the hill and burning the buildings of the original mission. Zeisberger immediately turned his horse about and plunged back into the river. When he reached the other side, he consulted quickly with Mack, Sensemann, and Partsch, attempting to get as many particulars as possible. Then he set out for Bethlehem with the grim news as fast as his tired horse could travel.

The lonely midnight ride was broken only by another brief interruption from the militia contingent that had detained him earlier in the afternoon. When they heard the tragic news, they immediately released him to continue his journey. At three o'clock in the morning he reached Bethlehem, awoke Spangenberg, and told him the horrible news. Within several hours the bishop sent a messenger to Justice William Parson at Easton. Zeisberger knew nothing about the incident beyond what he learned from Joachim Sensemann and George Partsch.[29]

Throughout the next day, the grim survivors straggled into Bethlehem. The first, Peter Worbass, knew little more than Zeisberger, having spent the early evening lying sick in the Brethren's house. Hearing the first shots, he looked out the window and saw a woman fleeing to the cellar outside the house and back into the sister's room, chased by an Indian with drawn tomahawk. He heard the screams of the burning martyrs as the fire in the building reached the loft. Sometime during this period, his hiding place was discovered and a guard was placed at the door of the Brethren's house. A shout distracted his guard momentarily, and Worbass managed to escape through a rear window, run toward the Mahoning Creek, and elude his captor. All night long he limped toward Bethlehem.

Early in the afternoon, Sensemann arrived in Bethlehem with thirty of the converts who had been hiding in the woods. He had persuaded the frightened Indians to return to the village with him. But Sensemann knew little more than Zeisberger. Several hours later, Martin Mack and his wife arrived, accompanied by Bernard Grube and his wife, Schmick, Joseph Powell and his wife, and a party of fugitive Indians. All had been on the east side of the river. Mack was heartbroken and near collapse. Gnadenhutten had been his project since its inception in 1746. For eight years, he had tenderly cared for and dearly loved all of the converts. They were equally attached to him. He had assigned the colony of Brethren to the west bank, and he had encouraged them to remain firm and stand courageously through the recent danger. The weight of those lost lives was now on his shoulders.

In the afternoon of November 26, two days after the massacre, George Partsch and his wife, Susanna, arrived at Bethlehem, along with Sturgis. Zeisberger had talked briefly with Partsch and Sensemann, but nothing had been heard from Partsch, and the Brethren concluded that his wife had been killed. From these survivors they learned the full details of the horrible affair. After Sensemann left the Pilgrim house to lock the chapel, the barking of the dogs increased. Footsteps were heard just outside the door of the Pilgrim house. Suspecting that the militia had returned, several of the men, including young Sturgis and Martin Nitschmann, opened the door. Before them stood a party of painted Indians. They fired instantly, and Nitschmann fell in the doorway riddled by several bullets. Sturgis had been grazed along the face and retreated back into the room. The Indian party poured into the cabin and began indiscriminate firing. The second volley quickly felled John Lesley, John Gottermeyer, and Martin Presser. Presser's body was discovered some months later in the woods near the village where he had crawled and finally perished.[30] Martin Nitschmann's wife, Susanna, cried out, "O Brethren! Brethren! help me!" That was the last they heard from her, and she was presumed to be dead.[31]

The other Brethren in the room ran for the second story dormitory in the garret and closed and bolted the door. Temporarily they were safe. There were now eight people in the garret: Gottlieb Andres, his wife, Joanna, and their infant daughter; Susanna, wife of George Partsch; Anne Catherine, wife of Joachim Sensemann; George Christian Fabricus; George Schweigert; and Joseph Sturgis. Sensemann's wife sank down on the edge of the bed and sighed, "Dear Saviour, this is what I expected!" For a quarter of an hour the Indians shouted and fired through the windows and the floor of the upstairs garret, but no one was injured. The prisoners screamed for help, hoping someone would come to their rescue, then suddenly all became quiet. No one was seen from the upstairs window. Sturgis seized this opportunity to leap from the window, landed safely on the ground, and escaped. Susanna Partsch followed him and also escaped. The third and last attempt was made by Fabricus. Unfortunately, he was discovered, and as he dropped to the ground a tomahawk was instantly buried in his head. The five remaining in the attic did not have to wait long before discovering their fate. Smoke began to filter through the cracks in the floor and the crackling flames could be heard from below.

Susanna Partsch had arrived at Gnadenhutten the week before, was unfamiliar with the surroundings, and did not know which direction to take after jumping from the window into the darkness. She hid behind a tree in an elevated spot above the village where she could observe the grim proceedings going on below. In horror, she watched the war party systematically burn the buildings: first, the barn, filled to the loft with new hay and precious corn and other grain essential to their livelihood the coming winter; then the kitchen, bakery, and the single men's dwelling. Before burning the store, the Indians looted the building of everything edible, along with food in the kitchen, bakery, and spring house. During the conflagration they feasted by the light of the burning buildings. The final building torched, with some difficulty, was the chapel or Gemeinhaus. Sometime near midnight the twelve warriors left the village and faded into the night toward Wyoming.[32]

The terrified Susanna Partsch had witnessed it all from behind her tree. Groping her way down to the river, she discovered a large hollow log, where she spent the rest of the night. Her husband, George, fled back into the mountains where he found Joseph Sturgis. The two spent the night in a vacant cabin on the side of the mountain. George had a premonition that Susanna had escaped the massacre. When daylight approached, he and Sturgis crept down from their hiding place, crossed the river, and came upon the tree where she was crouched, cold and frightened. The three then returned to explore the scene of destruction and desolation. Smoke rose slowly from the burned buildings. Lying along the side of the charred Pilgrim house lay the scalped and brutally mutilated body of George Fabricus, the brilliant young and talented Indian language scholar. As they approached, his faithful dog, who had guarded the body all night, whined and raised his head as if to say, "Look what they have done to my master." Nearby, on the stump of a tree, lay a blanket and a hat, pierced by a knife, Indian symbolism for "This much we have done, and are able to do more."[33] The Gnadenhutten mission was gone. The three young people could barely comprehend the scene. The sorrowful trio set out on the journey to Bethlehem. Across the river on the east side at New Gnadenhutten the faithful John (Bull) Schebosch maintained a lonely vigil, the last of the Brethren to remain at the mission, waiting and hoping that more converts would return to the village.

The day following the massacre, Anton Schmidt and Marcus Kiefer, the fearless blacksmiths from Shamokin, left Bethlehem to check on the situation at Gnadenhutten and deliver a message from Justice Horsfield to the militia roaming in the area. They spent the next two days gathering the bodies and making coffins. Today, from the side of that lonely little hill overlooking the green valley of the Lehigh, the small communities of Lehighton and Weissport below, one can see the spot where the two blacksmiths buried the martyrs of that black Monday.

· 8 ·

The Peacemakers, 1755–1761

ALTHOUGH A deep despondency prevailed in Bethlehem on the morning of November 25, the Brethren had little time to grieve and mourn their disaster. Indian war parties roamed at will throughout the countryside, north, east, and west of the village.

With the exception of the New York colony, whose Indian allies were firmly under British control, all across the six hundred miles of colonial frontier the Indian war had begun. The middle colonies, especially Pennsylvania and Virginia, were particularly vulnerable. Their western frontiers consisted of three distinct belts of white occupation that lay between the Indian territories on the west and the more populated eastern centers of white civilization. The farthest outposts were the crude huts of the "borderers"—wild and graceless souls who chose to flee the confining aspects of society. Many were outcasts evading the long arm of the law. For the first several seasons of occupation they grew no crops, usually because they detested the plodding employment or because their nearest neighbors, the Indians, resented their presence and occasionally forced them to flee eastward, back toward the settlements.

The second layer of inhabitants, who settled twenty-five to thirty miles further east, were log cabin dwellers. Cattle, sheep, horses, and hogs were their principal products, raised in the broad meadows and hills of the Pennsylvania and Virginia uplands. In many respects they were similar to the ranchers of the Far West one hundred years later. Another layer fifty miles further east, yet many miles from the thickly settled, prosperous eastern villages, consisted of the small, rough holdings of the pioneer farmers and their large families, averaging ten to fourteen children. They grubbed a meager existence from the virgin lands.[1]

When the attacks began, many terrified frontier souls straggled into Bethlehem and Nazareth. Half-dressed and barefoot, they were aroused in the middle of the night by Indian intruders and arrived without any provisions, hungry and exhausted. By the end of the year the refugee numbers grew to well over three hundred, not including the seventy Christian Indians from the Gnadenhutten mission.[2] The logistics of providing them with bare necessities—shelter, food, and clothing—sorely taxed the resources of the Moravian communities. Ironically, many of these refugees were the same people who, just a few months earlier, had heaped ridicule and scorn on these "French-connected, Indian-loving papists."

What course should the Moravians now pursue? They seemed to have two options. Either they could abandon their pacifistic, nonmilitary principles, take up arms, and aggressively fight to defend themselves, or they could load no guns, adopt no measure of defense, post no guards, and say, "We are the Lord's People, he will protect us." They were not extremists, either as *Kriegerisch* (disposed to fight) or as *Quakerisch* (of Quaker mind). They would not organize aggressive activity against the Indians but would certainly defend themselves and those who desperately depended on them. The pragmatic Spangenberg had a solution: guards would be posted round the clock in each community where hostile activities were reported. If the enemy was sighted, the orders were to shoot to wound, not to kill.[3] They knew well the Indian psyche and methods of fighting. Zeisberger once wrote, "They (the Indians), are courageous where no danger is to be found, but in the face of danger or resistance they are fearful and the worst cowards."[4] Zeisberger missed the point. The Indians fought on their own terms with the only resources they had. Ambush and surprise, concealment, and attack were the essence of Indian strategy, but only against a force over which they clearly had a numerical superiority. Spangenberg's defense procedure proved effective. During the entire French and Indian War, no serious attack was made on any of the Moravian white villages.

Events now moved rapidly. In Philadelphia, on December 18, fifty provincial cavalrymen and three Conestoga wagons set out for Bethlehem. In the procession were James Hamilton, the former governor, now a member of the governor's council; Joseph Fox, the chairman of the assembly's new committee of accounts; and Benjamin Franklin, a member of the committee. By rank, Hamilton was the leader of the expedition. But after a week or so of deference to the man of rank, Franklin, the man of genius, took charge with his son as his aide. Fat and fifty, Franklin, with his usual resilience, took to the coming campaign like the proverbial duck to water.[5]

Franklin conceived of a series of forts, beginning at Easton on the Delaware River and continuing along the southern side of the Blue Mountains southwest to the Susquehanna. The most vulnerable site was the gap at the Lehigh. Any hostile penetration at this point put the enemy less than one hundred miles from Philadelphia. Only the Moravians at Bethlehem stood in the path.

In January 1756, the refugee count peaked at 556 persons crowding into the Moravian settlements. There were 205 at Bethlehem, 134 at Nazareth, 104 at Friedensthal, and the remainder at other settlements surrounding Nazareth.[6] But by the beginning of March, Forts Allen, Norris, and Franklin were in place, and some of the refugees began to filter back to their homes, alleviating the crowded conditions in Bethlehem.[7]

Governor Morris, his patience exhausted, finally declared war on the Delawares on April 14, 1756. He did so against the advice of James Logan, a member of his council and the former proprietor's secretary.[8]

The Moravians, while not declaring their stance publicly, were so concerned that Spangenberg traveled to Philadelphia in late April to confer with the governor. He suggested that several of the prominent Delaware chiefs, now in Philadelphia, be sent to the Wyoming Valley where they could confer with Teedyuscung and encourage him to work with them to find a peaceful solution to their mutual problem. After consulting for several days with Spangenberg, the governor agreed to the embassy. On April 29, three chiefs, led by Captain Newcastle, a son of old Queen Alliquippa, left Philadelphia for the valley. Newcastle was accompanied by Jagrea, a Mohawk, and William Lacquis, a Delaware.

The party arrived in Bethlehem on May 1, where they received supplies. Augustus (George Rex), the former national assistant at Meniologameka, and David Zeisberger joined them as escorts. Within twenty days they returned to Bethlehem, where Augustus reported that the Delawares might be ready to talk peace.[9] Continuing on to Philadelphia, the delegation reported to Morris on June 3. Encouraged by the results of the Newcastle mission and Augustus's hope for peace, the governor issued an armistice, effective for thirty days, that protected all Delawares living east of the Susquehanna River and instructed Newcastle to return to Tioga and invite the Delawares to a council in July at Easton.[10]

The Brethren at Bethlehem and Nazareth provided much of the impetus for the negotiations and were largely responsible for their success. But most of their efforts were made behind the scenes and so went unnoticed and unheard. Zeisberger, the eyes and ears of Spangenberg, attended all the sessions, sometimes as an interpreter but usually as an interested bystander. He knew many of the Delaware and Iroquois personally, and his quiet behind-the-scenes diplomacy helped create a positive atmosphere.[11]

The first conference was held at Easton from July 27 to 31, 1756. Teedyuscung became the principal spokesman for the Indians. At the first meeting at Easton, he entered the crude shelter dressed in a fine, dark brown cloth coat laced with gold braid, which matched his ruddy complexion. (The coat was a recent gift from the French at Niagara.) A well-built man of fifty, he was an imposing figure playing his newfound role of "king." For the next six years he would monopolize the Pennsylvania peace-seeking process, even though he was disliked by many of his own people, despised by the Iroquois, and barely tolerated by the English. Teedyuscung had found his destiny and played his role to perfection.

In November the conference participants began to gather at Easton. In the interim, Governor Robert Hunter Morris, at the suggestion of the proprietors, had resigned his post and was replaced by Colonel William Denny. Haughty and overbearing, with no experience in dealing with Indians, Denny was ill-equipped to face the ordeal of the coming months.[12]

Several days before the beginning of the November conference, the governor and his entourage arrived in Bethlehem without a guard and proceeded on to Easton. Included in the governor's party was Benjamin Franklin, some of the commissioners, and Israel Pemberton, leading a dozen Quakers who hoped to cause trouble for the new governor. Zeisberger was there with the entire male Indian population of Bethlehem.[13]

The conferees sat down for business on November 8. Negotiations proceeded satisfactorily until November 12, when, against Weiser's strong objection, Governor Denny opened a "hornet's nest." Prompted by the Quakers, he naively asked the Indian negotiators, "Have we, or the people of Pennsylvania done you any kind of injury? . . . Speak your mind plainly . . . tell us if you have any just cause for Complaint, what is it, that I may obtain a full Answer to this point, I give this Belt?"[14]

The wily Conrad Weiser, who accompanied the Pennsylvania delegation, knew exactly why the question was asked and the political consequences of the answer. The ingenious mind of Israel Pemberton was again at work. The Quakers were determined to escape the charge of Pennsylvania's unpreparedness, for which they were responsible, by blaming the war on the proprietors and raising the ghost of the Walking Purchase.[15]

"Honest John" Teedyuscung, prompted that evening by Pemberton, took the bait. When the sessions opened the next day, a controversy over that infamous purchase began that raged on for the next three years. The conference lumbered on for the next five days, closing inconclusively on November 17.

The year 1756 proved to be inconclusive for the English cause as well. On August 1, the Delaware Indian Captain Jacobs had attacked and burned Fort Granville, killing some of the garrison. The soldiers not killed were taken into captivity to his village at Kittanning. Fourteen days later, the Marquis de Montcalm, the new French commander at Montreal, captured and burned the English fort at Oswego. To counteract these French successes, Colonel John Armstrong, the brother of the commander killed at Fort Granville, attacked the Kittanning village on September 8 and avenged his brother by killing Captain Jacobs and burning the village.[16]

It was also a busy year for David Zeisberger. In May he made a trip to the Brethren's settlement of Wachovia (now Winston-Salem), North Carolina, to deliver dispatches for Spangenberg, returning to Bethlehem in July, just in time for the conference at Easton. Following the Easton meeting and during the winter, he carried Spangenberg's intelligence dispatches to the governor in Philadelphia.[17] The next five years would be agonizing for the missionary. Forced by the Indian war to remain near the safety of the white settlements, he spent most of this period living at Christianbrunn completing his Onondaga Indian dictionary.

The Peace Process Begins to Bear Fruit, 1757

In May 1757, Zeisberger traveled to Lancaster to attend a council called by George Croghan, Sir William Johnson's new deputy Indian agent. Zeisberger was one of the official interpreters. Both Croghan and Johnson wanted the eastern Delawares to take up the hatchet for the English cause. Teedyuscung refused to attend the council, opposed Johnson's suggestion in a letter to the delegates, and insisted that the Delawares remain neutral. Because of his absence, little was accomplished at Lancaster and the conference closed on an indecisive note, although they did agree to reconvene again in July 1757 at Easton.[18]

Following the council at Lancaster, Zeisberger returned to Bethlehem in time to participate in discussions about a new Indian village to be built near Bethlehem. Since the destruction of Gnadenhutten, housing and feeding the ever-growing Indian population was becoming a serious challenge. They had been temporarily housed at Bethlehem's Indian house on the west bank of the Monocacy, but since the massacre, the population there had increased to nearly the size of the original group at Gnadenhutten. New quarters were essential.[19] Teedyuscung spent the latter part of June and the first week in July rounding up his contingent for the third treaty conference. By July 6, 1757, a boisterous crowd of Indians had arrived at Fort Allen, much to the discomfort of Jacob Orndt, the commander. The next day they headed for Easton, escorted by a small party of Orndt's colonial guard. It was a hodgepodge group of over 150 Delawares, Mahicans, Nanticokes, Shawnees, and a sprinkling of Senecas. Fifty of Teedyuscung's followers tagged along.[20]

Governor Denny arrived on July 20, and official deliberations began the next day. Zeisberger attended each session but did not stay in Easton, commuting back and forth each day to Bethlehem. Unlike the former council meetings, he was surprised to discover that he knew only a few of the Indians who attended.[21]

Teedyuscung had decided before coming to Easton not to bring up the subject of the land fraud, preferring to wait until the question of peace was settled. Denny, however, insisted that the subject be discussed, and it consumed the delegates' time for the next twelve days. Teedyuscung demanded that he be permitted to see the original Delaware deeds from the Walking Purchase treaties of 1736 and 1737 and the Iroquois treaty of 1749. The governor eventually agreed, but his secretary, Richard Peters, refused, stating that it would violate his sworn trust to the proprietors. The review of the former treaties seemed to satisfy all parties temporarily. The chief, however, pressing his luck, insisted that the governor build a complete village in the Wyoming Valley for his people, setting the land aside forever for the use of the Delawares. After both Croghan and Weiser approved, the governor granted the request. The last several days of the council were devoted to settling the final details of the peace. A satisfactory resolution was reached on August 7, and the council closed with a victory celebration of feasting, dancing, and much drinking around a huge bonfire.[22]

A great step had been made to restore order, but many months would be required to forge a lasting peace. Throughout all of these treaty negotiations, Teedyuscung claimed to speak for ten nations (the Six Nation confederacy, along with the Delawares, Shawnees, Mahicans, and Nanticokes), but Weiser, Croghan, and most of the colonial officials knew that he spoke for a mere handful of Delawares in the Wyoming Valley. Even there he had wavering support. Most of the other tribes, including the

Iroquois, were anxious for peace and were content to humor the old braggart, permitting him to play out his role and patiently awaiting their opportunity to set the record straight.

Much to the chagrin of the Moravians, Teedyuscung returned to Bethlehem on August 9 following the conclusion of the Easton treaty.[23] Worse, he planned to remain there for the winter rather than return to Tioga in hopes that being near Philadelphia would assist in implementing his treaty promises. Spangenberg and the church officials were not pleased by this decision, but they could see the wisdom of his request. He was finally given permission to stay, and the Moravians constructed a small cabin on the south side of the Lehigh as his family quarters.[24]

If the peace was to become a reality, all parties had to secure the cooperation of the western tribes, which were principally responsible for sending the war parties against the eastern settlements. Pennsylvania officials agreed to send a peace delegation to the western tribes to seek their acceptance. Teedyuscung had received several small delegations of western Delaware chiefs, "the Beaver," and his brother Shingas, who indicated that they would entertain peace overtures. This was an encouraging sign. Both Teedyuscung and the colonial officials agreed that such an embassy would be perilous because the French controlled the western tribes.[25] After a deliberate search, both white and Indian negotiators finally concluded the Moravian missionary Christian Frederick Post would be the ideal ambassador to the Indians.

The Nain Mission

As the dark winter months of 1757–58 passed and the first signs of spring appeared, the Brethren at Bethlehem began to construct the new Indian mission at Nain. The village, several miles northwest of Bethlehem, was laid out in a square with houses built on three sides. Construction continued throughout the summer months, and on October 18, they dedicated the new chapel.[26] The converts were delighted with their new accommodations and within several years the population grew to well over 125 converts, eclipsing the size of the former Gnadenhutten.

The advent of spring in 1758 brought additional Indian incursions on the frontier, sending refugees to clog the streets of Nazareth, Gnadenthal, and Christianbrunn. Also that spring, Teedyuscung shook off his winter lethargy and left the banks of the Lehigh. In early March, he was in Philadelphia again conferring with the governor and colonial officials. Despite his faults and efforts to seek personal glory and public esteem, Teedyuscung did understand the essential ingredients necessary to bring the Indian war to a successful conclusion. In Philadelphia, he urged the government to "send a messenger to my Delaware Indian friends on the banks of the Ohio and the Allegheny. Warn them to sever their allegiance with the French and join me in my peace efforts." This appeal was a direct result of his previous year's conference with Beaver and Shingas. It was the first move toward implementing the daring mission of Christian Frederick Post to the western Indian tribes of Ohio. When leaving Philadelphia, Teedyuscung returned to his home in the Wyoming Valley, much to the relief of the Brethren at Bethlehem. They were pleased to be relieved of his disrupting rhetoric.[27]

Following Teedyuscung's suggestion, the governor called Post to Philadelphia and gave him instructions. Post made four trips in 1758 on behalf of the Pennsylvania government. Two were to the Wyoming Valley, the first to advise Teedyuscung of the conference at Easton to be held that summer and the second to deliver a Cherokee peace message that seemed to allay Teedyuscung's suspicions of his old enemies. The third journey, the first to the Ohio Country, began on July 15 from Philadelphia, only five days after Post returned from his visits to Wyoming. He returned to Philadelphia on September 15 in time for the Easton treaty conference. The fourth trip, again to the Ohio Country, would be made during the dead of winter immediately following the Easton meeting. It began on October 25 and culminated with his return to Philadelphia on January 10, 1759.[28]

These last two journeys rank among the finest acts of courage and patriotism displayed by any man during the course of the American experience. Only Post's supreme religious faith and shrewd knowledge of Indian life and customs enabled him to make his journeys successful. The ultimate success of the fourth Easton conference, which began on October 8, 1758, can be largely attributed to Post's mission to the western Delawares. Without their cooperation, the negotiations would have failed. Credit must also be given to Pisquetomen, the oldest brother of Shingas and the Beaver. Without his protection during the trip it is doubtful Post would have returned alive.[29]

The Grand Council at Easton

David Zeisberger represented the Moravians at the Easton council in 1758. It ranks among the most important Indian treaty councils of the eighteenth century. When the official deliberations began on October 8 with a speech by Governor Denny, more than five hundred Indians were present, many of them Zeisberger's friends. All members of the Six Nation Iroquois confederacy were represented, in addition to the Delawares, Conoys, Tuteloes, Nanticokes, and Shawnees. Among the white delegates were Governor Denny, members of the provincial council, and the Pennsylvania colonial assembly. New Jersey was represented by Governor Sir Francis Bernard and his retinue. Two of the most important delegates were the Indian colonial agents, Conrad Weiser and George Croghan. Israel Pemberton led his Quaker associates.

From the beginning of the conference, there was no question who was in charge of the Indian contingent. It was a Six Nations affair with Weiser carefully guiding their deliberations. The most powerful hereditary chiefs in America sat among the delegates dwarfing the "imposter king" Teedyuscung. Indian affairs would now be put in their proper order.

After several days of the customary "wiping the sweat from their eyes, and clearing the sand from the ears," the delegates settled down to business. The agenda dealt mainly with land purchases. First, the Albany purchase of 1754 was amended, returning to the Indians all the land west of the Allegheny Mountains; the Six Nations agreed to the treaty grant confirming the remaining disputed lands. The second topic on the agenda was a land dispute between the Munsees and the New Jersey colony, which was settled by a gift of £1000 from Governor Bernard. The third and most delicate point dealt with Teedyuscung's squabble over the Walking Purchase claim. The discussion, ominously, began on Friday the thirteenth with a series of angry speeches by the representatives of the Iroquois. All the speeches were cast in the same vein, asking one question: "Who made Teedyuscung a king?" Both governors responded with raised eyebrows and shrugged shoulders, denying any responsibility for appointing him as such. When it came Teedyuscung's turn to respond, he rose, a pale, drawn, and sobered man, to address the delegates. As he began to speak, all the Iroquois representatives quietly rose and left the council shed, silently expressing their disgust for this imposter. It was a critical moment for the deliberations. Fortunately, Conrad Weiser intervened in the last great moment of his illustrious career, suggesting the conference delay for several days until tempers could cool.

On Friday, the twentieth, when the council reconvened, Teedyuscung, to his credit, withdrew his claim to land on the Delaware River, in fact, to any land at all. He threw himself on the mercy of his uncles, the Iroquois.[30] His "bird on a Bow" response was done with dignity and skill and is one of the great recorded Indian speeches of all time. The old "king" concluded his remarks: "I sit here as a bird on a Bow [bough]; I look about, and do not know where to go; let me therefore come down upon the ground, and make that my own by a good Deed, and I shall then have a Home for Ever; for if you, my Uncles, or I die, our Brethren the English will say they have bought it from you, & so wrong my Posterity out of it."[31]

With the land questions settled, the conference quickly moved to its conclusion. Pisquetomen delivered the belt which Post had received from the western Delawares, signifying their willingness to discuss peace. Once arrangements were made for another council to be held in Easton the next year, the last three days were spent rejoicing with speeches, presents, and rum in abundance. The conference came to a successful conclusion. On October 25, Post was back on the trail to deliver peace belts to the western Indians.

Following the conference, George Croghan requested that Zeisberger escort the head Mohawk, Chief Nichas, as far as the Schoharie Valley. From there Zeisberger proceeded to the struggling mission at Pachgatgosh in New York where he preached and taught in the mission school. At the close of the year, he returned to Bethlehem.

At the beginning of 1759, with the French influence seriously diminished, settlers began to return to their plantations north of Bethlehem, and peace reigned in the Lehigh Valley. The Indians temporarily sheltered at Nazareth were moved to Nain, swelling the population of the burgeoning village to record numbers. In March, a measles epidemic raged through the village. But fortunately, though forty-seven people contracted the disease, none died.[32] In August, Zeisberger again returned to Wachovia, North Carolina, carrying dispatches from Bethlehem, and returned to the village in November.

The month before Zeisberger left for Wachovia, George Croghan, William Trent, and Thomas McKee met the western Indian tribes at the newly constructed Fort Pitt to explain the terms of the Easton treaty. This was the first of many conferences at this emerging center of English power in the West. The Delawares were represented by Shingas, King Beaver, Delaware George, John Killbuck, Sr., and Captain Pipe, all of whom later played prominent roles in the life of David Zeisberger. Guyasuta led the Iroquois delegation. Croghan explained the provisions of the Easton treaty, and the Indian delegates confirmed the terms without conditions, agreeing to return their white prisoners.[33]

The Wechquetank Mission, 1760

The French capitulation of Montreal in 1760 effectively ended the war in the West. With the peace, a new effort was made to expand Moravian mission work. In February, Martin Mack and Joachim Sensemann attempted to relieve the crowding at Nain. They crossed the Blue Mountains to inspect a site for another Indian mission near the former Meniologameka. The land, now vacant, was subsequently purchased by the Brethren. By April, Sensemann and Schebosch (Zeisberger's friend John Bull), with more than thirty of the Nain Indians, moved to the site, planted crops, and began building the new village to be called Wechquetank. By the first week in May, they erected the first cabin. Sensemann was appointed the head missionary and Schebosh the general warden.[34] The opening of Wechquetank immediately relieved the congestion at Nain.

Other events saddened the Brethren, however. On July 15, 1760, they received news of the death of their old friend Conrad Weiser. Over the past few years relations had become strained, but he still remained their friend. Had he lived, Weiser might have anticipated one of the greatest of all Indian dramas that was about to begin—the uprising of Pontiac. Despite the apparent peace, Weiser knew that these Indians were restless and dissatisfied with the terms of the peace. He knew they hated the British, and he knew the woods were no longer free as he and his friends had known them but "closed to white men, storms rising, limbs falling, brains being knocked out, horses fighting in the moon, and the white people being all driven into the sea." But these were the events of the future; whites and Indians would sorely miss Conrad Weiser's wise counsel.[35]

Zeisberger was absent from Bethlehem for the last ten months of 1760 and all of 1761. In April 1760 he had been assigned to the superintendency of the Brethren house at the new Moravian settlement of Litiz (now Lititz, Pennsylvania).[36] He spent the next fifteen months at that post, except for several weeks in 1761, when he was called by a special invitation of Governor Hamilton to serve as an interpreter at the Indian conference at Easton.[37] The purpose of the conference was to settle the terms regarding the prisoners taken during the late war and explain the previous treaties to the Indian delegates. Following the meeting, Zeisberger returned to Litiz and remained there until December 1761, when he resigned as superintendent and returned to Bethlehem.

Meanwhile, four hundred miles to the west of Bethlehem, in the valley of the Muskingum (now the Tuscarawas in the Ohio Country), Christian Frederick Post was felling trees and building a cabin beside the beautiful winding river, dreaming of a Christian mission among his Delaware Brethren and thinking of David Zeisberger.[38]

· 9 ·

Pontiac and His Indian War, 1761–1763

THERE WAS an audible sigh of relief as news of the British victory at Montreal on September 5, 1760, slowly passed across the British colonies. The war was over. As the fleur-de-lis of Louis XV was replaced by the Union Jack of George II, the one-hundred-year fight for possession of the continent was settled. King George had only forty-seven days to enjoy his victory. He died on October 25 and was succeeded by his twenty-two-year-old grandson, George III. The fighting had ceased, but it took the diplomats more than two years to thrash out the terms of the Treaty of Paris, signed February 10, 1763. The French ceded to the English all of the territory they held east of the Mississippi. The western section of the Louisiana territory was transferred to Spain. The peace briefly ended Indian incursions against American frontier settlements, and the westward movement of white pioneers resumed at an accelerated pace.

The war had devastated the Moravian missionary program. In one cataclysmic stroke, the war and the resultant Indian insurgency destroyed the thriving mission at Gnadenhutten and the struggling mission at Shamokin. Any new missions among the Iroquois seemed highly improbable in the near future. The Moravians continued to operate Nain and, across the Blue Mountains north of Bethlehem, the new mission of Wechquetank.

Of the three former New York missions, only Pachgatgoch remained, and many of those converts had recently moved to Wechquetank.

It had been six years since David Zeisberger, now forty-one, roamed the forest, preaching to and teaching prospective Indian converts. On March 16, 1762, he left Bethlehem bound for the Wyoming Valley and carrying a commission from Sir William Johnson and Governor Hamilton to Teedyuscung, asking his attendance at yet another conference at Easton in June 1762. The governor of Pennsylvania and Sir William Johnson would make one final attempt to settle the nagging question of the Walking Purchase Treaty of 1737.

After delivering his message to Teedyuscung, Zeisberger turned his attention to the former converts now living in the valley. He visited a number of the apostates, including Augustus (George Rex), the former national assistant at Meniologameka, and Abraham, who had caused so many problems at Gnadenhutten. Zeisberger was back in Bethlehem on March 24, pleased with his reception at Wyoming.

The visit to the Wyoming Indians stirred David's missionary blood. He longed to renew his ministrations among the Indians. In August, Zeisberger and Gottlob Sensemann returned to the valley, responding to an urgent message received in Bethlehem from Abraham: "Brethren, let a teacher come to see me ere I die."[1] The old man had returned to Nain four years earlier, appealing to the Brethren to forgive him and accept his repentance. They refused, and he returned brokenhearted to his home in the Wyoming Valley. Abraham was now trying to make amends and to be forgiven for all the contention he caused. Fortunately for him, Zeisberger and Sensemann arrived before he died. Assured of the Brethren's forgiveness, he recalled the good times. In his mind, he was welcomed into the arms of the Savior, and he died early in December with a smile of contentment on his face.[2]

The missionaries were also in time to comfort the dying Augustus. He had traveled to Wechquetank in May, appealing to Bernard Grube for forgiveness and requesting permission to return to the Brethren. The passionate Grube was far more tractable with Augustus than the Nain Brethren had been with Abraham and granted him permission to return. The happy former national assistant and brother-in-law to Teedyuscung returned to his home in the valley and prepared to make the move. But in September he became seriously ill. The visiting Zeisberger spent several weeks administering medicine and caring for his old friend, but his ministrations were unsuccessful. The old chief died on October 12, 1762, content to have been exonerated by the Brethren. Zeisberger and Sensemann returned to Bethlehem on November 13, saddened by the loss of the two old apostates but content with the progress they had made preaching to other Wyoming Valley Indians.

Abraham and Augustus are representative of those Indians who faced an agonizing sociological dilemma by becoming Christians. Despite the Brethren's attempt to minimize the shock of converting to the white man's culture, the Indians had great difficulty making the transition. They were forced to comply with European economics, religious laws, and living conditions and asked to repudiate and reject their independent aboriginal lifestyle. Zeisberger recognized this dilemma and attempted to ease the transition, but the change still remained a perplexing problem. Francis Jennings alludes to the question in *The Ambiguous Iroquois Empire:*

> Their [the missionaries'] assumptions led to actions designed deliberately to weaken traditionalist (Indian) government and leaders . . . they withdrew converts from participation in the rituals by which the tribe confirmed its unity; they instigated converts to attack the institution and leaders of traditional society. . . . Some missionaries were heroic in their faith, some less so. All were undeniably dedicated, and the irony is that their dedication wrought devastation in ways unintended and unforeseen.[3]

Jennings's observation was directed at missionary programs in general.

The Post-Heckewelder Muskingum Mission

Four days before Zeisberger left Bethlehem to deliver Governor Hamilton's message to Teedyuscung, two solitary travelers bid farewell to their friends at the small Moravian village of Litiz. On March 12, 1762, Christian Frederick Post and John Heckewelder, who turned nineteen that day, departed from the new settlement, bound for the virgin forests of the Ohio Country. Post, who had become friendly with the Delaware chiefs during the treaty negotiations in 1758, conceived a plan to found a mission on the banks of the Muskingum (now the Tuscarawas) River. Strategically located, the proposed site (Bolivar, Ohio) lay at the Great Crossing Place, a junction on the Indian trail from Fort Pitt to Detroit and the trail from Lake Erie to the Upper Shawnee villages on the Scioto (Columbus, Ohio). It was also the site of the village of Beaver (Tamaque), the new head chief of the Delawares, and his brother Shingas.[4] Post had spent the summer and fall of the previous year building a small cabin at the proposed mission site, then returned to Bethlehem during the winter, searching for a partner for his new venture. The Bethlehem elders denied him official sanction, but they did applaud his effort and helped him secure Heckewelder's services.

Winter still hung heavy in the western skies as the two missionaries left Litiz. Their route followed the Forbes Road through Carlisle, Shippensburg, Fort Bedford, and Fort Ligonier, across the Laurel Hill and Chestnut Ridge to Pittsburgh. Leaving Fort Pitt on April 5, they arrived six days later at the Great Crossing Place on the Muskingum River.[5] The cabin Post had constructed the previous summer was on a high bank, seventy feet from the north side of the river (in Stark County, Ohio). Across the river, a mile to the south, was the trading post of Thomas Calhoon, whom Heckewelder described as "a moral and religious man." Nearby stood Beaver's Delaware village.[6]

Before he left Pennsylvania, Post had promised the governor that he would urge the western Delaware chiefs to attend the treaty conference to be held at Lancaster in August and assured him he would accompany the delegation and act as their official interpreter. He further promised the elders at Bethlehem that he would not, under any circumstances, leave Heckewelder alone on the Muskingum.

As the months passed, it become increasingly evident that all was not peace and harmony with the Delawares. As soon as the missionaries arrived, disputes arose over Post's proposed missionary project. Many of the tribal chiefs opposed the project, believing it to be another attempt by white men to steal their land. As the time approached for Post to leave for the conference, the two missionaries discussed his departure. Despite Post's promise, they resolved that Heckewelder would remain alone at the cabin to guard against any attempts to destroy it, while Post would accompany the chiefs to Lancaster, then return after the conference ended. Heckewelder recorded the decision in his journal: "He [Post] laid the whole matter before me; and we at last agreed that I should remain."[7]

It was a harebrained idea. Why Post, who was aware of Indian instability at this time, would leave this nineteen-year-old man in the wilderness is difficult to understand, especially since he had promised the Bethlehem authorities just the contrary. Heckewelder could not speak the language, had no knowledge of the perils of the wilderness, had virtually no food, and was living among inhospitable natives.

He stayed until October, living "mostly on nettles which grew abundantly in the bottoms." Twice friendly Indians warned him to "leave the country" because war was about to break out. But, he wrote, "I remained in happy ignorance of my dangerous situation." On a cold afternoon in early October, one of trader Calhoon's men called from across the river; Heckewelder quickly gathered his few possessions and left immediately "as Calhoon wished to speak to me of a matter of great importance."[8] When he arrived at the trader's store, Calhoon told him that a friendly Indian woman had disclosed that the Delawares planned to visit Heckewelder's cabin that evening and kill him. For the next few days he remained under Calhoon's protection, regained his strength, then, furnished with a horse, returned to the settlements, protected by traders who were transporting a load of furs to their eastern market. He arrived at Bethlehem shortly after the first of November, thin and emaciated, almost unrecognized by the Brethren. John Heckewelder survived; God and David Zeisberger had plans for this young man.

While Post and Heckewelder had been scratching out a meager existence deep in the forest of the Ohio Country, a major change took place at Bethlehem following news of Count Zinzendorf's death. Spangenberg was called to assume new duties on the General Governing Board of the church in Europe. Spangenberg sailed from New York on July 1, 1762. The American Brethren would miss him. Bishop Nathaniel Seidel replaced him at Bethlehem.

When Zeisberger returned from his Wyoming trip on November 13, Heckewelder waited for him with a note from Post. In Seidel's presence, Heckewelder delivered the concise message, which read: "Cast in your lot with me. We will go out as independent evangelists, establish God's kingdom among the Indians, and extend it as far as the Mississippi." Without hesitation, Zeisberger replied, "Post is free to undertake what he pleases; I am not. I belong wholly to the Church of the Brethren."[9]

The Beaver and Shingas, with their Delaware delegation, returned in September to their Muskingum village from the conference at Lancaster. But when the austere Indian policies of the king's new commander in America, Lord Jeffery Amherst, became known among the western tribes, their hostility increased. Any hopes the English might have had that the western tribes would accept the general's new program were based on an ignorant assumption of Indian credulity. The uniform kindness and urban civility of the French contrasted strikingly with the harsh manners and rude treatment they now received from the English, who clearly disliked them. The systematic perfidiousness of the English traders and the continuing advance of the pioneer settlers who stole their land further inflamed them.[10] The Indians were proud and intelligent people; such treatment

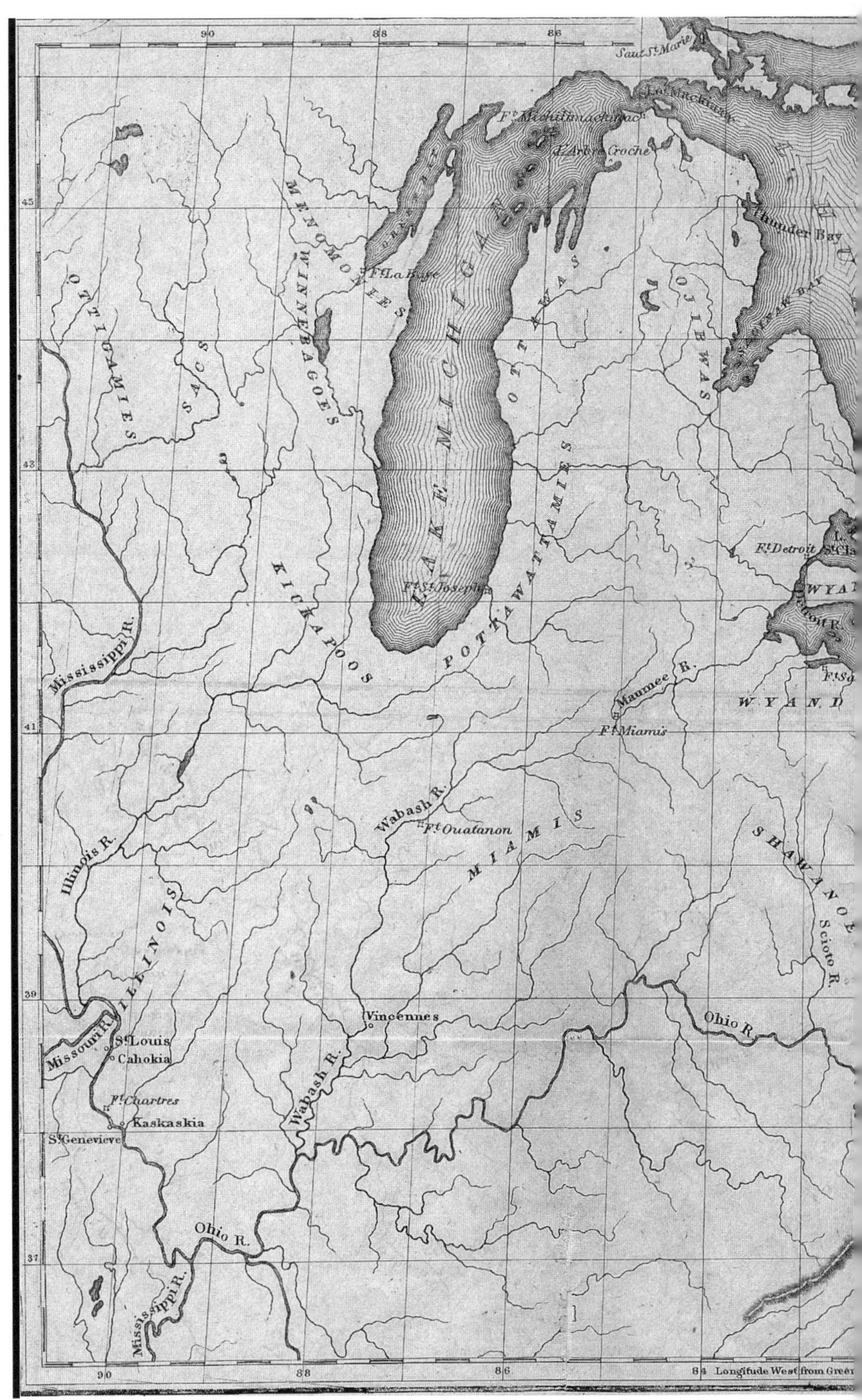

Forts and Settlements in America, 1763.

From Francis Parkman, *The Conspiracy of Pontiac* (Boston: Little Brown, 1893).

attacked the very roots of their character. Rumors were rampant among the western tribes. Their patience neared the breaking point. The American colonials were soon to incur the wrath of an Ottawa Indian named Pontiac and his allies.

Amherst, in New York, remained smug over his new policy of stringent control of Indian gifts and presents. He longed to be back in England. Peace reigned, and on the surface everything seemed tranquil. It was all an illusion.

The Pontiac Uprising, 1763

Within five months after the beginning of the new year the former French territory west of the Allegheny Mountains would explode in bloody violence, death, and destruction. Pontiac would lead the Ottawa nation and its allies, the Chippewas (Ojibwa), Pottawattomies, and Wyandots, in a combined attack against Detroit on May 9, 1763. Within a few weeks the Delawares, Shawnees, Senecas, and Miamis joined in the carnage. It was the largest single Indian uprising in the history of the North American continent. Their objective was to drive the English into the sea.

One week after Pontiac's forces attacked Fort Detroit, they murdered the fifteen-man contingent at Fort Sandusky, sparing only the commander, Christopher Pauli, who later escaped and returned to Detroit. Pontiac had made a hollow mockery of Amherst's remark to Sir William Johnson when Johnson cautioned the general about building the fort at Sandusky: "I must and will . . . have one at this place."[11]

On May 25, a group of Pottawattomies attacked Fort Saint Joseph. All but six of the fifteen men stationed there were killed. Those six were taken captive. Following the same pattern at Sandusky, the Pontiac-led warriors plundered and burned the fort. Then using stealth, intrigue, and help from the Miamis, the Indians overcame the garrisons at Fort Miamis and Fort Quiatenon on May 27 and June 1. Sixteen men were killed; those who survived were taken as prisoners to Fort de Chartres, one of the remaining French forts on the Mississippi.

On June 2, the Chippewas, using the ruse of a ball that went over the wall of the fort during a game of baggataway (lacrosse), gained entrance to Fort Michilimackinac and launched an attack. By the time the slaughter was over, twenty-six of the thirty-five men in the garrison had met a gruesome death.[12]

Except for Detroit, which continued to hold out against Pontiac and his allies, the only British fort still standing west of the Ohio River was Fort

Edward Augustus on Green Bay, commanded by Lieutenant James Gorrell. His Indian neighbors, the Sauk, Fox, Menominee, and Winnebago tribes were never friendly with the French so were not interested in Pontiac's uprising. They agreed to intercede with the Ottawas and Chippewas on Gorrell's behalf and succeeded in securing his release. The entire Augustus garrison finally found safety in Montreal.

Word of Pontiac's exploits soon reached the eastern tribes of the Delaware, Mingo, Shawnee, and Seneca, who joined in the attack. The first three tribes began a siege against Fort Pitt on May 29, while the Senecas turned their wrath against the forts to the north. On June 16, they attacked Fort Venango, killing the entire garrison of sixteen men. Two days later, they attacked Fort Le Boeuf, but the thirteen-man garrison held them off until evening, then, under the cloak of darkness, escaped to Fort Pitt.

The Senecas then moved up to Fort Presque Isle, a much stronger post, garrisoned by twenty-nine men and commanded by Ensign John Christie. They began an attack on June 19, but Christie and his men held out for two days before surrendering to a combined force of Senecas and two hundred Ottawas, Wyandots, and Chippewas sent by Pontiac. Christie gained Fort Pitt commander Henry Bouquet's everlasting disfavor for his "disgraceful surrender." Except for one man, who was turned over to Major Gladwin at Detroit, we know nothing of the fate of the others.[13] By the end of June 1763, the only British forts remaining west of the Allegheny Mountains were Detroit, Pitt, and Niagara.

Machiwihilusing

Near the end of April 1763, as Pontiac and his chiefs made their final plans to attack Fort Detroit, David Zeisberger descended the southern slope of the Blue Mountains, returning to Bethlehem from Wechquetank. Both Nain and Wechquetank were now flourishing missions, and the Brethren had great hopes for their continued success.[14] But Zeisberger longed to expand the work, especially in the Wyoming Valley.

For over four years, Papunhank, the Indian conjurer at Machiwihilusing, had been petitioning the elders at Bethlehem to send a teacher to his village. He and his people lived at the foot of Browntown Mountain near the present city of Wyalusing, north of the Wyoming Valley. Following his visit to Nain in 1759, Papunhank became entranced by Christian philosophy and Nain village life. David Zeisberger was appointed by the Mission Board to investigate his request for a teacher.

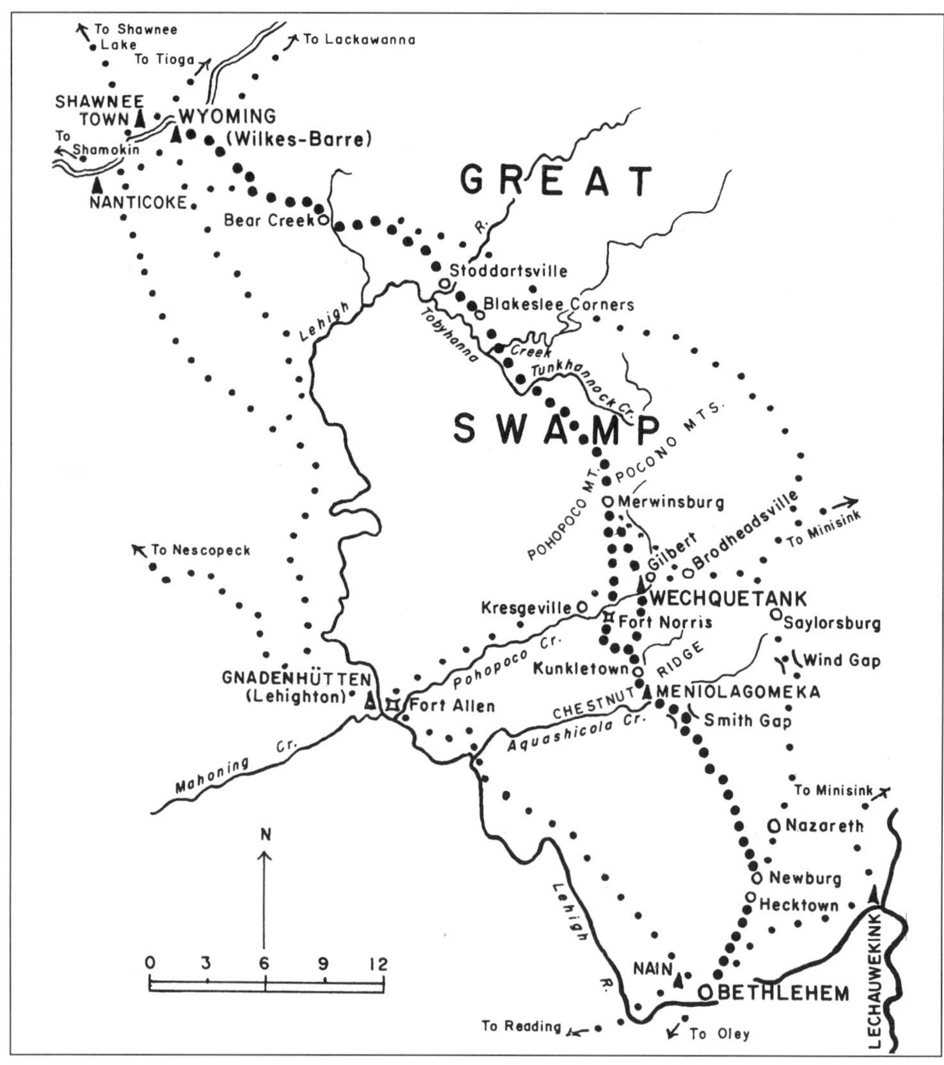

Wechquetank Path. From Paul A. W. Wallace, *Indian Paths of Pennsylvania,* Pennsylvania Historical and Museum Commission, 1965.

Leaving Wechquetank on May 16, Zeisberger and the Indian convert Anthony traveled north on what later became known as the Wechquetank Path.[15] It reached north from Bethlehem, crossed the Pocono Mountains, and plunged into the Great Swamp, an almost inaccessible maze of virgin forest and laurel bushes. After two days of hardship, amid drenching rain, through pathless forest and swamps, guided by only a pocket compass, they came down across the Wyoming Mountain into the beautiful Wyoming Valley to the village where Teedyuscung had lived.

The village lay in charred ruins. Only a handful of emaciated villagers remained to recite the gruesome tale of its destruction. On the evening of April 16, as the old chief lay in a drunken stupor, his cabin was set on fire from the outside and consumed in a fiery holocaust, along with its sleeping occupant. Within a few minutes, the twenty remaining dwellings burst into flames. In several hours the entire village lay in ashes.[16] Most of the remaining villagers fled in terror, some back to the mission at Wechquetank, some to Nain, and others to Big Island on the west branch of the Susquehanna. Those responsible for the destruction of Teedyuscung's village have never been positively identified, but suspicion points to the Connecticut settlers then invading the valley.

As Zeisberger passed through the valley, he recorded in his journal that he found the Indians "in great Consternation not knowing wither they moved" but all "in motion to leave the place."[17] Zeisberger and Anthony arrived at Machiwihilusing on the evening of May 23. Papunhank received them in his lodge.[18] Late the next morning they assembled to hear the "great word." Indian runners hastened up and down the valley to invite their brothers to come and hear the message. The preachers deeply impressed their listeners, especially Papunhank, who seemed more affected than his villagers. The missionaries stayed with the Indians for three days, then returned to Bethlehem with a message from the village council to the Mission Board requesting that a permanent teacher be assigned to the village.

Bethlehem responded by appointing Zeisberger as the missionary. During the second week in June, he left for Papunhank's village, accompanied by Nathaniel, a brother of Anthony. As they passed through the Wyoming Valley, they heard the first rumors of Pontiac's uprising in the West. The valley rang with the disturbing news as the friendly Indians prepared to move.

At Machiwihilusing he enthusiastically resumed his work. This was Zeisberger at his best, teaching, preaching, and praying with his "brown brethren." Shortly after the party arrived, Papunhank asked to be baptized. The whole town gathered on June 26 to celebrate the baptism. Falling on his knees, Papunhank was baptized by Zeisberger and renamed Johannes. He was the first of many native Indian prophets baptized by Zeisberger. Heckewelder later said, "He [Zeisberger] rejoiced more over this convert than he would have rejoiced had he inherited a kingdom."[19]

On June 30, a messenger arrived from Bethlehem with a letter from Seidel. He asked Zeisberger to return to Bethlehem immediately because the news from the West confirmed the rumors of an Indian war. Everything west of the Allegheny Mountains was in a state of terror. Although the mission's project appeared promising, continuing in Machiwihilusing would be foolhardy. Zeisberger and Nathaniel departed the next day and reached Bethlehem on July 10, 1763, happy to be safe again among the Brethren.

Bethlehem seethed with rumors. The May and June attacks by Pontiac's forces were well known, and rumors of Indian incursions against the new settlers in the Cumberland, Juniata, and Sherman Valleys were beginning to deluge the village. In the interim between the close of the French and Indian War and the beginning of the Pontiac uprising hundreds of white pioneers crossed the Susquehanna and flooded into the lush, green, fertile valleys to the west. Within four months, according to George Croghan, the Indian agent, more than two thousand of these settlers would pay with their lives or be taken into Indian captivity for long periods.[20]

During Pontiac's uprising, most of the Indian attacks against white settlements occurred west of the Susquehanna River. Thus, with several exceptions, Bethlehem was spared the fear and terror experienced during the late hostilities. But the settlement was not free from turmoil. Hostile war parties still roamed the countryside near Bethlehem. In some respects, the residual effects of Pontiac's action proved to be more damaging to the mission program than any previous event. When the uprising was finally subdued, the mission program around Bethlehem would be in shambles. Never again would Christian Indians gather in villages near Bethlehem.

By far the most devastating result of the Pontiac uprising was a change in the attitudes of the white population. An intense hatred of all Indians began to form in the minds of many of the white settlers. The idea that "the only good Indians were dead Indians" was first manifested among the large population of Scotch-Irish settlers, who developed a fierce hatred of all aborigines. Like a plague, the idea drifted across the countryside until some white men committed acts of violence that exceeded the brutality and savagery of the bloodiest Indian massacre. Many of the white settlers firmly believed the Indians were the Canaanites of the Western world. Had not God commanded Joshua: "When the Lord thy God shall bring thee into the land wither thou goest to possess it, and hath cast out many nations before thee. . . . And when the Lord thy God shall deliver them before thee; thou shall smite them, and utterly destroy them, thou shall make no covenant with them, nor shew mercy unto them"?[21]

During the summer months following his return from Onondaga, Zeisberger took up residence at the single Brethren house at Christianbrunn. Much of his time was spent carrying messages from the Mission Board to the missions still operating at Nain and Wechquetank.

On July 22, 1763, the Christian converts sent a message to Governor Hamilton requesting protection. To safeguard them from his own scouting parties, the governor suggested that some means be devised to identify the "Moravian Indians." Timothy Horsfield, the justice of the peace for the area, drew up eight articles describing their appearance and regulating the Indians' conduct when meeting white men. Horsfield's instructions were simple: "They are always clothed; they are never painted; they wear no feathers, but hats and caps; they let their hair grow naturally; they carry their guns on their shoulders, with the shaft upwards; when meeting a white man, they call him, salute him, and in coming near carry their gun on the shoulder in a reversed position. When they go hunting they will have a pass from either Horsfield, Johann Jacob Schmick, the superintendent at Nain, or Bernard Grube, his counterpart at Wechquetank." How galling these instructions must have been for the fiercely independent and spirited Indians.[22]

During the night of August 20, a series of events began that eventually destroyed both missions. Zachary, a former convert, with his wife and child, and Zippora, a member of the Wechquetank mission, were returning from Wechquetank to Long Island, Zachary's village on the Susquehanna River. They had stopped at a barn where they would be under the protection of a detachment of soldiers, billeted there for the evening and led by Captain Nicholas Wetterhold, the commander at Fort Allen. The captain, normally a responsible officer, let the off-duty activities of the soldiers get beyond his control. Late that evening, in a half-drunken lark, his men decided to murder their Indian guests. Arriving at the barn, they threw the sleeping Zippora on the threshing floor and brutally beat her to death. Aroused by the noise, the Zachary family fled from the barn only to be pursued by the soldiers. Zachary was eventually caught and knifed to death along with his wife as she pleaded in vain for the life of her child.[23]

Zachary had four brothers living at Wechquetank. When the news of the massacre flashed across the countryside, the whites immediately came to the conclusion that the Wechquetank Indians would rise up and ravish the area. To foil any possible Indian retaliations, the militia approached the village fully intending to prevent such action. Only through Grube's skill as a negotiator were they dissuaded from attacking and destroying the mission. Wetterhold and his militia troops had nothing to fear from the Wechquetank Indians, but other forms of retribution were in the making.

Early on the morning of October 8, the same militia unit that participated in the Zachary incident, but now led by Captain Jacob Wetterhold, a brother of Nicholas, was encamped in the Irish settlement eight miles north of Bethlehem, at the tavern and home of John Stenton. The unit had spent the previous day in Bethlehem and was returning to Fort Allen. Wetterhold retired for the evening, unaware that his men had been scouted by a party of hostile Delaware Indians led by Captain Bull, the son of Teedyuscung. As the first dawn light began to break across the Lehigh Valley, the captain's servant opened the door of their quarters to gather the horses and begin breakfast. A shot rang out, and he fell to the ground. The captain rushed to the door. A shot tore through his body, and he fell badly wounded on the doorsill. Sergeant Lawrence McGuire, in an attempt to drag the captain from the doorway, also received a dangerous wound. A lieutenant advanced to help when an Indian warrior, jumping on the two bodies in the doorway, drew a pistol, which was deflected by the lieutenant and discharged over his shoulder. The Indian fled from the house and the lieutenant closed the door. The war party had now surrounded the house and were firing in the windows. As Stenton was getting out of bed, he was shot but rushed out the door and ran for over a mile before dropping dead. Mrs. Stenton and her children hurried into the basement and, despite repeated gunfire, escaped unscathed. Wetterhold dragged himself to a window and killed one of the Indians who was attempting to set fire to the dwelling. Having accomplished their objective, the Indians gathered up their dead companions and retired from the scene. Loading their captain and the other wounded in a wagon, the militiamen hurriedly returned to the Crown Inn in Bethlehem, where the captain died the next day. Jacob Wetterhold was a brave and energetic officer who deserved a better fate.[24]

A storm of fury swept over Northampton County following the Wetterhold massacre and other killings the same day. Again, the militia mobilized and marched toward the Wechquetank mission, and mobs began to gather with the avowed purpose of destroying both Wechquetank and Nain. Fortunately for everyone, a violent late evening rainstorm quenched their ardor; the missions were safe for a few more days.

At midnight on the same day of the massacre, Grube received a message from the Mission Board informing him of the catastrophe and advising him to take immediate measures for the Indians' protection. The missionary ran a tight ship at Wechquetank. He knew the danger of the smallest suspicion that one of the converts left the mission to participate in any hostile activities against the white population. A ledger was kept of the converts' daily activities, and every evening he checked to be sure that each convert had returned to the mission.[25] But it was all in vain. Grube now knew it was time to leave Wechquetank. On October 11, he sadly led his little band south to Nazareth and temporarily housed them in the widows' house. Zeisberger took charge of the displaced converts, while Grube, accompanied by Horsfield, Schmick, and Frederick von Marschall, went to Philadelphia to report to the governor and seek his aid for the harassed Christian Indians in their charge. Something had to be done immediately to protect the converts or they would be murdered by the aroused white population. In the meantime, Zeisberger and the Brethren encircled Nazareth with a stockade to prevent any assault by hostile Indians or enraged whites.

Refugees again began to flock into Bethlehem. On October 25, a general meeting of the citizens put into place the same defensive measures used during the Indian war. Guards were mounted around the clock and stockades were constructed. Watch houses were built in the same corners as before. On November 18, the oil mill mysteriously burned, and on the same day the deserted Wechquetank mission was destroyed, both acts probably committed by disgruntled white enemies of the Brethren.[26]

On October 28, three days after the general alarm meeting in Bethlehem, the sheriff of Northhampton County, John Jennings, appeared at the village with a warrant for the arrest of Renatus, a young member of the Nain mission. The widow of John Stenton accused him of being one of the Indian party that killed her husband. Renatus's old father, Jacob, was the last survivor of the first three converts baptized at Oley.

George Klein, Jennings's deputy sheriff, arrested Renatus the following day. He then deputized missionary Schmick to take the prisoner to Philadelphia for incarceration.[27] Schmick, the prisoner, and his father, Jacob, left Bethlehem the same day. Renatus's subsequent trial became a cause célèbre and was one instance when justice prevailed in an otherwise charged and dangerous situation.

Schmick and the two Indians arrived in Philadelphia on October 30 just as the residents were recovering from a mysterious alarm. A loud roaring noise had passed over the city, shaking and rocking the buildings and frightening the inhabitants. It was probably a mild earthquake. In the midst of this excitement, John Penn, the thirty-four-year-old grandson of the colony's founder, stepped ashore from a vessel onto the High Street wharf. He had just arrived from England. Penn did not realize that he had just been dropped into a sea of trouble.[28]

· 10 ·

The Philadelphia Incident, 1763–1765

ALTHOUGH THE situation on the frontier was explosive, in Philadelphia little planning had been done to receive the Moravian contingents from the missions of Wechquetank and Nain. Most of the pressure on the young governor to confine the Indian converts was coming from the dissatisfied western pioneer counties and the Quaker-controlled assembly. All of these parties were primarily concerned with political considerations that had little to do with the welfare of the Indians.

Back in Bethlehem, Nathaniel Seidel, Spangenberg's replacement, dispatched his assistant, Frederick von Marschall, to follow the Schmick party to Philadelphia.[1] Marschall arranged the legal defense of Renatus and, aided by the Moravian attorney Lewis Weiss, presented a plan to the governor that would protect the refugee converts now living at Nain and Nazareth. William Logan placed the plan before the governor's council, but it was quickly rejected for an alternate arrangement calling for the disarmament and removal of the converts to Philadelphia. With little dissent, the letter plan was approved by the assembly.

Governor Penn sent a messenger to Bethlehem directing the converts to make immediate preparations to move. Though distressed at the thought of being confined in the city, the converts obeyed the order with astonishing "patience and resignation," relinquishing their weapons to Sheriff Jennings several days later.[2]

The three-day journey to Philadelphia proved tormenting. On the morning of November 8, 1763, the 44 former Wechquetank converts, led by the faithful missionary Grube, arrived in Bethlehem from Nazareth. After a short church service, they proceeded to Nain. By the middle of the afternoon, eight wagons, each under the charge of one of the Brethren, pulled away from the little Nain village just northwest of Bethlehem. The wagons carried the aged, sick, women, and children, supervised by Margaretha Grube and Marie Roth; the men followed on foot, led by David Zeisberger, Bernard Grube, and Johann Roth.[3] Of the 125 converts bound for Philadelphia on that day, almost half would not return alive.

Governor Penn had designated the Philadelphia barracks, which extended from Tammany to Green, between Second and Third Streets, as quarters for the refugees. He assigned Joseph Fox, the commissary, to provide provisions for the Moravian party.[4] Unfortunately, the British commander and his troops were not advised of the governor's orders.

On the morning of November 11, Frederick von Marschall, missionary Schmick, George Neisser, and commissary Fox met the procession.[5] The first wagon approached at 9:30 A.M., filled with women and children. It passed through the gate, followed by others. Suddenly the soldiers understood the meaning of the visit. Seizing their muskets, they surrounded the wagons and stopped the others that had passed through the gate from entering the grounds. The soldiers, threatening to fire if the wagons continued, demanded that they leave immediately. All persuasion and consultation were of no avail. Fox rushed off to inform the governor.

Meanwhile, a crowd began to gather, which quickly grew into a howling mob. Second Street rang with invectives heaped on the poor converts and their white leaders. Bloodthirsty remarks were heard: "Shoot them! Hang them! Scalp the damnable trouble-makers!" Zeisberger, Grube, and Roth did their best to calm the converts. From ten to three o'clock in the afternoon they endured this abuse. As the afternoon wore on, many Quakers, in sympathy with the Indians, came along and offered comfort to the stoic Indians.[6] By three o'clock, Fox returned with some members of the council and advised the British commander that the converts would be moved to Province Island rather than risk an armed confrontation with the citizen rabble. Surrounded by the howling mob, the wagons and men proceeded down Second Street to the wharf, where they were loaded into several flatboats and taken to the island.

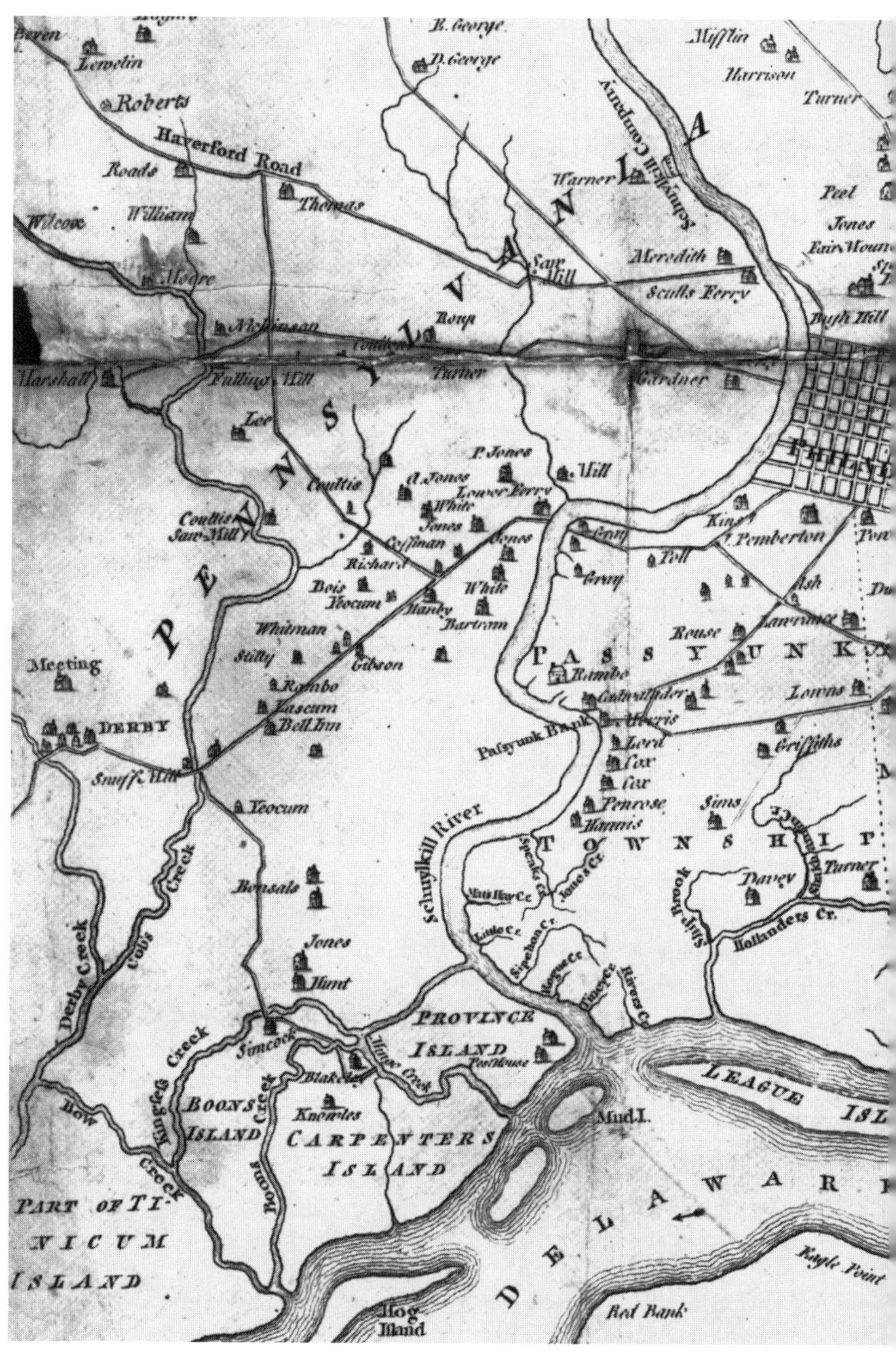

Philadelphia and the surrounding area, 1777.

From the Map Collection (MG-11) of the Pennsylvania State Archives.

Province Island was south of Philadelphia at the mouth of the Schuylkill and Delaware Rivers (just north of the present site of the Philadelphia International Airport). During the eighteenth century, Province Island was the summer smallpox quarantine area for Philadelphia. The Indians, under the supervision of Zeisberger and Grube, were housed in two large hospital buildings on the island. The first few weeks were busy times for Zeisberger, who acted as superintendent and officiated as minister and purveyor of provisions when Grube became ill.[7]

Shortly after the converts arrived in Philadelphia, they were joined by Johannes Papunhank and his family from Machiwihilusing. By the beginning of December the converts were adjusting to their new quarters. The atmosphere in Philadelphia returned to a semblance of order, and Johann Schmick again joined the island Indians on December 8, replacing Zeisberger, who returned to Bethlehem on December 21. But this relative tranquillity was only temporary.

The Paxton Boys

On the morning of December 21, 1763, Governor Penn received a message from Lancaster. The peaceful village of twenty Conestoga Indians had been attacked on December 14 by a party of Scotch-Irish settlers from Paxton (Harrisburg).[8] Fortunately, only six of the villagers were at home at the time of the attack. The rest were hunting in the surrounding woods. All six villagers were bludgeoned to death and their homes burned. The fourteen survivors were gathered together by Sheriff John Hay and confined in the Lancaster jail for their own safety.

Thirteen days later, the augmented gang of sixty "Paxton Boys" returned to the Lancaster workhouse to complete their grisly task. William Henry, a thirty-four-year-old resident of Lancaster and later a prominent judge, described the horrible event:

> The first notice I had of the affair, was that while at my father's store, near the court house, I saw a number of people running down street towards the gaol, which enticed me and other lads to follow them. At about sixty yards from the gaol, we met from 25 to 30 men, well-mounted on horses, and with rifles, tomahawks, and scalping knives, equipped for murder. I ran into the prison yard, and there, O what a horrid sight presented itself to my view!!—Near the back door of the prison, lay an old Indian and his squaw (wife) particularly well-

> known and esteemed by the people of the town on account of his placid and friendly conduct. His name was Will Sock; across him and his squaw lay two children, of about the age of three years, whose heads were split with a tomahawk, and their scalps taken off. Towards the middle of the gaol yard, along the west side of the wall, lay a stout Indian I particularly noticed to have been shot in the breast, his legs were chopped with a tomahawk, his hands cut off, and finally a rifle discharged in his mouth; so that his head was blown to atoms, and the brains were splashed against, and yet hanging to the wall, for three or four feet around. This man's hands and feet had also been chopped off with a tomahawk. In this manner lay the whole of them, men, women and children, spread about the prison yard: shot—scalped—hacked and cut to pieces.[9]

The Conestogas, the last of the once great tribe of the Susquehannocks, had resided in the area for over one hundred years and for the past sixty had lived peacefully with their white Pennsylvania neighbors. The seven adults and seven small children were the last remnants of that tribe.

When the news reached Philadelphia at the end of December, it had a galvanizing effect on the Pennsylvania authorities. Lancaster County sheriff John Hays and Edward Shippen had written to Penn describing the details and further noted, "It is rumored that a Superior Force intend an Attack on the Province Island, with a view to destroy the Indians there."[10]

On the evening of December 29, the governor and his council met in emergency session and ordered three flatboats delivered to Province Island. If the converts were threatened, they could escape to nearby League Island.[11] They also dispatched messages to Edward Shippen advising him to secure intelligence as to the movement of any force toward Philadelphia.

The governor's two urgent proclamations appealing for the arrest of the offenders, one on December 22, 1763, and the other on January 2, 1764, brought no responses, despite the offer of a reward of £200 for the apprehension and conviction of the Conestoga murderers.[12] There was a good reason for the silence. Complaints about Indian depredations east and west of the Susquehanna had fallen on deaf ears in Philadelphia for months. Throughout the year the proprietary government and the assembly remained deadlocked as to how to respond effectively, quarreling over who was to pay for organizing the response to the Indian incursions.[13]

Most of the animosity was directed toward the hostile Indians, but the Quakers, because of their nonresistant principles and their ability to control the assembly, received much of the criticism. The center of this frontier resistance was found in the Scotch-Irish settlements. Some of their complaints were certainly justified, but most went beyond reason into the realm of fanaticism.[14]

The news of the Conestoga massacres reached Bethlehem on December 31, along with rumors that hostile mobs were moving toward Philadelphia to attack Province Island. That same evening the Mission Board sent Zeisberger and Horsfield to Philadelphia to protect the converts.

Rumors that mobs were converging on the city continued to flow into Philadelphia. At the insistence of Joseph Galloway, the governor appointed Cornelius Sturgis and Nicholas Garrison, Jr., to travel to Lancaster County and ferret out the facts.

Garrison returned from Lancaster with disturbing news. The insurgent contingents could be expected to arrive in Philadelphia soon. He also learned that popular opinion in the backcountry was running strongly in favor of the Paxton Boys. The governor submitted an urgent message to the assembly along with a petition from Lewis Weiss asking for immediate action. For once, the assembly did not object and voted, on January 4, to give the governor £1000 to be used as he pleased.[15]

Events were now moving so rapidly that prudence was replaced with panic. The governor, with advice from the council and the approval of the converts, decided to send the Indians to William Johnson in New York, under the protection of Captain Robinson's Highlanders. He had written Johnson on December 31, but sufficient time had not passed for a reply. In January, he fired off a message to Governor William Franklin of New Jersey, advising that the Indians were on their way to his colony and begging him to grant them proper passports. The next morning, expresses were leaving by the hour: one to the New York governor Cadwallader Colden, another to Sir William Johnson, and the last to General Thomas Gage in New York City.

Zeisberger brought the governor's order to Province Island late in the afternoon of January 5. The Indians were most agreeable to the plan. By 2:00 A.M. they received the prearranged departure signal from across the Schuylkill River. Boarding the flatboats, they crossed the river where Lewis and Jacob Weiss were waiting to lead them down Second Street to the Moravian church at the corner of Second and Race Streets. They entered the church undetected at 5:30 A.M. on Thursday. Here, a hearty breakfast had been prepared and was enjoyed by all. Rev. Marschall remarked, "It seemed like the passover-supper in Egypt."[16]

As the faint glow of the cold January morning began to appear, five large wagons pulled up in front of the church. Quietly boarding the wagons, the party proceeded north out of the city. Several miles beyond the city limits they were joined by Captain Robinson and their escort of seventy Highlanders. On January 9, they reached the port of Perth Amboy, where they were to sail the next day in two sloops to New York City.

The northward procession of Zeisberger's Indian contingent had reached its meridian. Just as they were about to board the boats, a dispatch arrived from New York for Thomas Apty, who accompanied the expedition. New York's Governor Colden, having received Penn's letter of January 5, immediately met with his council. Their response was direct and to the point. The citizens and government of New York wanted nothing to do with Susquehanna Indians.[17]

Apty immediately sent several dispatches to Governor Penn and New Jersey's Governor Franklin, asking for instructions. Zeisberger and his Indians spent the next eight days cooling their heels in the barracks at Amboy, holding their religious services as usual and becoming somewhat of a public novelty. Even Captain Robinson's war-hardened soldiers, who had fought off Pontiac's attackers at the Detroit siege, began to show respect.

Penn laid the problem before his assembly on January 16: "I am under the Necessity of ordering those poor Creatures to return again to this Government & am heartily disposed to do everything in my power to afford them that protection & security which, under the Circumstances, they have an undoubted right to expect and claim from us."[18] Four days later, Isaac Norris, the Speaker of the assembly, notified the governor that his body concurred with the action.

During the intervening period, General Gage had replaced the Robinson contingent with another company of Royal Americans commanded by Captain Schlosser, who proceeded south with the converts as far as Trenton. There, Schlosser received the governor's instruction and proceeded on to Philadelphia through a driving snowstorm, arriving without opposition at the army barracks on the afternoon of January 24.

The three-week journey proved to be a harrowing experience for both the Indians and their Moravian teachers. Caught in the intricate web of colonial diplomacy, the Moravians had successfully held the converts together, averting any tragedies. Margaretha Grube and Johanna Schmick, along with their husbands and Zeisberger, braved the cold winter storms and white ridicule and reproach to remain at the side of the Indians, counseling them and sharing the hardships of the journey. Three days after they arrived in Philadelphia, Zeisberger returned to Bethlehem.

With the Indians back in Philadelphia, there was an immediate renewal of white hostility. Self-appointed orators again took to the street corners haranguing the crowds against both Indians and Quakers. On January 28, four days after the converts returned to Philadelphia, the governor received reliable intelligence reports that a force of fifteen hundred men was gathering in Lancaster to march on the city and destroy the Indian contingent. The governor responded on February 2 by requesting that the assembly enact the English Riot Act, augmenting his presentation with a letter just received from Sir William Johnson. Johnson warned the Pennsylvania authorities that his current peace negotiations with the Six Nations would be doomed if harm came to the Indians under their protection. The governor appeared before the assembly the next day and signed the new Riot Act bill.[19]

Events moved quickly. In the forenoon of February 4, Penn sent instructions to Captain Schlosser to remove the Indians to the second floor of the barracks, sent carpenters to improve the defense of the structure, and ordered Schlosser to mount eight cannons on the stockade.

Shortly after lunch, a general town meeting was called, attended by the governor, former governor Hamilton, the council, and the members of the assembly. Benjamin Franklin and Benjamin Chew addressed the gathering.[20] The Riot Act was read and a call was made for volunteers to uphold the law. Five hundred citizens responded to the call. The ringing of the town bells was the signal to indicate the approach of the insurgent forces. At midnight, the governor visited the barracks and assured the converts that all precautions had been taken for their protection.

Fortunately, the next day was Sunday and the city remained calm. Late in the evening, the governor received intelligence reports indicating that the insurgents were approaching the city in two bodies, one from Reading and the other on the Lancaster road. The council was immediately called and met until 1:00 A.M., when the general alarm was sounded. As a cannon was fired at the barracks, the city bells began to peal, candles appeared at windows, and the volunteers hurried toward the statehouse to accept their arms. Franklin and Hamilton were hard-pressed to maintain discipline and bring some semblance of order among the crowd that surrounded the building. Only a miracle prevented an accidental shooting during the night as the zealous citizens milled about the area awaiting their assignments. By daybreak, most of the six hundred volunteers had marched to their posts.

Undetected by the citizen militia, the insurgents, led by Matthew Smith and James Gibson, crossed the Schuylkill River at Suetts Ford west of Philadelphia, the only one of the three fords left unguarded. (Smith and Gibson were reported to have led the attack on the Lancaster jail.) The

Lancaster contingents, having heard of the preparation made for their arrival, turned north and spent Monday night in Germantown. Early on Tuesday morning, another alarm was sounded, and again the citizen army rushed to its posts.

Amid protests from the volunteers, who eagerly looked forward to the engagement, the governor sent Benjamin Franklin and several other commissioners to parlay with the insurgents and persuade them to disperse. Franklin received a surprisingly respectful hearing. The insurgents had prepared a list of nine complaints against the government, which six days later was presented to the governor in a lengthy written remonstrance.[21] But in the meantime, a quick outline was given to Franklin, who promised that the government would do all in its power to "redress their grievances." The principal complaint charged the government with harboring Indians supposedly known to have participated in many of the depredations and killings. Franklin granted permission for an unarmed representative to be escorted to the barracks to identify the offenders. The others were to return to their homes. Temporarily satisfied, most of the insurgents returned to Paxton. The crisis had passed, and Philadelphia began to return to a normal routine, shops opened, and business was transacted as usual.[22]

The next day, February 9, Commissioner Huse of Philadelphia County rode out to Germantown and returned with the Paxton representative charged with identifying the Indian murderers among the congregation. All the converts were assembled. After close inspection, the representative confessed that he did not recognize a single person. Pleased as the converts were at their exoneration, the day ended on a sad note. The first evidence of the plague that would eventually devastate the congregation struck one of their beloved elders. Jacob, Renatus's father, died of smallpox and was buried in the potter's cemetery.

The governor, the assembly, the newspapers, and the citizens of Philadelphia and the backcountry spent all of February and most of the next several months discussing the fate of the Indian converts confined in the barracks of the city.

On February 17, Penn met with a committee of the assembly to discuss the remonstrance presented by Smith and Gibson.[23] Although the discussions were fervent, little concrete action resulted. The remonstrance was well-written and clearly set out the complaints and the prevailing public opinion of the frontier counties of Lancaster, Berks, Northumberland, and especially those on the west side of the Susquehanna River, York and Cumberland. Residents in the latter three areas had suffered the most from the Pontiac uprising. A few citizens, though not condoning the Lancaster murders, protested the lack of support they had received from the colonial government, which remained stymied over who was to support the war financially.

As the weeks and months passed, the controversy subsided, but a smallpox epidemic ravaged the ranks of the converts.[24] By the first of June, pressure was building to resolve the accusations against Renatus, who had been confined to the Philadelphia jail for the past eight months. During his incarceration, his father, wife, and baby daughter had died of smallpox. Only the frequent visits from his lawyer, Lewis Weiss, and the missionaries Zeisberger, Grube, and Schmick kept his spirits up. Numerous witnesses over the previous eight months had submitted testimony to the government which disputed his complicity in the Stenton murders, but public pressure demanded a trial. Since the crime was committed in Northampton County, he was taken to Easton on June 14. Tension among the white residents was at a fever pitch. Most were demanding his conviction. The trial began on June 19 and lasted four days. On the morning of June 23, after an all-night deliberation, the jury brought in a verdict of not guilty.[25] Considering the public opinion, it was a courageous decision. The next day Schmick carried the good news to Philadelphia. It took all the resources of the county sheriff to maintain order in the little village of Easton and prevent the mob from attacking the acquitted defendant. For his protection, Renatus was again confined to the jail. Early on the morning of July 4, he and Johann Roth quietly left the village and returned to the safety of the Philadelphia barracks.

After July, the smallpox epidemic reached its climax. By the end of September, more than fifty-six of the converts were released from their worldly cares and were buried in potter's graves, an appalling 40 percent of the original group who came to Philadelphia. But their suffering was nearing an end.

With the possibility that the converts might soon be released, Bethlehem began to plan for their removal. It was obvious that the days of missions near Bethlehem were at an end. A location secure from white molestation had to be found. The Bethlehem authorities decided to settle them on the former Machiwihilusing site near the Susquehanna. To their joy, on February 26, 1765, they "obtained leave to depart" from Philadelphia. During the following days, the government liberally supplied them with necessities. A statement of gratitude and thanks was sent to the governor on March 18, signed by Papunhank, Joshua, Anthony, and Shem Evans. Commissioner Joseph Fox, who had cared for them from the beginning to the end, was showered with expressions of affection. He responded to Schmick with tears in his eyes, "I have willingly done what I could, knowing their innocence."[26]

On March 20, the heavily loaded wagons pulled away from the barracks on Second Street bound for Nain just northwest of Bethlehem. Here they would rest for a few days before beginning the trip to the Susquehanna.

· PART 3 ·

The Age of Controversy, 1765–1774

· 11 ·

Indian Missions: A Critical Reappraisal, 1765–1766

THE PERIOD immediately before the American Revolution, 1765 to 1775, has been called "The Age of Controversy," ten years of conflict and contention between American colonials and the British Empire. Pennsylvania provides a good example of the clash of divergent political and economic concepts that created the turmoil.

From the vantage point of the late twentieth century, it may be difficult to appreciate, let alone understand, the political, social, and economic issues that split the colonies and produced intracolonial strife. The cohesive ingredients of nationalism or "the American maturity" developed after the Revolution, finally flowering during the nineteenth and twentieth centuries. Historian Merrill Jensen, in his *Founding of a Nation*, sums up the problem: "Once one goes behind the superficial word-screen of a common political language, unity is replaced by an amazing diversity of motives, thought and local interest."[1]

The pluralism found in the thirteen colonies was a result of the various European cultures represented among the population. The English-speaking people were the largest group and were probably slightly in the majority, with the exception of Pennsylvania. But as early as 1646, more than eighteen European languages were spoken in the Hudson Valley alone.[2] Pennsylvania 120 years later was a microcosm of this diverse population. There were myriad native Indian groups, and the settlers consisted of Germans, English, Scotch-Irish, Scots, Swedes, Finns, Dutch, French, Welsh, Swiss, and black Africans. There were more religious denominations than European groups, among them English Quakers, German Quakers, Scotch-Irish Presbyterians, German Pietists, Mennonites, German Baptist Brethren, Schwenkfelders, Moravians, Lutherans, Reformed Germans, Anglicans, Dutch Reformed, Jews, Roman Catholics, Huguenots, and smaller sects such as Conrad Beisel's Seventh-Day Baptist Monks and Nuns at Ephrata.[3]

Although the three major European ethnic groups were English, German, and Scotch-Irish, any accurate estimate of the size of each group is difficult to make. A fair projection would be 40 percent English, 30 percent German, 20 percent Scotch-Irish, and 10 percent other groups.[4] During the first half of the eighteenth century, most of this population lived in the four counties bordering the Delaware River. By 1760, the list of taxables in the five backcountry counties in Pennsylvania had reached 15,443, as compared to 16,221 for the original seaboard counties. Yet those frontier counties had only 26 percent of the representatives in the colonial assembly and could easily be outvoted on any bills brought before the lawmakers (see Chapter 10, note 21). This sectional imbalance, which produced conflict, was further complicated by the religious diversity. The Quakers actively promoted Indian trade with presents, treaties, and general leniency. They also encouraged missionaries to work among the Indians, hoping to make them less warlike. During the periods of peaceful relationships between the Indians and the colonials, the plan worked and the Indian trade flourished.

Most of the frontier people were Scotch-Irish Presbyterians—belligerent, rough, generally crude and impatient people. They received little assistance from the Quaker-controlled assembly during the Indian wars of 1755 to 1763, and any attempts to reach agreement between the contending parties always ended in impasse. Many Germans also lived in the frontier counties, and though they were more moderate, they generally agreed with the Scotch-Irish on the Indian question.[5] It was within these conditions that the Moravian Brethren maintained their settlements and sought to extend their influence among the tribes.

Bethlehem, 1765: A Reanimation

The life span of the Moravian missionary movement in America can be likened to the human birth-to-death struggle, or "rites of passage" from one stage of life to another. The movement had grown from its inception with the New York missions in 1740, through its childhood during the Gnadenhutten mission in 1746, to young adulthood in 1755 during the French and Indian War period. As the movement moved toward maturity, the Bethlehem Brethren needed to reappraise their entire missionary program. No longer could they minister to the Indian flocks in or around Bethlehem. The effort must be removed from the corrupting influences and "civilizing" effect of white society. Beginning in 1765, David Zeisberger was the point man for the Moravians' missionary efforts. From then until his death some forty years later, he led the constant struggle to flee from the white man's debilitating interference in his mission program.

Wyalusing Mission

On March 22, 1765, in the midst of a heavy snowstorm, the Philadelphia converts arrived back at their lonely and empty mission. Nain was not the same bustling little village it had been with its green gardens and clean streets. The snow lay two feet deep as cold March winds blew the creaking doors of the cabins to and fro, a haunting reminder of those who had left the settlement with happy, expectant faces many months before and now lay buried in silent, unmarked, pauper graves in Philadelphia. Of the 125 converts who left the village in November 1763, 83 returned. But the survivors were not to remain in their desolate little village. The Mission Board's plan called for them to be removed to Papunhank's old village at Machiwihilusing (Wyalusing) on the banks of the Susquehanna.[6] The converts welcomed the decision and applauded the appointment of Zeisberger as the resident missionary.

They spent eleven days resting and recuperating from the trip, then, led by Zeisberger, departed from Nain early on the morning of Wednesday, April 3, 1765. The route the party traveled is now Pennsylvania Route 115, at one time the turnpike from Easton through Smith's Gap to Gilbert, Fernridge, Stoddersville, and Wilkes-Barre. Reaching the Susquehanna, they borrowed canoes and arrived at Wyalusing on May 9, five weeks after their departure from Nain. Through sheer determination, without horses or wagons, ninety adults and many children had forced their way through the tangled wilderness, then braved the rushing waters of the Susquehanna to arrive safely at their new home.

Since leaving Bethlehem, securing sufficient food for the contingent had been a constant problem. On arriving at their destination it became

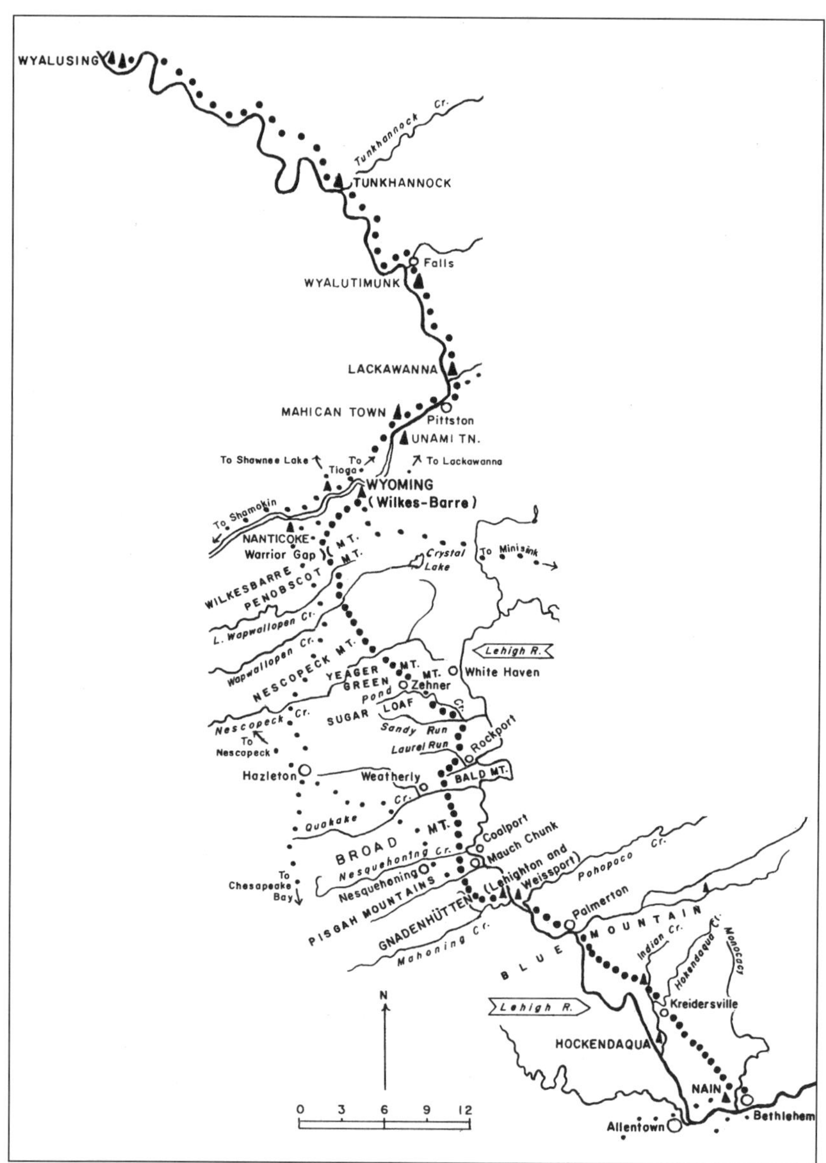

The Bethlehem and Wyalusing Trail. From Paul A.W. Wallace, *Indian Paths of Pennsylvania*, Pennsylvania Historical and Museum Commission, 1965.

their top priority. Twelve days after their arrival, Schmick and a party of twenty-eight Indians set out for Bethlehem for additional supplies. On May 31, John Heckewelder and a party of Brethren arrived from Bethlehem.[7] They carried additional provisions and were driving four cows, the first of a thriving herd that would become a mark of distinction at Wyalusing.

Shortly after they arrived in May, a message was sent to Togahaju, the Iroquois sachem, who controlled the area for the Six Nations from his village on the banks of Cayuga Lake. It was essential that they have his approval to live within his jurisdiction. Within a month, a string of wampum arrived summoning Anton, Joshua, and Johannes Papunhank to Cayuga. Zeisberger instructed the delegation: "Explain to the Six Nations, that the Mahican and Delaware here were not as other Indians, and that they desired to have their teacher reside with them." Since Joshua was not at home, Andrew accompanied the party. On June 12, they left the village for Cayuga. On June 27, they returned with a mixed report. Togahaju, though pleased to have the "praying Indians" under his jurisdiction, preferred that they move farther north to the headwaters of Cayuga Lake. "Wyalusing," he said, "is stained with blood," a reference to the long-ago battle between the Iroquois and Andastes.[8] Papunhank, who had lived in this area since 1752, observed that they had no objection to the chief's suggestion but pointed out that there was no game in the Cayuga Lake area. The converts, nevertheless, promised to lay his suggestion before their people and respond "when the corn was ripe." In the meantime, Zeisberger began a discreet program to change Togahaju's mind.

On July 20, another Cayuga chief, Tajanoge (Ta-jan-NO-ga), a friend and councillor of Togahaju, visited the village for several days. He was also an old friend of Zeisberger's from his years spent with the Iroquois. They discussed the proposed migration, and the chief agreed with Papunhank's observation. Since there was an absence of game and the Indians were meat-eaters, the Cayuga Lake location would be unsatisfactory. Zeisberger delayed his answer to Togahaju and proceeded to build his new village.

The new year began with an unusually cold January. Chilling snow-laden winds blew down Browntown Mountain, covering the valley with deep drifts of snow. Zeisberger recorded, "The Susquehanna froze solid." "Wild Indians" who visited the new village became an ever-increasing problem. Zeisberger recorded a meeting between the convert Anton and one of the visitors, Nanticoke Sam. It illustrates one reason why such visitors were not welcome: "We hesitated to receive him, for when a

Nanticoke dies, his friends come, disinter the body, cut off all the flesh from the bones, and carry them away. Recently such a spectacle passed through here."[9]

Shortly after the first of the year, they received another message from Togahaju, their landlord at Cayuga. Using Johannes Papunhank's "ripened corn" terminology, he left no question in the missionaries' minds that he expected a quick response to his directive that they move the village to Cayuga Lake: "Cousins! What kind of corn have you at Machiwihilusing? You promised an answer to my proposition when your corn would be ripe. My corn has been ripe long ago. It is nearly consumed. I think of soon planting again. Why do you not fulfill your promise?"[10]

Why Zeisberger postponed the response to the Cayuga chief remains a question. The diaries are silent on this issue. With the receipt of Togahaju's second message, however, the village sprang into action. Zeisberger appointed Anton and Johannes Papunhank to visit the Delaware chiefs Newallike and Echgohund to solicit their assistance in dealing with the Cayuga chief. Both "declined to advise us."[11]

Zeisberger could no longer delay his response to Togahaju. But first he made a quick trip to Bethlehem to consult with the Mission Board. He left Wyalusing for Bethlehem on the last day of March and returned on April 13.[12] Ten days later, he gathered the Indian leaders of the mission, Anton, Abraham, Jacob, and Johannes Papunhank and set out for Cayuga to settle the matter.

Their route was the familiar trail Zeisberger first traveled with Cammerhoff in 1750. After two days they arrived at Chief Togahaju's village, where they received a pleasant and cordial welcome. He promised to call a meeting of his council the next day.

The council began with opening remarks by Togahaju. Johannes, one of the converts, followed the chief, presenting five strings and two belts of wampum at the beginning of his speech. Using the typical Indian metaphor, he assured the council, "The path had been cleared and cleansed from Wyalusing, from whence they came." Anton followed and presented a belt of ten rows, explaining "they were different (men) from others and wished for a separate town." Johannes then delivered the main speech, presenting a large and impressive belt:

> Uncle! You made known to us last year that you wanted to remove us from Wihilusing [*sic*] and place us at the upper end of the Lake. Now, however, it is our desire that you would permit us to remain at Wihilusing. We have already built houses, and the place which you

> cleansed for us a year ago is agreeable, and we like to live there. As we can live there quietly and undisturbed.[13]

Togahaju responded:

> Up to this time you have had no abiding place, but now I will take you and seat you permanently. You can therefore remain there and the land shall be yours; and as your number is many and may increase, so I have further thought of you. We will, therefore, give you all the land from Wihilusing [*sic*] up to some distance beyond Tioga, (which is by land a good two days' journey).[14]

The council was an unqualified success, in no small part because Zeisberger was respected by the Iroquois. Leaving the Cayuga village on May 2, they arrived back in Wyalusing on May 5.

Friedenshutten "Huts of Peace"

There was a new zest to the church services that evening as the Delaware hymns were sung with gusto by the men, and the clear voices of the Indian women rose from the Susquehanna Valley celebrating the "glad news." The following day, Zeisberger called a meeting of the Indian helpers and leaders of the congregation.[15] Finding a more convenient location for the settlement was discussed. Accordingly, they began to prospect for the new site. More permanent and substantial buildings were required that would be located nearer the sources of wood and water and their plantations. The mission diary for May 6 records: "We finally selected a site near our present town and resolved to lay it out regularly."[16]

On May 22, with plans for the new village completed and construction under way, Zeisberger and Johannes Papunhank left Wyalusing to attend a synod at Bethlehem and report the results of their embassy to the Cayugas. Several important decisions were made at this June 1766 synod. Johann Jacob Schmick and his wife, Johanna, were to replace Zeisberger as head missionaries at Wyalusing; Roth was to be recalled; the name of the new village would be Friedenshutten (Huts of Peace).[17]

Zeisberger returned to the new Friedenshutten settlement on June 23, carrying the news of the synod and the plans to turn the operation over to the Schmicks. Three days after Zeisberger returned to the village, Roth left for Bethlehem, happy to return home. All of the converts who had been at

Philadelphia were intimately acquainted with both Johann and his wife, Johanna. The Schmicks were experienced missionaries, good administrators, and well-adapted to mission life. They remained at Friedenshutten for the next six years and were primarily responsible for the success of this mission.

In those six years, Friedenshutten grew to over 150 inhabitants who were housed in twenty-nine well-built log structures with glass windows, doors, and outside chimneys similar to the homes of white settlers. In addition, there were thirteen secure Indian-style bark huts, for a total of forty-two buildings. The village formed one street with houses on each side. The thirty-two-by-twenty-four-foot shingled-roof chapel was in the center of the street, flanked on one end by the schoolhouse. Directly opposite the chapel was the mission house. Behind the houses, which stood on thirty-two-foot lots, each two separated by a ten-foot alley, were individual gardens and orchards stocked with fruit trees and vegetables. The entire town was surrounded by a post or rail fence. The women passed daily through the streets and alleys, sweeping with wooden brooms to remove rubbish. The streets were always kept scrupulously clean. The physical layout and methods of operation at Friedenshutten became a familiar pattern for future villages laid out and operated by David Zeisberger, especially the Schoenbrunn mission in the Ohio Country.

Stretching from the village to the river were more than 250 acres of flat, well-tilled farmland and meadows, enclosed by over two miles of fence. Near the river, the village fleet of canoes, usually one to a family, was securely moored. Over the years, they had bred a large collection of cattle, hogs, and poultry to provide food for the village. Friedenshutten became the "jewel of the Susquehanna," rivaling any white settlements of similar size.[18]

The Schmicks' appointment became official on June 23. They left Bethlehem several days later, arriving at Friedenshutten on July 7 to a joyous and lighthearted welcome. Less than one month later, Schmick assumed responsibility for keeping the mission diary. Zeisberger stayed at the village until the first of September, then returned to his favorite haunts at Christianbrunn near Nazareth.

On July 21, before leaving Friedenshutten, Zeisberger received an Indian visitor who carried a disturbing rumor: "An Indian, who arrived today related, that at a recent council of the Six Nations, the Cayuga chief was taken to task for permitting us to settle at Wyalusing."[19] Little was made of the incident at that time. By the end of September, however, the Mission Board concluded, on Zeisberger's advice, to check the authenticity of the report. David welcomed the opportunity to "renew old friendships" at Onondaga.

He left Bethlehem on September 30, shortly after the Mission Board conference. Accompanied by twenty-one-year-old Gottlob Sensemann, he set out for Onondaga. In Zeisberger's words, "It was a tiring and difficult journey on account of the swollen streams."[20] But after ten days, they arrived at Friedenshutten. They stayed at the mission for five days, leaving on October 14, accompanied by four Nanticokes who were returning from Philadelphia.

Pushing up the swollen Susquehanna, they arrived at the Nanticoke village of Zeniinge on October 19. Here they received a friendly welcome from the head chief, who remembered David from his visit thirteen years earlier.[21] Otherwise, the news was not encouraging. The only open route to Onondaga was by water; the foot trail was closed. But Zeisberger's luck held. "We also looked up our Brother Samuel [one of the converts at Friedenshutten], who had, several weeks ago, come here to bring back his wife. He was glad to meet Brethren here, and at once offered to go with us to Onondaga, which pleased us very much, as otherwise we would have had to take a strange Indian."[22]

After Samuel received thorough instructions from the Nanticoke chief on the proper route to take, the trio left the village on October 21 and arrived at Onondaga by noon on October 26. One-half mile from the village, the party met an Indian who immediately recognized David and escorted them into the town. It was a surprisingly cordial welcome after an eleven-year absence.

The council convened the next day. Zeisberger, now confident of his position as one of the brothers, began with a surprisingly frank speech. It was Zeisberger at his best—a brilliant soliloquy to the distinguished chiefs who sat before him. He began with a complete history of the Christian converts: their removal from Nain and sheltering by the Pennsylvania authorities at Philadelphia, then their difficult journey to reach the new mission site at Wyalusing. He explained in detail his spring trip to Cayuga and the results of the council with Togahaju, describing the chief's decision to let them stay permanently at Friedenshutten. He then listed the various Indian tribes represented at the mission: Mahican, Delaware, Munsee, and Nanticoke. The speaker interrupted at this point. "What! are there also Nanticoke with you?" Zeisberger responded by pointing to Samuel, "There sits one of them." The Nanticokes had a reputation for being great drinkers and troublemakers, which accounted for the speaker's surprise. Zeisberger finished by requesting the council to confirm the Togahaju grant. They gave him permission to go to Cayuga and speak again with the Cayuga chief.[23]

The day following the council, Zeisberger and Sensemann were on the trail to the Cayuga village. They arrived the next day, October 30. As they approached Togahaju's dwelling, they could see the chief standing in front of the door, his arms folded and a slight smile on his face. "Welcome," he shouted, "I have always believed you would come, for I dreamed about you."[24] They talked throughout the day and long into the night. The rumors reported in Bethlehem were all a misunderstanding. The message brought by the Indian to Friedenshutten had been delivered incorrectly. In the spring, shortly after Zeisberger and his party had left the Cayuga village, the chief heard that traders had arrived at Friedenshutten and planned to build storehouses. In his words, "At first I did not wish to believe it, however, as so much about it had come to my ears I sent the message." He then admonished Zeisberger: "Cousins! I have given you the land, but not for the purpose of allowing the white people to build storehouses thereon. Therefore adjust yourselves to what we have decided with each other. Do not give the traders place among you, and do not permit them to build houses."[25] Zeisberger assured him that no traders lived at the mission, nor would such activity be permitted at Friedenshutten. Traders had appeared and requested permission to trade but were quickly asked to leave.

Togahaju further assured Zeisberger that the council of the Six Nations had approved his actions and had placed him in complete control of the area. The converts were to look to him as their landlord and not to any of the local Delaware chiefs, especially Newallike. There was complete understanding among the three men.

By noon on October 31, they were back on the road to Onondaga, arriving the next day. Chief Tianoronto, the speaker, called the council together on November 2 and delivered the following message to Zeisberger and Sensemann:

> Brother Ganousseracheri [Zeisberger]! The question which you have asked us we have considered, and will now give you our ideas about them. . . . We let you know herewith that the matter which Chief Togahaju, in Cayuga, treated and concluded with you, meets with our and the whole house's consent, and we all know what he has done. We are not only all satisfied therewith, but it pleases us very

> much that you live in Friedenshutten, and that you shall have a council fire there, which is entrusted to you, and which is no small matter. We have heard your mind in regards to living among the Indians; you are their teacher, and you do well that you instruct them in good things. They need it, for the Delaware, our cousins, are very much inclined toward the bad. This could be plainly seen in the late war [a reference to the Pontiac uprising in 1763].[26]

Pleased with the results of the embassy, Zeisberger prepared to leave. But the council would not let him go until he promised to return. He responded, "If it please the Lord and I live, I will see you again." Unfortunately, this was the last time his voice would be heard in the great council of the Six Nations.[27]

To this day, it is a mystery why the Moravian Church authorities gave up their effort to found missions among the Six Nations, especially the Onondaga. I have questioned numerous church officials, and all are at a loss to provide an answer. Edmund De Schweinitz, a long-standing and respected bishop of the church, who wrote the only definitive biography of Zeisberger, published in 1870, noted: "None of the authorities we have examined explain this change in the policy of the Church."[28] Zeisberger and Sensemann left Onondaga on the morning of November 3 and arrived back in Bethlehem on November 22.[29]

In the two years Zeisberger spent establishing the Friedenshutten mission, he traveled a conservative estimate of sixteen hundred miles. During that period he made six round trips from Bethlehem to Friedenshutten; one trip from Friedenshutten to the Cayuga village near Union Springs, New York; and one round trip from Friedenshutten to the Onondaga castle near present Syracuse, New York. After his return from Onondaga, he spent the winter and spring at Christianbrunn.

· 12 ·

Westward to the Delaware Country, 1767

AFTER RETURNING from his Onondaga trip in November 1766, Zeisberger spent the next ten months at Christianbrunn relaxing from his missionary labors, although he was restless and longed to return to the missionary field.

Early in 1767, the western tribes along the Allegheny requested a white Christian teacher. The source of the message, Zeisberger wrote, "was somewhat untrustworthy."[1] He would later discover that the invitation came from residents on the Allegheny who had friends at Friedenshutten and were impressed with the teachings at the Susquehanna mission. Since the Moravians were not generally known in the Allegheny area, the Mission Board approved a tour to investigate. Zeisberger, their most experienced missionary, was chosen to make the trip. He left Bethlehem on September 20, 1767, traveling north to Friedenshutten, and arrived four days later.[2]

The trail his party would take to the Allegheny region was known as the "Forbidden Path" of the Seneca Nation.[3] No white man had successfully traversed it. Christian Frederick Post and John Hays had tried in 1760 but were turned back when the Indians threatened to cut off Post's ears.

The country Zeisberger was about to travel through was wild and foreboding, and the resident Indians were a cantankerous and ill-humored lot. Yet he had some knowledge of them. During his July 1750 trip with Cammerhoff to Chenussio, Zeisberger had a disagreeable meeting with Hagastaes, the controversial old Seneca chief.[4] Remembering that occasion, he had no illusions of an easy success. Although the proposed route lay south of the more populated Seneca country, he knew he might meet with the same hostility and mistreatment as in 1750.

Zeisberger chose two of his most trusted lieutenants to accompany him, Anton and Johannes Papunhank.[5] They left Friedenshutten with a packhorse and a pet dog on the morning of September 30, 1767.

The party arrived at Goschgoschunk on October 16, seventeen days out of Friedenshutten. According to Zeisberger's journal, they were "heartily welcomed in the town and given lodging in the house of one who was a close friend of Johannes." The mountains come down hard on the west bank of the Allegheny, leaving little space for the broad alluvial plains normally required for plantations of corn, squash, and beans, which were usually found near Indian villages. Zeisberger noted, "Goschgoschunk consists of three towns. We had arrived at the middle one, another lies two miles up the river and the third, four miles down." Two days later, he wrote that the people were scattered, "but the nature of the region is such that not many could dwell together in one place."[6] This entry gives some indication of the limited agricultural area surrounding the villages.

Immediately across on the eastern side of the broad, meandering Allegheny, the topography rises in gentle slopes, certainly a more suitable site for villages. All three towns were located on the west bank. There were strong reasons for these locations, going back to King George III's proclamation of 1763 and the long-standing grievance between the two factions of the Seneca Nation. The Allegheny Indians' landlord was the western Geneseo-Allegheny Seneca and their white-hating chief, A-gaus-tos or Hagastaes, "Mud-eater," who lived on the Genesee River north of the Allegheny. "Mud-eater" had a truculent relationship with his eastern Seneca counterparts, who were allied with the Iroquois League centered at Onondaga. At one point he considered seceding and forming a league of his own. Only the lack of a proper treasury of wampum belts prevented his doing so. At the heart of the dispute was the usurpation of the league, which claimed to have exclusive rights to sell land to the whites and distribute the proceeds among themselves. Since the Allegheny Indians did not know precisely where the boundary would finally be cut, they were suspicious. After all, many of them were here because their old homes had

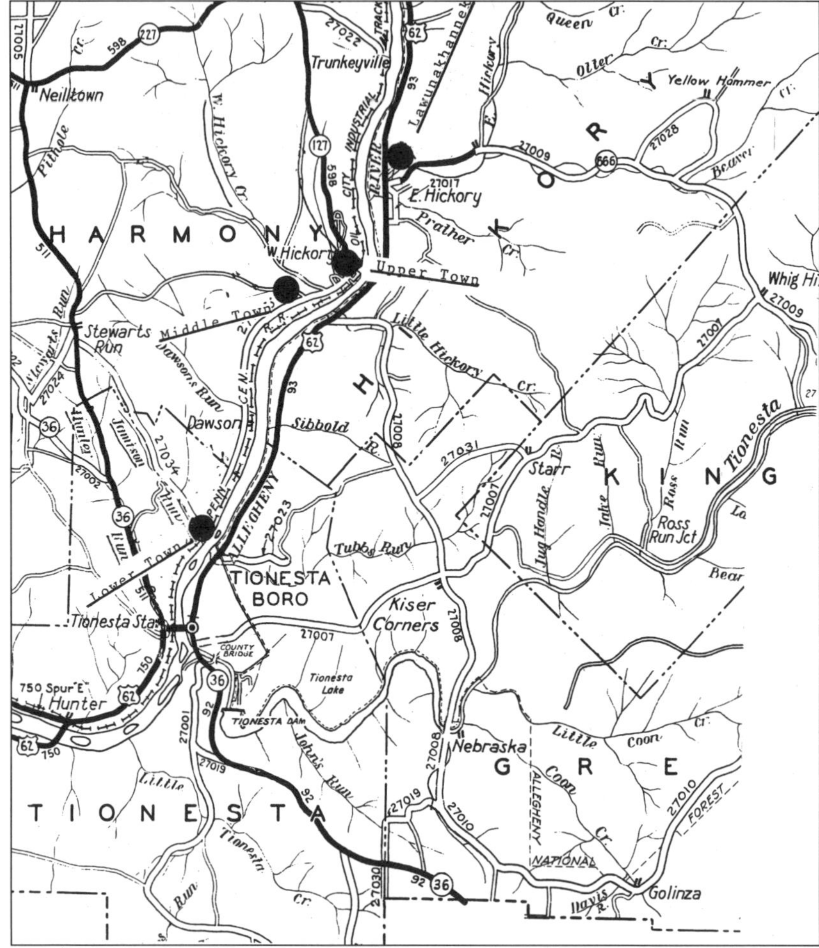

The Allegheny Region, Forest County

been sold out from under them by the Iroquois council, and they did not wish to repeat the experience. Therefore, why should they build on the east bank?[7]

Prophetically, Zeisberger recognized another problem: "The chiefs [here] appear to exercise little authority." From years of experience he knew that without a close-knit council and a strong head chief there would be lax discipline and virtually no organization among the three native villages.

Zeisberger noted that the villages were founded "only two years ago last spring. All the inhabitants are Munsee or Minissink Indians, who on account of the last war moved hither from Wihilusing on the Susquehanna as well as from Assinissink and Passigachgungk on the Tioga [Cowanesque Creek]." During his short stay at the village, he found that it contained other Indians: Cherokee, Fox, Mahican, Shawnee, Missisauga, Nanticokes, Chippewa, even a "baptized Jew from New England." Such a conglomeration was not unusual on the Allegheny below Geneseo. These were the remnants, the dissatisfied, and the rejected of the westward Indian migrations. They were the tenants of the Geneseo Senecas and were always to behave as "women," that is, they were not to speak for themselves in council, nor were they to meddle in the affairs of international diplomacy conducted by the council at Geneseo. To ensure their obedience, "Mudeater" stationed a chief a few miles downriver at Venango, at the mouth of the French Creek, to make sure they did not involve their landlord in a war or other troubles. It was a delicate situation and required adroit diplomacy, all forerunners of future problems for David Zeisberger.[8]

Their eight-day stay was frenzied. Before nightfall on the day of their arrival, runners were sent to the other towns. The villagers quickly gathered for the preaching that evening. Through the misty, smoke-filled room of the council house, the pungent odor of Indian cooking permeated the air. Young and old filled the room to capacity and others crowded at the doors. Zeisberger began by explaining the reason for his visit. Then his words began to fill the room: good news, bloodshed, death and resurrection, from darkness into light, salvation, eternal life, the soaring promises of the Christian faith. From his faithful companions, Johannes and Anton, came similar words. The preaching continued until very late in the evening.[9]

For eight days the sermons continued. "They relish the message concerning the death and sacrifice of the Redeemer, though it is new teaching to them," Zeisberger wrote on the eighteenth. "It is with them, as it is with all the Indians at the beginning, they hear the words, can understand and comprehend but little of it, yet they always ask to be taught more. They cannot understand until spiritually roused, then their understanding is cleared and they are able to receive what is taught them."[10] But alas, he had to admit that not all of them were mesmerized by his message. The younger people of the villages continued their heathen practices, going every evening to the native dances.

Zeisberger's first opposition came from Wangomen, the local native divine. He insisted that Indians should reject the white man's ways, especially Zeisberger's views on heaven. Wangomen preached that there were three levels of heaven, insisting that when an Indian dies he enters the first heaven, where he remains for one hundred years, living a more

The Power of the Gospel, from the 1862 painting by Charles Schuessele, now located in the Moravian Church Archives Building in Bethlehem, Pennsylvania.

comfortable life than on earth. Then he enters a second heaven for the next one hundred years, where he enjoys a better life. From there, he enters the third heaven, filled with fat deer and bear aplenty, much fatter than those on earth. The Indian would then be given a choice. He could remain with God or return to earth. If he chose the latter, he would be born anew into the world. Zeisberger conceded, "Such preaching the Indians enjoy." But he found the practice loathsome and noted, "They constantly use the name of God in connection with their most revolting heathenish abominations." "I must confess," he concluded, "that nowhere else among the Indian have I found such desperate heathenism. Here Satan has his power, he sits enthroned, here he is worshipped by the heathens and accomplishes his work in [and among] the children of darkness."[11]

After six days of preaching, Zeisberger and his Indian companions began to detect a slight break in the "heathenistic armor." Some of the villagers' remarks indicated that Wangomen was beginning to understand the Christian teachings. "As I have heard from the Indians," Zeisberger wrote, "the Indian preacher recognized Anton's worth and is reported to have said that he believed, concerning Anton and myself, that we know God." On the evening before their departure, the Moravians held their final meeting. The council house was jammed and the overflowing crowd crushed the doorways. Again Zeisberger repeated his doctrine of universal salvation for all men, regardless of color or race. He concluded his remarks by requesting that all the adult men meet with his party "on the morrow to consider various things."[12]

They met the next day, and Zeisberger explained that he had been commissioned by his Bethlehem elders to bring the word of God to the Allegheny valley as they had previously done among their fellow brethren along the Susquehanna at Friedenshutten. Over the past seven days "we have become convinced," he told them, "that many here were anxious to hear the gospel message. Would they welcome another visit?" One after another, the villagers stood and enthusiastically endorsed the request. Especially outspoken was the blind chief Allemewi. Here, Zeisberger's message had fallen on fertile ground. From this soil would grow one of his most productive converts. Allemewi soon became the convert Salomo (Solomon).[13]

But support that morning was far from unanimous. At the rear of the room sat the grim-faced Wangomen, vigilantly maintaining his silence despite several attempts by villagers to have him speak his mind. Only after Zeisberger finished his remarks and left the council chambers did Wangomen rise to speak. What immediately followed was one of those moments in Zeisberger's life when he displayed the deep courage that so ingratiated him with the Indians.

Although Allemewi was one of the subchiefs in the village, Wangomen was as close as one could find to being head chief among the Allegheny Munsees. He wielded great power among his people. Conversely, Zeisberger was almost a complete stranger and a white man. To challenge this man openly could mean great danger, even death, if Wangomen's followers were so inclined.[14]

Standing on the outside of the council house and conversing with some of the Indians, Zeisberger could hear the rising voice of the Indian preacher within the building. He reentered and observed that Wangomen "was speaking in a very excited manner and with great show of authority." He noticed, too, that Anton did not know how to respond. Quickly Anton repeated what had happened in Zeisberger's absence. Wangomen had told the Indians that there were two ways to salvation, one for the white and one for the Indian. He had symbolized his statements by drawing a design on the ground showing that the Indian route was much more direct. During a pause in the prophet's remarks, Zeisberger interrupted: "I told you clearly enough several days ago that there is but one way of salvation, and the Saviour is Himself that Way. All men, be they white, black or brown, desirous of being saved, must come to him, as poor lost sinners, who know and feel that they are sinners and are seeking forgiveness."[15]

A perplexed look passed across Wangomen's face. It was clear that he did not comprehend Zeisberger's words, but he continued to assert that the Indian had two separate ways to heaven. He insisted he had known God for many years and had spiritual conversations with him. Zeisberger then asked whether he knew the Lord who had been wounded and shed his blood for our transgressions.

He replied, "No, I know nothing of Him. Otherwise I know all things. I knew in advance that you would come here, but that God should have become man and shed His blood, as you say, of that I know nothing. This cannot be the true God, since I know nothing of this." Zeisberger noted that since his arrival he "had dealt tactfully with this man," hoping to win him to his side, but his patience was now exhausted. He turned to Wangomen and with anger mounting in his voice and fire in his eyes, he pointed an accusing finger at the Indian and retorted:

> If you do not know, I do know and will now tell you. The devil is your god, whom you preach to the Indians, for you are his servant. He is the father of lies and from him all lying proceeds. For this reason you can tell the Indians nothing but lies to deceive them. You declare that you are concerned about God, but this is not true. When you celebrate Kentckey [a native Indian feast] and you pray, whom do you worship? It is surely the devil; do not imagine that you have any part of communion with God, for you must not think He has any pleasure in your pretended worship, since this is an abomination before Him.

The intensity gone from his voice, a somewhat subdued Wangomen responded almost pleadingly, "But I cannot understand your teaching, it is something quite new and I cannot understand it." For a moment neither man spoke. They stared intently at each other. A deadly silence permeated the room. A faint, almost imperceptible smile passed across Zeisberger's face. Without the slightest movement, his eyes riveted on Wangomen, Zeisberger slowly began to speak.

> I will explain that to you. Satan is the king of darkness and dwells in no light. Where he is there is darkness. He dwells within you, him you feel and not God as you say. For this reason your understanding is so darkened that you can understand nothing concerning God and his word. For several days I have been preaching to you. I have endeavored to make the message clear. Yet you cannot understand it. Were I to devote months, even years, to preaching to you, you would not be able to understand the gospel tidings, even though the words are not hard words, but may be understood by a child. But if you will turn from Satan and his teachings and will give up your Indian abominations and come to the Saviour as a poor, wretched lost man, who knows nothing and plead with him for grace and mercy, then He may have mercy upon you and deliver you from the power of Satan. In that case it will be possible that you will learn to understand something of God and his word. Now it is impossible. Yet there is opportunity; if you turn to the Saviour help can be granted. But do not delay, make haste and save your soul.[16]

A seemingly endless amount of time passed before someone spoke. From the rear of the room a questioner arose and asked Wangomen to answer Zeisberger's question. Should he return? Quietly Wangomen arose and replied he would be glad to hear more because he was a poor man. The meeting over, the audience filed from the council chamber. Allemewi and some of his followers remained, assuring Zeisberger of their allegiance.

Generally pleased with the overall response, the missionary party departed from the village on October 23, 1767, returning via the same route they had come to the Allegheny. On November 5, Zeisberger and his friends reached Friedenshutten. Eleven days later, they strolled into Bethlehem to file their report with the church elders.[17]

· 13 ·

Frustration on the Allegheny, 1768–1770

ANY HONEST assessment that David Zeisberger may have made of his recent four-month trip to western Pennsylvania must have led him to an enigmatic conclusion. If he returned to the Allegheny it was going to be risky. The first trip had been exhausting, mentally more than physically. He looked forward to a long winter's rest at his favorite haunt at Christianbrunn, headquarters of the single Brethren's choir, located a few miles north of Bethlehem. In his twenty-eighth year, he had led the first group of twenty-two men to the new village on December 17, 1749, and served as their first leader and elder-counselor.[1] The cold but lazy winter months of 1767 and 1768 provided the rest and reflection he needed to decide his future course of action.

By the beginning of May, responding to the call of the Bethlehem elders, Zeisberger and his assistant, Gottlob Sensemann, were at the Friedenshutten mission on the Susquehanna, preparing to keep his promise to return to the Allegheny. The Zeisberger party, consisting of Anton and his wife, Johanna, Abraham and Salome, Peter and Abigail, and the boy Christian, the grandson of Anton, departed on May 9. Exactly one month later, toward evening on June 9, they reached Goschgoschunk, stopping at the uppermost town. "To our surprise," Zeisberger recorded, "the Indian preacher (Wangomen) took us into his house, the largest one in the village, until we should be able to put up for ourselves. He lodged his family elsewhere and turned the house over to our service."[2]

They were also pleasantly surprised by the friendly reception from most of the inhabitants. After a quick inspection that evening, however, Zeisberger found Goschgoschunk changed considerably from the previous year. The middle village, two miles downriver, was almost entirely deserted, the former residents scattered up and down the river. Though not the designated chief, Wangomen remained the head man over this intermingled body.

The Moravians' first order of business was to build a permanent home for their company. Eleven days after arriving, they began to gather wood for a log cabin. Zeisberger called it a "blockhouse." Ten days later it was finished and they moved into the commodious twenty-six-by-sixteen-foot structure.[3] It quickly became a combination residence and meeting house, located one-half mile from the Indian village to provide a degree of privacy. The location also provided sufficient space for huts of other friendly Indians.

Wangomen attended the missionaries' meetings regularly but usually remained silent. Yet Zeisberger detected a rising tide of opposition against his teachings.[4] On July 6, he noted in his diary: "Children are forbidden to come to us. Our place is avoided by many, is hated by them and a cause of vexation. Many are afraid to visit our house during the day-time and come only at night. Others do not come at all, fearing disgrace. Yet we continue to hold our meetings. There are always some present."[5]

By the middle of July, Wangomen no longer attended their meetings, supposedly administering to his dying sister, who was reputed to have said that if her brother continued to attend the Moravian services it would cause her death.

Within the next several weeks a threatening message arrived at the native village directed to Zeisberger. He wrote:

> On the 1st of August a great Bunch of Wampum (that is as many Strings of Wampum as one can hold in the hand) arrived with the following message from the Seneca chief [Mud-eater]: "Cousins, who dwell in Goschgoschunk and along the Ohio and you Shawanese [the Shawnee Indians]! I have arisen and looked about me, to find out what is going on in the land. I have seen that *somebody in a black*

> *coat has arrived, beware of the black coat.* Believe not what he tells you, for he will pervert and alienate your hearts." In conclusion, he desires that we should let him know what our intentions was [*sic*].[6]

It was an ill omen. Zeisberger did not recognize its significance at the time, but it haunted him for the rest of his life.

Allemewi, the reigning chief in the valley, had dispatched a message to the Seneca chief on July 20, several days before the arrival of the message warning of blackcoats, explaining that his people had invited the missionaries to come to the Allegheny, but the invitation had not reached Hagastaes's Seneca village at Zoneschio.

The turmoil and confusion surrounding his Indian village was beginning to take its toll on Allemewi. The weight of the political responsibility and the limitations caused by his blindness and his advanced age were more than the old man could take. He came to Zeisberger on July 26 and begged to be accepted as a convert, thus giving up his role as chief.[7] That evening Zeisberger recorded his response: "We counseled him not to give up his office to another but to seek to serve the Lord while discharging its functions they fear him. . . . He tells everyone openly that he is of the same mind as we are."[8]

To compensate for Allemewi's concern, Zeisberger, on July 29, suggested that he move from the native village into Zeisberger's house at the Christian mission until they could build a permanent cabin for him at the mission. Several weeks later, however, Zeisberger began to build a new house for the missionaries. On September 13, they moved into the new building, and Allemewi and his family moved into the missionaries' original combination home and meeting house.

By the first week in August, the antagonism had escalated to such a degree that Zeisberger discontinued the evening meetings "until such a time when there will be more calm and quiet."[9]

On August 11, the diary contained this entry: "The sister of Wangomen died today. Up to the end she remained hostile toward us and was the means of causing much mischief among the Indians." The death of the sister marked the turning point of Zeisberger's work on the Allegheny. Her enmity to the missionaries and her influence with her brother were now removed.[10]

Shortly after Wangomen's sister died, the preacher mysteriously left the native village and remained absent for about two months. After he left, the evening services began again and attendance improved noticeably. He did not return until October 7. In the meantime, after a prolonged discussion, Zeisberger convinced both Allemewi and Gendaskund that a delegation should visit the Seneca chief at Zoneschio and deliver a response to his August 1 message.[11] Since the threat had been directed toward the Moravians, Zeisberger agreed to lead the delegation.

The five-member party left the mission village on October 11, 1768: Zeisberger, Sensemann, Abraham, and two other Indians. They spent nine days on the road before arriving at Zoneschio, four days in conference with the Senecas, and seven days on the return trip, for a total of twenty days. Their efforts were inconclusive, and none of their problems with the Senecas were resolved. Chief Hagastaes was absent, attending the treaty sessions at Fort Stanwix, so Zeisberger was forced to deal with lesser chiefs. Both Abraham and Zeisberger presented forceful arguments for their case and received in return polite but indecisive answers. In reality, it made little difference. Within less than seventeen months, the question of their residency on the Allegheny would be moot. But in the short term, it was essential that they not make any precipitous moves without the approval of the Seneca chief. In the meantime, they would await his answer.

Zeisberger's party returned to Goschgoschunk on October 31, 1768. On the same day Allemewi received a reply from the message he had sent to Packanke advising the Beaver River chief of Zeisberger's Zoneschio visit. It was exciting news. Zeisberger's diary entry shows his exhilaration:

> On this very day a welcome message [to Allemewi] had arrived from Chief Packanke in Kaskaskunk. . . . This was his answer, "It pleases me very much that you should inform me of your aims and how you intended to live in the future. . . . I think it would be very good if the Christian Indians will move thither [to the Kaskaskunk], in order that if more Indians of this region or of my people would become Christian, they might join you and you would be able to welcome them. Move thither, therefore, and build a good-sized town. Take your teacher with you." This message is the more remarkable, because I have always heard and hear yet that Packanke is not a friend of the gospel. Of this, however, one cannot be sure until a visit to his town can be made, for the testimony of the Indians is not always reliable.[12]

To add to Zeisberger's euphoria, another message arrived for Allemewi the following day. This one was from King Beaver, the Delaware head chief on the Muskingum at Tuscarabi, the site of present Bolivar, Ohio. Zeisberger recorded:

> I am very glad to hear that you are minded to believe in God and that you have received the Moravians who have brought to you the good word of God. Be steadfast and hold to your resolution. Then he addressed all the Indians saying, Hear, all ye inhabitants of Goschgoschunk, Men, Women, Children and You Young people! It will be an excellent thing if you will all believe in God and live a decent life. Therefore, listen to the Moravians and believe what they tell you. I should like, if possible to hear the Moravian brother who is among you. I have heard the Indian preachers often and see that there is nothing in their words. Believe the Moravians and follow them, they know the right way.[13]

If David Zeisberger was surprised and pleased with the message from Packanke, he must have been astonished by the reaction from King Beaver. Within a period of two days, the prospect for success among the Indians in western Pennsylvania reversed dramatically. He was fully knowledgeable of the influence of these two men and the power they wielded among western Indians. But he also knew that the people who sat in the councils and surrounded the villages of these Delawares were of superior intelligence to those who resided on the Allegheny. But ever cautious and prudent, he knew Indians and determined to let time reveal the direction of his next move. The remaining months of 1768 were spent consolidating and evaluating his position at the Goschgoschunk mission.[14]

Throughout January 1769, attendance at the daily services increased. Then on February 4, Wangomen returned. Shortly after he arrived, Zeisberger began to experience interference from the native population. He noted on February 5, "No one but our own converts attended the services, because since Wangomen's return the Indians have avoided our company." The old preacher had a great deal of influence over his people.

On February 10, Zeisberger wrote, "Wangomen is supposed to have said that he would wait and see who could attract the greater audience, he or I. For that reason he holds many celebrations, hoping that the Indians will attend them rather than our own meetings."[15]

On the evening of February 25, a young Indian in the neighborhood brought rum into the native village. This was the final blow. No longer could the two villages, both called Goschgoschunk, one native and one Christian mission, just half a mile apart, remain compatible. Zeisberger "realized that this means the end of our residence here, and that we shall go elsewhere, even if we do not receive an answer from the Seneca Chief."[16]

Present site of Lawunakhannek mission, 1769–1770. Photograph by the author.

Despite his fear of possible retaliation from the volatile Seneca Nation, which would certainly oppose any removal beyond the immediate area, they decided to locate upstream but on the east side of the Allegheny. The new location, three miles from their previous site at Goschgoschunk, would be called Lawunakhannek. It took a few months to organize the logistics for the move.

The most urgent need was for canoes. By March 14 they had completed nine. Sugar making interfered briefly with their moving plans, but by March 28 Zeisberger called the converts in from the sugar camps, and two days later they made the first trip to the new location.[17]

After inspecting the proposed site for the village, they returned. Three days later, they were back on the river again. Zeisberger describes the trip and the village site:

> April 3: We all went along up the river to Lawunakhannek, about three miles from here upon the east bank of the Allegheny; inspected

> the locality where we want to build; divided it up and began to fell trees. . . . Our plantations, for which we have to make the land arable yet, are quite near to us, and very good land. However, we do not consider this place as a permanent residence, only until our condition has become straightened out.[18]

The recent invitations from the western chief burned in his mind like a welcome beacon.

By April 7, the move was completed and they began building new homes to accommodate eight adults and an unknown number of children. During these three hectic weeks of construction, Gatschenis and his wife were among the visitors and assisted with the work.[19] Since their arrival on the Allegheny, they had visited the village regularly and attended services. On this April visit, he again pleaded with Zeisberger to be allowed to join their congregation. Within less than eight months, the Munsee Indian and his wife would become the first converts on the Allegheny.

Another respected Munsee was a regular visitor. Gendaskund, a captain in the Indian council of Chief Allemewi, first visited Goschgoschunk on September 18, 1768. He next appeared on December 18, complaining that his relations with his Indian friends were strained because of his interest in Zeisberger's teaching. They called him a Schwannak (a white man). The frequency of his visits increased until he was attending the chapel services regularly. His close connection with colonial Indian traders and his involvement in the politics of the Indian council caused Zeisberger to be wary of the depth of the Indian's faith.[20]

June 7, 1769, marked Zeisberger's first meeting with one of the most important Indians in his life. On this date the famous Chief Glikhikan arrived at the native village of Goschgoschunk to visit his brother Wangomen and conduct official Indian business in the area.[21] Highly respected among the Delawares of Chief Packanke's tribe on the Beaver River, he was the leading warrior captain and principal spokesman of the tribe, in short, a man of considerable power. The native Indians eagerly awaited his confrontation with Zeisberger. His oratorical skill would certainly destroy the white missionary's efforts. Even Zeisberger sensed the coming drama and clearly anticipated the encounter.

The following day the chief arrived at Lawunakhannek, accompanied by his brother Wangomen and Gendaskund. Zeisberger was on his plantation at the time, and the party was welcomed by Anton. When the missionary arrived, he found the visitors listening intently to a sermon by Anton. He stood for a few minutes on the edge of the gathering until Anton noticed him and called on him to speak. Greeting Glikhikan cordially, the missionary remarked, "I can add nothing to what Anton had already told you." The meeting continued for a short time and finally broke up into small conversational groups. Zeisberger observed:

> "He [Glikhikan] paid very much attention to all we told him and we could see that he was thinking about it. At least he expressed his joy to have heard us, adding, that he could not say anything against it, because he believed that it was the truth, that he would be thinking it over, at the present he could not say definitely whether he wanted to believe in the Saviour or not."[22]

Returning to Goschgoschunk that evening, Glikhikan met with the native villagers. Using his enormous powers of persuasion, he laid before the Indian audience his reaction to the afternoon visit:

> Surely that which we heard in Lawunakhannek today, is the truth; if anything can be true. The brethren have the right doctrine and preach the right way to happiness. Indians of Goschgoschunk: Esteem it of great importance to have the brethren with you. Go out of your way to hear them. If I lived here I would go and live with them at once, and I hope that I shall live to see the day when I shall live with them and believe in the Saviour.[23]

His remarks stunned the audience, including Wangomen. The following day marked the first-year anniversary of Zeisberger's arrival on the Allegheny. With the visit of Glikhikan, he had crossed his Rubicon.

On June 14, five days after Glikhikan's visit, Wangomen and three of his chiefs arrived at the Lawunakhannek mission to speak with Zeisberger regarding an appropriate response to Packanke's invitation to move to his area. The alert Zeisberger immediately noticed a difference in their attitude:

> He [Wangomen], as well as all the other Indians, have been quite different since Glikhikan's arrival and are much more friendly than before, because they, as well as we, have heard the truth from him namely—that the Three Chiefs in the west—Packanke, King Beaver, and Netawatwes, are not against the brethren but for us, and although many Indians are opposed to the preaching of the gospel, many of them, and especially the Chiefs in the west, are in favor of the Saviour's cause.[24]

The question of moving to Packanke's Beaver River area was complicated further by the news of the death of Hagastaes, the Seneca chief. No information from that quarter could be expected until a new appointment was made, which could take many months. Rather than get directly involved in Iroquois politics, Zeisberger conferred with Allemewi. An appropriate acknowledgment of the death was prepared for the Senecas and delivered by Gendaskund.

On the last day of August, the mission village had an unexpected visitor. Glikhikan arrived from Kaskaskunk. He quickly assured Zeisberger, "I did not come for business, but rather to tell you what was in my heart and on my mind. It is a matter which concerns my well-being and that of all the Indians." Gathering the villagers in the meeting house, Glikhikan told them of how he first met the Moravians. At that time, "I became fully convinced that your message was the only way to life and happiness." Returning to his village of Kaskaskunk on the Beaver River, he testified to Chief Packanke and the other Indians that if they wanted to hear the truth and the right doctrine, they should go and hear the Brethren. "I can assure you," he told Zeisberger, "I, and many Indians want to hear the gospel, not only in Kaskaskunk but also in Gekelemukpechunk [Kuh-kee-luh-mook-pa-kunk], and Tuscarabi [Tus-ca-raw-bi]."[25] He also told Zeisberger that "Chief Packanke, and his council have arranged, subject to your approval, a separate site away from other Indians to be set aside especially for your village. He has pledged all drunken Indians will be kept away from your village so they will not disturb you." He closed by saying, "I for my part intend to live with you and have already informed my friends that I want to hear the Gospel and to be converted, even if nobody else wants to." Benjamin, an apostate from the old Gnadenhutten of 1750, now living with the natives, had accompanied Glikhikan and confirmed his statement.[26]

It was now Zeisberger's turn to respond. For almost twenty-five years he had lived among the Indians. He had learned that prudence and caution were the most desirable attributes when holding discussions with the Indians. Arbitrary and expeditious action could only spell disaster. Slowly and carefully he crafted his reply. "I hear your words and understand them very well. We are glad to hear that the Indians want to accept the word of God." As for coming to Kaskaskunk, he cautioned, "We do not like to promise more than we know for sure we can keep, and we keep any promise that we have made." He assured Glikhikan that Packanke's invitation had not been considered "superficially." But several obstacles must be removed before they could proceed. First, they had been commissioned by the Bethlehem elders to come specifically to Goschgoschunk on the invitation of their chiefs to preach the Gospel. At that time, neither the Allegheny chiefs nor the Moravians knew of any other Indians who wanted to hear their message. "These are our friends," he explained, "and they were the first to act, therefore we do not want to leave them without their permission. Their wish will decide us." Second, they would need the permission of the Bethlehem elders before making such a move. The request has already been made, and an answer was expected within a few months. After Zeisberger asked Glikhikan several questions, which could not be answered until he talked to his council, the meeting closed on a friendly tone. Glikhikan remained overnight at the village, attending the evening service and talking late into the night with Anton.[27]

In September Zeisberger consecrated the new assembly hall, and by the middle of October they completed the fall harvest, bringing in a bumper crop of corn. An unusual and mystifying incident occurred in November—one of those spiritual awakenings that challenge mortal understanding. It had been just short of seventeen months since Zeisberger and his small party arrived on the banks of the Allegheny—seventeen months of antagonism, frustration, and disappointment. There was nothing unusual about the day, the thirteenth of the month; it began as usual with the regular morning gathering. Shortly after the service began, an unseen force seemed to pervade the atmosphere and be diffused over the entire congregation, especially affecting Zeisberger. "We were elated and tears were shed which comforted us. Today I felt especially happy, which I had not been until now; so happy, that I thought it was now time to think of baptizing, because since we have been here, I have never had that feeling, there was always an obstacle in the way, so that I did not have enough confidence to undertake it."[28]

Twenty days later, they baptized their first convert. Zeisberger wrote elatedly on December 3, "We lived through a day which cannot be compared to any other since we have been here." The faithful Indian Gatschenis, his wife, and their eight-month-old son were baptized, "unto Jesus' death," as Lucas, Pauline, and Israel.[29] The ceremony was repeated on Christmas Day, and their friend since the inception of the mission, the blind chief Allemewi, was baptized as Salomo. At the close of the year twenty-five villagers lived at the mission.

The new year began with Zeisberger in a sanguine mood. He wrote, "Who would have thought it possible that we would come to live through such blissful days here." The baptisms continued, and on Sunday, January 21, during the afternoon service, Tschechquoapesch and his wife were baptized as Jeremias and Anna Caritas, and the following February 25, Beata, the mother of Lucas, was baptized.[30] A total of seven converts had been baptized on the Allegheny.

Wangomen continued to do his utmost to prevent his people from attending the services at Lawunakhannek by resurrecting the old familiar lies and other cleverly designed tricks of chicanery. According to the diary, he even "resorted to making himself another Bible, because he can see that the old one does not suit his purpose."[31]

An incident occurred shortly after the first of the year that further added to Wangomen's frustration. It also shows how seriously Indian conversion disrupted the structure of the native political system. Abraham's sister, who resided at Goschgoschunk, visited the mission, bringing gossip from the native village. One item had a most sinister ring. Zeisberger's diary explains:

> From there we also learned that the message or the bunch of wampum, which was received here from the Seneca Chief on August 1, 1768, with the words: BEWARE OF THE BLACK COATS! and which since then has traveled around in the land of the Indians, has now reached us again on the way back, and they [the native council] now have to give an answer, which is causing them difficulties because they have no chief. Their chief is our *Salomo* [formerly Allemewi, now living with Zeisberger's converts], and they do not like to come here for advice, so when they hold a council they fail as a rule to reach a decision, because they have no one in authority and no one will accept anybody else's suggestions.[32]

Because there was no strong chief in charge at the native Indian village of Goschgoschunk, its decisions had little effect beyond the village. The "Black Coats" belt traveled among the Indians as far west as the Mississippi River and among the Great Lakes Indians around Lake Michigan, damaging Zeisberger's reputation.

Near the end of January the converts discovered a plot to kill the missionaries. A drunken Indian, probably from Damascus and one of the hostile chief's sons, arrived at the far woods on the opposite side of the river, where, having lost his way, he spent the night. Fortunately, the next morning he had sobered up, lost the desire to kill, and returned home. Zeisberger heard of the attempt and called the chiefs from Goschgoschunk into council. He was angry. "Are you not those who wanted me to come here?" he cried. "You agreed upon it in your council and dispatched two messengers to Friedenshutten saying that I should come. Why are there people now who try to kill me?" Sheepishly, the chiefs gave the standard response: "Had the Indian been sober he would have not attempted the act." That was not good enough, and the missionary sharply responded, "That was hardly sufficient." Then he told them, "If you do not put an end to this trouble I shall have to use a different means and lodge a complaint about your bad treatment with the chiefs in the west which they certainly would not like." Within a few days, the council sent Gendaskund and several of the chiefs back to the village with apologies, assuring him it would not happen again. "He told me," Zeisberger recorded, "They were afraid of receiving a harshly worded message from the chiefs and be considered disturbers of the peace."[33] This was the final episode in the long string of events designed to interrupt Zeisberger's work. He had made up his mind. He would rid himself of this ungovernable lot on the Allegheny. He had been more than patient throughout the time he spent there. Before he had received Packanke's invitation to move to the Beaver River, he had few options. Now he had the luxury of an alternative.

Zeisberger held a lengthy conference with his congregation, and they decided to leave Lawunakhannek and move to the Kaskaskunk region on the Beaver River. The converts spent the remaining days of February and March making canoes for the trip. On April 8, Gendaskund visited the village, accompanied by Glikhikan, who had just arrived from the Beaver River. Everyone at Lawunakhannek was overjoyed by their visit and excitedly advised Glikhikan of their plans. "As a matter of fact," Zeisberger said, "We plan to leave in a few days." Both men shared their enthusiasm.[34]

Four days later, Zeisberger and his Indian helpers had their final council with the chiefs at Goschgoschunk. It was a memorable meeting. Zeisberger was accompanied by Sensemann, Anton, Abraham, Lucas, and Glikhikan, who had remained at the village to be with them over the Easter holiday on April 15. Wangomen began the conference on a penitent and apologetic tone. He went through a standard litany of his misdeeds and regretfully expressed his contriteness, telling Zeisberger that he had appointed a mediator to discuss any future problems he might encounter. It was then Zeisberger's turn to reply.

For the first time since he arrived on the Allegheny, he felt relaxed and confident. The decision had been made to leave and was supported by Packanke and his Delawares on the Beaver River. Now he could express his feelings without fear of retribution from Wangomen. The pressure from Wangomen's brother Glikhikan and the other western chiefs who outranked him in the Indian hierarchy had made it clear that he was to stop interfering with the "praying Indians." He also knew that many of his people would follow Zeisberger and his band of converts, diminishing Wangomen's already meager population.

Zeisberger began by thanking the chief for his frankness. "I have," he said, "often wished to have the chance to speak to you in such a manner." He then chronicled the events since their arrival, beginning with the unanimous invitation of the Indian council for the Moravians to come to the Allegheny and ending with regret for the lack of support from Wangomen's people. But, he acknowledged, "the Indians are a free people and can do as they please." He held no grudges, no hostile feelings, and assured Wangomen, "If anyone has spoken evil of you, it was not I." Almost pleadingly he said, "Even if you cannot approve of our religion, let us live together in peace, and let us not speak evil of one another." He did not think it was necessary to appoint a mediator, but if Wangomen desired such an arrangement, he would recognize his surrogate. Again, he conceded, "We do not want to have anything to do with affairs of state, that is not our business. We are glad if only we can live unmolested and be at peace with everybody."[35]

The speech closed with one of Zeisberger's most powerful statements. It strikes at a complicated but basic problem that plagued white missionary relations with the Indians. To Zeisberger, the problem was simple: Forget the color of our skin! Don't judge us as other white men! Listen to what we say, and the message that we bring.

> I have on several occasions told you we are a people different from others, and I wish that you could understand what I am going to say. We are not able to live as other Indians do, we do not like heathenism, on the contrary we abhor it. We live only to please the Saviour and to do his work. It is the same with us white brethren. We are separate from the world. *There are only two kinds of people in all the nations of the world; Namely, children of the world and children of the Saviour; the former are on the way to eternal destruction, the latter on the way to eternal life*. I have often heard that many of you have said: Why should we believe in the white people, they look quite different than we do, because their skin is white and ours in brown. We do not want you to believe in the white people but in the Saviour, because you could learn very bad things from the white people, things which are even worse than what you do. You call me Schwannak, which means white man; we can see that you do not make any difference

> between us and all other white people. *Try and use your intelligence and judgment which God has given you and open your eyes, then you will see the difference!* I take it you realize that my way of living is different from that of other white people. We are children of God and all those who believe in God and His five wounds are our brothers and sisters, whether their skin is white, brown or black. . . . All together we form *one* people of God.[36]

He closed with a final plea: let us "depart in peace with hope that we shall see you again some time. We would like to be friends with you and live in peace with you."

After a brief interval, Wangomen arose and assured the missionary party that nobody objected to their leaving. "We are ready," he said, "to let you go in peace." He had no other alternative. Within a few days almost half of his village would join the missionary party and leave the Allegheny for Kaskaskunk.

· 14 ·

Lagundo Utenunk on the Beaver, 1770–1771

A WARM spring rain fell on the mountains and passed eastward, delaying the departure of Zeisberger and his converts from Lawunakhannek on the morning of April 17, 1770. By noon the weather cleared and fifteen canoes pushed off from the banks of the river. Spirits were high as they glided down the wide Allegheny toward the Indian village of Goschgoschunk. As the village came into view, a lone canoe pulled away from the crowded banks of the river. Gendaskund and his family had made their decision. They would join the Christians. Others would soon follow. The old mission site was deserted. Abraham served as quartermaster and traveled ahead each day to find a suitable camping site.

The following day they passed the mouth of the French Creek, where during the French and Indian War, the English had built Fort Venango, now deserted except for a small village of Mingoes. The same day, Glikhikan left the party, returning by land to Packanke's village. He would announce their coming. Three days later, toward evening, they arrived at Fort Pitt and camped a mile above the fort.

At noon on April 22, they continued their journey, canoeing downstream on the Ohio, and by noon of the next day they entered the mouth of the Beaver River. Leaving the Ohio, they passed three miles up the

Beaver and encountered the first waterfalls (now Beaver Falls, Pennsylvania). The next three days were spent portaging around the falls, and on the twenty-eighth Glikhikan arrived with horses.[1]

Two days later, Zeisberger recorded: "In the morning we came to a women's town consisting of five or six huts, where only single women live who do not want to marry."[2] (Unfortunately, Zeisberger fails to say why these women chose a single lifestyle.) The following day they located a large plain on the east side of the river, unloaded their baggage, and, with Glikhikan's help, inspected the site, which seemed satisfactory for their prospective village.

That evening they called a conference to discuss what to do for the next few days. An immediate visit to Packanke's village was planned. "Hardly had we finished," Zeisberger noted, "when a mounted messenger arrived from Packanke inviting us, or as many as were desirous to come, to a feast. We replied that we had already intended to visit him tomorrow and speak to him."[3] They arrived at the Kaskaskunk village on May 5. The town was situated on a big plain and consisted of twenty huts scattered along the Shenango River at the junction of Neshannock Creek (now New Castle, Pennsylvania).[4]

Zeisberger described his meeting with Packanke: "We went into the Chief's house and he seemed pleased to see us welcoming us very cordially. He is already well advanced in years, his hair is grayish white, but he is active and of a happy temperament."[5]

Before Zeisberger described their formal meeting with the chief and his council, he explained in the diary a problem discussed at the village mission conference the previous evening. It was a matter of Indian protocol, or how their speaker would address Packanke. Should he be called "brother" or "sister"? He wrote:

> Several of us were reluctant to call him brother for the following reasons: 1. The Indians are wont to call him brother and they make war on each other. 2. It might occur to them sometime to ask our Indians to go to war with them if they are called brother. But the name sister would make this impossible, it is also best suited for the Delawares because they know quite well and are not ashamed of the fact that they are women and therefore should not go to war. So it was unanimously decided to call him sister. This is nothing unusual for the Delawares. But some, in particular the warriors, are ashamed of it and do not want to be women, therefore they prefer to call one another brother.[6]

A council of Packanke's advisers was promptly called, and Abraham, the mission's speaker, was the first to address the assembly. Using the agreed-upon appellation of "sister," he began. The message was a brief summary of all the incidents leading up to their arrival. Strings of wampum were presented at the appropriate time to confirm each point (see Appendix C).

Now it was Zeisberger's turn to speak. He repeated what he had said to Wangomen and his council back on the Allegheny earlier in the year. Again he emphasized the unique status of the Moravian missionaries compared to all other white men, especially their disdain of profit, land, and riches. "Our only purpose here," he assured them, "is to show the Indians the way to eternal life, so that they shall not be lost." He closed by imploring Packanke not to believe the many lies and rumors that were being spread among the Indian people about the Moravian missionaries but to come to him for the truth.[7]

Packanke rose and repeated each of the remarks connected with the appropriate belts and strings and passed each to the members of the council, demonstrating the Indians' phenomenal ability to remember the intricate and various points spoken and then confirmed by strings of wampum. The chief acknowledged his invitation to the missionaries to remove from Lawunakhannek to the Kaskaskunk, was pleased with everything they said, and promised that they could live in peace and not be molested. He also said he would confer with the chiefs on the Muskingum and inform Zeisberger when he received their reply.

Although the council was productive, Zeisberger nevertheless reflected: "The preaching of the Gospel is encountering much opposition here too and if Packanke's enemies were not afraid of him, we would not fare any better here than we did in Goschgoschunk. Unofficially we hear of enough things which are said against us. The [blackcoat] message of the Seneca Chief 2 years ago has gone all round the land of the Indians and not done any good work, we hear of it everywhere."[8]

Despite the auspicious results of their first meeting with Packanke and his council, Zeisberger knew how fickle Indian diplomacy could be. Experience had taught him to be wary. But little time could be spent on such musings.

On May 3, believing "that our way of life was the only one to redemption," Glikhikan and his family moved into the village. Zeisberger knew this would provoke a reaction among the native Delawares and especially from Packanke.[9]

By the end of May the fences were finished and numerous temporary huts were completed. But Zeisberger was concerned about the village site.

The flat alluvial plain made fine farming ground for their plantations, but it could be subject to flooding. Glikhikan had shown him an alternative and much improved site on the west side of the Beaver just opposite the present village. Here there would be no chance of flooding. The only potential problem was its proximity to the Indian women's village. After consultation with the women leaders, who expressed no objections, Zeisberger decided to build the permanent village on this raised ground on the west bank. He sent Abraham and Lucas to Packanke with this message:

> We find that our settlement has not yet a name. To prevent other Indians from giving us a name which we may not like we are herewith informing you that this settlement is to be called Lagundo Utenunk. (In German, Friedensstadt; or, in English, Town of Peace) Kindly make this known within the boundaries of your district. The men were well received by Packanke and he promised to make it known throughout his entire district.[10]

Hereafter, Zeisberger would always refer to the village using the Indian name Lagundo Utenunk.

Over the previous month the number of native Indians living at the mission village had steadily increased. Attendance at the daily services reached forty or fifty persons.

Packanke was becoming increasingly disturbed over the interest shown in Zeisberger's teachings, especially among his own villagers. The defection of Glikhikan, his head captain, was a serious blow to the morale of his council and impinged on Packanke's ability to carry on his functions as head chief. The captain and all ten of his family, including his children, were now living at the mission. But other members of the chief's village were also regularly attending the meetings, including two of his own sons. The aggravation came to a head on June 19.

Glikhikan had gone to Kaskaskunk to handle several personal chores and arrived during a meeting of Packanke's council. He was invited to attend. A message had just been received from Netawatwes suggesting that they invite the New Jersey Delawares to come to the Ohio Country and bring their white Christian teachers. Packanke was angry and told his council, "I would never ask white people to live with me. We already have white people here. Who has asked them to live with us? Not I. I only invited the Indians, and if I am called to account for it by the Six Nations, the Cherokees and other nations I shall say, One of my young and imprudent people has done that." The speech continued in a similar vein, but

Present site of Lagundo Utenunk mission, 1770–1773. Photograph by the author.

finally he turned to Glikhikan and declared angrily, "You have left our council and have gone to theirs. Are you hoping by any chance to get white skin there? Not even one of your feet will become white, let alone your whole body. Were you not a brave and honored man when you sat beside me in council? You despise all that now and think you have found something better, but as time goes on, you will find you were deceived." A saddened Glikhikan rose slowly to his feet, looked around the room, finally fixed his eyes on his chief, and said, "I have gone to them and where they are, there I will stay."[11] It must have been with a heavy heart that he returned to the mission village the next day. Within a few days Packanke's anger subsided and he became resigned to Glikhikan's defection.

During the hot summer days of July and the first two weeks in August, the converts worked at constructing temporary huts in their new location on the west side of the Beaver River, and by August 13 they had moved. Seldom did a day pass that one or more Indian or white visitors did not stop at the village. Packanke's two sons and his grandson were frequent guests. All three expressed a desire to join the congregation, but Zeisberger demurred. The defection of Glikhikan had caused enough antagonism among Packanke's council, and he did not want to create aggravation among the other tribal chiefs. On August 13, he briefly noted, "I am on the whole not very keen to have many Chiefs and men in authority living with us, I would rather have them stay where they are and be good friends with us all the same."[12]

Early on the morning of October 28, Johann and Anna Margareth Jungmann arrived "unexpectedly" at the mission. Zeisberger knew the couple was on the road from Friedenshutten, but he had not expected them for several weeks. Zeisberger was jubilant, and that evening he wrote, "It is impossible for me to describe my joy." (Both of the Jungmanns were experienced in missionary work, knew the Delaware dialect, and were close friends of Zeisberger.) Shortly after their arrival, Gottlob Sensemann, who had been with Zeisberger since he arrived on the Allegheny in 1768, returned to Bethlehem.[13]

Toward the year's end, an important event took place. On Christmas Eve, Zeisberger baptized two of his most famous converts: the captain warrior Glikhikan, called Isaac, and the Munsee captain Gendaskund, baptized as Jacob. Both men, but especially Isaac, would become major players in the following years of the Moravian Indian missions. More than eighty persons attended the service. Since coming to the western theater in 1767, Zeisberger had baptized ten converts.

The year closed at Lagundo Utenunk with seventy-three permanent residents living at the village—forty-four adults and twenty-nine children. The most prominent group (thirty-six) were former residents of Goschgoschunk, the Munsee village on the Allegheny.[14]

The Jungmanns' presence and quick orientation to the mission routine permitted Zeisberger to give some attention to plans for expanding the missionary program. He had received numerous invitations to visit Chief Netawatwes at Gekelemukpechunk on the Muskingum. This was the heart of the Delaware Nation and its capital. On February 7, he sent a runner to the village with a dispatch saying "we would visit them in the near future and we were especially anxious to speak to the Chiefs and Captains there."[15] The decision to visit the Muskingum was probably prompted by the rising tide of opposition against the missionaries at Packanke's village. If their relationship with Kaskaskunk should turn sour, Zeisberger wanted the option of remaining at Lagundo Utenunk or moving to the Muskingum.

But there was another reason for concern regarding the permanency of the Beaver River location. Almost a year earlier, Packanke had spoken to Zeisberger about the possibility of moving the Indians at Friedenshutten to the Beaver. Since Zeisberger and his people had arrived, Packanke had his eye on the additional two hundred Indian converts living at Friedenshutten. If he could convince them to move, it would increase his Delaware population and substantially enhance his power and prestige as a chief.

For many months Zeisberger had been aware of Packanke's solicitations to Friedenshutten. Shortly after he arrived on the Beaver, the rumor had been rampant in Indian circles. On one of the chief's frequent visits to Pittsburgh, he stopped at the mission and Zeisberger talked with him about the subject. He told the chief, "I thought there were a few snags in his proposal. First, I could not see a convenient locality in the area and they certainly will not leave one place without being sure of another. Second, their teachers must accompany them. Third, they would not like to go to a place where they are hated or ill-treated, and finally, it depended on what the Six Nations would say to it, reminding him, the Cayuga chief in Gajuga has taken them into his arms and loves them much more than their own nation does in this district."[16]

After thoroughly discussing the proposal, both agreed that Zeisberger should write a letter to the missionary Johannes Schmick explaining the situation. Unknown to Packanke, problems were developing at Friedenshutten. The Six Nations had recently sold the land occupied by the mission to the Pennsylvania proprietors, and white settlers were rapidly following the surveyors into the area. It was only a matter of time until the mission Indians at Friedenshutten would be forced to move. If Zeisberger could find a suitable location in the Muskingum Valley it would solve both problems. In the meantime, he must hasten to talk with Netawatwes and his council.

Fortunately, by the first week in March, the weather had moderated and on the fifth, Zeisberger and his party left the village bound for the Muskingum. Accompanying him were three of his staunchest allies, Anton, Jeremias Papunhank, the brother of Johannes, and Isaac Glikhikan.[17]

The snow was still heavy and drifted in the valleys, making travel treacherous, but on the fifth day out, they reached the Muskingum, crossing over on rafts and almost losing two horses that became tangled in driftwood as they swam across the river. Early on March 13, they arrived at Gekelemukpechunk. Most colonial officials usually referred to the village as New Comers Town. (Netawatwes was called "New Comer" by the English, but the Indian name translates as "One who is a skilled adviser.") The party was housed in the chief's cabin.

Zeisberger recorded one of the most detailed accounts we have of the village.

> Gekelemukpechunk, which is situated on the Muskingum River, is rather a large Indian town and is said to consist of 100 houses which I think is quite likely. Most of them are block houses. The Chief's house is a studded house with a floor and stairs of cut wood. It has a brick chimney, a shingle roof and is the biggest one in the town. A few other houses have shingle roofs too. The countryside is beautiful and consists of a vast plain. The land on both sides of the river is good. The river "here" is about as wide as the Delaware near Easton, but 6 miles further down a tributary flows into it which is just as wide. Tuscarabi, which is now uninhabited, is situated on a "branch" of this river and approximately 40 miles north of here; from Pittsburgh they often come here by water, which however, is a long detour. Many Indians are supposed to live along the river, Delawares, Mahicans, and Shawanese. About 50 miles N.W. is a town of Dalamattenos [Wyandots]. Most of the Indians here were Unami and belong to the Turtle Clan. There are a few Munsee, part of them came here only a year ago, namely from Goschgoschunk where they several times attended our services and were very friendly to us.[18]

The next two days were a whirlwind of activity. The most interesting discussions, however, were the private conversations with the chiefs between preaching sessions.[19] The major topic discussed in these meetings was a letter written by two Indians from the Muskingum village. Zeisberger recorded this meeting in some detail on March 14. He began the discussion by reading the letter. He had distinct reason for discussing the subject.

> We have heard that our sister has gone to you and has accepted your religion and way of living. We, the undersigned, are herewith informing you that we are seriously asking you to send her back to us. If you do not comply with our request we shall come and take her back by force which should not be very pleasant for you. We are finally determined not to let her stay with you and it would be wise of you to send her back to us before we come and fetch her.[20]

Exactly when Zeisberger received the letter is unknown, but he did indicate it had been "some time ago," and apparently it was not acknowledged. After reading the letter, he noted:

> I told them it was not sensible and quite unnecessary to use such harsh words because they had not even asked why the woman was with us. I said, the woman in question who had been baptized and is now our sister, did not come nor is she now staying with us at our request. She has followed her inclinations, and as she wanted to hear about the Saviour, and as we thought the Indians were free people and not obliged to live in one and the same town (as a matter of fact we know that you often change residences) we saw no reason for sending her back. I assured them our sister was not desirous to go back to them, that she did not even want to be reminded of them, and that she thought only of her soul's salvation. I said if they wanted to know more about her they could ask Isaac (Glikhikan), who is her dearest brother.[21] [The woman in question was Gertraut, baptized January 20, 1771, and a blood brother of Isaac, who sat in the audience.]

Zeisberger closed his remarks to the chiefs by saying, "The best piece of advice I can give you is to accept the Word of God [in your village] and have it preached to you so that whoever wants to come here, will have the opportunity to do so. Then they will not need to leave your town. This is my advice to you."

Needless to say, the issue turned into an embarrassment for the chiefs, especially when the writer of the letter proved to be young Killbuck (Gelelemend), the grandson of Chief Netawatwes, who had forged the signatures of the two men and sent the letter without authorization from the council. Zeisberger had made his point. If the missionary group were to move into this area, they must be permitted to live in peace, undisturbed by the native villagers. Furthermore, the chiefs must not interfere with the free access of the natives who might wish to join the Christian congregation.

An abashed Netawatwes responded to Zeisberger's remarks, apologizing for the letter but admitting he had no knowledge of it. Later Killbuck's culpability would be discovered. Obviously, Killbuck never thought the letter would come to the attention of the council. The chief said: "If anyone of us wants to go to you and to hear the word of God I will not prevent him, on the contrary, I shall be pleased because I like to hear it myself."[22]

The next evening, Zeisberger had another talk with the the council members, again stating his position and emphasizing the importance of being "unmolested" from the "gambling, dancing, drinking and constant noise" of the native village.[23] During this meeting, he also had a "long conversation" regarding the messages Packanke promised to relay to the Muskingum. He was dumbfounded to learn that none of these had been delivered to the Muskingum council. Both parties were embarassed, and the discussion was quickly dropped.

On the afternoon of March 17, Zeisberger and his party departed for the return trip to Lagundo Utenunk, arriving just in time to celebrate Easter.[24] During Zeisberger's nineteen-day absence, the snow-filled valleys and ice-clogged river had been thawed by the first warm rains of spring. Baptisms continued at the mission and the Sunday services filled the temporary assembly hall to capacity, but rumors of additional problems at Packanke's village continued to circulate. On April 8 Zeisberger recorded, "Life there was really miserable and they had been drinking continuously for three weeks."[25]

Of all the vices introduced by the white man into Indian culture, none was more debilitating than the use of intoxicating liquor. Excessive indulgence runs like a devastating theme throughout the postcontact era of the American Indians. The bottle provided one brief moment when they could escape from their frustrations and forget the many problems that plagued their lives, only to awaken the next morning and again face the reality of their world. The diaries from Lagundo Utenunk provide a graphic example of this destruction.

With the coming of the Christian villages, the Indians were confronted with a perplexing problem. Should they leave their relations and friends, accept this "word of God and save my eternal soul," or remain among their native friends and take their chances? These problems remained the same throughout Zeisberger's career, but he discusses them more during this period. One of Packanke's sons provides an excellent example. From the beginning of Zeisberger's stay on the Beaver, the son and his wife had visited the mission regularly. In April, Lucus had talked with the son at Kaskaskunk and discussed the possibility of his religious conversion. He told Lucus:

> I have spent all my money on alcohol and my wife and I have nothing wherewith to dress. I know and believe that you preach the truth, and like to listen to your sermons. But there are many who are opposed to your religion and we are afraid of those in authority. I hope

> that soon we shall all be at liberty to do as we please, because I want to live with you and be converted, but as long as I am here I cannot accept the word of God, for I am not a free man.[26]

Certainly the reference to "those in authority" meant his father and uncles, all members of the Kaskaskunk council. Four days later, he and his wife paid another visit to the mission to hear the Sunday sermon. They were back again on the following Wednesday. After the service, they had a long conversation with Zeisberger. The missionary asked the man if "he had decided to believe in the Saviour or not." He replied, "I often think of him, but I am afraid of the other Indians." "I told him," Zeisberger responded, "that no one who believes in the Saviour needed to fear man, that everyone should make his own decision regardless of what other people thought and that the only thing which should matter to him was to have his soul saved."[27] While Zeisberger may have truly believed the faithful "needed [not] to fear man," this young man obviously had strong connections to his own family.

Four days after this incident, in a seemingly unrelated entry, Zeisberger recorded a conversation he had with Isaac, who had just returned from hunting. During the hunt in the woods, Isaac had met Packanke's brother, a captain in the council at Kaskaskunk and the son's uncle. The captain told of a recent conversation he had had with his grandmother.

> My grandmother came to me the other day, told me that she wanted to hear of the Saviour and asked me what I would do in her place. I replied that I could not give her any advice because she was old and sensible enough and could do what she thought was best for her. Then she saw her son, Packanke, and ask him the same question. Packanke answered: "If you do that you must realize that all of your children, grandsons, granddaughters and all of your friends will follow you which will leave me here without friends." At those words she became afraid and dropped her plans.[28]

These few conversations illustrate both the intimate nature of the native Indian family and the perplexing decisions faced by any member of the clan who chose to leave the native village and move to the Christian mission. Notwithstanding the worthiness of the Christian missionary program, it released destructive forces upon the native culture. Although Zeisberger may not have wittingly created this Gordian knot, he left its unraveling in the hands of the native Indian, who was faced with finding a solution, torn between his family and, according to the missionary message, the salvation of his soul.

It had been just over three years since Zeisberger had been to Bethlehem. The leaders there now called him back for consultation. Leaving Lagundo Utenunk on July 1 and traveling alone, he would be absent from the mission a few days short of four months. Fortunately, the Jungmanns could carry on in his absence, but it was to be a crucial four months.

The diaries kept by Jungmann from July through October contain frequent entries describing the sordid events at Kaskaskunk. Suicides, murders, and family altercations became weekly occurrences, all connected with the increasing consumption of liquor. Even Packanke admitted that he was beginning to lose control of his own people. Unfortunately, those affairs were not confined to the native village and spilled over into the mission. The convert Lazara's father-in-law was killed at Kaskaskunk in a drunken melee with his son. Only the hasty intervention of Abraham prevented Lazara from killing the son, thus avenging the old man's death.

To everyone's relief, Zeisberger returned from Bethlehem on October 21, accompanied by twenty-eight-year-old John Heckewelder, a recent recruit to the mission field. Heckewelder would become one of the major players in Zeisberger's life in the next fifteen years, and his influence would have far-reaching effects on the literature handed down to us regarding the Moravian missions in America.[29]

John, born on March 12, 1743, was the first of four children of David and Regina Heckewelder. The other children were David, Christian, and Mary. They immigrated to America on the ship *Irene* in 1754. His parents subsequently were assigned as missionaries to the Danish West Indies, where they both died, leaving John and his siblings orphans at an early age. He lived in Bethlehem until 1756, when he was transferred, on his fifteenth birthday, to the single Brethren's house in Christianbrunn. Two years later he returned to Bethlehem and was apprenticed to William Nixon, a cedar cooper.

Though of German descent, the family had lived in England since 1742. John was born in Bedford and raised in an English-speaking home with limited knowledge of German. Since only German was spoken in the Moravian settlements, his teen years were difficult. His education progressed slowly, and he became dispirited, primarily because of his limited knowledge of German and the loss of his parents.

In 1762, after receiving Spangenberg's approval, he accepted Christian Frederick Post's invitation and began his trip to the Muskingum (see Chapter 9). Emaciated and in poor health, he returned to Bethlehem in

November 1762. On his arrival in Bethlehem, after an absence of only nine months, he found the community and his life radically altered. His employer, William Nixon, had moved to New York, making it impossible to finish his cooper apprenticeship, and his close friend Spangenberg had been called back to Europe. He was disheartened and depressed and on the point of leaving Bethlehem with the intention of returning to Europe. He later wrote of this period, "My anguish and distress of mind having increased beyond endurance, I again resolved to quit Bethlehem for ever." After arriving in New York, he changed his mind and returned to Bethlehem.[30]

When Zeisberger returned to the Bethlehem in 1771, he applied to the church elders requesting Heckewelder's services as a potential schoolmaster at Lagundo Utenunk. This was the beginning of Heckewelder's involvement with the missionary program. It would be another seven years (1778), however, before he was ordained a deacon. He served for the next fifteen years directly in the mission service, although for several years during this period he was sent back to Bethlehem because of hostile Indian action in and around the missions. In 1786, while residing with Zeisberger at Pilgerruh on the Cuyahoga River, he and his family left the mission service never to return except for several visits to various missions.

Zeisberger took almost two weeks to evaluate conditions at Lagundo Utenunk, then sat down on November 4 and wrote Nathaniel Seidel, the Moravian leader at Bethlehem. It was a long and detailed letter outlining the mission's position and possible alternatives. He concluded with a "suggestion":

> I have another idea, namely, as we have to plant, clear land and make fences for our Indians from Friedenshutten next spring, would it not be better and save much work, if one group of us went to Gekelemukpechunk (the Muskingum) in the spring, planted as much as they could and began to build, after we have arranged everything with the Chiefs. Then, when the Indians from Friedenshutten came here, the second group could split up, so that perhaps some stay here and the others go there. Because I already know many who would like to stay here, partly because of their friends, partly for other reasons. But in that case we ought to know for sure that they will come here in the Spring. If conditions change, and if they decide differently they ought to let us know in time. That is what I wanted to tell you about Gekelemukpechunk. If you want to remind us of anything, or if it were not in the interest of the Saviour, let us know soon, and especially because of the invitation there, Either "yes" or "no."[31]

The-end-of-the-year diary summary reveals the mission's progress. There was a new assembly hall, replete with a bell and a picture of Christ. On November 22, when the picture was installed, Zeisberger wrote the following revealing entry.

> Yesterday we hung the church bell on our Assembly Hall and today we put up the painting of our Saviour's passion and crucifixion. Children and Adults wept because they had never seen anything like this in all their lives. The other day a baptized woman told us with tears in her eyes that she had never seen the Saviour and could not image what he looked like. Today, when she came out of the Assembly Hall, she exclaimed: "I had no idea that the Saviour looked like that! I cannot take a look at him yet, because if I do I must cry too much."[32]

Statistics at the end of the year were encouraging. Over the previous year, the mission's population had increased by 50, including men, women, and children, to a total of 124.

· 15 ·

The Die Is Cast, 1772

ALTHOUGH THE final decision to move to the Muskingum had not been made officially, David Zeisberger, in his heart, knew an affirmative decision was imminent. Early in 1772, the congregation at Lagundo Utenunk approached the numbers currently at Friedenshutten. The question of how to move both settlements to the Muskingum that year filled his thoughts with logistic nightmares. With 124 Delaware and Munsee converts on the Beaver, 151 Delawares at Friedenshutten, and another 50 Mahicans from Schechschiquanunk just north of Friedenshutten, he knew how difficult it would be to organize such a move.

Unfortunately, the incidence of drunkenness in the neighborhood of Lagundo Utenunk continued to increase. On January 10, Zeisberger sent Isaac with a dispatch to Packanke and his Kaskaskunk council. The tone of the message was close to an ultimatum. He said Packanke had been asked on behalf of all the inhabitants of the missionary town to keep his young people in check and to see that the village was not molested by drunken Indians. If this continued, they would be obliged to live somewhere else.[1]

The chief promised to respond in a few days. Normally, a "few days" could mean several months or longer. Surprisingly, three days later a reply was delivered by Gulpikamen and four other Indians from Kaskaskunk.[2]

> My friends and inhabitants of Lagundo Utenunk: I am indeed sorry that you are molested by drunken Indians and have to hear their abusive talk and threats. Do not worry about the evil words which the wicked children say about you. Do not think I am hand in glove with them; I do not know anything about it. . . . Do not take any notice of the ill deeds of these children, for they are disobedient people. Remain quiet and let not anything interfere with your services. As regards your request to clear your neighborhood of the Indians who have settled too close to your town, I cannot comply with it. For this is not the land of the Delaware Indians where they were asked to settle. But turn your faces to Gekelemukpechunk, that is the land of the Indians, and that is where you, too, were invited to settle. If you want to live there, nobody will molest you, because all the Indians will be told to leave you in peace and not settle too near you, but this I cannot do here.[3]

A string of wampum was presented to the converts to confirm the remarks of the speaker. Then, surprisingly, he presented a large and impressive belt of wampum which had been sent from the Delaware capital on the Muskingum. This was the long-awaited belt from Netawatwes and his council. Routed through Packanke and his council, it had been delayed for more than a year, probably intentionally, by the Kaskaskunk council. The speaker continued:

> Hear the words of Netawatwelemeny [Netawatwes], the chief of Gekelemukpechunk! You are herewith informed that I have cleared a straight road from here to the Susquehanna which is safe and which you can use without fear. [This was a tactful invitation to both Christian congregations to come to the Muskingum.] The land in Kaskaskunk and along the Beaver Creek does not belong to the Delawares but to the Mingoes who still maintain their claim. The land of the Delawares is here on the Muskingum River, from the mouth of the river up to Cayahaga [River]. You came to Kaskaskunk because you did not know of another place at the time. Send this message and this belt to Newallike on the west branch [of the Susquehanna] so that he can pass it on to Friedenshutten and Schechschiquanunk not to go to Kaskaskunk but to Gekelemukpechunk where they will be cordially welcomed. There they shall live in an isolated place where nobody will drive them away nor molest them and where they will not be bothered by wild and drunk Indians. This stretch of land has been given to us by the Dalamattenos [Wyandots] and belongs to us.[4]

The truth had emerged. The Delawares and Munsees at Kaskaskunk were living on borrowed land and resided there at the pleasure of the Mingoes, Senecas of the Six Nations. Why Packanke refused to pass along the belt from Netawatwes remains a mystery. Perhaps he believed the Moravian settlements increased his prestige among the Delaware Nation and thus was reluctant to reveal the invitation from the Delaware council at Gekelemukpechunk. Zeisberger wrote that evening, "This probably explains why Packanke has never given us a plain answer, because it is not he who invited us, but the Chief in Gekelemukpechunk [Netawatwes]. He [Packanke] only gave his consent to send us the message. Not he is the master of this land, but the Mingo, of whom he is afraid."[5]

The messengers left the village after attending morning services the next day. Following their departure, the missionaries gathered the congregation together to discuss the previous day's conference. Almost unanimously they agreed "to not stay here another year." Zeisberger noted in the diary, however, "We decided not to make a definite decision for the time being but to await further events."[6] But privately, he began to make plans to visit the Muskingum. If the proper terms could be made with Netawatwes, they would move in the spring.

The months of January and February 1772 were especially severe, and Zeisberger's planned January departure for the Muskingum was delayed until March 11. It was essential that he quickly work out all of the many details of the forthcoming move. To prevent disputes with Netawatwes similar to those they had encountered with Packanke, a clear understanding must be forged with the chief and his council.

Zeisberger, Isaac Glikhikan, Lucas Gatschenis, and Petrus Sapen departed early on the morning of March 11, traveling by horseback.[7] Their route to Gekelemukpechunk was entirely different from that used in the spring of 1771. Traveling west-southwest from Lagundo Utenunk and using the "Great Trail," they struck the Sandy Creek near the present town of Dungannon, Hanover Township, Columbiana County, Ohio, and followed it to just before it enters today's Tuscarawas River (Muskingum). Immediately off to their right was the old Indian village of Shingas and the Beaver, now Bolivar, Ohio. On the morning of March 15, leaving the Great Trail, they turned south on the eastern bank of the Muskingum and continued for approximately twelve miles, crossing the Muskingum twice. "Toward evening," Zeisberger noted, "we came to a nice neighborhood which we liked very much. At first we went through an extensive plain, several miles long. The plains here are different from those in Wajomik [Wyoming Valley on the Susquehanna River in Pennsylvania], they have hedges but no trees. The soil seems to be very good. After having traversed the plain we came to a beautiful forest. It is located on a stretch of land which is rather elevated but even. We camped there and inspected the neighborhood. . . . But there was a great drawback! We had not yet found any water except river water."[8] They were probably in the plains now covered by the cities of Dover and New Philadelphia, Tuscarawas County, Ohio.

On the morning of March 16 they continued the journey southward along the eastern side of the river. Shortly after leaving camp, they came to another plain. The Zeisberger party had arrived at the future site of the proposed mission. His own words clearly show his excitement:

> We inspected the country further down the river which is many miles long, nice and even, and well supplied with wood, which is just what we want at the town-place, and because the lowland in between is very wide, so that the town comes to stand rather far from the river, and because it is a little inconvenient on account of the canoes which we cannot dispense with, this is substituted by the spring which is very big and forms a little lake which flows into the river, so that it is possible to take the canoes right up to the town and to have a safe harbor for the canoes at the same time. The lowland is very rich and good, and the river has plenty of fish, just as the Indians [at Gekelemukpechunk] have described it to us. There is plenty of game, in short the locality offers everything which the Indians need for their comfort. It is very spacious so many Indians can live there, because they will not need all the land for plantations. Unfortunately there are no stones in the river or on the land, but several miles away there are nice stones along the river which can easily be transported in canoes. A long time ago, a hundred years or more, Indians used to live there who have fortified their towns because the walls are still distinctly visible. We found 3 such forts at distances of several miles as the whole town was fortified where there is no dense forest in the middle of the place and nobody knows any more what nations lived there. But from all appearances they must have fought great wars. [The site is on the eastern corporate limits of New Philadelphia, Ohio.]
>
> After having inspected this neighborhood we went down the east bank of the river until we reached the "Fork" where the Gekelemukpechunk empties into the Muskingum. [This was the Big Stillwater Creek just south of present Midvale, Ohio.][9]

On the morning of March 18, they reached their destination, the village of Gekelemukpechunk. The previous evening they had sent an Indian messenger to announce their arrival. They were expected, and the principal chiefs were quickly assembled for their first meeting. Zeisberger wasted no time. The plan called for a small contingent of Indians from Lagundo Utenunk to move to the Muskingum immediately, lay out and build a village, and plant the spring crop. When the contingent from Friedenshutten, expected that summer, arrived on the Beaver, they would move to the Muskingum as soon as arrangements could be made. He explained the complicated logistics of moving some three hundred or more people, saying that it could take up to a year to complete.

This time Zeisberger would make sure there was no misunderstanding. All the terms must be clearly understood by both parties before the fact. There must be a quid pro quo. His final remarks to the council follow:

> There is one more thing which we must insist, namely that when we are in your neighborhood no other Indians shall settle anywhere near us because we are afraid that they will drink and bother us. We want to live by ourselves; not that we intend to monopolize the land but we find it impossible to live among drunken Indians. If those Indians did live near us they would corrupt our children and the young people, they would persuade them to drink and dance with them. That is why we have to live alone. We shall not prove troublesome to anybody, on the contrary we will endeavor to be at peace with everyone. We expect the same from you, namely that you will not be hostile to us but let us live our lives the way good Converts should. We also want to inform you that the Indians from Friedenshutten are going to bring their teachers with them. . . . We would like to start our return journey as soon as possible as time is short before the spring planting.[10]

This was one of Zeisberger's most straightforward and plain-spoken speeches. There could be little doubt in the minds of the council members concerning the conditions under which the missionaries would make this move. There was a delay of a few minutes while Netawatwes consulted with the council. Apparently Zeisberger's terms conformed to those set by the council in its discussions before the party had arrived. Netawatwes arose and responded:

> I am very pleased to hear that you want to live in peace with us. All of us have often hoped that you would accept our invitation, and not

> only you but the Indians in Friedenshutten and Schechschiquanunk. We are very glad that you have now accepted it. We had already thought that the locality at the great spring would be convenient for you. Many Indians can live there, and the site is isolated from other towns. The land from the mouth of the Gekelemukpechunk Creek to the Tuscarabi shall belong to the converted Indians and we will not permit any other Indians to live there. When you establish your residence with us, all the Indians will be told to be friendly to you and be well-behaved. They will also be told that anyone who wants to hear the Gospel and to live the way you do, will be at liberty to do so.[11]

Zeisberger's party left on the afternoon of March 20 after a long conversation with the chiefs. Exploring the west side of the Muskingum, they arrived again at the proposed site of the new mission on March 21. Zeisberger had now seen the area on both banks of the river, and estimated the distance between Schoenbrunn and the Delaware capital to be approximately thirty miles (actually it is slightly over twenty miles). Before leaving, they made some small improvements and planted corn. They spent the night near the Great Spring and in the morning departed, heading overland in a straight line for Lagundo Utenunk, arriving on March 26.

The die had been cast. Zeisberger had laid the groundwork for the most successful years in his long missionary life. The next seventeen days were a whirlwind of activity and excitement. Members were chosen to be in the first party to move, and all worked feverishly to pack for the journey. That first contingent was scheduled to depart on April 14.[12]

The morning of April 14 dawned bright and clear. As the warm spring sun rose above the horizon, it greeted a flurry of activity. The canoes lined the banks as the supplies were loaded aboard. The party was intentionally small: only twelve Indian converts and two other Indians. There were children in the party, but none were mentioned by name.[13] They were divided into two groups, one to travel by water and the other to guide the horses and cattle overland through the wilderness. Zeisberger's two previous trips to the Muskingum had given him a general familiarity with the region, but this founding party took an entirely different route than he had taken on each of his previous visits. He chose this route because more than half of the journey was by water and considerably less tiring than land travel.

After following the Beaver River as far as the Beaver Falls, they spent the night above the rapids. The following day they passed over the falls with difficulty, almost losing one canoe and its cargo. Originally they had planned to take the cattle overland from this point. They abandoned that idea and decided to have the land party travel near the river so that each evening the two groups could be together in their "night quarters." By the evening of April 17 they had entered the Ohio River and, traveling westward, had reached the mouth of the Little Beaver River. On the afternoon of April 21, continuing down the Ohio, they arrived at Mingo Town (now Mingo Junction) at the mouth of Ohio Cross Creek.[14] In the meantime, a messenger had been sent to Gekelemukpechunk to notify Netawatwes that they were on their way and he should send horses as promised and meet them on the Ohio. They would wait at Mingo Town for the return of the messengers.

Zeisberger had a low opinion of the Mingoes, which was shared by many of his white and Indian contemporaries. He recorded in his journal:

> These Mingoes, who are Senecas, told us that, when they heard that we were leaving Lagundo Utenunk, they had resolved to go and take possession of our town, but having learned later that only a few of us were leaving that place, they went some of them up the Ohio and some down the stream, and the few who are left here are minded to leave in a few days; they have received [orders] from their captains and chiefs to betake themselves away from here, as many complaints have come in against them, because they are wretched people who do nothing but rob, steal and commit murders among the White people.[15]

The Zeisberger party remained at Mingo Town for three days and during the entire time, to everyone's surprise, was treated cordially. On April 24, the messengers returned from Gekelemukpechunk with disappointing news. An embarrassed Netawatwes had to report "that hardly any of the Indians were at home, and because of scarcity of victuals they had scattered in the woods hunting and they could, therefore, not see how they could help us." He did suggest, however, that a small party take the heavy baggage in several canoes down the Ohio to the mouth of the Muskingum, then travel up it to their new location. In the meantime, perhaps the chief could send help for the remainder of the party as soon as the men returned from the hunt.[16]

Following Netawatwes's suggestion, on the afternoon of April 25 John Heckewelder, leading a separate party of canoes with the heavy baggage, began the long, roundabout journey down the Ohio and up the Muskingum to the new mission location.

Traveling by land directly westward, the rest of the party crossed over the headwaters of the creek and came down into the Muskingum watershed near present Cadiz, Ohio, to the Standingstone Creek, a branch of the Little Stillwater Creek. This area is now covered by Tappan Lake, one of the many lakes of the Muskingum Watershed Conservancy District.

On the morning of April 29, just as they were about to break camp, Echpalawehund, one of the leading chiefs of Netawatwes's council, and several other Indians from the village arrived with horses to help on the remaining journey.[17] They followed the Little Stillwater until it finally became navigable and spent the night of April 30 there. The next morning, they made a large bass canoe to carry the baggage and the children. This is the first mention of children in the Muskingum-bound party. Most of the land contingent continued on through the woods, "where there was neither way nor path."[18] Sometime on May 2 they reached the Muskingum River, and shortly after, the men, with the children, arrived in the bass canoe. It would be a few more days before the Heckewelder party arrived with the heavy baggage. They were now only a few miles from their destination. The next day they began the final leg of their journey.

Zeisberger's journal describes their arrival:

> The 3rd. Toward noon, to our great joy, we arrived at our destination by the great spring, on the very same day as that on which, three years before, we had come to Lagundo Utenunk. Our hearts were glad and thankful that the Saviour had so graciously helped us through the difficult journey. Here we encamped and even on this day reared huts for ourselves and looked over the ground again for the most suitable place for our town; we found no more suitable or better location than on which we had formerly determined.[19]

The Moravians had arrived at the Muskingum. Here they would reap their greatest harvest.[20]

· 16 ·

Chosen by the Lot, 1772

THREE WEEKS before David Zeisberger arrived on the Muskingum, he celebrated his fifty-first birthday. Never were his prospects so bright or external conditions so good. Now, in the prime of his life, he was separated from the debilitating influences of the white pioneers and had been assured by the Delaware chief Netawatwes of protection against unwanted native interference.

On May 4, the day following the converts' arrival at the new village site, they began clearing the land and building traditional Indian huts to provide shelter until more permanent log cabins could be constructed. A single street running east and west was laid out and the lots assigned. Although it was late in the planting season, there was still time to sow the crops and expect an adequate harvest in the fall. A portion of the workers began to build the temporary round-log church that would also serve as a home for Zeisberger.[1] On June 9, just three weeks after they felled the first tree, the cabin was completed.

Four days after the party reached its destination, an Indian runner appeared announcing the arrival of the Heckewelder contingent at Gekelemukpechunk, Netawatwes's capital on the Muskingum. (This was the canoe party that continued on down the Ohio carrying the heavy baggage.) Four Brethren were dispatched to assist the party on the final leg of the journey. Heckewelder's party arrived at the new settlement two days later.

Echpalawehund, a leading chief in Netawatwes's council and the guide of the Muskingum-bound land party, paid several visits to the village. During his visit on August 7, he brought Zeisberger news he had long expected. The Friedenshutten Christians had arrived on the Beaver River at Lagundo Utenunk. The chief had just returned from the Beaver River mission carrying a letter from John Ettwein, Zeisberger's close personal friend from Bethlehem.[2] There were three separate traveling groups. Two were from Friedenshutten. One group of 54 converts headed by Ettwein traveled by land. The second, led by Johann Roth, the head missionary at Friedenshutten, consisted of 140 converts who traveled part of the way in canoes.[3] The third party of 17 converts, led by Josua, Sr., came from the mission of Schechschiquanunk and arrived several weeks later, making a total of 211 converts from the eastern Susquehanna missions.

Ettwein, a superb organizer, had long desired to visit Zeisberger and his mission operations, and their recent correspondence convinced the Moravian leaders at Bethlehem that the church was about to embark on an entirely new missionary opportunity on the Muskingum. The principal purpose of his visit was to join with Zeisberger and the others in a conference at Lagundo Utenunk to develop the tactics for the missions on the Muskingum in the coming years. The first meeting began on the day of Zeisberger's arrival and was attended by the white missionaries: John Roth, Ettwein, Zeisberger, and Johann and Anna Margareth Jungmann.

More than three hundred converts now lived at Lagundo Utenunk, and Josua's Mahican contingent was expected momentarily. The missionaries faced questions such as: What to do with these people this coming winter? Who goes to the Muskingum and who remains here? Will all converts be moved to the Muskingum in the spring?

Customarily, most of these questions were resolved by using the lot, but there were exceptions. The usual three slips were prepared. The first question was, "Shall we move from Lagundo Utenunk next spring? The lot indicated that the Saviour does not approve that we proposed to leave this place next spring." The next item proved to be more complicated and somewhat embarrassing, especially to Zeisberger. For the last few years there had been increasing resistance from the Mahican and the Delaware converts, who preferred to live in separate villages. This issue had been solved by establishing two separate missions for the Susquehanna Christians. The question now was whether to establish two separate villages on the Muskingum. Since Zeisberger had done all the previous negotiating with Netawatwes and his Delaware council, no mention had been made of two villages.[4]

The minutes of the conference indicate that there had been some problems with Josua, the leader of the Mahican group at Schechschiquanunk, still on the road from the Susquehanna. As his contingent moved west across the Pennsylvania wilderness, he had been dispatching personal messengers to Netawatwes, apparently trying to negotiate a deal directly with the Delaware chief to have a Mahican village separate from the Delawares. The minutes explain:

> Old Josua has sent messengers and belts to the Chiefs [Netawatwes], in the name of the Mahicans and has undertaken separate negotiations with them. We have noted very clearly in the course of the journey that the old differences between the Mahicans and the Delawares is still existing and comes to expression on the part of the Mahicans, at least, in the case of Josua. In Bethlehem the matter has already been considered, whether now, perhaps, there would be an opportunity to separate them. We, therefore, came to an agreement to inquire of the Saviour whether we should propose a separation.

The slip drawn showed "*________," a blank. The secretary noted, "We shall, therefore, watch the matter, how it develops."[5]

But all the day's work was not lost. The missionaries asked the Savior to pick the name of the new village from a list of four: Bethel, Enon, Goshen, and Schoenbrunn. He chose the latter. Schoenbrunn was German for *beautiful spring*, or in Delaware, *Welhik Thuppeek*. Zeisberger, in most of his diary entries, used Welhik Thuppeek.

Interestingly, they took no chances on the lot for the last item on the agenda, the appointment of the missionaries to the various villages. Zeisberger made the decision. The Jungmanns and Heckewelder were assigned to Schoenbrunn, and the Roths were placed at Lagundo Utenunk. This would not be the only time when Zeisberger refused to consult the lot. As in this instance, it is difficult to explain why Zeisberger thought the use of the lot was or was not appropriate.

The missionaries met again on August 15 and, using the lot, decided on several minor questions concerning baptism and receiving new members into the congregation. The conference assembled again on August 17. This was the most productive of the three meetings, and the lot was not used. Zeisberger was reaffirmed as the leader, or "Oecononus," of the entire enterprise in the western theater and was admonished to visit all the missions frequently.

The second item of the meeting dealt with how to handle John Heckewelder, the new and untried assistant missionary, whom Zeisberger had brought from Bethlehem the previous year. The secretary recorded:

> Brother Heckewelder is here to learn the language and to help in all externals. Care is to be taken, however, that he may not become backward and weary and, for that reason, he is to be asked to conduct a service occasionally, but he is not able to sing. He is to conduct the boys' school in Welhik Thuppeek.

The conferees returned to the persistent problem of Josua's Mahicans and his insistence on negotiating directly with Netawatwes. The secretary wrote:

> As we do not know what Josua expects to do with the Mahicans, we can resolve nothing concerning them. . . . If Josua comes and inquires after Ettwein and Zeisberger are gone he is to be told that we should have been glad to see him, because one had heard all sorts of things concerning him, that the Brethren would have nothing against it, on the contrary, would rather favor it, if he would with the Mahicans and a few Delawares start a separate settlement.[6]

The discussion of Josua's role as a leader of the Mahican delegation contradicts a previous record of him in Moravian journals, which indicates that he had only a passive role in Moravian Indian negotiations. It further explains his later conduct during the unilateral negotiations with Netawatwes and his council and illustrates why the official diaries alone cannot be relied on for a complete account of incidents in the lives of the converts and the missionaries.

Discussions also concerned the horses and cattle as individual property. "Everything should be for the mission. Whatever a brother has spent of his own must reasonably be returned to him. If a head of cattle is sold, whatever may be gained by raising cattle shall be applied to the mission as a whole, for example, for salt, flour, coffee, tea etc." Zeisberger had his own ideas about this decision. The later diaries indicate that this regulation was never implemented, especially the community ownership of cattle.[7] The final items dealt with the assignments of native officers and the members of the Helpers' Conference at both Schoenbrunn and Lagundo Utenunk.[8]

Zeisberger stayed at the Beaver River mission until August 19 and was ill most of the time.[9] He returned to Schoenbrunn at noon on August 23, accompanied by Ettwein, Heckewelder, and a large complement of Indians and their families.[10] The next eleven days were a flurry of activity, hampered only occasionally by Zeisberger's continued sickness.

At Schoenbrunn, Ettwein was euphoric. Much of his life had been spent as an administrator back in Bethlehem. He was well known and respected among colonial officials and would direct the church's operations during the Revolutionary War. He comes down in Moravian history as an intelligent and lucid writer, particularly adept at planning and organizing the mission operations. Along with his voluminous correspondence he left a record of his trip to the Muskingum which is filled with tantalizing details, especially his observations of the Indians. Much of the information covering the next few days comes from his written record.[11]

Anticipating the arrival of the Friedenshutten Indians now living at Lagundo Utenunk, the missionaries laid out another street at Schoenbrunn running north and south, perpendicular to the existing street. The two streets resembled a cross, with the church located at the junction of the streets or the top of the tee. Additional lots were surveyed and staked. Each lot was three rods wide (forty-nine feet six inches) by six rods deep (ninety-nine feet), which was a standard size in most of the Moravian missions. There were now forty lots in the village. The missionaries' houses were on each side of the church. During Ettwein's stay at Schoenbrunn, he drew two maps of the village. The first was a rough sketch and the second a more detailed drawing showing the site of the church and several Indian houses and the names of the owners. These maps were discovered in the Moravian Archives in 1922. They became the critical ingredient in the reconstruction of the village, which was partially rebuilt in the 1920s. The proposed site of the cemetery was also shown. Both maps are still extant. The bell, brought from Friedenshutten, which had first been located at Gnadenhutten on the Mahoney, was hung on a scaffold near the temporary meeting house. It was purported to have been cast in 1747.

Because of Zeisberger's lingering illness, Ettwein left without him on August 26 to attend his scheduled meeting with Netawatwes and his council. Indian protocol and good manners demanded that all "great men" who visited the Delawares pay their respects to the head chief, Netawatwes, the host of the land. This was nothing more than a courtesy call.

Ettwein wrote a brief description of the Delaware village: "New Comers Town lies on the west [actually the north; the river here runs east to west] side of the Muskingum river. I counted between 40 and 50 houses very irregularly built. Some miles upstream and some miles down, stand many more houses and huts, which are reckoned as belonging to the town. It is a fine region, but they have no water other than the river."[12] His party left the capital the next morning and arrived back at Schoenbrunn on August 28.

Zeisberger, Ettwein, and the members of the Helpers' Conference spent the next day completing the final draft of the rules and regulations for the new Schoenbrunn village. The original drafts had been drawn up at the conference in Lagundo Utenunk and represented the first written statutes or codes of law regularly enforced in an organized village in the Ohio Country. From this point on they would be regularly read and subscribed to by all mission residents. Although similar rules must have been in effect at previous missions, this is the first time they were codified and recorded in the diaries.

1. Whosoever wishes to live here must worship God, our creator and Saviour, as the one and only God and must look for everything good, to him alone.
2. Nobody can live with us, who intends to go to heathen feasts and dances held at other places.
3. Nobody who wishes to bring rum here to get drunk, or to make others drunk, or who runs after rum at other places.
4. Nobody who keeps whores or attempts to seduce the wives of others.
5. Nobody who deserts his wife, nor a wife who runs away from her husband.
6. No son or daughter who, after thorough admonition, wantonly disobeys parents.
7. No thief, nor any person who is in the habit of stealing.
8. Nobody who would abuse or strike his neighbor.
9. Nobody who employes objects of heathen superstition in hunting or in curing diseases, or gives them to others.
10. We will keep the Sunday holy, and will not hunt or work on Sunday, except out of love of neighbor, or from dire necessity.
11. Whosoever tells stories about others' preparing poison, hunting people at night, and practicing witchcraft, must prove this before the committee, and he of whom such things are proved shall not live with us. If, however, the accuser has been found lying, we will regard him as a tool of the Devil who tries to destroy our love and our peace, and we will not tolerate such a person among us.[13]

These rules were subject to revision as circumstances might require.

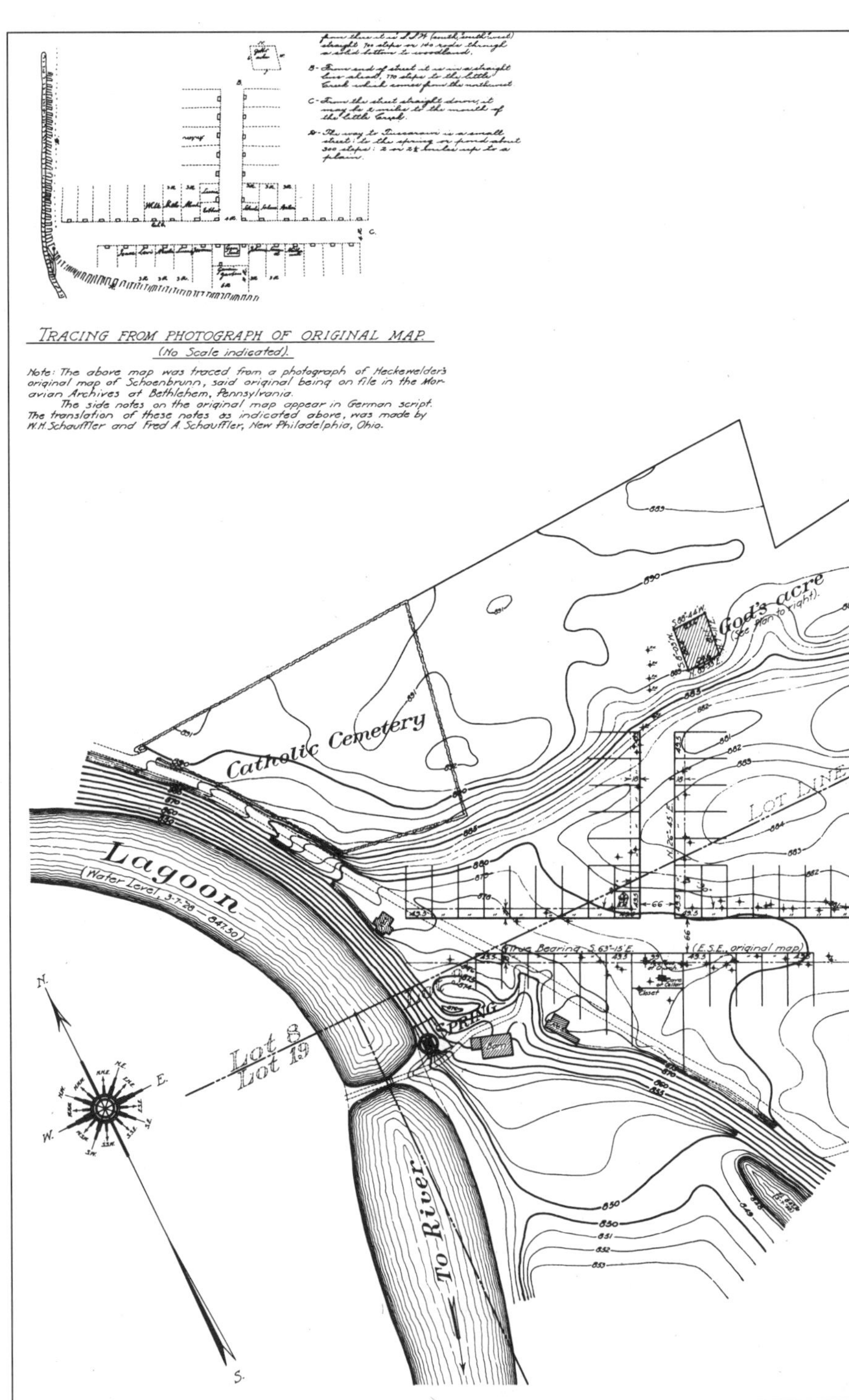

John Ettwein's 1772 map of Schoenbrunn, superimposed over a topographical map.

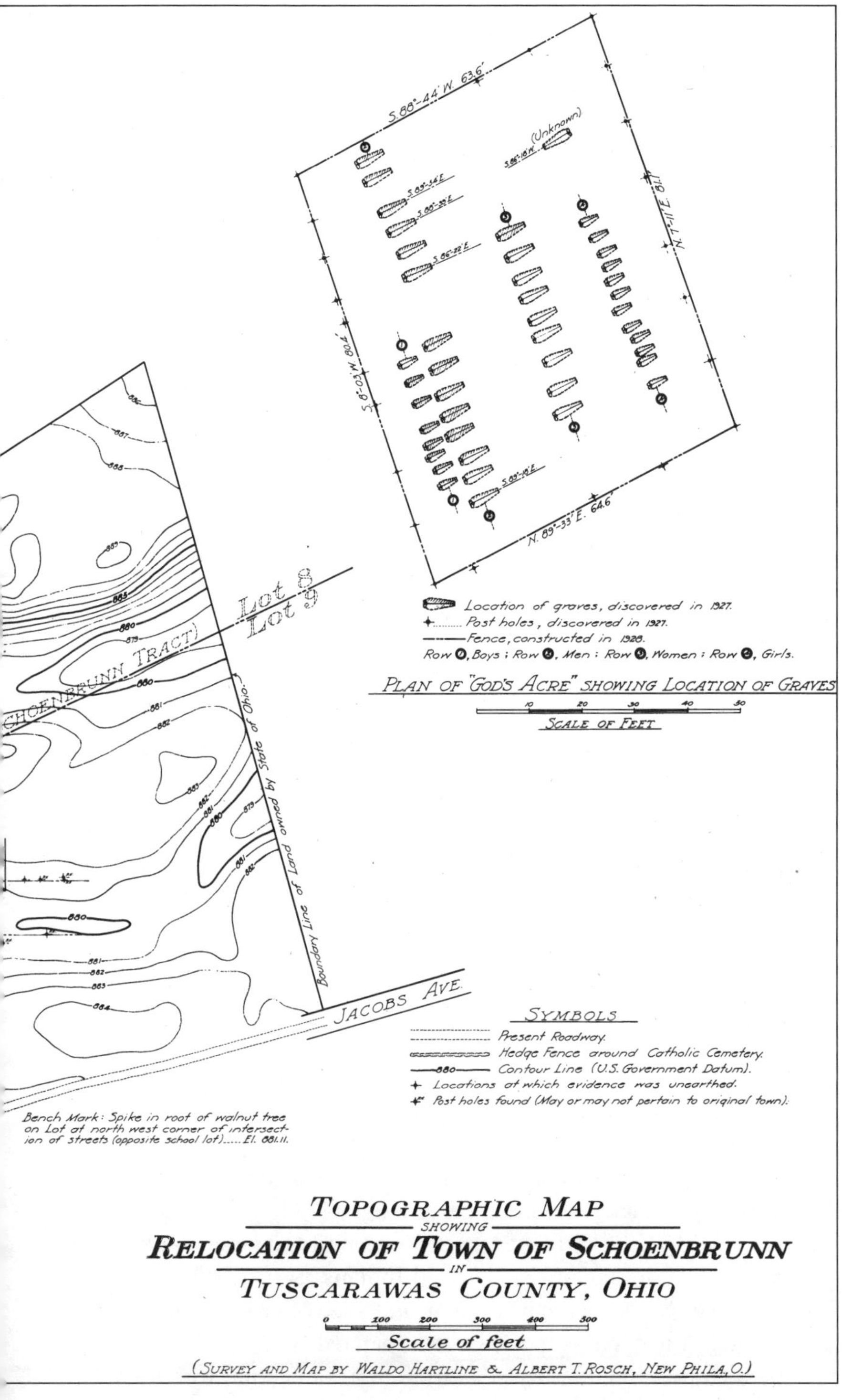

S. 88°-44' W. 63.6'
(Unknown)
N. 7°-11' E. 81.1'
S. 8°-03' W. 80.4'
N. 89°-33' E. 64.6'
Lot 8
Lot 9
SCHOENBRUNN TRACT
Boundary Line of Land owned by State of Ohio
JACOBS AVE.
Location of graves, discovered in 1927.
Post holes, discovered in 1927.
Fence, constructed in 1928.
Row 1, Boys ; Row 2, Men ; Row 3, Women ; Row 4, Girls.
PLAN OF "GOD'S ACRE" SHOWING LOCATION OF GRAVES
SCALE OF FEET
SYMBOLS
Present Roadway.
Hedge Fence around Catholic Cemetery.
Contour Line (U.S. Government Datum).
Locations at which evidence was unearthed.
Post holes found (May or may not pertain to original town).
Bench Mark: Spike in root of walnut tree on Lot at north west corner of intersection of streets (opposite school lot)..... El. 881.11.
TOPOGRAPHIC MAP
SHOWING
RELOCATION OF TOWN OF SCHOENBRUNN
IN
TUSCARAWAS COUNTY, OHIO
Scale of feet
(SURVEY AND MAP BY WALDO HARTLINE & ALBERT T. ROSCH, NEW PHILA, O.)

Courtesy of the Tuscarawas County Historical Society.

On Sunday, August 30, following the regular services, Zeisberger and Ettwein had a long discussion with the members of the Native Helpers' Conference. After the discussion they decided, by lot, that Zeisberger should begin, as soon as possible, a quick proselytizing trip among the Shawnees, their nearest neighbors. Perhaps he could find additional converts for the Lord.

Ettwein reluctantly left Schoenbrunn on September 3 and began his return journey to Lagundo Utenunk. When he returned to the Beaver several days later, a letter from David McClure was waiting for him. McClure was a young missionary who had recently graduated from Yale College and was now on a proselytizing trip among the Indians sponsored by the Scottish Society for the Furtherance of the Gospel. He promised to visit Lagundo Utenunk in a few days.[14]

McClure arrived near dusk on September 7 and was heartily welcomed by Ettwein. That evening the young missionary recorded this journal entry:

> It was a neat Moravian village, consisting of one street & houses pretty compact, on each side, with gardens in the back. There was a convenient Log church, with a small bell in which the Indians assembled in the morning and evening prayer. . . . They received me with great hospitality. At the sound of the bell, the Indians assembled in the church for evening prayer. It was lighted with candles around the walls, on which hung some common paintings of Jesus in the manger of Bethlehem with Joseph & Mary; Jesus on the cross & the resurrection &c. On one side set the elderly men & boys by themselves, & on the other the women & girls.

McClure stayed in the village for several days and left one of the most insightful and charitable observations ever recorded of a Moravian mission.

> The Moravians appear to have adopted the best mode of Christianizing the Indians. They go among them without noise and parade, & by their friendly behavior conciliate their good will. They join them in the chase, & freely distribute to the helpless & gradually instill into the minds of individuals, the principle of religions. They then invite those who are disposed to harken to them, to retire to some convenient place, at a distance from the wild Indians, & assist them to build a village, & teach them to plant and sow, & carry on some coarse manufactures. Those Indians, thus separated, reverence & love their instructors, as their fathers, & withdraw a connection with the wild or drinking Indians.[15]

Before Ettwein left the village to return to Bethlehem, Josua and his Mahicans arrived at Lagundo Utenunk. Ettwein spoke at length, first privately with Josua and later to his entire congregation, advising them that his plan to live separately from the Delawares had been approved and further encouraged by the missionaries. Josua and his congregation could expect the missionaries' full cooperation, and Ettwein assured him that a permanent missionary would be provided to his village as soon as possible. In the meantime, they were to go to Schoenbrunn for their communion or Zeisberger would come to them. Ettwein explained that he (Josua, Sr.) and Johannes Martin were to be head laymen (*Gemein-Diener*) of the congregation and that they would belong to the Helpers' Conference of Schoenbrunn.

Josua had sixteen families in his congregation, most of them former inhabitants of Gnadenhutten on the Mahoney. They proposed two names for the new village, Nain and Gnadenhutten. The Savior, by lot, preferred the latter.[16]

John Ettwein left the Beaver River valley on September 9, by way of Pittsburgh, and arrived at Bethlehem on September 25. He had been absent from Bethlehem since May 18. It had been an epic visit, unfortunately never to be duplicated in his lifetime.

On September 4, the day after Ettwein left Schoenbrunn, the converts vigorously began clearing lots and felling trees. Five days later they began the first round-log structure to be used exclusively for a meeting house, or church. The building was completed on September 19. Zeisberger continued to use the original structure built in June as his home.[17]

Josua's contingent of thirty-six Mahicans and a few Delawares arrived from Lagundo Utenunk on September 18 and spent the next few days exploring the neighborhood for a suitable site for their new village. They chose a location, temporarily to be called Upper Town, a few miles north of Schoenbrunn and on the west side of the Muskingum, near or possibly on the same location of present Dover, Ohio. News of the new village site had reached the Delaware capital, however, and Netawatwes was not pleased with the location. John Killbuck, Sr., a principal counselor to Netawatwes, visited the Upper Town on October 2 and told Josua: "That is not your proper place, and you will do well if you move; we are desirous of having our Grandchildren dwell near us. . . . We have decided on, and arranged for you a choice site to settle namely, the old town below Gekelemukpechunk Creek [the present Big Stillwater Creek]." Perplexed by the message, Josua checked with Zeisberger on how to respond. "We advised him to say that we were considering the words of the chief and that we would send him an answer in a few days."[18]

The Mahicans visited Netawatwes's proposed site on October 5 and were delighted with it. The site had a special ceremonial significance to the Delawares. It was there in 1769 that their previous head chief, Tamaqua, the Beaver, had lived and chosen to be buried. It was on a broad alluvial plain some fifty feet above the river and had some negative elements, which were quickly recognized by Zeisberger when he visited the site on October 10. The only water available was from the river, and the plantations would have to be located across the river from the village. Originally this land was not included in the grant given to the Moravians, but during Ettwein's visit, the chief had extended their territory to include the proposed new village. It was also some eight miles from Schoenbrunn, which would make it difficult for the missionaries to supervise. Despite his few objections, Zeisberger agreed with the selection and proceeded to the capital at Gekelemukpechunk with Josua and a delegation of his people to announce their acceptance of the site to the Delaware council. All the arrangements for the new village, to be called Gnadenhutten, were completed the next day to everyone's satisfaction.

Since the Jungmanns had arrived at Schoenbrunn on September 30, Zeisberger was free to begin the first of his two proselytizing trips to the Shawnees, which had been proposed by Ettwein and the Helpers' Conference. Before beginning the trip, it was politically necessary for him to consult the Delaware chief. In a private conversation with Netawatwes he suggested that he make such a visit and received a warm approval from the old chief. He left the capital on October 12, accompanied by Isaac Glikhikan and Joseph Peepe, both of whom spoke fluent Shawnee.

It was to be an informative five-day visit. Their destination was the Shawnee town of Wapatomica located on the Muskingum (near present Dresden, Ohio), approximately thirty-six miles below the Delaware capital. The village was referred to by the Indians as "Vomit Town." Vomiting, a symbolic gesture to purify one of sin, was induced with the aid of "Violent emetics." The Shawnees were not alone in this practice.[19]

Proceeding down the north bank of the Muskingum, near the forks, they encountered the old camp of Colonel Henry Bouquet. He had brought his army to this area in 1764 to subdue the Delawares and Shawnees following the Pontiac uprising.

The next morning, they arrived at the first Shawnee village. Ironically, the cabin they entered was the home of the son of the late chief Paxinosa, Zeisberger's old friend who lived in the Wyoming Valley back in 1754. The son recognized Zeisberger immediately and welcomed him with outstretched arms. They spent the evening in his home, talking of the Savior late into the night.

Toward noon, accompanied by their host, they arrived at Wapatomica, their destination. The little village contained seventeen cabins and huts, and nearby were three smaller Shawnee villages. The main Shawnee groups and the home of the head chief were on the Scioto River near present Chillicothe, Ohio.[20]

They spent two days with the Shawnees at Wapatomica and were treated with unusual warmth. Before leaving Wapatomica on October 16, Zeisberger had accepted a promise from the Shawnees that they would accept the Christian message, and he, in turn, pledged to do all in his power to send a missionary to their area. Leaving the village in high spirits, the travelers arrived back at Gnadenhutten on October 17 and were home at Schoenbrunn early in the evening to find that the first baby had been born there two days earlier to Anton and Julianna. He was baptized Joseph that evening. Two days following their return, Zeisberger, Isaac, and Schebosh traveled to Gekelemukpechunk to report the results of the Shawnee trip to Netawatwes.

The first of many white traders visited Schoenbrunn on November 16. Two days later, the annual fall hunt began. Most of the temporary homes required for the winter had been completed, but on December 22, enough hunters had returned to begin building the schoolhouse.[21]

The Christmas Eve love feast and the annual lighting of candles for the children preceded the baptism of three additional converts on Christmas Day. Communicants from Gnadenhutten arrived the following day and forty-nine converts took Holy Communion.

The joy of the holiday was somewhat dampened three days later with the first death at the new village. Catharina, the daughter of Samuel, died on December 28. After the consecration of the new cemetery, God's Acre, the little three-year-old was laid to rest.

Zeisberger closed his Schoenbrunn diary with the traditional year-end statistics. Johann and Anna Margareth Jungmann, with Heckewelder, had 92 converts at Schoenbrunn, Josua, Sr., supervised 94 at Gnadenhutten, and 115 remained with Johann and Marie Roth at Lagundo Utenunk. That made a total of 301 Moravian Christian Indians under Zeisberger's charge.[22]

· 17 ·

An Organizational Nightmare, 1773

David Zeisberger faced three formidable tasks at the beginning of 1773. Transferring the 115 converts from Lagundo Utenunk to the Muskingum Valley was the first priority. Adequate housing at both Gnadenhutten and Schoenbrunn had to be quickly built to accommodate these new arrivals. Second, another missionary must be sent from Bethlehem to cope with the rapidly expanding population at both villages. Temporarily, Johann Roth, who was coming from Lagundo Utenunk, could fill in at Gnadenhutten until the new man arrived. Finally, new and larger split-log community buildings, including churches, schoolhouses, and missionary homes, had to be built to accommodate the new activities at both villages.

Living conditions at Lagundo Utenunk were deteriorating because of drunkenness and general rowdiness. The weather had moderated sufficiently by the middle of March to begin preparations to relocate the converts. On March 24, Heckewelder, who is seldom mentioned in the Schoenbrunn diary during this early period, led a party of brothers and sisters to the Beaver River mission to assist the moving operation.[1] By April 13, both parties were on the trail to the Muskingum Valley. One party, led by Roth, traveled by land; the other, led by Heckewelder in twenty-two canoes, traveled by water.[2] The Roth contingent arrived at

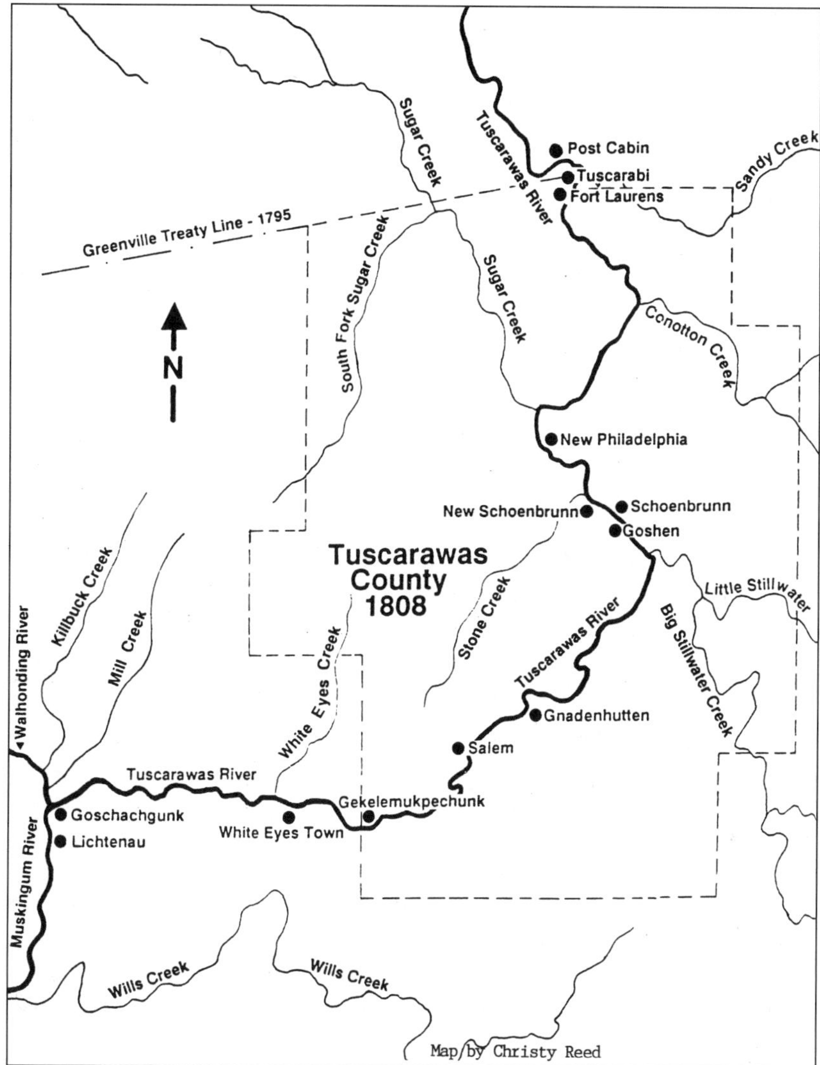

Moravian mission sites in the Tuscarawas Valley, 1772–1821. Courtesy of the Tuscarawas County Historical Society.

Schoenbrunn on April 24, the Heckewelder canoe party eleven days later.[3] The exact number of converts who made the move is not known, but there were 115 living at Lagundo Utenunk at the end of 1772.[4] Most of them were probably now at either Schoenbrunn or Gnadenhutten. Certainly the Mahicans followed Josua and resided at the lower village.

Heckewelder left a record of his waterborne party's travels down the Ohio and up the Muskingum, similar to the trip he had made with the original Schoenbrunn travelers in April the previous year.[5] They pushed away from the banks of the Beaver on April 13 and reached the Ohio River four days later. Along the eastern side of the river, they noticed occasional cabins and plantations of white settlers. The Zane brothers, Ebenezer, Jonathan, and Silas, lived at Wheeling, where they had staked out a claim three years earlier. Michael Cresap and his family, who had moved from Maryland, lived near Grave Creek, at present Moundsville, West Virginia. In the last five years the western-bound settlers had reached the eastern banks of the Ohio. But Heckewelder discovered no whites living on the western banks in what was clearly recognized as Indian territory.[6]

By April 19 they passed the present location of McMechen, West Virginia, just south of Wheeling. That evening they camped on the western shore of the river. Shortly after they arrived, six white men called to them from the eastern bank. Since the river was too wide to hear what they were saying, Heckewelder, Anton, and Boas, another convert, paddled across and spent several hours in conversation. The river residents were full of questions about the converts. What kind of Indians were these? Where were they going? Were they the Moravian Indians? Were their ministers with them? Of what religion were their teachers? Did they receive a salary from the king or from a certain society? How were they supported? Could their teachers talk with them in their language? Did they truly believe that there is a God in Heaven? Did they let themselves be baptized? For the next hour Heckewelder answered such questions. Finally, as night approached, they told Heckewelder, "It cannot in the least be questioned that God is with you and blesses your work."[7]

The next day, they were running short of food when they passed a small island in the river. Using a favorite Indian ploy, they encircled the island with the canoes and put "some people with a few hounds [first mention of dogs] ashore whereupon at once four deer jumped into the water, three of which we obtained."[8] By noon on April 22, they had reached the mouth of the Muskingum, having traveled by water some 160 miles.

Now they were traveling upstream, and fatigue began to take its toll on the paddle and pole men. By noon on April 25, they stopped and set up camp beside a huge rock that protruded into the river. Heckewelder observed: "Some of the Brethren at once built a sweating-oven, to sweat out their fatigue; others went out hunting and encountered buffaloes, at which they shot, but without success."[9]

Three days later they camped at the junction of Salt Creek and the Muskingum, near the present site of Duncan Falls, Ohio. They had experienced several severe rains so the grain they were carrying had become damp and was beginning to sprout. Two days were spent drying the precious seeds, the source of next year's food supply. During this time, Heckewelder explored the Indian salt springs in the area. He also noted outcroppings of coal.[10]

On April 30 they visited the Shawnee town of Wapatomica, the same village Zeisberger had visited the previous October. The following day they visited another Shawnee town. Heckewelder noted, "I visited a white man who is living there, and who has a white wife; she had been a prisoner and cannot talk anything but Shawnee." Heckewelder had met Richard and Polly Conner, who would later play an important role in the Moravian mission history. Three days later they arrived at the Delaware capital of Gekelemukpechunk. Heckewelder wrote that he "counted 106 spectators" on the banks of the river. They visited both Netawatwes and Killbuck, pressed on to Gnadenhutten on May 4, dropped off several families, then continued on to Schoenbrunn, arriving on May 5.

Even before the Heckewelder contingent arrived, Zeisberger had begun to reorganize the two villages, designating Roth and his wife to minister at Gnadenhutten. The Roths left Schoenbrunn for their new assignment on April 26. For most of the previous year Zeisberger and Jungmann had been traveling regularly to Gnadenhutten, sharing the ministerial duties at both missions. To the great relief of both men, on May 1, 1773, Johann Roth began his tenure at the Gnadenhutten mission.[11] Only four months into the new year, Zeisberger had completed two of his major tasks for the year. The Beaver River converts were safely in the Muskingum Valley, and the Gnadenhutten mission had a temporary missionary.

Zeisberger now turned to the third item on the year's agenda, the construction of the permanent split-log private homes and community buildings. Like all previous Moravian missions, there were four classes of Indians living at the mission villages: the communicants, the baptized, the candidates for baptism, and natives given permission to live at the village as long as their behavior complied with the rules of the missions. To accommodate all these residents, each community required private homes and outbuildings, public structures such as the schoolhouse and church (Gemeinhaus) as well as semipublic homes for the missionaries. Fences were also required to guard the town site, the plantations, and a cemetery.[12]

In 1773 permanent split-log public structures were built at Schoenbrunn. Most were traditional Indian huts and round-log buildings such as the temporary church. Because of the varied configurations of round logs, the temporary buildings were difficult to caulk and were not secure against the elements. This problem was overcome in the permanent buildings by using split or square-hewn logs that were easier to caulk. The tools for doing square-log construction had been left back at Grand Island (Lock Haven, Pennsylvania). On September 9, Zeisberger dispatched two of his most faithful converts, Nathanael Davis and Anton, the son of Joseph Peepe, to bring the tools. They returned on October 9. On September 14, the Brethren began cutting trees for the new church. After the tools arrived, the building, forty by thirty-six feet, was completed, including the shingle roof and a cupola that held the bell. On October 24, forty-one days after they cut the first log, the new church was completed and dedicated.[13] Zeisberger noted sometime later "that the Schoenbrunn church could accommodate 300 worshipers." Four glass windows adorned the building, the glass having been requisitioned from Bethlehem and the frames made by the village carpenters.[14]

The diaries are less specific about the construction of the Schoenbrunn school. The building was begun on December 22, 1772, and completed July 29, 1773.[15] The split-logging tools did not arrive until October 1773 so this was certainly a round-log structure. On December 4, 1775, Zeisberger wrote that "nearly one hundred children" attended the session that began that day.[16]

Zeisberger's diaries give little information on the construction of fences. On May 15, 1773, he noted that fencing had been completed, enclosing eighty acres of plantation. On March 3, 1774, the fence surrounding the cemetery was completed. Archaeological excavations in the 1920s, 1930s, and 1950s indicate that the entire village was encircled with a fence, which was the normal practice for all mission villages.

Now that the Moravians were firmly ensconced on the Muskingum, the Christian converts looked to the Delaware capital to confirm their status as approved and legal residents of the Delaware Nation. The initiative came from the Helpers' Conference, not Zeisberger. On June 1, he recorded: "For quite some time our Indian Brethren had considered it good and necessary that we should convey another declaration [message] to the Chief in Gekelemukpechunk because he had not replied to all of our words, and we had been waiting for a good opportunity to express our opinion. . . . It was the proper time to define our stand."[17] Traditional Indian protocol required that the Delaware council grant formal approval, which it had not yet done.

Zeisberger delegated Johannes Papunhank, Isaac Glikhikan, Wilhelm (Billy) Chelloway, and Joseph Peepe to carry the request to the Delaware council. Isaac was appointed as the spokesman. They stopped at Gnadenhutten, where two additional converts joined the party. They were prob-

Reconstructed Schoenbrunn Village, 1982. Photograph by Carl Kempt.

ably Johannes Martin and Marcus, the Mahican who usually represented Gnadenhutten at the council meetings. Strangely, Josua, Sr., the most powerful convert among the Mahicans, refused to join the group. Roth, who was now the head missionary at Gnadenhutten, does not explain why. On June 3, the delegates appeared before the full council.

Isaac's remarks were straightforward, with none of the restraint shown in traditional council oratory. He reviewed the historical relationship between the Christians and the native Indian groups up to the previous year, then continued:

> A year ago we gave a declaration to the same effect to you in your council, when our friends and brethren from the Susquehanna arrived here whom you invited; all of which, I'm sure, is still in your memory. Yet, you have replied to us not a single word although it is almost a year since. . . . Friends, we want to inform you that we have accepted the holy and saving words of God, not only with our mouths but with

> our entire heart. The word which God has sent us we have brought along with us here and we shall hold on to it as to a great treasure which we have found, and shall continue to do so until the end of our lives. Now who ever among the Indians wishes to hear and accept it willingly, let him come to us. We are going to take great pleasure in giving him instructions.

He then presented a beautiful belt of wampum and admonished the Delawares to send it to their grandchildren, the Shawnees, and to their uncles, the Wyandots. He closed his speech by informing the council members of the pending arrival of the Schmicks, who would replace the Roths as the missionaries at Gnadenhutten.

> My friends, your grandchildren, the Mahicans, who live near you [the Gnadenhutten converts], had for quite some time been obliged to be without a teacher because they had left theirs behind when they moved out here from the Susquehanna. The one who came to them only a little time ago has only been lent to them since we had compassion on them because they had to be all by themselves. Let us tell you, therefore, that soon they are going to call for their teacher and bring him here.[18]

The following day the council responded to Isaac's speech. Echpalawehund was the speaker. He told the Christians that their messages had not been forgotten and said that the council would send a wampum belt to their respective grandchildren, the Shawnees, and their uncles, the Wyandots, and await their reply. He advised, "I consider it unnecessary that my grandchildren, the Mahican, want to have another teacher, and if they bring some more these will preach to them the same thing." (This was probably not Echpalawehund's own opinion because he was a special friend of the Moravians. He undoubtedly had been instructed to respond in this fashion.) Isaac answered the last remark by telling the council, "All we have wished to do was to inform you about this. Whether your grandchildren are satisfied with your reply or not, we do not know. Let them speak for themselves." Since Josua, their usual spokesmen, had not accompanied the delegation, the matter rested. This question was resolved four days later, when Josua, Isaac, Marcus, and Johannes returned to the capital and received Netawatwes's reluctant permission for the missionary to be stationed at Gnadenhutten.

This conference was remarkable for the frankness and sense of confidence displayed by the Christians. At least for the present, they seemed to be in charge of their own destiny. We must remember, however, that Zeisberger, the author of the diary, was not at the conference and received his information from his delegates. If the meeting was objectively reported by Isaac and dispassionately recorded by Zeisberger, it seems reasonable to conclude that Isaac's remarks were delivered from a position of strength.

On June 10, five days after the conference, Johannes Martin and Wilhelm Chelloway were on the road again, accompanied by Nicholas Smaan. They set out for Bethlehem, where they would meet Johann and Johanna Schmick and escort them to their new missionary assignment at Gnadenhutten. Martin, Chelloway, and Smaan arrived with the Schmicks at their new pastorate on August 16. Accompanying them was John Jungmann, the twenty-four-year-old son of the Jungmanns, who served at Schoenbrunn. He was about to learn his father's profession.[19]

During the latter part of July and the first week in August, a delegation of Quakers arrived at the Delaware capital to talk with the old chief and request permission to send several preachers to the village. Never one to pass up any opportunity, Netawatwes expanded the discussion to include not only ministers but artisans who would teach the Indians "all kinds of trades and crafts so that they might become orderly people." In recent months the chief had become obsessed with the idea of going to England and having a "man to man" talk with the king. He "demanded" that the Quakers assist him in this project. Quickly retreating, the Quakers excused themselves, saying "that it was neither their business nor within their competence" to become involved with such a scheme. In reporting the incident, Zeisberger wrote, "The Indians are not so much concerned about hearing the Gospel as they are by means thereof to secure presents and under the appearance of good intentions to seek to profit in externals."[20] Thus ended the Philadelphia Quakers' interest in the valley Indians.

The Schmicks, who arrived on August 10, settled in quickly at Gnadenhutten. Johann visited Zeisberger two days after they arrived, and the two men spent the day planning their strategy for the coming months. They had known each other intimately for twenty-two years. Schmick, perhaps one of the most underrecognized of all the Moravian missionaries, was an ordained minister and a graduate of Koenigsburg University in Germany. He first met Zeisberger in 1751.[21] When Nathaniel Seidel and Zeisberger visited Zinzendorf at Herrnhut in the summer of that same year, Schmick had returned with them on the *Irene*. This was the beginning of a long and successful, but on rare occasions, stormy relationship. Each had great respect for the other's talents. Schmick had been in the mission field for most of the twenty-two years he had been in America and had just finished a six-year stint at Friedenshutten. Most of the Indians now at Gnadenhutten

Johann Jacob Schmick (1714–1778) and Johanna Schmick (1721–1795). Courtesy of the Moravian Church Archives.

had been in his former congregation. He was also an accomplished musician with a charming voice and a skilled carpenter. But he had an independent personality and at times seems to have chafed under Zeisberger's supervision.[22] Otherwise it was a combination that worked well.

Schmick's organizational skills were promptly put to use, and a bustle of building activity consumed his time over the next several months. By August 23, seven days after his arrival, plans for the new church had been completed. The building, constructed in less than twenty days, was 32 feet long and 27 feet wide and, like the Schoenbrunn church, had a cupola with a bell and four glass windows. The 854-square-foot structure was slightly smaller than the 1,440-square-foot Schoenbrunn house of worship.

The schoolhouse at Gnadenhutten was not started until early in 1774. Schmick's diary notes: "Jan. 3rd, the Brethren decided to build a school house and to start a collection of deer skins for defraying of public expenses. Jan. 4th, they squared logs for the school house. Some of the Brethren carried those to the building site and began to block up the structure."[23]

Reconstructed Gnadenhutten Church. Photograph by the author.

Reconstructed Gnadenhutten Cooper House. Photograph by the author.

By February 16, 1774, Schmick wrote sadly, "The school house is not yet completed." Apparently the building was finished sometime during May. As with the Schoenbrunn school, there is no record of the size of the Gnadenhutten building.[24]

While Schmick was getting his house in order at Gnadenhutten, Zeisberger, at Schoenbrunn, continued working on his own agenda. The decision had been made to make another visit to the Shawnees. On September 17 Zeisberger, accompanied by Isaac Glikhikan and Billy Chelloway, two of his most trusted assistants, left on that mission. Arriving that afternoon at the Delaware capital, they spent the rest of the day at the village. It would prove to be one of the most rewarding days of Zeisberger's life because that evening he met for the first time Captain White Eyes, Koquethagachtoon (Coo-quet-ha-kex-toon). White Eyes, who lived six miles up-river from the Delaware capital, was one of Netawatwes's most trusted counselors. In the next five years, he would play a prominent role in Zeisberger's life and would also dominate political discussions at the Delaware council.[25]

White Eyes was a complicated man, full of contradictions, which sometimes drove Zeisberger to distraction. Extremely intelligent and ambitious, he mastered the English language and numerous native dialects. Christian Frederick Post met him in 1762 and described him as "one of the cleverest Indians I ever met." David Jones, during his first trip into the Indian country in 1772, wrote, "He was the only Indian I met within my travels that seemed to have a design of accomplishing something in the future." Zeisberger called him "a sensible man."[26]

White Eyes had just returned from a trip down the Ohio and the Mississippi to New Orleans, then by boat to New York, returning home via Philadelphia. When he arrived in Pittsburgh, he met the Quaker party mentioned above and guided them to the Muskingum.[27] His trip to New Orleans, New York, and Philadelphia dramatically changed White Eyes's life. He had observed white culture and civilization and longed to bring some of this way of life to his own people. This trip was the source of White Eyes's dream someday to propose a separate fourteenth colony to be set aside especially for the Indians, which was never to come to fruition.

The Zeisberger party arrived at Wapatomica on September 20, where they met one of the principal Shawnee chiefs, Kishenatsi, a known enemy of the Gospel. The chief and his party were on their way to the Delaware capital for a conference with Netawatwes. Zeisberger's meeting with the Shawnee chief proved to be a disaster. Pointing his finger at the missionary, the chief recited a long litany of abuses the Indians had suffered at the hands of the white man. Most of his charges were true, although he did not condemn Zeisberger personally. The next day he permitted Isaac and Zeisberger to speak in a formal council, but no minds were changed. The chief finally said, "You might as well go to our towns. I will not forbid it." Then he turned to Isaac and Chelloway and said, "You may conduct him there, but you must expect that they will brain him." Zeisberger was a brave man, but he was not a fool. They stayed for several more days, then departed for home on September 22 and never again attempted to preach to the Shawnees.[28]

At the end of the year Zeisberger and Schmick recorded their customary statistics and a summary of principal events. The population figures at each village were as follows:

Village	*Baptized*	*Communicants*	*Miscellaneous* *	*Total*
Schoenbrunn	56	50	78	184
Gnadenhutten	52	31	25	108
Total	108	81	103	292
Percent of total	37	28	35	100

* Candidates for baptism and/or persons given permission to live at the village (see Appendix E).[29]

Of the fifteen deaths during the year at Schoenbrunn, one is of particular interest. Anton, who died on September 5, represented the first of two generations of Indians that passed through David Zeisberger's life. Over the next several years, many more would be buried alongside Anton in the Schoenbrunn cemetery, but none played a more prominent role in Zeisberger's life than he did. He was baptized in Bethlehem on February 13, 1750, by Bishop Cammerhoff. From the day of his baptism, he seldom left Zeisberger's side. In all the Zeisberger missions Anton was always with his "beloved teacher." When Zeisberger made his first trip to the Allegheny in 1767, Anton was his guide. When they returned in 1768, Anton followed Zeisberger until they arrived at Schoenbrunn in 1772, where Anton served as one of the missionary's principal advisers. He was seventy-six at his death, and Zeisberger closed his long obituary: "Although his demise is painful to us, yet we are glad for him to have found peace and the great happiness of being at home with the Lord. His body was buried, on the 6th, in the presence of numerous people."[30] His grave was one of the first uncovered during the excavations in 1927.

· 18 ·

Lord Dunmore and His Shawnee Indian War, 1774

A GREAT feeling of optimism permeated the Muskingum Valley at the beginning of the new year. Both Schoenbrunn and Gnadenhutten continued to receive new residents, and additional baptized converts were added to the ever-growing congregation.

Chief Newallike, their old nemesis on the Susquehanna, arrived at Schoenbrunn on March 11, after almost a two-year journey from his home at Grand Island on the west branch of the Susquehanna, bringing his entire family.[1] At a meeting of the Helpers' Conference a few days later, he explained, "For three years, they had thought about it, feeling a call in their hearts to come to us and believe in the Savior." They were welcomed with "open arms" by the residents. Zeisberger baptized him Augustinus on May 12. Newallike had played a prominent, albeit rather contentious, role in Zeisberger's life during his stay at Friedenshutten. But he was an important subchief of the Delaware Nation and his presence added prestige to the mission village. Zeisberger and the Helpers' Conference could hardly refuse his request to join them. Three years later, they would regret that decision.[2]

The general aura of optimism that pervaded the valley for the first three months of the year was brought to a sudden end in April and May. On

April 30 Jungmann and Schebosh returned from Pittsburgh with information that shocked the residents at both villages. Zeisberger noted:

> Through them we received the news that there had been a change in the government there, so that henceforth it should belong to Virginia. We learned also, that conditions among the Shawnee were looking serious, for it is suspected that they will attack the new settlements of the white people down by the Ohio, across from them, for it is a thorn in their flesh. A message has, however been sent by [Sir William] Johnson to the other nations, warning them not to ally themselves with the Shawnee.[3]

The change of management at Fort Pitt might cause political problems for the missionaries, and a war with the Shawnees could threaten the safety and existence of both missions, especially if the Delawares became involved. The intelligence that Jungmann and Schebosh received at Fort Pitt proved to be accurate.

The controversy between Pennsylvania and Virginia regarding the land on which the fort sat had its origin in the grants from the English monarch. Virginia relied on its charter granted by James I in 1606 and modified in 1609. Pennsylvania's claim came from the charter granted by Charles II in 1681. Pennsylvania contended that its western boundaries extended several miles west of Fort Pitt, while Virginia insisted that its land embraced not only the fort but all of the country west of the Laurel Hills, including Ohio.[4] As long as the crown forces occupied the land following the French and Indian War, the controversy between the two colonies never came to an open dispute.

In 1774 the dispute broke into the open. The British government in London, searching for any opportunity to reduce the expense of maintaining armies in the West, made the decision to abandon Fort Pitt and sell off the king's property at the site. On October 10, 1772, the British commander, Captain Charles Edmondstone, began to dismantle and dispose of the crown property.[5] A few days later, leaving behind a corporal's guard of three men to protect the remaining fortifications, he returned to the East. This divestiture of the last royal interest at the forks created an ownership vacuum between the colonies of Virginia and Pennsylvania.

Shortly after Captain Edmondstone departed, a citizen of Pittsburgh, Captain Edward Ward, occupied the decaying fortification. Ironically, he was the same man who, as a twenty-one-year-old ensign, surrendered the fort to the French in April 1754.[6] Ward remained at the site undisturbed for a year. Then late in 1773, Dr. John Connolly stepped into the void created by the departure of the British force.[7]

Connolly arrived at the fort commanding a contingent of Virginia militia under the authority of Lord Dunmore, the governor of the colony of Virginia. He seized the installation, renaming it Fort Dunmore and, as the self-appointed commandant, issued a proclamation calling for the people to meet him to organize a local militia on January 25, 1774. In response, Arthur St. Clair, a magistrate of Westmoreland County, Pennsylvania, which included Fort Pitt, issued a warrant for Connolly's arrest and tossed him into the Hanna's Town jail.[8] Connolly posted bail and was released. He left for Staunton, Virginia, where he was sworn in as a justice of the peace of West Augusta County, which, as Virginia claimed, embraced the land surrounding Fort Pitt. During the latter part of March, he returned to Pittsburgh armed with both civil and military authority to put the laws of Virginia into force in the Pittsburgh area.[9]

In the meantime, a messenger was sent to Philadelphia to inform Governor Penn of the new developments. On January 31, 1774, Penn wrote a diplomatic letter to Governor Dunmore requesting him to refrain from appointing officers at Pittsburgh until a temporary line could be drawn to clarify the situation.[10]

While Penn and Dunmore corresponded, the regular session of the Pennsylvania court met at Hanna's Town on April 5, 1774. Just after the session began, Connolly appeared with a militia of 150 men and stopped the court's deliberations. The three Hanna's Town justices, Eaneas Mackay, Devereux Smith, and Andrew McFarlane, returned to their homes in Pittsburgh on April 8 and were arrested the following day by Connolly's sheriff. They were carted off, under guard, to Staunton, Virginia. Mackay was given permission to go by way of Williamsburg to confer with Dunmore, who released the three men with assurances that he would be "personally answerable for appearance in case it be required." The three men were back in Pittsburgh by early June, and Mackay fired off an angry letter to Governor Penn on June 14: "The deplorable state of affairs in this part of your government, is truly distressing. We are robbed, insulted and dragooned by Connolly and his militia, in this place and its environs."[11] Mackay's letter was written shortly after Jungmann and Schebosh had visited the fort.

By the spring of 1774, both Lord Dunmore and his agent John Connolly were planning the events that would soon precipitate Dunmore's War with the Shawnee Nation. Zeisberger's and Schmick's diaries give a picture of how these activities affected both the Shawnee and Delaware Nations and the Christian missions during this period.

Lord Dunmore, 1732–1809. From the *Ohio Archeological and Historical Society Publications*, 1899.

It had been eleven years since the Pontiac uprising, and during that time relative peace reigned along the Indian frontier. Immediately following the Pontiac uprising, George III's ministers issued the Proclamation of 1763. It was an idealistic dream, which was supposed to constrain the westward movement of white settlers beyond the Allegheny Mountains into Indian territory. The Treaty of Fort Stanwix, signed in 1768, extended the original proclamation line westward to free all of the land east of the Ohio River

William Crawford, 1732–1782. From the *Ohio Archeological and Historical Society Publications*, 1898.

for white occupation, including a large portion of the Kentucky country down to the Tennessee River. Unfortunately, that treaty was negotiated with the Six Nation confederacy, whose ancient claim of ownership gave them the title, not the Shawnee Nation, which considered the land its personal hunting grounds. In October 1770, another treaty at Lockabar, negotiated with the Cherokees, also granted Kentucky land to the white settlers. Again the Shawnees were not consulted.

Lord Dunmore was at a loss to explain the insatiable demand for land by the westward-bound American pioneers. He once wrote to Lord Dartmouth, his immediate superior, "They acquire no attachment to Place: But wandering about seems engraved in their Nature; and it is a weakness incident to it, that they Should for ever imagine the Lands further off, are Still better than those upon which they are already Settled." He seems puzzled by the settlers' lack of respect for a government of laws in the vast "uninhabited" land that lay to the west. "They do not conceive that government has any right to forbid their taking possession of a vast tract of Country, either uninhabited, or which Serves only as a Shelter to a few Scattered Tribes of Indians. Nor can they be easily brought to entertain any belief of the permanent obligation of Treaties made with those people, whom they consider, as but little removed from brute Creations."[12]

Most of the settlers referred to in Dunmore's letter were the pioneer backwoodsmen of either German or Scotch-Irish origin then living on the edge of white civilization. They were scattered along the banks of the Ohio River or traveling across the Cumberland Gap and the Wilderness Trail bound for the new Kentucky territory. Dunmore's assessment of them was accurate. These were tenacious people, fiercely individualistic, and with virtually no respect for the law.

Wheeling, founded in 1769 by Ebenezer Zane, was a small backwoods settlement with a handful of permanent residents. The frontier town was the western terminus of the Cumberland and Redstone Trail and in the spring of 1774 was jammed with Kentucky-bound immigrants. The Cresaps seemed to be in charge. Connolly wrote to them from Pittsburgh informing them that a war with the Indians was feared at any moment. On April 24 or 25, another letter with a more urgent tone arrived from Connolly. The frontiersmen took it as a declaration of war. Connolly's letter was addressed to the inhabitants of Wheeling and reported that he "had been informed, by good authority, that the *Shawanese* were ill disposed toward white men" and that he expected the people to be ready "to repel any insults that might be offered" by the Indians.[13]

Jungmann and Schebosh had left Schoenbrunn in the heart of the Indian country for Pittsburgh on April 20. They would have been in the city by April 21 during the time Connolly wrote these letters. They probably left Pittsburgh on April 29 and arrived back in Schoenbrunn April 30. Not one entry in either the Schoenbrunn or the Gnadenhutten diaries during the first four months of 1774 contains any reference to hostile activities by the Shawnees against the settlers on the eastern frontier. After May 1, 1774, hardly a day went by without some reference to the impending war in both diaries.[14]

Although the Shawnees had molested settlers floating down the Ohio during the previous year, it would appear that Connolly had manufactured the recent reports about Shawnee depredations so as to inflame the frontiersmen. Twenty-two-year-old George Rogers Clark would later write: "The reception of this letter was the epoch of open hostilities with the Indians. A new post was planted [as a Shawnee declaration of war], a council was called and the letter read by Cresap. All the Indian traders being summoned on so important an occasion, action was had and war declared in the most solemn manner; and the same evening two scalps were brought into camp."[15]

The two scalps mentioned in Clark's letter were taken on the same day that Cresap and his men recognized the declaration. The attack probably took place on April 25 or 26. In the first blood spilled during the war, one Delaware and one Shawnee were killed.[16] The following day, the Cresap men received intelligence that a party of fourteen Indians had stopped at Cresap's plantation at Graves Creek (Moundsville, West Virginia), approximately fourteen miles below Wheeling. Cresap and his men set out in pursuit. They attacked the Indians and killed one Shawnee chief and a white man and collected considerable plunder. It would appear that this was a Shawnee delegation returning from a conference with Alexander McKee, the British Indian agent at Pittsburgh.[17] Zeisberger, in Schoenbrunn, received the news on May 8. He noted, "A Shawnee Chief had been killed by the white people along the Ohio, and another had been wounded."[18]

The day after the attack on the Shawnee chiefs, the Cresap party decided to march on Chief Logan's camp at the mouth of Yellow Creek (near present Wellsville, Ohio), some forty miles above Wheeling. Logan was a Mingo, the celebrated son of the famous Chief Shickellamy, who was a close friend of David Zeisberger. These Indians were members of the Six Nations and had committed even less offense than the Shawnees. As the Cresap party proceeded up the river and approached the village, their hostility began to diminish. After all, these Indians did not have anything to do with Kentucky land. They finally turned around and returned home.[19] But Logan and his family and friends were not to escape the wrath of their white neighbors across the river at Baker's plantation.

For some time the Logan camp on the west side of the river had carried on amicable relations with the Bakers, their neighbors across the Ohio.

The Indians frequently crossed the river to get liquor and other supplies for the men of the tribe and milk for the children. One of the babies was the son of John Gibson, a popular trader with the Indians, and his Indian wife, the sister of Logan.[20]

On April 30, two Indian men and two women, one of them Logan's sister with her baby, crossed the river to make a friendly visit and buy supplies. Exactly what happened next is open to speculation. All accounts claim the Indians were drunk and were fired upon by the whites after they had discharged their guns in a shooting match. All were killed except the baby. As the day passed, two more Indians crossed the river to check on the first party, and they were shot, which aroused their friends on the other side. Five more soon crossed and met fire that killed two and wounded three. At least eight and possibly thirteen Indians were murdered. Most accounts list the fatalities at twelve. The killings have been attributed to a party of settlers led by Daniel Greathouse.[21]

The slaughter at Baker's plantation evoked genuine shock and revulsion among the white community, especially in the eastern settlements, but there was little or nothing that could be done. Most citizens knew it was all part of Connolly's plan to incite the Shawnees.

Zeisberger received the news on May 8, eight days after the massacre. A special messenger was sent by Netawatwes from the Delaware capital informing him that "white people along the Ohio had killed nine Mingoes and wounded two." The message also contained word from the Shawnee chief, who advised the Delawares to remain calm and permit the traders to come to their villages. The Shawnees further advised, "Do not put anything in their [the traders'] way nor in the way of other white people who were here."[22]

The following day an embassy from Pittsburgh, led by Captain White Eyes, arrived at Schoenbrunn. The captain had been employed by George Croghan and Alexander McKee in hope of counteracting or at least partially circumventing the plans of the ambitious Connolly. McKee was the deputy Indian agent at Pittsburgh, and Croghan had previously held the same office. White Eyes commanded great respect among the neighboring Indian tribes, and that was why the Indian agents employed him to conduct negotiations with the Shawnees and Mingoes. He also was to try to keep his own tribe, the Delawares, neutral. Ultimately, the plan worked, but it played directly into Connolly's hand by isolating the Shawnees, leaving them to fight their battle alone. McKee and Croghan were primarily concerned with the safety of a large body of white traders still living among the Shawnees. Accompanying White Eyes were the trader

John Duncan and the Quaker Indian trader John Anderson, who was highly respected by the Moravians.

The Moravian diaries for the next six months clearly show the important role the Christian Indians played in assisting White Eyes with his negotiations. The captain's friendship with the convert Isaac Glikhikan was especially useful. These men were long-standing and intimate comrades. They had worked together in numerous efforts to maintain peace among the various local Indian tribes, and both commanded the respect of the Shawnees and Mingoes. Both men had great influence with their own tribe.[23]

On May 10, Whites Eyes's peace delegation departed from Schoenbrunn bound for the Shawnee villages. After leaving the Delaware capital, the party was fired on by Mingo warriors. Fearing for their safety, White Eyes instructed Duncan and Anderson to remain behind at New Comers' Town, where they were taken under protective custody, and the captain continued on alone to the Shawnee village at Wapatomica.[24]

At this time, the main Shawnee villages, called the lower towns, were located on the Scioto River near present Chillicothe, Ohio, where their head chief, Cornstalk, lived. A smaller set of upper villages, those that Zeisberger had visited the previous year, were at Wapatomica, near present Dresden, Ohio. On arrival at the upper villages, White Eyes received a less than cordial welcome and was peremptorily ordered out of the territory. The hostile attitude that he encountered was nurtured by the numerous Mingoes, who had just retreated to this area following the Logan massacre and were now living among the Shawnees. Many had lost relatives and friends at the Yellow Creek massacre. He did learn, however, that the lower villages were peaceful and not inclined toward war.

White Eyes was back in Pittsburgh on May 24, bringing with him ten white traders who had been held by the Delawares for eight days under protective custody at New Comers' Town. These were a few of the traders whom the Shawnees had protected while working their way back toward Pittsburgh.[25] He reported to McKee and Croghan the latest disappointing news from the Shawnee country along with assurances of neutrality from the Delawares. He also brought word on the activities of the Mingo chief Logan. The chief had not been at Yellow Creek during the massacre of his family. Upon hearing the news, he vowed to seek retribution in kind. Furthermore, he promised not to talk to any of the chiefs until he had done so.[26]

Logan was not long in finding easy victims to satisfy his lust for revenge. A typical attack occurred on June 6, 1774, at Muddy Creek, near where the Cheat River empties into the Monongahela. A man, his wife, and their three children were brutally killed and scalped; three other children were captured and later found dead. The incident was attributed to the Logan band.[27] By June 22, intelligence reached Pittsburgh that "Logan's party was returned, and had thirteen scalps and one prisoner: Logan says, he is now satisfied for the loss of his relations and will sit still until he hears what the Long Knives [the Virginians] will say." Eight days later, Schmick recorded at Gnadenhutten, "Logan and his family passed through the village on his way to live with the Shawnee."[28] His killing days were over—he would sit patiently under the elm and await the Virginians, who would surely come.

In the meantime, White Eyes, returning from Pittsburgh, arrived at Schoenbrunn on June 9. Zeisberger recorded that he came from the fort, again on his way to the Shawnee, on state business, stayed for a few hours and made an agreement with a few of the Indian brethren to be in readiness to go with him to Wapatomica as soon as he would send a messenger from New Comers' Town. He also brought two other Indians as far as Tuscarabi who left for the Wyandot country carrying a message from William Johnson and the Six Nations with the following contents: "We are stopping one of your ears so that you will not listen to it how the boys [the Shawnee] fight. They are like immature boys; have nothing to do with them. Rather incline your other ear here toward those who preserve peace (namely, the Delaware, the Six Nations, the English) and, with us, hold on to it."[29] Sir William Johnson was attempting to isolate the Shawnees and confine the war to them alone.

The following day, White Eyes sent word for Isaac, Jacob, and Cornelius and three of the Brethren from Gnadenhutten, including Petrus and Josua, Sr., to join him for the embassy to the Shawnees. Seven days later, on June 17, the news of their conference had arrived back at Schoenbrunn. Little progress had been made to change the attitude of the Wapatomica Shawnees, but White Eyes's party had interceded and protected the white traders who arrived at the village while the conference was in progress. They were accompanied by lower Shawnee guides, and when they arrived at Wapatomica the local Mingoes threatened to kill them. Using the Shawnee guides and his own Delaware party as a shield, White Eyes physically stood between the two parties, preventing the Mingoes from harming the traders. There were between eighteen and twenty white men escorting a 120-horse pack train.[30] Continuing north, the traders arrived at Gnadenhutten on June 18, escorted by John Gibson and a party of friendly Delawares. Two days later, the traders left for Pittsburgh without stopping at Schoenbrunn and reached their destination safely.[31]

After the Shawnee conference at Wapatomica, White Eyes returned to the Delaware capital to join Netawatwes, who had called a grand conference to be held in the village. Delegates from the Wyandot, Twightwee (Miami), Cherokee, lower Shawnee, and Gachnawage Indians in Canada were invited.[32] Though they were invited, neither the Mingoes, nor the upper Shawnees at Wapatomica were represented. On June 21, the conferees reached a decision to keep the peace. Cornstalk, the lower Shawnee war chief, had been detained and did not arrive before the conference closed. The delegates were admonished to ask neighboring tribes to the north, south, and west to abide by their decision. The noose had been tightened around the Shawnees.[33] The conference produced a written transcript dated June 21, 1774. For the Indians, the document was signed by Netawatwes, the head chief of the Delawares, Captain White Eyes, Killbuck, Sr., Augustine Newallike, and Petrus Echpalawehund (the latter two Christian Indians). For the whites, the signers were Thomas McKee, son of Alexander McKee, William Anderson the trader, and Simon Girty. The document was addressed to George Croghan, Alexander McKee, and John Connolly.[34]

White Eyes returned to Pittsburgh to make his formal report to the authorities there on June 29. After speaking to a large committee of Pittsburghers, he was back on the road again and arrived at Schoenbrunn on July 10.[35] This shuttle diplomacy continued for several more months, but his main mission had been accomplished with the agreement at the Delaware capital. The Shawnees now stood alone against their hated enemy, the Virginia "Long Knives." When the time came, they fought gallantly.

When White Eyes arrived in Schoenbrunn, he found the villagers in a state of turmoil. News had just arrived from New Comers' Town that the Virginians were marching toward the Big Kanawha River. Netawatwes was in a panic, seriously considering taking his people and fleeing westward up the Walhonding. To compound the problem, numerous Shawnee war parties were leaving daily to attack the eastern settlements.[36] There was equal panic among the Christian villages.

Much of the agitation at New Comers' Town can be attributed to the Delawares' fear for their own safety now that they had cast their lot with the strongest party and against the Shawnees. For years they had harbored a mortal fear of the Shawnees, who now looked upon them as traitors. Early in the month they had received a threatening message from a Shawnee war captain advising that he headed a war party to strike the Virginians and would then blaze a road to New Comers' Town and see

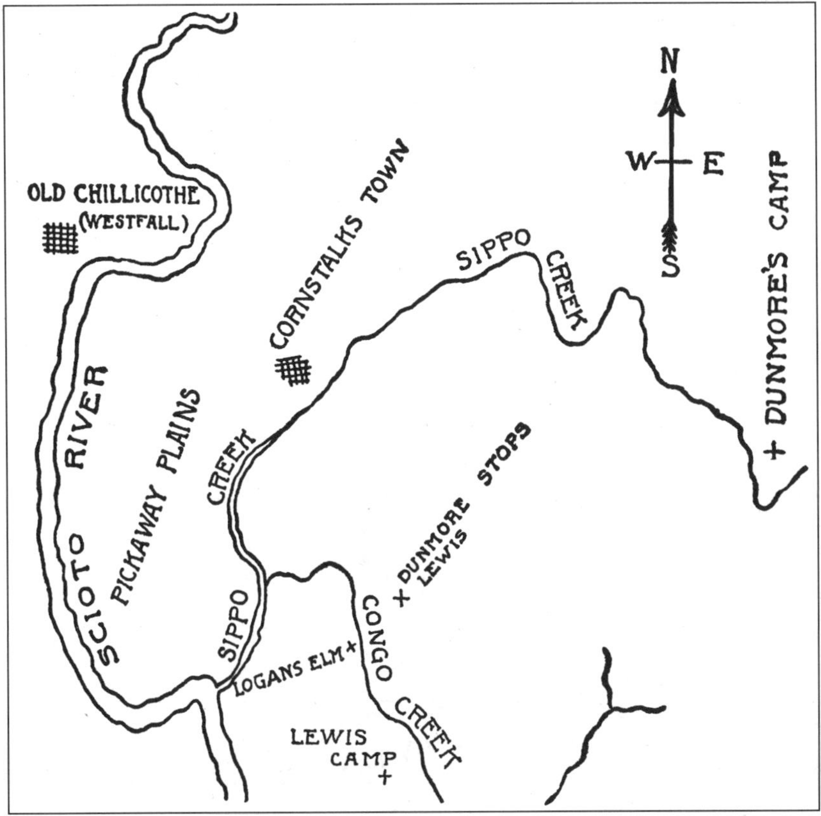

Dunmore's Camp in Shawnee Country. From the *Ohio Archeological and Historical Society Publications*, 1903.

what mischief he could do there. "We will see then," he said, "whether the peace between the whites and the Delawares is as strong as pretended."[37]

By the second week in July it became clear that the Virginians were on the march toward Shawnee territory. As early as June 10, Dunmore had ordered out the militias of the western counties of Dunmore and Fincastle with instructions to defend the Ohio River boundary line. At the same time, he ordered a series of forts to be constructed to defend the Virginia borders.

Returning to Pittsburgh on July 23, White Eyes warned McKee and his other friends, "When you have thrown down the Shawanese Brethren, we desire you to look no further, nor sit down there, but Return To the

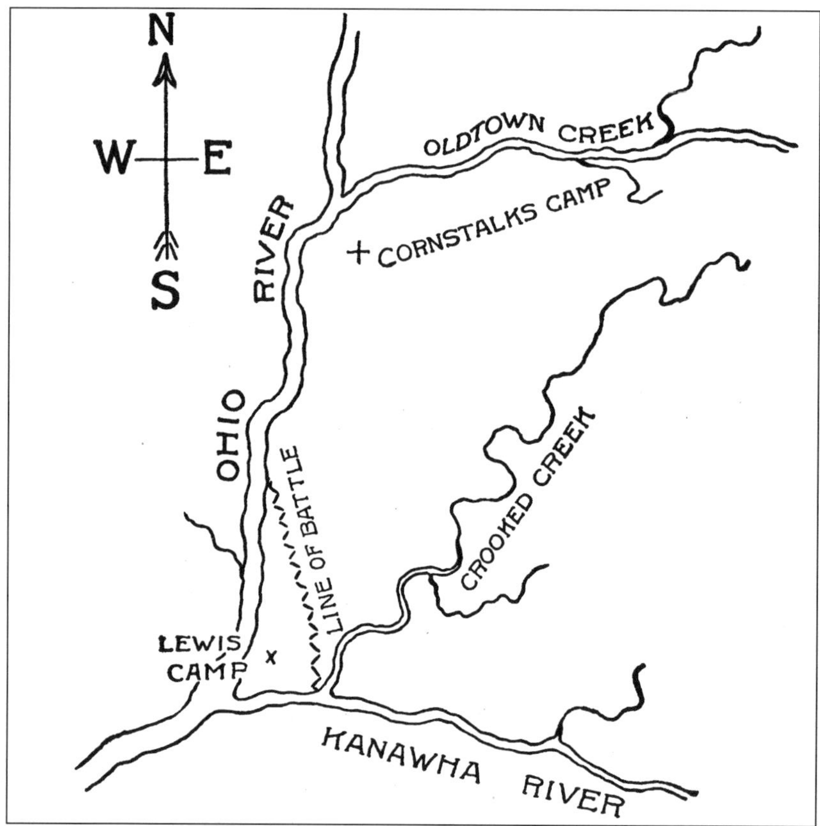

Battle of Point Pleasant, October 10, 1774. From the *Ohio Archeological and Historical Society Publications*, 1903.

Kannhaway [Kanawha] or South Side of the Ohio, the place that you rise from."[38] He further warned that any attempt by the militia to invade the Delaware country would be considered a breach of the peace and a violation of their agreement.

In response to White Eyes's appeal, McKee sent "John Gibson and another white man" to reside at the Delaware capital for several weeks in the event any of Dunmore's armies approached the Muskingum villages. Zeisberger noted his arrival in the Schoenbrunn diary on July 31. Gibson reassured the missionary that he had been present when the troops left Pittsburgh traveling down the Ohio and had read their instructions, which prohibited the army from molesting the Delawares.[39]

Dunmore's orders had reached his field commanders by the end of June. They called for the militia to meet at three strategic locations on the Ohio. Colonel Andrew Lewis was to proceed to the mouth of the Great Kanawha (now Point Pleasant, West Virginia) and construct a fort. Angus McDonald, then at Pittsburgh, was to move down the Ohio to Wheeling and occupy Fort Fincastle, built the previous June by William Crawford. On arrival at Fort Fincastle, McDonald was to march westward some one hundred miles and strike and destroy the upper Shawnee villages. Dunmore wrote that he would proceed to Pittsburgh and meet Lewis at either Wheeling or the Great Kanawha.[40]

McDonald moved first. Leaving Fort Fincastle on July 26 with four hundred Virginians, he crossed the Ohio and proceeded to the upper Shawnee and Mingo villages in and around Wapatomica on the Muskingum. Five villages were burned and seventy acres of corn destroyed. No attempt was made to push on to the Delaware villages fifteen miles to the north. Both of the Dunmore and Lewis columns continued to plow through the western wilderness toward their destination on the Ohio. Dunmore was the first to arrive, reaching Pittsburgh the first week in September with seven hundred men.

When White Eyes returned to Gnadenhutten on September 30, Matthew Elliot, the assistant Indian agent to Alexander McKee, was with him. After informing Chief Netawatwes of their proposed attempt to intercede to try to bring about a peaceful settlement, they proceeded south to Shawnee country, Elliot to join Cornstalk's warriors and White Eyes to meet Dunmore's army, both as peace ambassadors.

Lord Dunmore left Pittsburgh on September 17 and proceeded down the Ohio (partly by land and partly by water). Near the end of the month he stopped at the mouth of the Hockhocking River to build Fort Gower, pick up an additional five hundred men commanded by William Crawford (the old McDonald group), and await news of Lewis's brigades, which arrived at the Great Kanawha on October 6. Dunmore was joined at new Fort Gower by White Eyes, accompanied by a small contingent of Delawares and John Montour.[41]

Meanwhile, Lewis came under attack at Point Pleasant. Disregarding the advice of Cornstalk, who continued to argue for peace, some seven hundred Shawnees crossed the river on the evening of October 9 and early the next morning slammed into Lewis's surprised army. Throughout most of the day Cornstalk's men fought gallantly, but by nightfall they had not dislodged the Virginians and had suffered substantial casualties. That evening the Shawnees gave up the fight, recrossed the river, buried their dead, and carried the wounded back to their villages. At a council that evening, it was obvious they had little fight left in them. Caustically Cornstalk suggested, "Shall we go back to the villages, kill all the women and children, then turn on the enemy and fight until we are all slain?" He received no response. "Then I will go and make peace."[42] The day following the battle, Cornstalk sent Matthew Elliot to Dunmore, suggesting that they negotiate.[43]

Six days after the battle at Point Pleasant, Zeisberger heard the news. The dispatch also confirmed that White Eyes, acting as an adviser, was with the Dunmore troops moving westward toward the Shawnee villages.[44]

Dunmore caught up with Elliot on October 15 on the Pickaway plains a few miles east of the Scioto River. His troops were now in the heart of Shawnee territory on the banks of Scippo Creek and approximately six miles south of present Circleville, Ohio. Here he constructed a crude enclosure and placed a large wooden slab marked with red paint in the center of the camp and called it Camp Charlotte after the English queen.[45]

Meanwhile, leaving a guard to care for the wounded, Lewis left Point Pleasant and, by forced march, headed toward the Shawnee villages. Dunmore learned of Lewis's approaching army when the negotiations were nearly completed. He immediately sent a runner to order Lewis to return to the Ohio. The runner returned several hours later advising that Lewis refused to obey Dunmore's command. The governor hastily left his camp accompanied by White Eyes and fifty of his own men to stop Lewis. He caught up with him at dusk on October 17, just a few miles from Cornstalk's Shawnee village on Congo Creek. Lewis and his army had suffered some seventy casualties at Point Pleasant, and he was determined to destroy the Shawnees. A nasty scene ensued. The governor drew his sword and threatened the colonel's life if he did not obey his command. His Lordship's party stayed for the night with a double guard to protect him and White Eyes. The following morning Lewis's dejected army began their march back toward the Ohio, and Dunmore returned to Camp Charlotte to complete the negotiations.[46]

The Shawnees agreed to all the conditions imposed by Dunmore. The Mingoes, however, refused to attend any of the sessions. Dunmore learned the location of their villages from several Mingo prisoners. A detachment of 250 men under William Crawford was sent to attack their camps (near present Columbus, Ohio) and bring in their war captains. The mission was completed the evening of October 19 after Crawford plundered and destroyed as many as five small villages. He returned the following day with twelve Mingo prisoners, including their head captain.[47]

The terms of Lord Dunmore's treaty were lenient. The Shawnees agreed to forfeit their hunting rights to the south side of the Ohio in the Kentucky country and not to molest settlers traveling on the Ohio River. In return, the whites agreed to refrain from hunting north of the river. The Indians' access to traders was limited "to such regulations, for their trade with our People, as Should be hereafter dictated by the Kings Instructions." All stolen property was to be returned, and the Shawnees were to surrender four hostages to be held until a final treaty was signed in Pittsburgh in the spring. The Mingoes refused to negotiate, and eleven of their leading men were taken as hostages, also to be held in Pittsburgh. Their refusal to negotiate would have grave consequences for the Moravian missions in the next several years.[48]

Later, Lord Dunmore was savagely criticized by his Virginia army officers for his lenient treatment of the Shawnees, particularly from Andrew Lewis. There is little question that the combined forces could have decimated the Shawnee nation, but Lord Dunmore recognized that such action would have destroyed the fragile Indian peace he had carefully crafted among the Delaware, Wyandot, Twightwee, and Six Nation tribes. The Shawnee treaty led eventually to the three-year peace that kept these nations from joining the British during the early part of the Revolutionary War.

White Eyes had been absent from the Muskingum Valley since September 30, when he left Gnadenhutten with Matthew Elliot to join Dunmore's forces on the Ohio. The Delaware villages evinced a genuine concern for his safety. At first, rumors of his death and the destruction of the Shawnees filled all three towns with wild stories of the Long Knife army on the march to destroy the mission villages. Then the opposite scenario prevailed—that the Shawnees had destroyed the Long Knives and were coming to take revenge on the Delawares for not joining in the Shawnee cause.

At the Delaware capital, the Christian Indians were condemned either way for causing all these problems. During the previous few months the Shawnees and a small contingent of renegade Munsees who lived at Assinink south of the capital had been taunting the Delaware residents at New Comers' Town, calling them "Virginians" and "Shwonnak" (a white man). This was perhaps the most insulting epithet an Indian could use against another Indian. On several occasions, Netawatwes had cautioned both groups of his people not to use these terms. Thoroughly disgusted with them, he sent another message objecting to this treatment, but this time the dispatch carried a new twist. If these names were applied to the

Delawares because the missionaries were living with them, he wanted to assure his friends that "*they had not been invited by him and must have been invited by other foolish and unreasoning people*." Furthermore, he made it clear that the Delawares were not embracing the Christian cause and that "*they would never accept the Word of God, let alone live the way they [the Christians] did*."[49] Oblivious to the incendiary nature of these two comments, he again, as in the past, denied any connection with the Christians. But the times had changed, and this time he would reap the harvest of his deceit. Unfortunately, the dispatch never reached the Shawnees, but it was read by the Assinink Delawares.

White Eyes arrived back at New Comers' Town on November 4. The whole village turned out to welcome him. Messengers were sent to the two Christian towns to summon their representatives. Billy Chelloway and Augustine Newallike represented Schoenbrunn and Jo Peepe and Petrus Echpalawehund arrived from Gnadenhutten. The following day, White Eyes made his report. Zeisberger's diary entry for November 5 covered twelve pages, an unusually long description for one day's activities.

The captain's account of the last month of Lord Dunmore's campaign agrees almost completely with those of other colonial eyewitnesses, but historians have generally ignored his prominent role. Zeisberger, however, explains in detail the role the captain played in the final negotiations at Camp Charlotte. He emphasized in particular how White Eyes helped to moderate the hostile attitude toward the Shawnees among Dunmore's officers. Zeisberger reported that the governor, after praising the Delawares for their peacekeeping effort, had told the Shawnees that "they owed it to the Delaware that they had not been annihilated during the summer for their Grandfather, [the Delaware], had not wished to stain his brother's land with blood and had not wished [us] to deal too harshly with them."[50] One month later, in his report to Lord Dartmouth, Dunmore confirmed this statement and recognized the captain's contribution: "The Delaware remained Steady in their attachment; and their Chief, named Captain White Eyes, offered me the assistance of himself and the whole tribe . . . and I received great Service from the faithfulness, and firmness and remarkable good understanding of White Eyes."[51]

But White Eyes's report to the Delaware council on November 5 went well beyond Dunmore's negotiations with the Shawnees. After relating the incidents connected with the transaction, he turned to Netawatwes and delivered a scathing denunciation. The chief's dispatch to the Shawnees and Assinink Delawares was intercepted by White Eyes before it reached the Shawnees. He was incensed when he read it. Clearly it was a breach of Indian diplomatic protocol. Since he was the leading war captain, all diplomatic exchanges had to be approved by him and the council before being dispatched. The head civil chief (Netawatwes) was not permitted to initiate such action. Netawatwes had violated an ancient custom of the tribe. But it was the contents of the dispatch that enraged White Eyes. Netawatwes's statement that "foolish and unreasoning people" were responsible for the Christians living among them and that they would never accept the word of God or live like the Christians was a sheer deceit. Of course, the council, with the chief's approval, had invited them to come to the Muskingum, and the second statement regarding the acceptance of the Christian religion had never been proposed, debated, or decided by the council. After a long and bitter discussion, citing his lengthy and exhausting effort that summer to keep the Delawares neutral, White Eyes threw Netawatwes's belt at the chief's feet, resigned his post as war captain, and left the council house. Bewildered and embarrassed by the whole affair, Netawatwes asked the Brethren to mediate the dispute.[52]

The crux of White Eyes's complaint lay in Netawatwes's rejection of the Word of God and in his refusal to recognize the Christian Indians as a separate and distinct group to be granted their own land and to be protected from interference from the native Delawares. True, initially the Christians had been invited to move to the Muskingum, but that had all been a ruse. The original plan called for the move, and after the converts had arrived, the missionaries were either to be forced to leave or be killed, leaving the converts behind to swell the Delaware population at the capital. During the course of the original discussion before the invitation, Petrus Echpalawehund and Jacob Gendaskund, both now converts, admitted to Zeisberger the truth of this statement because they had been present during the council meeting when the plan was conceived. "They had been blind," Netawatwes said, "you yourselves had joined them and, although I have always waited for it, you have not yet said to us; Now it is time to drive the teacher out." "They laid the snare for us," Zeisberger wrote, "in which they themselves were caught. They had intended to betray us and to trap us shrewdly, but they themselves were trapped."[53] The council had woven the web, only to be caught in its own deception.

The total Christian population between the two villages was rapidly approaching four hundred. If the missionaries were forced to leave, the converts would probably follow them. Another nation, perhaps even the Wyandot, could send them an invitation. Such thoughts were common among the Delaware councillors.

Zeisberger closed the year by commenting, "We were visited by strangers more than ever during this year, not only from the local region, but also from more distant places, by Shawnee, Cherokee, Dalamattenos

[Wyandot], and Mingo."[54] Most of this increased activity can be traced directly to the Delaware Nation's involvement in the activity before and the peace process following the events associated with Lord Dunmore's War. Dunmore and his colleague John Connolly carefully crafted the events leading up to open hostility. To Dunmore's credit, he did, at the end of the fighting, negotiate at Camp Charlotte a treaty that protected the integrity of the Shawnee Nation. But the bloody events of Baker's plantation would never be erased from the minds of the Mingo warriors.

· PART 4 ·

That All Men Are Created Equal,
1775–1782

· 19 ·

A Hard, Bloody, and Tragic Business, 1775

THE CONCEPTS of liberty and equality, the central theses of classical liberalism, have deep roots in Western culture. They can be traced back to the ancient Greeks and the Judeo-Christian tradition. Later they were confirmed and expanded by the reformers in the sixteenth and seventeenth centuries. The thoughts of the American founders were shaped by eighteenth-century Enlightenment writers such as the Englishman John Locke and the Frenchmen Montesquieu, Diderot, Rousseau, and above all Voltaire. Their writings inspired Thomas Jefferson to sound the call, "We hold these truths to be self-evident that all men are created equal." In the twelve years preceding the Revolution, the caldron of political and social discontent had been boiling. Now, in 1775, it spilled over and marked the beginning of a new world epoch.[1]

Bruce Catton, writing about the Revolution, said, "A romantic haze has settled down over the whole affair, and when we look through it the facts tend to be a little blurred. And what is most worth remembering—the thing that so often escapes us—is the fact like all of history's wars, the war of the American Revolution was a hard, bloody, and tragic business—a struggle to the death that we came very close to losing."[2]

Near the end of January 1775, Zeisberger gave the first indication of the rumblings back east: "From traders who had come from Pittsburgh we heard many things about the serious conditions in the colonies of this country."[3]

During the second week in February, Netawatwes called all of his chiefs and head men together at New Comers' Town for a grand council. They were to discuss the disputes regarding the Christian Indians and the native Delawares. Captain Pipe, representing Chief Packanke and the Kaskaskunk council, passed through the village on his way to the council meeting the first week in February and stopped again at Schoenbrunn twelve days later on his way home but refused to reveal the details of the discussions. The Schoenbrunn delegation returned from the grand council on the twenty-eighth, accompanied by White Eyes, who carried the official report.[4] It was good news. According to the captain, the council had capitulated to the various demands Zeisberger had laid out during his first visit to the capital in 1771. White Eyes recited the list:

That from now on they will make common cause with them.
That they would accept the word of God.
That the believing Indians with their teachers should enjoy, in the Indian country, all liberties and equal rights and privileges.
That the country from now on should be open to us, and the believing Indians should have the same rights and claims to the land as have the non-believing ones.
That whosoever of the Indians wants to turn to the Brethren and become believers, he shall have the liberty to do so and should not be hindered.
No Indian should settle in the neighborhood, and those already there have been enjoined to move down the river toward them.[5]

It was a complete renunciation of the council's previous attitudes and seemed almost too good to be true. Normally, when Zeisberger received unusually good news, he expressed his pleasure in his diary. On this occasion he was reticent. He closed the diary entry: "The chief and White Eyes with their council have thus professed, in the name of the entire nation, that they are willing to accept the Christian faith and, although many Indians are against it, in fact, hostile to it, yet by this measure they will be silenced and they can no longer rise against us openly."[6] The operative word here is "openly." The ever-cautious Zeisberger approached the coming months with considerable circumspection because he recognized the potential for deception.

The council also announced that the capital would be moved to the forks of the Muskingum (now Coshocton, Ohio), approximately fifteen miles downstream and west of Gekelemukpechunk. The move was to be made immediately. Netawatwes also requested that another mission village be established near the site of the new capital, giving the native Indians living at his village easy access to Christian teachings. This dramatic change in attitude can best be explained in the council message from Netawatwes and delivered to Zeisberger through White Eyes. Zeisberger wrote: "This was what he wished to announce to us since he was a very old man and did not know how long he would live in this world . . . he was glad that he had been able to complete this work so that it would benefit their children and their childrens' offsprings. Now, he said, he could leave this temporal life whenever it pleases God."[7]

A close analysis of Zeisberger's diaries during this period reveals a sense of pessimism, almost as if he had concluded that the council was saying: Now that the old man was approaching ninety, let us simply defer to his wishes. True, he had been a good man in his day, but he will not be with us for many more months. After his death we can do as we please.

Early in March, Zeisberger received word that the Mingoes had been ordered by the Six Nations to detach themselves from the Shawnees and move to the northern part of the Ohio Country near Lake Erie. They were a very small group, principally of Senecas; Zeisberger estimated their strength at not more than eighty warriors. But they were undisciplined, combative, and a warlike people who vowed, following the Logan massacre during Dunmore's War, never to lay down the war hachets against the colonials, especially the Virginians, the hated Long Knives.[8]

Indian diplomatic protocol required that after receiving the grand council's message, the Christians prepare appropriate belts to be delivered to the Delaware capital and sent to the western tribes. With White Eyes's assistance, the proper belts were prepared. On April 6, Isaac Glikhikan and Billy Chelloway representing Schoenbrunn and Johannes Martin and Jo Peepe from Gnadenhutten delivered the belt to Netawatwes and his council. Zeisberger explained:

> Each belt was a half fathom long [three feet], and proportionately wide. The belts were not made according to the Indian manner, but plain without figures, with a road running along the middle lengthwise and a [Christian] cross above it. . . . The nations would immediately see that they signified something different from others and came from the believing Indians, from which they could at once

conclude that the believing Indians had been received and were recognized and looked upon as their friends.[9]

Each of the mission villages prepared a separate belt for the Delawares, and another set was sent to be passed among the Dalamattenos (Wyandot), Tawa (Ottawa), Twightwee (Miami), and Wawiachtano (Kickapoo). The presentation took place at the new village site of Goschachgunk (Ko-shock-ach-kunk), also frequently referred to as the Forks of the Muskingum.[10]

During their visit, Netawatwes requested Isaac Glikhikan's help in laying out the new town. Most Indian villages were helter-skelter affairs with cabins and huts placed at the whim of the residents. The new village would have an organizational touch, courtesy of the Moravians and Glikhikan. Each tribe and clan was to have its own separate street.

Despite Zeisberger's melancholy attitude, a steady stream of new converts continued to join the Christian villages. On Easter Sunday, April 16, more than three hundred attended the Schoenbrunn service, certainly a capacity crowd for the little church.

Three days later, on April 19, back east, red-coated men and those dressed in homespun were fighting for possession of a small bridge "that spanned the flood" in the small village of Concord, Massachusetts. The shot "heard around the world" had been fired and the American Revolution begun. In the Muskingum Valley, oblivious to the roar of the battle, Zeisberger closed the month recording that "there prevailed a blissful feeling of His presence, and of the Peace of God."[11]

A stalwart Christian, Johannes Papunhank, died on May 15. It was a particularly sad occasion for Zeisberger. Johannes had been the "first fruits" of his missionary work on the Susquehanna. They had been close friends for twelve years, and Papunhank was deeply mourned.[12]

On June 1, Zeisberger, Joseph Schebosh, and several other Brethren left the valley to visit Bethlehem. They would be gone for two and one-half months. The diaries give no indication why the trip was made, but almost certainly Zeisberger had received the news of the Battles of Lexington and Concord. The information had reached Fort Pitt the last week in May.[13]

With the beginning of open hostilities between the British and the colonials, the attitude of the Indians toward the rebel cause became a primary concern to residents of the western borders. The Dunmore treaty, signed at Camp Charlotte, had been only a provisional agreement to be supplemented by a final treaty in the spring. But Dunmore, now a hostage aboard his own ship at Newport, was in no position to conclude these arrangements. The four Shawnee prisoners were still in his hands, and the twelve Mingoes were held at Fort Pitt by Major Connolly, now a professed Loyalist, who was still in charge at the fort. Connolly asserted that his "first work was to convene the Indians to a treaty, restore the prisoners, and endeavor to incline them to espouse the royal cause."[14]

Responding to Connolly's call for the treaty conference, Netawatwes, White Eyes, and the Delaware delegation left the capital and stopped briefly at Gnadenhutten on their way to Schoenbrunn, arriving on June 14. The chief stayed for three days, then left for Pittsburgh. White Eyes remained another two days, then followed the chief to the fort.[15] The Shawnee delegation was delayed, but by the last week in June they had left their villages on the Scioto and were also on the road. Cornstalk and his delegates, bound for the fort, also stopped at Gnadenhutten, on July 2. Enthralled by the village, they spent six days leisurely talking to Schmick, attending church services, and inspecting the village, even briefly visiting Schoenbrunn. On the eighth, they left for the fort.[16]

On May 16, several weeks before the news of the war arrived at Pittsburgh, a West Augusta County committee of correspondence had been organized. These committees were groups of colonial citizens who communicated with other like-minded men in the neighboring counties to keep informed of the rapidly developing events.

Connolly met with the Delaware and Mingo delegation (the Shawnees had not yet arrived) during the last week in June. One contemporary account reported: "The Committee of Correspondence as well as Major Connolly's most inveterate Enemies all agree that he Conducted the affair in the Most Open and Candid Manner." Following the meeting the delegates were assured that a large formal treaty conference would be held that fall to discuss a final resolution of their differences.[17]

In Williamsburg, it became clear to the members of the final session of the Virginia House of Burgesses that immediate action must be taken to keep the Indians on the Ohio frontier friendly to their cause or at least neutral. Meeting for the last time on June 24, at the same time Connolly was talking to the Delawares and Mingoes, the burgesses passed a resolution appointing a committee of five men to serve as commissioners to meet with the Indian tribes at Pittsburgh in September. James Wood was chosen to leave promptly "to visit each Indian town and give notice of the conference."[18] He left Williamsburg the next day and arrived at Pittsburgh on July 9, shortly after Connolly had finished his deliberations with the Delawares and Mingoes and seven days before Cornstalk and the Shawnees arrived at the fort.

Shortly after Wood arrived in Pittsburgh, it became apparent that John Connolly's days on the western frontier were rapidly coming to a close. Earlier, Connolly had carried out instructions from Dunmore to abandon the garrisons at Fort Pitt and also those at Fort Blair near the mouth of the Kanawha. Connolly also met clandestinely with a group of his Loyalist friends and revealed a secret plan he had developed for seizing the western theater for the crown. The plan, later referred to as the "Connolly Plot," called for him to travel to Detroit, where a regiment was to be assembled from the local garrison and supplemented with some of the British troops then in Illinois. Using Indian allies, they were then to proceed from Detroit into the Ohio Country and capture Fort Pitt, thus securing the western frontier for the British.

Earlier, Dunmore had given Connolly a letter for Captain White Eyes whom they hoped would use his influence to persuade the Delawares to join the British. Connolly wrote to John Gibson, his newly appointed Indian agent at Pittsburgh, instructing Gibson to deliver Dunmore's letter to White Eyes. His letter to Gibson placed Connolly squarely in the Loyalist camp and insinuated that Gibson should likewise align himself with the supporters of the crown. But Connolly had chosen the wrong man.[19] Gibson turned the letters over to the local committee of correspondence, which promptly issued a warrant for Connolly's arrest. On November 13, while traveling up the Potomac River with his servant and two companions bound for Detroit, Connolly was arrested a few miles south of Hagerstown, Maryland. He was carrying the plans for the invasion of the western theater.[20]

When James Wood arrived at Pittsburgh on July 9, he took charge of Indian affairs and quickly filled the vacuum created by Connolly's departure. Seven days later, the Shawnees arrived and Wood assured the chiefs that the Mingo prisoners taken by Dunmore the previous year were well and would be returned in September when the official treaty conference was held.[21]

Wood was anxious to visit the various Indian tribes to invite them to the treaty conference. Several hours after talking to the Shawnees on July 18, he left Pittsburgh with his guide and interpreter, Simon Girty. He was on the trail for the next twenty-five days meeting with the Indians and was back in Pittsburgh on August 10.

During the course of his journey he visited the Delawares, Mingoes, Wyandots, and Shawnees at their respective villages and invited each nation to attend the conference in September.[22] On his way back to Pittsburgh he stopped at Gnadenhutten. He spent two days with Schmick and wrote:

> 6th August [Sunday] went to church with the Indians at which were present One-hundred and fifty of them who all Behaved with Greatest Decency and Decorum the Minister who resides at this town is a German of the Moravian Sect has Lived with them several Years has Acquired their Language and taught most of them English and German he prayed in the Delaware Language Preached in the English and sung Psalms in the German in which the Indians Joined and Performed that part of the Divine Service in a Manner really Inimitable the Church is a Decent Square Log Building with Plank floars [*sic*] and Benches Ornamented with Several Pieces of German Scripture Paintings has a Small Cupola with a Bell and a very Indifferent Spinnet on which an Indian played.[23]

Upon returning to his home in Winchester, he wrote to Peyton Randolph, the president of the Continental Congress, giving a full report of his experience among the Indians and advising that "there may be a general Confederacy building against the Virginia colony having been led to believe that we are a people Quite different and distinct from the other Colonies." He also cautioned that there was no garrison at Fort Pitt and that the neighborhood was defenseless. He estimated that more than five hundred Indians would attend the conference.[24]

The Pennsylvania and Virginia colonies had anticipated James Wood's warning. During the last week in July the delegates at the Second Continental Congress "united in a circular letter" urging the people living in the disputed area of the western theater to "unite in mutual forbearance," disband their armed bodies, and join together against the common enemy.[25] Thus temporarily ended the dispute between Pennsylvania and Virginia over possession of the Fort Pitt area. Two weeks later, the Virginia Provincial Convention, assembled at Williamsburg, appointed John Neville to lead a company of one hundred men to Fort Pitt and take possession. They arrived on September 11 and Neville took charge of the fort.[26]

In the meantime, back in the Muskingum Valley, discussions at the Delaware council focused on Netawatwes's desire that the Brethren build a third village nearer to Goschachgunk, the new Delaware capital. They finally decided to have White Eyes again present the proposal to Zeisberger and Schmick. On September 4, the captain stopped briefly at Gnadenhutten and explained his mission to Schmick and then traveled on to Schoenbrunn, where he spent two days discussing the proposal with Zeisberger, who, though not opposing it, outlined various questions it raised. The captain told Zeisberger that by the time the chiefs returned from the October treaty conference at Pittsburgh, he hoped to have a firm answer.[27]

During the last two weeks in September, both Schoenbrunn and Gnadenhutten were visited by dignitaries from the Shawnee and Delaware Nations, who were bound for the conference at Pittsburgh. The Shawnee delegation arrived at Gnadenhutten on the eighteenth. Their head chief, Cornstalk, was accompanied by twenty-six young men and six women and children. They spent two full days visiting with the Schmicks and the other members of the village, then proceeded on to Pittsburgh.[28]

The two Delaware contingents planned to assemble at Schoenbrunn. In all, the Delaware party consisted of more than fifty men and women. Netawatwes was ill and unable to accompany his delegation, but he sent a message to Zeisberger regarding the third mission village. It was a "formal request" and was accompanied by the appropriate string of wampum.[29] Now that a formal presentation of wampum had been made, Indian protocol made an answer mandatory.

The provincials who gathered at Pittsburgh were intelligent and experienced men and rivaled those who were then meeting at the Second Continental Congress in Philadelphia. Each had distinguished himself in events that traced back some twenty years to the French and Indian War. Each was eminently equipped to face the delicate task before him. Their objective was Indian neutrality, especially that of the Delawares and Shawnees, their next-door neighbors, so as to provide a buffer zone against the more hostile western tribes.[30]

Both the Indians and the commissioners had arrived at Pittsburgh by October 7. When the negotiations began, there were well over five hundred warriors, the largest Indian delegation ever assembled at Pittsburgh. The list of those in attendance, both colonial and principal Indian chiefs, read like a "Who's Who in America" for the latter half of the eighteenth century. Lewis Morris from New York and James Wilson from Pennsylvania, both of whom signed the Declaration of Independence nine months later, had been appointed by the Second Continental Congress. Dr. Thomas Walker, James Wood, Andrew Lewis, John Walker, and Adam Stephen had been appointed by the Virginia House of Burgesses.[31]

Among the Indians were the head chiefs of each nation, with the exception of the Delawares, who were represented by Captain White Eyes. Appearing for the Six Nations was Guyasuta. Flying Crow, a Six Nation chief, spoke for the Mingoes. Cornstalk and his brother Nimwha represented the Shawnees, and Shegenaba, the son of Pontiac, appeared for the Ottawas. The principal Wyandot delegate was the capable Half-King (Pomoacan), who would later play an important role in David Zeisberger's life. The Christian Indians were represented by Isaac Glikhikan, Billy Chelloway, Nathanael Davis, and Jo Peepe, who acted as an interpreter.

The conference met for two weeks, concluding on October 21 with a giant celebration and the distribution of many gifts. All delegates pledged to keep the peace and remain neutral. The only disagreement concerned the Shawnees, who continued to hold captives (both black and white) and horses taken during Dunmore's War. Cornstalk insisted that they had all been returned except those captives who refused to leave. Some of the prisoners had been forcefully moved to the settlements only to return later, preferring to live in the Indian villages. A delegation of some twenty men, led by John Gibson, was dispatched to the villages to validate the Shawnee statement. Jo Peepe and Captain Pipe were among those deputized.[32]

The Pittsburgh treaty had enormous political significance over the next two years of colonial history. By and large the Indians kept their pledge to remain neutral, thus freeing the frontiersmen to join Washington's army in its confrontations with the British on the eastern coast. Only the Mingo nation broke the pledge and continued to conduct incursions across the Ohio.

At the conclusion of the conference, the Delaware delegation traveled directly to the capital without stopping at either Christian village, thus delaying Zeisberger's formal response regarding the new mission village. The Moravian contingent, Chelloway, Davis, and Glikhikan, arrived at Schoenbrunn on October 29, bringing the good news that peace had been preserved. They were accompanied by six Wyandots and a Six Nation chief (probably Flying Crow, the Mingo representative). To everyone's surprise, White Eyes had proceeded on to Philadelphia. They had fully expected him to return to the valley. Zeisberger noted, "Many had assumed he had gone there to fetch either an English or a Quaker preacher." Three days after the Schoenbrunn contingent arrived, Jo Peepe returned to Gnadenhutten with more disturbing information about White Eyes. Schmick recorded:

> We also received from him [Jo Peepe] the unexpected news that Capt. White Eyes, after the treaty was over, had made a speech to the Quakers to request of them a preacher and a schoolteacher; our Brethren present at the meeting were supposed to be very amazed at his being of a different mind than before. Now that Captain White Eyes has gone to Philadelphia we will see whether this really was his request, and whether he will or will not receive somebody of them. I doubt it![33]

On November 11, John Gibson, the agent for Indian affairs for the Continental Congress, arrived at Schoenbrunn with the delegation to collect the horses and captives from the Shawnees. The party was accompanied by several Mingoes and the trader John Dodge on his way to the Wyandots and the other western Indians, carrying the splendid Congress belt, six feet long and over six inches wide.[34] The delegation remained at Schoenbrunn for six days, then went on to Gnadenhutten and the capital.

Throughout the month of November, both Indian and white visitors passed through the village, all discussing the treaty. On the nineteenth, Zeisberger wrote, "From Sandusky we learned that the Wyandot had returned to their homes not very satisfied with the Treaty in Pittsburgh and were not in a mood to talk about it. They are inclined to [align themselves with] the Commandant in Detroit."[35]

The same day Captain Pipe and his family came from his village at Kaskaskunk. Zeisberger wrote of this visit:

> His wife hears gladly of the Saviour, and he is not content, is conscious of an inner call, and is convinced that the Brethren preach the only way of salvation, but he cannot make up his mind to follow his impulse and give himself to the Saviour. Whenever he hears of Indians that they have a desire and inclination to come to us to hear the Gospel, he always counsels them to do so and not to suffer themselves to be dissuaded by anybody.[36]

The chief's dilemma was shared by other native Indians confronted with the Christian philosophy. It was an especially difficult problem for those who were politically active, heavily involved in the Indian government, and respected in the social community of the Indian nations. Captain Pipe and his family remained at the mission until December, then returned to their own village.

School opened again on December 4, and both Zeisberger and Heckewelder complained about the lack of textbooks. One hundred or more students answered the call of the school bell. They were now being taught in their own Delaware language. Schoenbrunn ended the year with 263 residents, an increase of 43 from the previous year. At Gnadenhutten Schmick counted 151 residents. The total population stood at 414. The year 1775 marked the zenith; never would the missions surpass this number.

· 20 ·

The Pasture of Light, 1776

WITHIN FOUR and one-half months after the beginning of the new year, Zeisberger was on the move to a new mission location. It was his eighth since he had founded Friedenshutten ten years earlier. No longer could he delay a response to Netawatwes, who, the first week in February, sent him another urgent plea to open a new village near his capital.[1] Four days after Zeisberger received Netawatwes's message, he was on the road with five Brethren to choose the site of the new mission. They arrived at Goschachgunk on the evening of the tenth to a rousing reception.

Zeisberger gives an amusing description of the new Delaware (Goschachgunk) capital housing plot plan. The previous year Netawatwes had asked Isaac Glikhikan to lay out the native village, using Moravian schematic formal arrangements.

> Their town lies on the east side of the Muskingum, just across from where the equally large Walhondink empties into it, is quite large but spread out, and consists, for the most part of huts. Although it was [originally] laid out and streets were marked off, I could not find a single street that was built to any degree of regular fashion; each

> [resident] had built according to his fancy, the length of the houses or the width toward the street, or obliquely, or even houses in the middle of the street.[2]

Nobody, chiefs notwithstanding, would tell the new residents where to build their houses. Who cares about symmetry anyway?

During their conversation, Netawatwes again expressed a desire for a mission close to the capital. Zeisberger carefully explained the problems that had arisen in the past when missions were close to the native villages. But, before continuing their trip down-river, Zeisberger and his party accompanied some of the Delaware councillors on foot to a location proposed by Netawatwes several miles below the capital. Arriving at the site, Zeisberger was amazed with what they found. His diary entry for February 11 reflects his enthusiasm for the site:

> We soon came to an extraordinarily fine piece of land and proceeded for three miles through the bottom land, the likes of which is not found near Schoenbrunn, Gnadenhutten, nor all the way down the river. . . . It is truly a fine location. . . . The place lies on the east side of the Muskingum, quite near the river, which is twice as broad as the Muskingum at Schoenbrunn. It is a beautiful plain, just as all the country from Goschachgunk to this place, about three miles level. Land can be cultivated either up or down the river from the building site.[3]

Zeisberger closed his diary for the day with a touching tribute to Netawatwes: "He is a dear, venerable old man, who is concerned about the well-being of his people and has great confidence and trust in the Brethren that they will make the Indian a happy people. May the Saviour grant it and let him witness it with joy!"[4]

Before leaving the capital on February 12, Zeisberger had a long conversation with forty-year-old Chief Gelelemend, the grandson of Netawatwes, whose father was John Killbuck, Sr. During previous months, Gelelemend had expressed a desire to become a Christian. He would not be baptized for another thirteen years, but from this point forward, Gelelemend became one of the principal Indians in Zeisberger's life.[5]

On their way back from Goschachgunk, the Zeisberger party stopped at Gnadenhutten and discussed the new mission location with Schmick. "Since for various reasons," Zeisberger wrote, "we found it necessary to discover the purpose of our dear Lord with respect to the new settlement. . . .

And, oh, to what great joy and thanksgiving we were stirred when it was manifested as His gracious will and pleasure" to proceed with the project. Again, they had consulted the lot, this time to everyone's satisfaction.[6]

The first order of business called for the building of a fleet of canoes to transport the heavy baggage down the river to the new location. Eight families of Brethren were designated to begin the new settlement. The departure date was set for the day following Easter.

By April 10 they pushed the canoes away from the riverbank at Schoenbrunn bound for the new mission, which had just officially been named Lichtenau, "Pasture of Light."[7] Remaining at Schoenbrunn were the Jungmanns, who guided the fortunes of the little village for the remaining twelve months of its life.

Accompaning Zeisberger were John Heckewelder, who was to be his new assistant, and seven Brethren and their wives. This was Zeisberger's first official acknowledgment that Heckewelder was now considered a full-fledged member of the missionary staff. These men and women were his stalwarts, the heart of his congregation and his most trusted lieutenants: Abraham Sakima; Billy Chelloway; Isaac Glikhikan; Jeremias, the brother of Johannes Papunhank; Thomas Gutikigamen, the grandson of Netawatwes; Ignatius, who tenaciously served Zeisberger for the next twenty years; and Joel, all accompanied by their wives. At Gnadenhutten, they picked up Christian and his wife. In addition, there were a single brother and a single sister, two widows, and fifteen children, for a total of thirty-five. They represented the seed congregation. As was the custom, the majority traveled by canoe and a small overland party managed the horses and cattle.[8]

On the afternoon of the second day they arrived at the Delaware capital of Goschachgunk amid shouts of welcome and hearty greetings from the native residents. The next morning they began staking out the new village.[9]

It was customary to clear any village site completely of timber. The fragile log cabins could be easily crushed by falling trees during the violent storms that frequently visited this area. Seven days after their arrival, they began to move into their new houses.[10]

The same day, Johannes and his wife and four children applied for and were granted permission to live in the village. He was formerly known as Netanewund, grandson of Netawatwes and the brother of Thomas.[11] On the twenty-second, Welapachtachiechen, "Erect Posture," frequently called "Captain Johnny," arrived at Lichtenau. Nearing sixty, he was currently serving as the head chief of the Delaware Turkey Clan at the village of Assinink (the place of the standing stone), near the headwaters of the

Hocking River some fifty miles below Lichtenau.[12] He was not a total stranger to Zeisberger. During the previous winter he had visited Schoenbrunn and became enamored with the Christian message. For the next five years, as a member of the Delaware council, he was deeply involved in various transactions with Zeisberger, White Eyes, Netawatwes, and Gelelemend. In December 1777, he became the Christian convert Israel.

By the first week in May, the purpose of Captain White Eyes's March visit to Philadelphia began to be revealed. A letter from him, written in Philadelphia, arrived at Goschachgunk describing his meeting with Congress and instructing the Delaware council to begin building a schoolhouse and church at Goschachgunk because "he would be bringing a preacher, schoolmaster, and also some other kind of help" to the village through a generous grant from the Congress. Zeisberger wrote, "The Chief [Netawatwes] received the news in silence and said neither anything in favor nor against it."[13] Five days later, in a conversation with Gelelemend, Zeisberger expressed his own opinion. He would be agreeable if the minister was a Moravian, but if not "we will raise a protest against his settling in Goschachgunk."[14]

On May 10, White Eyes arrived at Schoenbrunn. A messenger sent by Jungmann arrived the following day in Lichtenau to say that White Eyes had arrived with John Anderson, the trader, but he was not accompanied by a minister or a schoolmaster. Zeisberger recorded: "He, White Eyes, was first to discuss the matter [regarding the preacher, schoolteacher, and blacksmith] with his nations, and to come to an agreement with them, to what kind of a preacher they wanted to have. After that would have been done and they all would be in agreement, they should send some word, i.e., they should inform Congress about their decision."[15]

Wisely Congress had not given White Eyes a definitive answer but placed conditions on its assistance. He must clear the project with the council before Congress would give him full discretionary powers and the money to implement the proposal. Someone in the Congress understood the intricate nature of Indian diplomacy.

On the morning of May 15, Gelelemend arrived at Lichtenau. He told Zeisberger that White Eyes had just arrived at his home village, six miles east of Goschachgunk, and Gelelemend had come to invite the Brethren to the council meeting planned for the morning of the next day.

On the sixteenth, Zeisberger and five of the Brethren left for the capital. White Eyes arrived shortly after the Brethren and was greeted warmly. Zeisberger noted, "There was a meal at which much food was consumed, and White Eyes in between told about his journey and his business in Philadelphia and what there he had seen and heard. . . . He had been well received."[16]

Following the opening amenities, the council got down to business. Zeisberger was called on to translate the letter the council had just recently received from White Eyes. Zeisberger read the report issued by Congress and sent along with White Eyes's letter. The report was to be presented to the Delaware council for its consideration. In addition to asking for a preacher, schoolteacher, blacksmith, and "further assistance," White Eyes had made several other demands. Zeisberger read: "He [White Eyes] was further quoted as having demanded that arts and sciences should be introduced among the Indians. With the understanding, however, that this could not be done, except that qualified white people lived and settled among them from whom the Indians then might learn." Aid for these projects was contingent on the approval of the Delaware council.[17]

The report also contained concerns for the future peace in the area, suggestions for a possible solution to Delaware land claims, and news of the appointment of George Morgan as the new Indian agent. As Zeisberger read the report, the members of the council began to leave the council house until only the chief, several captains, and Zeisberger remained. He turned to the chief and said that it appeared that nothing more would be done that day, but before leaving, he wanted to tell the chief "that he would have no part of this matter that was now being dealt with . . . nor could he consent to it. If, however, they were willing to accept good advice, then we should be glad to give it to them, provided they asked for it."[18]

The following day the council met again, apparently without White Eyes but with some of the Brethren from Lichtenau. Netawatwes conducted a "thorough inquisition among his councilors" regarding the previous day's meeting. He wanted to get to the heart of the reason for White Eyes's trip to Philadelphia. One by one he questioned the councillors to learn who might have suggested the visit. All denied any connection with the trip and "were entirely in the dark about it," especially Captain Johnny, who was the head chief of White Eyes's tribe. The council then proceeded to discuss other business, and Zeisberger wrote, "This seems to be the end of it. The more so, since White Eyes cannot pursue the matter without the Chief's consent."[19]

The rejection of White Eyes's proposal was quickly dismissed and little open enmity seemed to remain. The question was never again discussed in formal sessions of the council. But animosity lingered under the surface. Over the next several weeks, Billy Chelloway and Isaac Glikhikan, White Eyes's close personal friends, had several private conversations with him that seemed to ameliorate the dispute. Zeisberger noted at the time, "White Eyes was kind to us even affectionate, yet he looked defeated and restless."[20] The captain was devastated by his rebuke, and his rancor would surface later.

Although any analysis of the captain's motivation remains speculative, his visits to the white settlements on the Mississippi in 1773 and to the East appear to have made a marked impression on him. The wealth and living standards of the white Euro-Americans, in contrast to the stark poverty of his own people, must have shaken his belief in the future of Indian society.

Zeisberger's remarks on May 17, the day following the critical council meeting, provide a clue to the captain's thoughts:

> His mind is entirely darkened and his concern with all kinds of minor matters and projects for great enterprises which he tries to carry out among the Indians in order to make them reputable and wealthy people and he entertained vain hopes that the great [men] of the country [Congress] will lend him their help. The Brethren and their cause, on the other hand, appeared to him too vulgar, to express it in plain English, and their poverty and lowliness do not suit him well.[21]

Zeisberger's reaction was predictable. The goals of the two men were at opposite extremes. White Eyes dreamed of a fourteenth colony set aside for the Indian nations, where white and Indian culture could coexist, while Zeisberger wanted isolation from both cultures, safe within in the arms of his Savior. The fates, however, would rule against both men.

During the first week in June, the new Indian agent, George Morgan, arrived, accompanied by Alexander McKee. The two men planned to visit the Delawares, Shawnees, and Mingoes, carrying invitations to another conference at Fort Pitt in the fall.[22] Netawatwes summoned the council and some of the Brethren from Lichtenau to gather in the afternoon to hear the new agent's report and credentials.

Morgan also brought up White Eyes's request for preachers and schoolteachers to assist the Delawares. "Congress," he told them, "was willing to help . . . they should think about it and consider the matter well."[23] He left

George Morgan, 1743–1810. From J. A. Morgan, *A History of the Family of Morgan*, 1902.

the capital on June 13 and stopped briefly at Lichtenau, then proceeded on to visit the Shawnees after spending two days with the Delawares.

Since Morgan had reopened consideration of White Eyes's proposals to Congress, the day following his departure the captain, John Killbuck, Sr., and his son Gelelemend visited Lichtenau to discuss the proposal with Wilhelm Chelloway, their close friend and confidant. They wanted his advice. By now Chelloway had had a bellyful of the whole affair. He unloaded his mind to White Eyes.

It was a stinging rebuke. All three men, however, appeared to be pleased with Chelloway's advice, especially White Eyes, who seemed to have discovered a way to extract himself from an embarrassing situation. He knew he had invited the hatred of his fellow tribesmen by going too far, too fast. Some of his friends had even told him so, saying that even though his clan was the smallest in the nation, he had appeared to assume the role of head chief, giving orders and forcing them to do something that made little sense to his tribal members. Some had even suggested he should be killed.

A canny Zeisberger detected the heart of his dilemma. That evening he closed his diary by writing: "What really aroused the Indians against him is this: they had seen that he intended not only to call into the country another minister but also a great many white people such as farmers and craftsmen, etc."[24] The Delawares hesitantly accepted the white missionaries, but the thought of additional white men was a threat to their cultural life, which they clearly recognized. Zeisberger certainly understood the danger in bringing additional white craftsmen to the area at a time when a general Indian war loomed on the horizon.

On July 13, George Morgan and Alexander McKee stopped at Lichtenau after visiting the Shawnees and Mingoes. Zeisberger had anticipated their discouraging news. He recorded: "It does not look at all favorable among the nations so that we could believe that we will have quiet and peaceful times, for something is working among them that we cannot quite understand at the moment. But it is generally believed that if an Indian war breaks out it will be more fierce than ever has been which Mr. Morgan believes also." It was during this visit that Zeisberger proposed to the agent that systematic and regular communications be set up between the Delaware capital and Pittsburgh "to keep each other informed." This became an extremely important factor in the future course of the mission and marked the first time Zeisberger directly offered help to the colonials. He recorded the conversation in the third person:

> Bro. David proposed to him to share with the Delaware the communication from Pittsburgh, so the lies would be stopped and the Indians would know where they were at. Mr. Morgan approved this idea and the next day talked to the council at Goschachgunk and they approved what he said, that every fourteen days or so, or as often as it seems good, to send a courier to the fort. This was begun immediately

> and continued as long as necessary. At the same time he [Morgan] requested of Bro. David that when the Chiefs had anything to report to the Fort, he would do it for them and this he promised to do.[25]

This new arrangement was the first time Zeisberger reversed his traditional policy of avoiding political involvement between the Indians and the new American government. Between this point and the time of their final removal of the converts from the Muskingum Valley in 1781, many letters were exchanged between Zeisberger, Heckewelder, the Delaware council, and the authorities at Pittsburgh.

The Delawares and Shawnees spent the last two weeks in July and all of August and September preparing for the coming treaty conference to take place at Pittsburgh the last two weeks in October. Little hope was held that the Wyandots would participate. They seemed to be under the control of the British governor at Detroit. The Delawares sent a runner to the Upper Sandusky chiefs. By August 11 the messenger reported that none of the western tribes had decided to declare war against the colonies despite unusual pressure from Governor Henry Hamilton at Detroit.[26]

There was no speculation concerning the Mingoes. Dunmore's War had filled their hearts with hostility and a desire for revenge against all white men. Morgan had some success when he talked with their delegation, which he met at the Shawnee villages on June 20, but Logan, their speaker, was far from convinced that they should abandon their bloody attacks on the western frontier. They would probably not attend the treaty conference in October, but they authorized the Shawnees to speak for them.[27]

The extent and frequency of these attacks can be traced in the mission diaries of Gnadenhutten and Lichtenau. Mingo war parties passed regularly through both villages, stopping for a free meal. Zeisberger estimated their warrior population to be approximately eighty, and the ferocity of their attacks struck fear in the hearts of the white settlers living along the frontier. A survey of these visitations between 1775 and 1781 gives some indication of Mingo activity, particularly during 1776 and 1777. During most of these visits to the missions they were either looking for white traders, carrying scalps of murdered victims, or escorting prisoners back to their villages, all to be delivered subsequently to British governor Hamilton in Detroit. The number of Mingo visits were as follows: 1775, 7; 1776, 30; 1777, 62; 1778, 14; 1779, 18; 1780, none; 1781, 3.[28]

By July, the Mingo war parties were ranging and killing in the white western pioneer settlements, but the Shawnees and Wyandots and, of course, the Delawares, had not strayed from their neutral position. It was impossible, however, for the chiefs of the neutral tribes to control all of their warriors, especially the younger men. Invariably, most of the Mingo war parties contained a few men from all three of the neutral tribes.

Shortly after George Morgan's return to Fort Pitt, the congressional commissioners dispatched John Anderson to Goschachgunk to set up a "listening Post" to monitor the political climate in that area. He arrived at the capital during the last week in August.[29]

Morgan had ordered William Wilson, a friend and local trader, to visit the Shawnees and request their assistance in encouraging the Wyandots to come to Pittsburgh in the fall. Wilson, now accompanied by John Montour and two parties of Shawnees and Delawares, arrived at the Upper Sandusky some time during the middle of August. They received a warm and friendly reception, but the local chiefs insisted that they must all proceed to Detroit to discuss the details with the governor. On arrival at Detroit, they were presented to Governor Hamilton, who, as expected, threatened Wilson, tore his message in small pieces, cut the belt to shreds before the eyes of the Indians, and ordered both Wilson and White Eyes to depart the village before nightfall under pain of death. Before leaving the Upper Sandusky, Wilson did receive a promise from many of the Wyandot and Shawnee chiefs that the decision to go to war would be made by them and not by Hamilton. White Eyes and the Delaware delegation returned from Detroit just in time to begin preparations to leave for the Pittsburgh conference.[30]

The first session of the conference began on October 26 after all the tribes had arrived. Represented were the Shawnees, Delawares, and a few chiefs from the Seneca tribe of the Six Nations. Neither the Mingoes nor the Wyandots sent delegations. Until recently, scant information on this conference was available. In 1976, through a distant relative of George Morgan, the documents covering this period of Morgan's life surfaced in California.[31] Fortunately, we now have the details of the conference as seen through the eyes of Morgan, the principal colonial delegate. The congressional commissioners, Jasper Yeats and Colonel John Montgomery, were also present.[32] With the Shawnees were Koketha and their head chief, Cornstalk, who was the principal speaker. The Delawares were represented by Netawatwes, Gelelemend, White Eyes, Captain Johnny, and Captain Pipe, the new head chief of the Wolf Clan. Wilhelm Chelloway and Isaac Glikhikan were present as the Christian mission delegates. The principal Six Nations chiefs were Flying Crow and Guyasuta.

Most of the formal discussions revolved around problems with the Mingoes, who appeared to be the principal cause for the disruption of the peace and the other problems confronted by the delegates. The first and most significant speech was made by Cornstalk, who referred to his recent meeting with Hamilton in Detroit. Morgan recorded Cornstalk's remarks: "The governor of Detroit spoke to the Indians in my presence and told them he did not desire they should strike the white inhabitants on the Ohio, and I tell the truth when I say that, if you blame him or the people in Detroit for what he has done you are wrong for no persons are to blame but a Banditti of Mingoes and those with whom they have intermarried at and near Pluggy's Town."[33]

The next few days of the conference were spent devising a program to deal with the recalcitrant Mingo raiders. On October 29, the delegates met again, and Cornstalk renewed his appeal to the Seneca chief Flying Cloud to assist in controlling his Mingo wards. Morgan recorded the chief's response: "We are determined to send the White Mingo and others to make them sit still—if they do not take our advice they shall repent it."[34]

On October 31, Netawatwes died suddenly, and the conference ended. The Christian Indians had lost a dear, valuable friend and the Delawares their head chief. His death was not entirely unexpected, but it proved to be a devastating blow to both parties. Zeisberger received the melancholy news on November 5 and sadly reported, "He was a true friend of the Brethren. May the Lord remember him and let him have a part in eternity in our homes."[35] Some historians have contended that Netawatwes was divested of his role as head chief sometime before his death. The diaries and conference records clearly show this contention to be totally erroneous. He remained solidly in control until the day of his death.

The vacuum caused by the death of any head chief among the Indians usually led to a power struggle. Gelelemend had been rumored as Netawatwes's replacement, but that misinformation had been passed on by white authorities at the Pittsburgh conference in 1775. Gelelemend, just forty at the time, was relatively young to be the head chief. He did, however, serve as the temporary head chief for the next few years, closely assisted by White Eyes, Machingue Pushies (the Cat), Buckongahelas (One Whose Movements Are Certain), and Tete Bokshke or Grand Glaise (One Who Is Split), all members of the Turtle Clan.[36] Another of his close associates was Captain Johnny, the head chief of the Turkey Clan.

It was a long, slow, sad journey back to the valley following the close of the treaty conference. White Eyes had gone to Philadelphia with a delegation of twelve chiefs on the invitation of George Morgan. He was absent from Goschachgunk for over two months, returning on January 4 of the next year.

During the fall months, some changes occurred at the Christian villages. William Edwards had arrived at Schoenbrunn to serve as an additional missionary assistant.[37] On December 11, Edwards was moved to Lichtenau to assist Zeisberger, and John Heckewelder was transferred to Schoenbrunn to work with the Jungmanns. Netawatwes's wife moved to Lichtenau, where she lived for the rest of her life. Captain Johnny also moved his family to Lichtenau from his former village at Assinink. Accompanying his family were twenty other residents from his village. Captain Johnny's wife, Rachel, was a white woman who had been captured as a girl in 1757 during the French and Indian War. She eventually married the chief and had lived happily among the Indians for nineteen years.[38] They had three children. Over the next few years the chief became a close personal adviser to Gelelemend and White Eyes.

On November 20, shortly after the Delaware delegation returned from the Pittsburgh conference, a Wyandot chief stopped at Goschachgunk to state that his tribe and some of the other western tribes had decided to go to war against the Americans. He was sent to the Delawares to get their reaction. After several hours of deliberation, the chief was instructed to return to his people and advise them that the Delawares intended to continue their neutrality. He was also cautioned to keep his war parties away from the Delaware villages. One month later, they received hopeful news from the Wyandot chiefs. Zeisberger noted:

> They [Wyandot], as well as the Tawas have accepted the Delaware message and explanation as to why they do not want to be involved in war. Likewise, they explained and announced that the Indians gathered from all Nations in Detroit, upon hearing the Chief from Sandusky's message of the Delawares peaceful sentiments, all returned home again and their aims to go to war against the white people were given up for the time being.[39]

During the previous months there had been a substantial influx of residents to the new village, especially since the people from Assinink moved to Lichtenau. On November 24, Zeisberger decided to read the rules and regulations of the village. The Helpers' Conference had added three new laws to the list:

1) Noone can live here who wants to be treated (medically) according to the heathen methods.
2) Noone can be here who thinks of going to war, or even to take part in war robbery.

3) Noone who wants to live here should paint himself, nor hang wampum, silver or anything on himself. Who wants to do that cannot be allowed here.[40]

At the end of the year the total Christian population on December 31, 1776, was estimated to be over four hundred.[41]

· 21 ·

A Conspiracy on the Muskingum, 1777

In the fall and winter of 1775, a rebel army led by Benedict Arnold and Richard Montgomery made a valiant but abortive attempt to capture Canada. Although Montgomery was successful against Montreal, the attack against Quebec failed.[1] But the invasion had the side effects of sealing the British supply lines to the interior and preventing Indian trade goods from reaching Detroit.[2] Lacking both men and material, Governor Hamilton had to be content with urging the Indians to conduct small, individual, and largely ineffective raids against the frontier.

With fewer than eighty English regulars under his command, Hamilton could do little to mount an effective offensive. Each of his prospective Indian allies had rejected his proffered war belts, primarily because the Delawares refused and other tribes followed their example. Only the Mingoes were Hamilton's willing allies. Smarting from their humiliating defeat during Dunmore's War, they refused to be placated by American agents.

With the lifting of the American blockade of the St. Lawrence River in early 1777, British supplies began to filter into Detroit, and the fragile peace carefully crafted by the United States agent at Pittsburgh began to disintegrate. Movements toward the British first began to appear among the Shawnees. By summer their loyalties were divided between their two principal chiefs, Cornstalk and Blackfish. Cornstalk pleaded for peace while Blackfish's young militant warriors joined the Mingoes in repeated attacks against the frontier settlements. Shortly after the beginning of the new year, Zeisberger received word that a party of sixty-four Shawnee warriors was headed for the western frontier to wreak havoc on the white settlements.[3] When the warriors returned from their attack on the last day in March, they were badly beaten up, had lost several men, and had taken only one prisoner. But despite their apparent failure, they were determined to resume their attacks.

On January 20, Zeisberger received word that the Mingo leader Pluggy had been killed on December 29 at McClelland's Station in Kentucky. Rather than diminishing the Mingo zeal, his death only exacerbated their hostility against the whites. The attackers regrouped under the leadership of Pluggy's son.

It was soon obvious to the missionaries and their converts that their principal enemies were the Mingoes, now augmented by a sprinkling of dissatisfied Shawnees and Wyandots and even some disgruntled Delawares, especially the Munsees, some of whom were still living among the converts. Heckewelder, who was now at Schoenbrunn with the Jungmanns, was keeping the diary. He wrote on February 13 that the Munsee convert Augustine, the former Newallike, had the previous month broken with the Brethren and was now living at Killbuck's town (present Killbuck, Ohio), fifteen miles northwest of the Delaware capital of Goschachgunk. Although Heckewelder admitted that the missionaries were always "painfully disturbed" to lose any converts, in this instance, he wrote, "we could not help but thank the Saviour for having rid us such a bad influence as Augustine had been."[4]

By March, rumors were rife that the Mingoes were planning to kill the missionaries, beginning first at Schoenbrunn when the converts were absent during sugar-cooking time. Zeisberger took the rumor seriously, and some of the brothers were instructed to remain behind in the village.[5] The day before Zeisberger received his warning at Lichtenau, Heckewelder and the Jungmanns at Schoenbrunn received a similar warning. Nicholas, the son of Thomas, the Mingo, visited their village carrying this message: "That a Mingo had come to him [Nicholas] into his house at Walhondink and had said to him that it had been decided that as soon as the weather would become warmer, so that one could boil sugar [when the villages would be empty except for the missionaries], a party of Mingo would come in order to take Brother Heckewelder and Schebosh prisoners or to kill them."[6]

Several days later Thomas, the Mingo, visited his son Nicholas, who in the meantime had moved to Schoenbrunn, warning him that within the next few days a party of nine Mingoes intended to raid the village and carry Heckewelder and the Jungmanns to Detroit as prisoners.[7] At Gnadenhutten, Schmick was also receiving similar threatening reports, and he posted guards in the schoolhouse at night.[8]

The Delaware council was also privy to these threatening rumors and became so alarmed that it issued a call for a meeting to begin March 8 and continue for four days or until some solution to the Mingo threats was found. "The main work of the chiefs," as Zeisberger noted on March 2, "was to devise plans to hold the [Christian] Indians together so that none of their people would be drawn into war by enemy Indians but that they remain calm so that the Delaware nation remains in peace." Zeisberger's main concern was the Delaware Munsees, many of whom were presently living in the mission villages. Were they possibly conspiring with the Mingoes against the Christians? He noted in his diary that the Munsees were "tottering and not very steady."[9] The council agenda included methods and procedures to protect the missionaries against attack.

While the action of the Mingoes during the previous two weeks appeared to be the main threat to the missionaries, the defection of some of the Munsees, particularly the former convert Augustine, would shortly prove to be equally ominous. Although he had defected earlier in the winter, Augustine continued to live off and on at Schoenbrunn, where most of his relatives and friends resided. During January and February, he convinced most of his people to question the preaching of the missionaries, creating doubt and confusion among the converts and problems for Heckewelder and the Jungmanns.

The council meeting at Goschachgunk began on the eighth of March and continued through the eleventh. Zeisberger briefly attended the first day's discussion, and the Brethren had representatives in attendance for all four days. White Eyes presided at the meetings.[10]

The Munsee apostates from Schoenbrunn attended the conference, represented by Newallike and Jacob Gendaskund. The former no longer maintained a home at Schoenbrunn, but Gendaskund continued to live at the village. Both were secretly leading the Munsee defectors and cooperating with the Mingoes. It was obvious to those who attended the council meeting that the Munsees were not pleased with White Eyes's strong defense and his continued connection with the Christians.[11]

While White Eyes and Gelelemend contended with the suspected dissension among the Delawares, the missionaries had to deal with defection among their own converts. It was a situation that demanded determined and skillful leadership. Unfortunately, when the crisis came, at Schoenbrunn, neither the Jungmanns or Heckewelder met the challenge.

On March 14, the Delaware council at Goschachgunk received another rumor of pending Mingo attacks against the missionaries.[12] The repetition and similarity of these threatening reports had all three missions in a state of panic. With the responsibility for over four hundred Indian men, women, and children as well as the missionaries on his shoulders, Zeisberger faced the greatest challenge of his life. He could rely on the majority of the Delaware council to maintain the peace, but he was still surrounded by enemies. Four days later, the diary noted, "We encouraged them [the converts] not to be dismayed and comforted them with words that everything done here among the Indians is God's work and not man's and therefore he will not allow his Indian congregation to be disturbed and destroyed . . . stand fast and do not give in."[13]

By March 21, the deadline for the Mingo attack against Schoenbrunn had passed, but tensions remained high. Zeisberger was called to Goschachgunk to confer again with the chiefs regarding a message they had just received from George Morgan pleading with the council to keep the peace. The message had been brought to the capital by James O'Hare, an assistant Indian agent working with Morgan.[14] O'Hare's visit is an important link to understanding the coming events.

Events of the next few days are clouded in mystery. After Zeisberger left the meeting, his Lichtenau converts, who were also members of the Delaware native council, were again called into session and told that the council had decided, in their absence, that all of the converts at Schoenbrunn and Gnadenhutten should be brought to Lichtenau until the threat of war was over. The diaries are silent as to when this decision was made. They further recommended that the missionaries, especially those with wives and families, should return to the settlement but left that decision to the missionaries' own individual judgment.[15]

Unknown to Zeisberger and his Indian councillors, the native council had agent O'Hare write and secretly send a message to Morgan seeking his opinion regarding their decision to consolidate the missions and send most of the missionaries back to the settlements. To emphasize its importance, Chief Gelelemend personally carried the message to Pittsburgh. It seemed obvious that the council did not want the Christians or Zeisberger to know of this dispatch. Normally Zeisberger wrote the council's messages to Morgan. Why was he not called to write this one?

The events that immediately followed were totally out of character for David Zeisberger. A wary and cautious man when faced with critical decisions, he usually deliberated and carefully thought out all of his options. Without checking with any of the principal chiefs, Zeisberger accepted at face value his own councillors' description of what they had been told at the council meeting. He left the next day for Gnadenhutten. Schmick noted:

> Contrary to our expectation Bro. D. Zeisberger arrived with Abraham and Isaac from Lichtenau. We and our members rejoiced cordially with this meeting. But soon after we learned the reason for their coming, namely that all our people from this place and all from Schoenbrunn should move to Lichtenau so that they in Goschachgunk, reinforced by them [the Christians], might be strong in case of war; that the chiefs and the councilors in Goschachgunk desire this; that they, the brethren therefore have been sent hither by them to tell us this and also what they thought with regards to their teachers and their wives, namely, that I and my wife, Brother Jungmann and his wife, Brother Heckewelder could return to Bethlehem since one brother would be enough for them.[16]

Zeisberger, who was going on to Schoenbrunn, would receive the Gnadenhutten converts' decision on his return visit.

Abraham, Isaac, and Zeisberger then moved on the Schoenbrunn. The same speech was made, first to the Helpers' Conference and then to the general membership. Heckewelder's entry is particularly interesting for the tart manner in which Zeisberger made the announcement. "He at once informed us about the purpose of his present visit, namely, that the chiefs, in view of the present warlike times, and dangerous circumstance, and for the sake of greater safety for us, were positively demanding that we, here in Schoenbrunn, as well as our Brethren and sisters at Gnadenhutten, should move to Lichtenau near Koshachkink [Goschachgunk]."[17]

In contrast to the Gnadenhutten reaction, the announcement was received with relief, except for the Munsees. Heckewelder recorded their reaction. "*They said briefly in one word, We are through believing.*" Not only were the Munsees opposed to the move, they were highly resentful of the speech made by White Eyes on March 9 pledging the Delawares' unqualified support for the Christians.[18] The move to abandon Schoenbrunn was to take place shortly after Easter Sunday on March 30, or as soon thereafter as possible.

Zeisberger returned to Gnadenhutten on March 24. Schmick noted in his diary, "It snowed all day." In keeping with the weather, the Zeisberger party received a chilly reception. Schmick and his people were unilaterally opposed to the move and in fact refused to comply, defying Zeisberger's order.[19]

Zeisberger arrived back at Lichtenau on March 26, consoled that his trip had been partially effective despite Schmick's objection. While the Mahicans at Gnadenhutten refused to make the move, the Delaware converts at Schoenbrunn, with the exception of the Munsees, were most willing. They had told Zeisberger at the time of the announcement, "We have waited long for this and hoped it would be said to them." But the orderly and systematic move envisioned by Zeisberger did not occur.

At Schoenbrunn, the Easter festival was celebrated with all the usual solemnity.[20] On Monday, March 31, the Brethren began to make the canoes needed for the move, and the Sisters repaired to their sugar lodges. The following day Schebosh and his family moved to Gnadenhutten.[21] It would be the last peaceful day in the five-year history of the Schoenbrunn mission.

That evening, a breathless Sem, a relatively new convert, ran into the Schoenbrunn village announcing that eighteen Mingo warriors were at the abandoned site of the old Delaware village of Tuscarabi, just fifteen miles north of the village, planning an attack against Schoenbrunn that evening. Heckewelder hastily wrote, "It was their intention to kill us white brethren and Sisters both here and at Gnadenhutten. Jacob Gendaskund and Nicolaus, who confirmed the validity of this news, also insisted that if we would not go, it would soon be to late."[22]

Why the Jungmanns and Heckewelder placed any credence in these reports is hard to understand. First, Sem, a convert baptized on Christmas Day two years earlier, had had a reputation for being unstable since arriving at the mission. Shortly after this incident he disappears from the diaries. Second, Jacob Gendaskund was a well-known troublemaker among the Munsees living at Schoenbrunn. His friend Nicolaus was a Mingo, the son of Thomas and Maria and the bearer of the earlier false rumors of Mingo attacks. All of these characters were known by Heckewelder and the Jungmanns to be unreliable sources. Nevertheless, with the receipt of this news, the great run-away from Schoenbrunn began.

In the dead of night, Abraham and Michael loaded the Jungmanns and the Conners into several canoes and headed downstream for Lichtenau.

Several trusted Indians led Heckewelder on foot to Gnadenhutten. They arrived at Gnadenhutten just after midnight, surprising the Schmicks. The river was high with the heavy spring runoff, and the Jungmann and Conner parties did not arrive until early on the morning of April 2. After eating breakfast, they proceeded with haste to Lichtenau.[23]

Later the same day, Gnadenhutten had another important visitor. Chief Gelelemend arrived from Fort Pitt carrying agent Morgan's response to the query regarding the status of the Christian missions and the white missionaries.

Gelelemend had been instructed by Morgan to stop at Gnadenhutten and let Schmick and his Helpers' Conference, especially Johannas Martin, read the dispatch. Schmick and Heckewelder gathered in Martin's cabin, and Heckewelder read the speech. Morgan first cautioned the Delaware chiefs to maintain the peace and admonished them not to believe all the recent reports "they heard regarding other Indians as so dangerous." Morgan then instructed the chief not to send the missionaries back to the settlements. He wrote: "Concerning the departure of the Brethren Schmick, Jungmann, and J. Heckewelder I can say nothing, provided it is their wish; they themselves will know what to do in this matter, for they have been sent by God. . . . Therefore it is my advice and wish that you should try and keep them and esteem them." Schmick added a footnote to his diary that evening which provides an important clue to the entire affair: "All of this Mr. Morgan wrote concerning us to the chiefs they did not permit to come to the ears of D. Zeisberger in Lichtenau but kept to themselves. For I asked Brother David [later] about it, but he knew nothing of it; and that is no good sign of friendship."[24] Neither Heckewelder nor Zeisberger mentioned this Morgan dispatch in their diaries; only Schmick referred to it.

Agent O'Hare provided one final clue in this strange episode. On the way back to Pittsburgh he stopped at Schoenbrunn on April 1, the night of the expected attack. Six days later, when he returned to Pittsburgh, he wrote to his friend Devereux Smith:

> Dear Sir: I arrived yesterday from the Indian country, and I must say that I have great reason to suspect that numbers of the savages are determined to annoy our frontiers as much as they dare. On the 2d day of this month, as I was preparing to start with my horses from the Moravian town [Schoenbrunn], their were three runners arrived from the Tuscarawas, about thirteen short miles off, with intelligence that there were a party of eighteen, consisting of fifteen Mingoes, two

> Shawnee and one Wyandot at that place, on their way to war, and that they intended to come for the ministers and other white people who live with the Moravians, upon which all the white people of the upper town fled that night to the principal Delaware town; *however I stayed till next morning and got two of the Moravian Indians to go meet the warriors and find out, if possible, what they intended to do*. We got for an answer that they looked on themselves as free men, that they had no king nor chief, therefore would do as they pleased, *and that in the first place, they would visit the neighborhood of Fort Pitt*. . . . The Muncies [Munsees] have in general turned off from the Delaware, and are much inclined to listen to the Mingoes. The Shawnees are divided, about one half of them have joined the Mingoes, the Wiandots seem more inclined for peace.[25]

Despite the threat to all white people living at Schoenbrunn, agent O'Hare remained at the village the night of April 1 and seemed to have had no difficulty finding reliable Delaware runners to hasten to the Tuscarabi and check out the rumor the next day. Why, then, did Heckewelder and Jungmanns not follow the same procedure but choose to flee?

The great runaway had dealt the Schoenbrunn mission a death blow from which it never recovered. On April 3, Heckewelder received word in Gnadenhutten that the so-called Mingo party had proceeded on to the eastern settlements. After hearing this report, Heckewelder returned to Schoenbrunn only to find that "all sorts of good-for-nothing rabble are assembling here and are rejoicing at our secession."[26]

Heckewelder resumed the church services at Schoenbrunn, but the old spirit was gone. Throughout the next seventeen days Zeisberger and Schmick provided men and canoes to move the loyal converts to Gnadenhutten or Lichtenau. On April 8, Jacob Gendaskund and his friends announced that they were moving into the village and began inspecting the various houses as potential homes. Two days later Newallike arrived. He had come from Goschachgunk, where he had informed the chief that he was moving back to Schoenbrunn and planned to be the reigning village chief. The following day the Munsees held a shooting match and Heckewelder noted that "the only thing left to be feared is that rum will be brought in."[27]

Zeisberger and a large party of men and canoes arrived at Schoenbrunn on Saturday, April 12, from Lichtenau. They spent the next seven days moving the last of the loyal converts. On April 19, Brother David conducted the final service in the church. Following the meeting, the building was demolished to prevent desecration.[28] The next day the last of the loyal converts left Schoenbrunn. Zeisberger's crown jewel was now occupied by his enemies.

Perhaps no other event in David Zeisberger's sixty-three years among the Indians created more controversy than the closing of Schoenbrunn. Johann Schmick became his sharpest critic. Within the next four months the Schmicks would leave the valley and return to Bethlehem. In a letter dated May 24, Schmick wrote to his friend Matthew Hehl in Litiz. The disappointed missionary poured out his sorrow about the move with remarkable candor. His main complaints centered on Zeisberger's failure to use the lot in making the decision and his willingness to accept the suggestion of the Delaware chief that the missions be consolidated. He criticized not only Zeisberger but also the Jungmanns, whom he felt fled in an unseemly manner "in such a cunning way through the machinations of the evil enemy." "They could have," he surmised, "quietly stayed there, as we did at Gnadenhutten, even though our people had also been requested by the Chiefs to move away." Schmick also complained about the arbitrary way the order to move was given. "There is nothing to deliberate about," Zeisberger had said, "you just have to get away; there is nothing else to do; you have to move down, it will be war." (Schmick's complete letter can be found in Appendix G.)

It is difficult to form any firm conclusions regarding the closing of Schoenbrunn. While Zeisberger may have overreacted, he may have been privy to information within the Delaware council not available to Schmick, and his main concern was the vulnerability of the Schoenbrunn mission thirty-five miles away from protection of those at the Delaware capital and Lichtenau. But the safety of those consolidated converts at Lichtenau depended entirely on the Delawares remaining at peace. If the nation broke its neutrality and joined the British, both the missionaries and the converts at Lichtenau were in extreme danger at the forks of the Muskingum.

Two major developments occurred the first week in June. Hamilton received permissory orders from Governor Guy Carleton at Quebec calling on him to press immediately for all Indian tribes to join with the British and accept the war belt and for colonial western inhabitants to submit to King George and take refuge within British posts, where land bounties would be given them for loyal service. It was a cunning invitation, mingling terror with reward in the hopes that the rebellion could be speedily crushed. The Indian raiders scattered these proclamations among the backwoodsmen as they made their attacks, often leaving them on the dead bodies of their victims killed during raids.[29]

active in Detroit, General Edward Hand arrived
to become the first United States commander of
possible assignment, considering the mere hand-
troops assigned to him by Congress. There was
the Indian war parties that ranged far and wide
g death and havoc along their trail.[31]

ssion stations were directly in the path of most of
ne first five months of 1777, thirty-five different en-
tivities of the Mingo war parties were recorded
chmick diaries. Time after time, despite instruc-
n the Delaware council, they passed through both
itenau, always announcing their arrival with the
oller." Most of the parties were accompanied by
boys and girls petrified with fear, the scalps of their
nging from the warriors' belts or mounted on poles.
the Delaware chiefs attempted to ransom the chil-
success. Zeisberger and his fellow missionaries were
vail endured by these young children, but nothing
n care for their immediate needs for food and cloth-

l Hand's arrival at Fort Pitt, Zeisberger began to correspond with him. In his first letter, dated July 7, 1777, he advised Hand to urge the Indian agent Morgan to come to Goschachgunk for the coming treaty conference in July because the Wyandots refused to come to Fort Pitt.[33] John Montour arrived at Lichtenau the same day Zeisberger sent his letter to Hand, bringing disturbing news from Detroit. Zeisberger noted, "It seems a full scale Indian war will break out. It remains to be seen what will happen when the Wyandot come here and what the Delaware nation can work out with them."[34]

During the afternoon of July 20, the Wyandot delegation of nineteen warriors, chiefs, and captains arrived, headed by their principal and powerful chief, Pomoacan (the Half-King). The following day the council began. It was a short and to-the-point meeting because the Wyandots were anxious to return home. Pomoacan presented the war belt to the Delawares, and strongly exhorted his cousins to follow his example and join in the war against the rebels. Two days later, the Wyandots received their reply. It was nearly a unanimous decision. Neither the Delaware chiefs nor the captains would comply, citing their pledge in the 1775 and 1776 treaties to remain at peace with their American friends. Not satisfied with the answer, a disgruntled Pomoacan returned the belt hoping the Delawares would change their minds in a few days. The Wyandot party was back on the road late in the afternoon. Several days later, the Delaware council again rejected the war belt and returned it to the Upper Sandusky.[35]

Most of the credit for the Delawares' prompt decision can be attributed to Captain Johnny, the head chief of the Turkey Clan. During the previous months he had moved from his home village of Assinink to Lichtenau and become an important influence in the council's deliberations. He used his position as one of the leading chiefs to keep the Delawares on friendly terms with the Christians and the colonials at Fort Pitt.

On July 29, Zeisberger again wrote to General Hand. Most of the letter discussed the conference between the Wyandots and the Delawares. Near the end of the letter he wrote:

> We wish that an Army might soon come out, this would, in my opinion, be the only Method to get a Peace settled among the Nations. . . . The Delawares flatter themselves that an Army will soon come out which is their only Hope yet, but should that fail I am afraid they cannot stand, & then surely all the Nations, that have not yet joined & taken the War Belt, will soon join them.[36]

During the thirteen days after Pomoacan departed, the frequency of war parties passing through the village accelerated and Zeisberger became concerned for the safety of the Jungmanns. On August 5 the question was submitted to the lot, and Zeisberger recorded the results. "He [the Lord] gave us the direction that the Jungmanns should be brought away from here to a secure place." The following evening, accompanied by five trusted guards, they left the village bound for Bethlehem. He wrote, "Their departure was moving and touching and our tears accompanied them."[37] They would both return four years later only to be caught in "the Great Dispersement" in 1781 and suffer great hardship. Heckewelder had been sent back to Bethlehem on May 27, shortly after the abandonment of Schoenbrunn. With the departure of the Jungmanns, Zeisberger and Edwards were left alone at Lichtenau.

The day after the Jungmanns departed, Zeisberger received word that more than two hundred Wyandot warriors led by Pomoacan were headed toward the western settlements, specifically to attack Fort Henry at Wheeling. He heard that they would stop at the Delaware capital en route. Zeisberger began to devise his strategy and knew he would be required to play the host because both White Eyes and Gelelemend were in Fort Pitt consulting with Morgan. Calling together all of the Brethren, they discussed how to feed so many warriors and how to help those at the capital in Goschachgunk entertain their guests.[38]

Well over one hundred warriors arrived the next day at Goschachgunk. Pomoacan and several of his leading captains were with the vanguard. The brothers organized a feast and the sisters prepared food for the hungry travelers gathered at Goschachgunk. After their meal Isaac was granted permission to address their guests. Totally in the dark as to Pomoacan's intentions, Isaac took no chances and stationed a runner at the door of the council house. The runner was instructed to go immediately to Zeisberger at Lichtenau if Pomoacan displayed any hostile action against the Christians so they could flee for safety.

Isaac delivered a short but friendly speech explaining that the Christian missions desired to live "peaceably" and keep their teachers among them and looked upon the converts "as their own flesh and blood." "What you do to them," he said, "you do to us, good or bad." The appropriate wampum was presented. Following the speech, Pomoacan responded, "My cousins, you Christian Indians. I am extremely happy to hear from you. Your words went through my ears to my heart." He asked for their patience until he could talk to his warriors and get their opinion. After a brief meeting with his captains, Pomoacan said:

> My cousins: It is very pleasing to me and I feel very good about it that you have cleansed my eyes, my ears and my heart from all the evil that the wind has blown in on this trip. I am a soldier and go to war, therefore many things come over me and many evil thoughts go through my head and even into my heart. I am happy, however, that my eyes are bright and that I can look at my cousins with open ears and can take their words into my heart.

He continued with the typical beautiful imagery of Indian speeches, promising that no harm would come to their teachers and requesting permission to meet them the next day at their own village. "I want to look upon your teachers as I do my own father across the Lake, yes as my own body. This I will make known to my warriors."[39]

The following day, true to his promise, Pomoacan and eighty-three of his warriors visited Lichtenau and talked with Zeisberger and Edwards. It was a cordial and friendly meeting, the first time the men met. Unfortunately, they would later have a stormy and hostile relationship ending tragically for Zeisberger.[40]

On August 10, the day after Pomoacan's visit, Zeisberger received a surprising letter by special courier from Gnadenhutten. The Schmicks advised Zeisberger that they were leaving that afternoon to return to the settlements. It must have come as a shock to Zeisberger because his diary contains no indication that Schmick planned to leave. Schmick's own Gnadenhutten diary runs through July 31 and then ends abruptly. It also gave no indication of plans to return to the settlements.[41]

With the wisdom of more than two hundred years of hindsight, it is still difficult to understand the particulars of Schmick's departure. Few facts remain about Zeisberger and Schmick's relationship during the months after the closing of Schoenbrunn other than the passages in his diary. It seems obvious that he violently disagreed with Zeisberger's action. His letter to Matthew Hehl clearly registers his feelings. It was a sad final chapter in what had generally been a pleasant twenty-six-year alliance. Schmick made a monumental contribution to the Moravian missionary program; as schoolteacher, musician, hymnologist, linguist, and missionary he had been in the missionary service since 1751. He died unexpectedly at age sixty-four, less than five months after his departure from the valley.

Pomoacan and his warriors remained in the valley until August 23. Each day additional men arrived to join his party until more than two hundred warriors roamed through the two villages, much to the discomfort of Zeisberger, who did his best to keep them fed. On the fifteenth he wrote, "All kinds of nations and languages now gathered here—Tawas, Chippewa, Wyandot, Mingo of all sorts, Shawnee, Frenchman, and Pottawattamie. Daily our houses are full of them, but they are all very orderly, shy, and show themselves to be our friends." White Eyes and Gelelemend arrived back from the fort on August 21, two days before Pomoacan's departure. White Eyes announced to the warriors that "soon they could expect a strong [United States] army in Indian land." Two days later most of the Wyandot contingent left for Fort Henry. With a sigh of relief, Zeisberger wrote, "Satan is loose and rests not a little. But the Saviour graciously helped us out of trouble and sent us on the 24th a peaceful day."[42]

Nathanael and Marcus had escorted William Edwards to Gnadenhutten the previous day to become the new missionary replacing the Schmicks. Edwards and Zeisberger were now alone in the valley with the herculean task of supervising almost four hundred Christian converts.

Upon his arrival from the fort on August 21, the wily White Eyes's casual comment regarding the coming of a American army caused quite a stir among the warriors, especially among the Mingoes. Over the previous several months, Patrick Henry, the governor of Virginia, had mentioned plans to send such an expedition against the Mingoes, but those plans were abandoned. Perhaps, thought the Mingoes, they were now being revised. They could not be sure and promptly panicked and withdrew from Pomoacan's expedition against Fort Henry, returning to their villages to protect their women and children. Some of the Wyandots even returned to their homes in Upper Sandusky. As a result, only 140 warriors accompanied Pomoacan to Fort Henry, substantially weakening his forces.

On September 5, Zeisberger received his first report of the attack on Fort Henry. He noted, "One Wyandot was killed and several wounded." Two days later he had a more accurate account. "A war party of over 100 men returned with 11 scalps. They had attacked the Fort in Wilunk [Wheeling] where, according to their knowledge 14 men were killed and made many people leave their homes which then they plundered. On the Fort, however, they could do nothing further."[43]

The Mingoes' abandonment of the Pomoacan army marked the end of major activity of this nation against the western frontier. Zeisberger noted only one more incident of a Mingo party stopping at Lichtenau during the remaining months of 1777 and but a handful for 1778 and 1779.

The month of September not only brought tension and nervousness among the Mingoes and some of the Wyandots, it also began to affect the Delawares, especially White Eyes. Late in the night on September 12, Zeisberger was summoned to Goschachgunk to read a series of letters just delivered by couriers from George Morgan and General Hand. The contents of the letters were similar to those they had received in the past; Zeisberger noted that "they sounded good and along with all earlier speeches sent to the Delaware." That was not the problem. Zeisberger explained the reason for White Eyes's panic.

> But what the couriers [verbally] told them was very terrible, namely, that a new General had arrived in Pittsburgh who gives no Indian pardon, be he friend or foe, but wants to "root out" all of them indiscriminately. Mr. Morgan told them secretly [the couriers advised the Delawares] they should arm themselves and fight as well as they can and do their best because the Indians have to die anyway, fighting or not. . . . The couriers also said that *the Virginians would be in Goschachgunk in a few days. That gave new confusion and panic.*[44]

It was all a pack of lies. There was no new general, no army on the march, and no change in United States Indian policy. Zeisberger told White Eyes and the council not to believe everything the couriers said but to send to the fort and get the facts. Furthermore, the letters conformed with Morgan's and Hand's previous communications. The only deviation was a suggestion by Morgan that they temporarily cease communications because of unsettled conditions in and around the fort and a fear that the messengers might be killed by disgruntled white settlers who indiscriminately hated all Indians regardless of what tribe they might belong to. White Eyes interpreted the verbal message as a severing of diplomatic relations with the Delawares, amounting to a declaration of war. To Zeisberger's amazement, the next morning he learned that the captain had burned the letters the previous night and ordered all the young people to war. He also told the Wyandots, who were camped near the village, that they should stay and "help fight, for they had begun the war."[45] Thus began the "Great Upheaval," two days of panic and confusion for all the Delaware Indians living in the valley, including the Christians.

The next evening Zeisberger sent Captain Johnny, Chelloway, and Isaac to Goschachgunk with a suggestion that White Eyes reconsider his decision to take the Delawares to the war. The following day, September 15, White Eyes visited Lichtenau and confirmed that he had accepted the suggestion. He also brought a disturbing message from William Edwards at Gnadenhutten. Most of the converts were abandoning the village and fleeing to the Walhonding and would arrive at Lichtenau later in the day.

The next few days were a time of sheer panic for everyone, including the native Delawares at Goschachgunk, Edwards and his Gnadenhutten converts, and Zeisberger, who burned his papers and joined in the rush up the Walhonding to escape the supposed advancing army from Pittsburgh. Within hours, the whole valley came unglued.[46]

Just before daybreak on the eighteenth a courier arrived from White Eyes. The captain had personally scouted the entire area east of the villages, especially the location where the Virginians were presumed to be camping. Here he found a herd of bush horses quietly grazing in a meadow but no army of Virginians. It was all a monstrous hoax, an example of the fear and terror that always lurked in the minds of Indians and whites who lived in the American wilderness. The Christians remained on the Walhonding until the next day, when the Lichtenau converts returned to their village. Zeisberger wrote, "So this was a slight change and more like a pleasure trip than a flight."[47] Edwards and his Gnadenhutten converts remained on the Walhonding until September 25, then returned to their village.

In the meantime, couriers broke through the veil of silence from Fort Pitt, arriving at Goschachgunk on September 22 with letters from General Hand and Morgan. They were carried by James Elliot, a local trader, and Robin George, hired by Morgan. They contained welcome news. General Hand reported the successes of the eastern American armies and Morgan confirmed his friendship with the Delawares and Zeisberger, admonishing the Delawares: "I commit Mr. Zeisberger to your particular Care. He is sent to you from Heaven for your own good, therefore be strong & do not let him suffer on any account." He closed, "I desire you will get Mr. Zeisberger to write for you."[48]

Both Zeisberger and White Eyes responded immediately. Zeisberger wrote two letters to Hand, and White Eyes dictated one to Morgan and another to Congress. Zeisberger lamented the difficulty in corresponding with the fort and hoped regular communications could be resumed shortly. He also assured Hand that the Delawares continued to support the Americans. In his second letter to Hand, he passed on confidential information he had received several days earlier from an unidentified man who had just returned from Detroit. He listed the number of militia and regular troops stationed at the fort, the number of cannon and their placement, the stores of provisions, the number of head of cattle, and the armed vessels regularly guarding the fort. His informant was probably John Montour.[49]

This whole incident caused Zeisberger to reflect on conditions at Goschachgunk. He noted in his September 27 entry, "White Eyes and the Chiefs have become weak-kneed and have no real strength, but Captain Johnny goes to great trouble to preserve the Goschachgunk people."[50]

Early in October, the remnant of Pomoacan's army began to arrive at Lichtenau, accompanied by the chief. They had been among the western settlements since August 23. Pomoacan remarked, "My children are doing evil for they have killed over twenty-seven white men." Pomoacan and his warriors had spent six weeks spreading havoc. They were responsible for the attack on Fort Henry on September 1 and probably for the Foreman massacre on September 26, plus numerous other raids and attacks on the homes of white settlers. Zeisberger wrote on October 6, "Half King [Pomoacan] and his army marched home again for which we were glad and thanked the Lord, for since the 8th of August, the day he came, there was no day free of warriors and we hoped that this won't happen again."[51]

On October 9, more letters were received from George Morgan and General Hand, dated October 1. Zeisberger noted, "All messages that we had from Mr. Morgan and the General were good and nice for us and the Delaware Nation. Morgan proposed that they build a fort in their land for their security, if they wished, and to lodge a garrison there so they wouldn't have to fear the other nations." This was the first mention of a possible fort among the Delawares. It would become a reality within a year, but not with the results predicted by Morgan.[52]

Morgan left Fort Pitt shortly after writing the October 1 letter. His Indian policies were now being criticized by his western contemporaries, and he was even being accused of treason. His trip back east was designed to repair the damage and consult with his friends in Congress, now meeting at York, Pennsylvania.

During the third week in October, Zeisberger wrote a foreboding entry in his diary describing an incident that would have far-reaching and disastrous repercussions over the next eighteen years on the western frontier. He wrote, "22nd White Eyes and Gelelemend came here with two Shawnee. . . . These brought the message here that their Chief Cornstalk was taken prisoner at the Fort [Fort Randolph] on the Canhawa [Kanawha River]."[53] On November 10, Cornstalk, a valuable friend of the colonials, his son Elinipsico, and two other men in his party were murdered at the jail at Fort Randolph in one of the many senseless killings of that era. Many men, women, and children on the colonial frontier would eventually pay the price for this despicable act. From that point on, many of the Shawnee Nation became implacable foes of all white Americans.[54]

Despite the sad events in November, the year in the valley closed on a happy note. On Christmas Day, Chief Captain Johnny finally received his wish and was baptized as the convert Israel. Zeisberger closed the diary noting there were 232 converts living at Lichtenau. William Edwards left no diaries during this period, but the Gnadenhutten population was probably approximately 125, making a total population of 357.[55]

The year marked a major turning point in the fortunes of the Moravian missions in the Muskingum Valley. The forced closing of Schoenbrunn, inspired by the conspiracy of Newallike and his Munsee converts, was but the first blow. The Delaware council's neutrality began to waver, causing Zeisberger to begin to question his close relationship with the council. Fortunately for the Moravians, Captain Johnny, now the new convert Israel, became a stabilizing voice in the Delaware council. The murder of Cornstalk placed the Shawnees firmly in the British camp but also saw the Mingoes retire from border excursions.

· 22 ·

Grasping at Straws, 1778

WHILE GEORGE MORGAN was enduring the charges and countercharges of his western Pennsylvania contemporaries, Zeisberger, back on the Muskingum, was continuing to minister to his Christian flock.[1]

During the first week in February, twenty Shawnee families accompanied by White Eyes and the Shawnee chief Nimho visited the mission village and attended church services.[2] More families were expected. These were the peace-minded Shawnees, who, despite the death of Cornstalk, refused to join the war parties planned for the coming spring. They were trying to induce White Eyes to intercede with the other chiefs of their tribe to keep the Shawnees neutral and out of the war.

Also in February letters arrived from General Hand and Colonel Morgan, written the previous October. Zeisberger noted, "We had no word from the Fort the whole winter."[3] Morgan's letter advised of the near victory of the American forces at Germantown. Unknown to Zeisberger and the Delaware council, General John Burgoyne had surrendered his entire British and German force of five thousand men at Saratoga. It was another two months before this information reached the valley. When the news from Germantown and Saratoga arrived in France, the French king Louis XVI signed a treaty of alliance with the Americans on February 6, 1778, thanks to the adroit negotiating of Benjamin Franklin.[4] It marked the turning point in the American Revolution.

Other events in February also proved to be the final straw in General Hand's tumultuous tenure at Fort Pitt. Early in the month he received word that the British had stored substantial "arms, ammunition, provisions & clothing at a small Indian town about 100 miles from Fort Pitt to support the savages in their excursions against the inhabitants."[5] The village was probably Captain Pipe's Cuyahoga River town. Hand promptly organized a small army to attack the storehouse. Marching north out of Fort Pitt, amid alternately heavy rains and falling snow, they attacked the camp, killing one old man and some women and children. From a captured woman they learned of another camp further north. Trying to disguise their chagrin and embarrassment, they went off toward the second camp. There they found four women and a boy, whom they dispatched, saving one of the women. Discouraged and disgusted, Hand reported to his friend Jasper Ewing, "You will be Surprised, in performing the Above great exploits I had one man wounded & one drownd'd."[6] The expedition became known as the infamous "Squaw Campaign."

Simon Girty was with Hand's contingent as a guide. It was the only time he marched against the foe under the American flag. The one man killed was Captain Pipe's brother, and his mother was slightly wounded, having the tip of her finger shot off, which certainly did not endear the general to Captain Pipe.[7] Hand's was the first armed force to enter the Indian territory since the beginning of the war. The general had had enough of the western theater. Shortly after, he applied to Washington to be replaced, and the request was granted.

When George Morgan arrived at Pittsburgh in April 1776 to assume his duties as the Indian agent, he surrounded himself with many men to assist him in his endeavors. Among them were Alexander McKee, Matthew Elliot, and Simon Girty, all rumored to be Loyalist sympathizers.

Alexander McKee, a respected former Indian trader and crown Indian agent, was married to a Shawnee woman. At the beginning of the Revolutionary War, he was a man of considerable means and influence in and around Pittsburgh. Nevertheless, as early as April 1776, he had been placed under house arrest by the Virginia Committee of Correspondence and forbidden to transact business with the Indians on behalf of the crown. Hand had renewed the parole in August 1777 and confined him to his home at McKee's Rock, near Pittsburgh.[8]

Matthew Elliot was little known among his contemporaries. He served as the Shawnee peace messenger during Lord Dunmore's War. Elliot, Irish by birth, came to America in 1761 and successfully engaged in the Indian trade at Pittsburgh, where he met McKee and the two became good friends. He played an important part in Zeisberger's later life.[9]

Simon Girty is one of the most maligned individuals in the history of the western frontier. His biographer, Consul W. Butterfield, in *History of the Girtys*, caught the true spirit of this man, calling him "a tragically romantic" character. He was born in Pennsylvania and at the age of fifteen was captured and raised by the Senecas. Though unable to read and write, he learned the Indian way of life and became a consummate Native American. Intensely independent, he served with success as a colonial scout and was considered to be reliable but occasionally eccentric. Few of the most scurrilous words in the English dictionary were spared by early American historians in describing Girty. But to the British, he was a "faithful servant." When he died at his home in Canada, at the mouth of the Detroit River, on February 18, 1818, they erected a monument to him and inscribed thereon "To Simon Girty, A faithful Servant of the British Indian Department for Twenty Years." The monument stands there today.[10]

Girty and Elliot, under the influence of McKee, decided to defect to the British. At Pittsburgh on March 30, 1778, General Hand wrote to General Horatio Gates, "Sir—I have the mortification to inform you that last Saturday Night (March 28), Alex. McKee made his escape from this place, as also Matthew Elliot, a person lately from Quebec on parole, Simon Girty, Robt. Surplus and a man named Higgins." Actually, the party consisted of McKee, Elliot, Girty, Robert Surphlit, a cousin of McKee's, one Higgins, and two Negroes belonging to McKee—seven in all.[11] They left McKee's home at McKee's Rock, Pennsylvania, just down the Ohio River from Pittsburgh, and headed directly for the Delaware capital at Goschachgunk. On the road they met White Eyes coming to the fort to discuss the fall treaty conference with Morgan. After some consultation, both parties returned to the Delaware capital.

Confusion and disorder reigned over the next six days. The McKee party tried to convince White Eyes, Gelelemend, and the council to break their neutrality by telling fantastic and outlandish tales of defeat and disaster among the American armies. Zeisberger recorded the scene in his entry of April 1, when McKee's party, accompanied by White Eyes, arrived at Goschachgunk. "Among them was Mr. McKee. . . . White Eyes, who met them on the way to the Fort and heard much bad news from the deserters, [the McKee party] came back with them. This caused difficult circumstances since the Chiefs were quite possessed with the bad news from the deserters."[12]

For three days, in constant consultations with McKee and his party, the chiefs wavered between believing or dismissing the chilling news the deserters had brought: American armies cut to pieces; remnants on the march to kill the Indians; no more Congress, some members hanged; Washington killed. These ridiculous rumors should have been rejected out of hand considering the recent reassuring letters the Delaware council had received from its trusted friend George Morgan and the congressional commissioners.[13]

At the beginning of the fourth day, Zeisberger and the Brethren stepped into the discussion, where he exhibited his ever-increasing power over the council.

> The 4th—Today and yesterday were two difficult days. We handed over to the Council a speech with which they [the Moravian Brethren] declared themselves in agreement, and [the chiefs] were to give us an answer. . . . We didn't find the Chiefs agreeing and they did not listen; they were all very insane and confused and not united among themselves; so that now at this stage it was in doubt and came to this whether they would decide for peace or war. *This was an anxious and distressing time for us and if they [the Delaware council] had not feared separation from us, with which we did threaten them plainly enough they would long since have split away.*[14]

To everybody's relief, the deserters left the village in the afternoon, going to spread their seeds of discontent and confusion among the Shawnees.

Johannes Martin, from Gnadenhutten, visited Zeisberger at Lichtenau on the same day to check on the negotiations. This provided an opportunity for Zeisberger to invite the converts from that mission to move to Lichtenau temporarily. If the rumors were true and an army was marching toward the Delaware villages, Gnadenhutten would be the first to be attacked.

The crisis came to a head on April 6. Zeisberger explains: "Before noon, a messenger came from Gnadenhutten with the unexpected but joyful news that the Brethren Heckewelder and Schebosh arrived there safely last evening." The messenger also brought two letters which Heckewelder had carried. Both were from Morgan, one to White Eyes and the Delaware council, the other to Zeisberger. These letters had been written on March 27, the day before the McKee party left Pittsburgh. Morgan wrote to White Eyes that he "rejoiced at this fresh testimony of your friendship." Hopefully, he told the chiefs, "This Tempest will be over in a few months.

You will then enjoy the Sweets of Peace." He then confirmed the glorious news of the surrender of Burgoyne's entire British army to General Gates. Morgan's letter to Zeisberger also contained the news of the Burgoyne surrender, and he further wrote that he was pleased "to hear that Capt. Pipe, Capt. White Eyes, Capt. Killbuck and all the other wise Delaware Chiefs resolved to remain our Friends."[15] But Morgan was unaware of the developments occasioned by the visit of the deserters and what was now going on at the Delaware capital.

Zeisberger's diary entry of April 6 noted:

> I went soon to Goschachgunk, read the letters to the council and made a speech, which gave the opportunity for White Eyes to express his doubts and objections, that we could hope that everything would be brought into order. In the evening Brother Heckewelder himself came with Anton to the joy of everyone, for we received the news that the brothers and sisters at Gnadenhutten had decided all would come here.[16]

The following day Zeisberger wrote: "White Eyes came with the Counsellors with whom Brother David wrote a message to the Fort." Regrettably, this letter has never been found, although we do have a copy of Morgan's response to the chiefs. Morgan's letter is dated April 13. "Brothers—We have received your Letter dated the 6th inst. We have considered the contents and are well pleased with your repeated professions of Friendship to the United States. It was to perpetuate our mutual happiness that we invited a few of you to meet us at our Council Fire at this place." Morgan apologized for the ten Indian deaths referred to in Zeisberger's diary entry of March 10 and noted that Captain Pipe was invited to join the Goschachgunk Delawares when they came to the fort. He closed the letter, "Be strong, for you may depend we will convince you of our Friendship."[17] Zeisberger's letter of April 6 draws the curtain on these six days of turmoil. Thanks to his effort, the issue came to a peaceful conclusion, and the Delawares continued to maintain the peace despite the efforts of McKee and his party.

Fortunately, most of the letters and all of the diaries written during this emotional episode are extant, and from them we can recreate an accurate version of events during these critical six days. To my knowledge, the only other recorded version was furnished by John Heckewelder. Writing in 1820, some forty-two years after it occurred, when he was seventy-seven years old, Heckewelder's account differs wildly from the contemporaneous ones. It has come down to us as "Heckewelder's Ride" and is a quintessential example of how fictitious historical legends are born.[18] It is important to note that Heckewelder did not arrive until the evening of April 6, when the negotiations were completed and the chiefs had come to an agreement on their future course of action. Also he came with Anton and not John Martin, as Heckewelder later wrote. Heckewelder's altering of the facts to place himself at center stage can probably be attributed to the forgetfulness of old age.

The defection of McKee, Elliot, and Girty had a great impact on the next twenty-one years of American and British Indian history. McKee shortly became the British Indian agent and played a major role in the future tumultuous years of Indian history on the western frontier.

Following Easter on April 19, Heckewelder and Edwards moved the Gnadenhutten converts to Lichtenau. Surprisingly, Zeisberger received little objection to his original plan to consolidate his people in one location. By the end of the month the move was completed and Gnadenhutten was deserted.[19] (It was reoccupied one year later.) Zeisberger wrote on April 30, "Yesterday and today the brethren helped those who had come from Gnadenhutten and continue until everything was completed. We made a new [separate] street for them and built a long cottage for the widows and made various sections."[20]

Shortly after the April crisis had passed, White Eyes, Isaac Glikhikan, Schebosh, and Wilhelm Chelloway again repaired to Fort Pitt as requested by Morgan and the commissioners to discuss the preliminary work on the treaty conference to be held in the fall. They returned to the capital on May 2. Zeisberger wrote, "They brought good news. . . . The best for us was that the planned military march into Indian territory, which would have been the most dangerous for us, was now put off. They would have done terrible things and neither friend or foe would have been spared." Schebosh brought Zeisberger a letter from Morgan, who "acknowledged the work of the brethren among the Indians as a benefit for the whole country. They [the Americans] are well aware of this."[21] He was referring to the defection of the McKee party and Zeisberger's role in keeping the Delawares at peace.

The coming of May brought balmy spring weather but also an increase of Indian war parties destined for the frontier. The Moravians' old "friend" Pomoacan, the Half-King Wyandot chief, arrived in the valley on May 5 with a large mixed party of Shawnees and Mingoes. They passed by the capital and landed on the banks of the Muskingum near Lichtenau. Zeisberger remarked, "The Wyandots and Mingoes were orderly and discreet but some of the Shawnee let their rudeness show."[22] Two days later, they left the valley bound for Fort Randolph at the mouth of the Great Kanawha and the Ohio. By June 9, Zeisberger received word that the party had been badly mauled by the Americans, losing a large number of men.[23]

Also in June, Zeisberger received word that General Washington had appointed General Lachlan McIntosh to command the forces at Fort Pitt, but this time with a new twist. Unlike General Hand, who had to contend entirely with local militia, the new commander would bring with him seasoned American forces from the eastern theater.[24]

On July 16, a party of eighty Wyandots passed through the valley. They brought a personal message for Zeisberger from Governor Hamilton. The Indians had been complaining to him that Zeisberger had been sending messages to Fort Pitt concerning these war parties. Hamilton wrote, "They were to cease this practice and not let it happen again." Zeisberger was being unfairly accused for the loss suffered by the Wyandots on their last excursion to Fort Randolph. Hamilton could not have known that during the entire time the Wyandots had been on the march, no couriers had passed between the Delaware capital and Fort Pitt. Zeisberger closed his entry for the day writing, "It looks very much on all sides around us as if a great storm was to come over us."[25]

Four days later he sent Anton and Samuel Nanticoke (known as Sam prior to his baptism) with two letters to Morgan, one a personal letter from him, the other written for White Eyes. Both letters expressed concern for their personal safety and that of the missions and the Delaware nation. While White Eyes was reserved in asking for assistance, Zeisberger was candid.

> Capt. White Eyes in his speech [letter] hath not spoken quite so plain, for which he hath reason enough; but I can tell you that he wishes an army might come out now—the sooner the better, for it is high time. All thoughts of bringing about a peace with the Nations, especially the Wyandots, are in vain, & time is only lost; therefore White Eyes thinks, that the only help you can afford him, is to send an army against the Wyandots & etc., except [unless] you should know another remedy.

Both letters warn that the information must be kept secret, undoubtedly a reaction to the message received earlier from Hamilton.[26]

Both Zeisberger and the council had completely changed their position from the beginning of May, when Zeisberger wrote that "any military expedition into the Indian country would have been the most dangerous for us." The developments of the past two months were beginning to affect his conservative instincts. Grasping at straws, he had mused at the end of July, "To all appearances it seems the total ruin of the Indian congregation is coming."[27] There was, however, adequate reason for his melancholy. In addition to the warning he had received from Hamilton, between May and the end of July nine Indian war parties of 350 warriors had passed through the mission on their way to the settlements, some returning with only a handful of prisoners and scalps to reward them for their time and labor, which only heightened their anger and determination.

Zeisberger wrote two more letters to Fort Pitt in August, one to Morgan before the agent returned east to consult with Congress and the other to the commissioners, who had arrived on August 1 to prepare for the treaty conference in September. In Morgan's letter he enclosed a message that the Delaware council had recently received from Governor Hamilton, who again threatened to destroy the Delaware Nation if they did not join the war against the Americans. He also told Morgan of a report from the Twightwee (Miami) Nation, "who had opened the road to Detroit & invited all the Nations to come shake hands" with the Americans. This is the first information Zeisberger had received about George Rogers Clark's invasion of British territory in Illinois. In his letter to the commissioners, he acknowledged the receipt of the newspapers they had sent but lamented that "I found not in them what I was most desirous to see and hear, namely that an Army was to come out." Although it "disheartened" him, he acknowledged that the messenger told him it "would be done." His final comments were a scathing denunciation of the Munsees. They have "always shewn themselves & are yet enemies to the white people, they ought therefore to be broken & no Chief of their own left them, cast out of the Council & deliver'd to the Delawares to be ruled by them, because they are not fit to be ruled by themselves."[28] Undoubtedly, some of Zeisberger's animosity against the Munsees can be traced to the problems he had encountered with Wangomen and his people on the Allegheny. They had always resisted the Gospel message. To heighten his rancor, the Munsees were now being led by Newallike and Gendaskund, who were former converts and had a great dislike for Zeisberger, a feeling that was mutual.

On the first day of September, the Delaware delegation left the valley to attend the treaty conference at Fort Pitt. Anton and Wilhelm accompanied the chiefs. Generally acknowledged to be the first treaty negotiated by the United States and the Indian nations, it proved to be a fiasco and set the tone for many that would follow. It was negotiated only with the Delawares, although a scattering of Shawnees attended in an unofficial capacity.

General Lachlan McIntosh was in charge of the negotiations. He had arrived at his new command on August 6. McIntosh's orders were to mount a campaign against Detroit. While Morgan agreed with the Detroit objective and thought it was not only practical but extremely desirable, McIntosh's personal plans were to expand the project and attack the enemy Indians en route, especially the Wyandots. Morgan, the expert in the field, knew that any attempt to strike the Wyandots would do irreparable damage and provoke the hostility of the other western tribes, especially the Delawares. Regrettably, Morgan was in the East when the conference was held, although his presence would probably not have changed the results. The Treaty of 1778 marked the abandonment of Morgan's policy of restraint toward the Indians. It also revealed the active hostility of his enemies in Pittsburgh and of the men responsible for the new strategy of dealing with the Indians.

The treaty session began on September 12 and concluded with the signing on September 19. After reading the treaty, Morgan scathingly commented, "There never was a conference with the Indians so improperly or villainously conducted." The terms of the treaty provided for an offensive and defensive alliance between the United States and the Delaware Indians and granted American troops free passage across Delaware land in order to advance against Detroit. It further provided for a fort to be built by the forces of the United States "for the better security of the old men, women and children . . . whilst their warriors are engaged against the common enemy." Gelelemend, White Eyes, and Captain Pipe signed the treaty for the Delawares, and the commissioners Andrew and Thomas Lewis signed for the colonials. The officers at Fort Pitt witnessed the signing.[29]

Morgan's characterization of the treaty as a fraud proved to be correct. It became abundantly clear in the next few months that the articles were misrepresented and that, in signing, the Delawares were "accepting the war belt." The work of the translator, Daniel Sullivan, was deficient and in some cases deliberately deceptive. He would later be charged with these offenses.[30]

Zeisberger's first reference to the treaty was in the diary entry of October 2:

> A great party of Munsee came here during the night to whom the chiefs announced that the General at the Fort did not speak favorably in respect to them and that he planned to visit [attack] them, over which they are dismayed and came therefore [to Lichtenau] to inquire about it. Without a doubt, we would now have many deserters from the "bad" people who would force themselves upon us [seek asylum with the Moravians]. But it is plainly forbidden in the Articles of the Treaty that the Delawares should not take in any deserters from the "bad" people who would force themselves upon us.[31]

Zeisberger was correct in his statement regarding "deserters." It was clearly spelled out in Article IV of the treaty, which indicates that he had read the copy given to the Delaware councillors. He was also aware that White Eyes, who had remained at Fort Pitt, was to be the army's principal guide when it marched into Delaware territory.[32]

The diaries for the final weeks of October and the first two weeks of November were again filled with rumors of expected attacks against the Delawares. Most of the reports came from the Munsees. It was a replay of the rumors during the Schoenbrunn upheaval, giving deadlines when an attack was to take place. The commotion was entirely among the residents of Goschachgunk. Now an old hand at analyzing such reports, Zeisberger on October 28 described the turmoil: "The confusion among the [Goschachgunk] Indians is indescribable; none can say why they are fleeing, and yet they go, leaving their corn that they have just harvested without considering; What shall we eat, and what shall we drink?"[33]

The deadlines for the attack passed, and by the first week in November village life was returning to normal. Pomoacan visited Lichtenau on November 7 after spending two days at Goschachgunk discussing the latest information with Gelelemend. It was a friendly visit, and he assured the Moravians that he had heard no rumors regarding an attack against the missions. Prophetically, he told Zeisberger "he wanted much to see him once again for he believed that he would not see them for a long time."[34]

Twelve days after Pomoacan left the mission Zeisberger received devastating news. "November 20th—Heard the advance party of the army came to the Tuscarabi night before last; likewise that Col. White Eyes died not far from Pittsburgh from an old illness plus smallpox."[35]

Death was common in the wilderness, and Zeisberger took White Eyes's demise calmly. There is no previous information regarding White Eyes's "old illness," although smallpox was common among the Indians, and a smallpox epidemic was raging on the western frontier at that time.

Zeisberger probably presumed that White Eyes had contracted the disease at Pittsburgh. Perhaps this was why he was so impassive.

Reports on White Eyes's death did not end with this one from Fort Pitt. In 1779, Morgan took three Indian boys to his home back east, and Congress agreed to provide them with a Christian education. The boys were George, the eight-year-old son of White Eyes, and two older sons of Gelelemend. Six years later, in an appeal to Congress for additional money to continue their education, Morgan revealed, in a letter dated May 12, 1784, to Thomas Mifflin, the president of Congress, that George's father "was treacherously put to death." He added, "I have carefully concealed, & shall continue to conceal from young White Eyes, the manner of his fathers death."[36] Morgan wrote one more letter to the Board of Treasury, on September 25, 1788, on behalf of the young man. Here again he refers to the "murder of Colonel White Eyes."[37]

How White Eyes died still remains an open question. Some historians have taken Morgan's version at its face value, believing he was murdered.[38] If so, how was the act so cleverly concealed? Could Morgan have been playing for sympathy from Mifflin to get his request for further funds from Congress approved? Additional information can be found in a little-known recollection of Stephen Burkam, who accompanied McIntosh's expedition. In 1845, long after the event, he was interviewed by Lyman Draper. He told Draper: "McIntosh took Capt. White Eyes and Bob Bee [Baubee] as pilots; Capt White Eyes at Fort McIntosh was taken with small pox, and was sent to Pittsburgh where he soon died. Bob Bee deserted at Fort McIntosh. None of the others had small pox."[39]

White Eyes's death had a profound effect on coming events, and even though he and Zeisberger had occasionally disagreed, White Eyes had been the one man most responsible for keeping the Delawares neutral and out of the war. Furthermore, he had the clout within the council to control the hostile element that opposed Zeisberger's peace policy. From this point forward, it became a different ball game, and White Eyes would be sorely missed by Zeisberger and especially by Gelelemend.

Movement of the American army into Delaware country proved to be a giant fiasco. The troops were not the conquering heroes earlier envisioned by Zeisberger and the Delaware council. Much of the blame for the failure can be attributed to General Lachlan McIntosh. He came not as the savior, so hopefully envisioned by Zeisberger, but rather as the occupying Caesar. Haughty and overbearing, when he arrived at the Tuscarabi on November 18, he carried some personal baggage that made him poorly equipped for his new role. His stern sense of duty and his strict idea of discipline appealed to Washington as qualities needed for a frontier commander. But those qualities clashed dramatically with the free and independent spirit of frontier militiamen. In his short tenure at Fort Pitt, he quickly became universally disliked, even hated.[40]

It had taken him fourteen days to march from Fort McIntosh, his new headquarters constructed at the mouth of the Beaver River, forty miles downstream from Pittsburgh. Daniel Brodhead, who later replaced McIntosh, called the fort the "Hobby Horse on the Beaver."[41] The march had been at a crab's pace. Normally it should have taken no more than six days to cover the distance of some eighty miles.[42] His army of twelve hundred men—three hundred regulars, nine hundred local militia—was so badly equipped that when they arrived on the Muskingum, the Delawares had to provide them with provisions. The deplorable condition of McIntosh's army was not entirely his fault. Organizing the campaign started back in March when Congress and General Washington devised an elaborate plan to capture Detroit. From the very beginning, the plan began to fall apart, and by the time McIntosh left his "Hobby Horse" on the Beaver, it was only a shadow of its original version. Most of the supplies required for the invasion and half of the men did not arrive at Fort Pitt by the September 1 deadline for departure. As they left Fort McIntosh, General Brodhead, the commander of the Eighth Pennsylvania Regiment, complained, "In vain was the nakedness of the men—the scanty supplies wornout—starved horses—leanness of the cattle and total want of storage, all difficult under [the best] circumstances of supporting a post at so great a distance into enemy Country."[43]

On arrival, the men were put to work building a new structure to be called Fort Laurens, named for McIntosh's mentor, Henry Laurens, president of the Continental Congress.[44] Four days later, McIntosh met with the Indians. It turned out to be a joke to all but the commander. He faced primarily a delegation of Delawares, with Gelelemend, Israel, and even Captain Pipe in attendance and perhaps a scattering of Shawnees, none in any official capacity.

Most of those in attendance had up until then been friendly to the Americans. It was an opportunity for McIntosh to glorify himself and reflect on the honor of the United States. Instead, he accomplished just the opposite.[45] Standing behind him was a ragtag army with torn clothing, short on supplies, horses dying for lack of forage, and few provisions for the coming winter. Assuming the role of conquistador, he delivered a bombastic and threatening speech to his audience. "I have ordered," he said, "Great Guns, wagons horses Cattle and flour enough to take that

Fort Laurens, 1778–1779. Courtesy of the Ohio Historical Society.

place [Detroit] and I am determined never to leave the country until that is done." He then threatened his spectators with dire consequences if they did not return in fourteen days and humbly submit to him, at which time he would dictate the terms of the peace, "and if any nations or Tribes refuse this offer now, I will never make it again nor rest or leave this country, but pursue them while any of them remain on the face of the earth for I can fill the woods with men as the trees, or as stones are on the ground." He then asked the Delawares for supplies, "all the corn you can spare . . . Horses, Cattle, hogs, deer skins, venison or anything else you can spare," promising to pay for them. After revealing his precarious position to the Indians by requesting supplies, he closed by saying "that any nation of people who would not afterwards join us heartily by taking up the Hatchet with us, and striking, such a refectory People Should be looked upon as Enemies to the United States of America." When he finished his remarks, the Indians were said to "Set up a General Laugh," and well they might.[46]

Even if his enemies agreed to his ultimatum, it was impossible for them to reach him in fourteen days or even in two months. In less than an hour, McIntosh came close to destroying all the years of painstaking work Morgan had accomplished with the Delawares.

Two days later, Israel and Gelelemend returned from Fort Laurens. Zeisberger wrote, "In the presence of all the Indians and the Generals, Gelelemend had declared Israel Chief as one on whom we depend." That evening Zeisberger admonished his Helpers' Conferences to "give all the help they could to Israel since he was now the head chief."[47]

In December, both Zeisberger and Heckewelder made several attempts to travel to Fort Laurens to talk to McIntosh, but each effort was aborted because of high water. Finally, Heckewelder was successful, but he reached the fort after McIntosh had departed. The general left a garrison of two hundred men at the fort under the command of Colonel John Gibson. Gibson and his men would live through hell during the next four months at Fort Laurens.[48]

The turbulence and unrest during the year are revealed in the closing year's statistics. On December 31, Zeisberger recorded a total of 328 converts. The Gnadenhutten villagers had joined Lichtenau in April, therefore Zeisberger's figures represented the total Christian population living in the valley. This was a far cry from the more than 400 in 1775.[49]

It had been a distressing year for David Zeisberger. Fortunately, George Morgan's frequent reassuring communications with the Delawares kept them allied with the Americans. But it took Zeisberger's influence to keep them cool and loyal to the United States. Even Zeisberger began to lose hope as the number of war parties passing through the valley increased. He was also deeply concerned about the warning he received from Governor Hamilton in July. The success of the eastern armies strengthened the American cause. But the arrival of General McIntosh and the building of Fort Laurens proved to be a tragic disappointment to both the Delaware council and Zeisberger, revealing the woeful weakness of the colonial forces. The year would mark a turning point in Zeisberger's life in the Muskingum Valley, and the most disastrous incident that contributed to this change was the sudden death of Captain White Eyes in November. None of the participants seemed to appreciate its importance.

· 23 ·

Estrangement among the Delawares, 1779

WITH THE beginning of the new year, the colonial military position on the western frontier began to deteriorate. Nevertheless, the western commanders made one more desperate effort to confront their British adversaries.

From the first of the year until August 2, when Fort Laurens was finally abandoned, there was a flood of military correspondence between the Muskingum Valley and the United States authorities at Fort Pitt and the eastern headquarters. More than eighty separate letters passed between Fort Laurens, Fort Pitt, Washington's headquarters, and Congress, to and from Zeisberger, Heckewelder, and the Delaware chiefs. From these documents a clear picture emerges of the complicated maneuverings occurring on the western frontier.[1]

The Delawares, desperately in need of trade goods, clothing, guns, powder, lead, and other supplies that could not be found at Fort Pitt, began to accept the proffered help from Detroit. This new development made Zeisberger increasingly concerned about Lichtenau's close proximity to the Delaware capital. With more than three hundred of his own people living within three miles of the Goschachgunk, the possibility of the Delaware defection, and his own alienation from the Delaware council, Zeisberger knew the Lichtenau converts must be removed from the forks of the Muskingum.

This rapid change in Delaware policy was attributed to the death of White Eyes and the deplorable condition of McIntosh's army. The dead captain's young successor, Gelelemend, at forty-two, lacked experience and the respect of his peers, which only added to the turmoil within the Delaware council. When White Eyes died in November, Captain Johnny, the convert Israel, was appointed head chief by Gelelemend, but his appointment had never been officially recognized or confirmed by the Delaware council. The council soon split into three quarreling factions unable to agree on a common policy.

Sometime during November of the previous year, shortly after they received the news of White Eyes's death, Captain Pipe and his Delaware Wolf Clan moved from their Cuyahoga River villages to the Upper Sandusky nearer the Wyandots.[2] Contrary to previous accounts, the diaries reveal that he remained loyal and supportive of the Goschachgunk council throughout this period. He was also friendly with Zeisberger and the mission program. But from this point forward he clearly was in the British camp. This left two contentious segments at Goschachgunk, one led by Gelelemend, Israel, Wingenund, and Machingue Pushies, counseling to continue their relationship with the Americans, and the other by Buckongahelas advocating defection to the British.[3]

Meanwhile, deplorable conditions were experienced by the men stationed at the newly built Fort Laurens on the Muskingum River. The appellation of "Fort Nonsense," given by the men assigned to occupy the fort, aptly described their experience.[4] The bombastic and threatening speech delivered by General McIntosh to the Delaware delegates in December set the tone for the fort's existence during the next six months—all bluff and bluster. The Indians quickly saw through McIntosh's charade. Even before he returned to his headquarters on December 9, the general had given up his plans to move on to Detroit, and the dwindling provisions at Fort Laurens required that the men be placed on reduced rations, a harbinger of future conditions.[5]

Colonel John Gibson and 152 men of the Thirteenth Virginia Regiment and 20 men of the Eighth Pennsylvania Regiment were left behind to garrison the fort. Three days before the end of the year, already short of provisions, Gibson sent his commissary, Samuel Sample, to the Delaware capital to secure supplies.[6] Zeisberger's diary noted his arrival on December 28.

> Mr. Sample, the quartermaster from Fort Lawrence [*sic*] was here to exchange cattle and all kinds of things from our Brothers and Sisters for merchandise. . . . He couldn't wonder enough over the order and quiet in our town, "I see," he said, "these are quite different Indians than those in Goschachgunk, they are neat and industrious people and I didn't expect such Indians in the woods. It is a good thing if one helps you."[7]

One month later, on Friday, January 22, Sample, accompanied by seven men of the Thirteenth Virginia Regiment, returned to the capital for supplies and received a hostile reception from the Delawares. One man was killed and scalped and another seriously wounded. Two days later, the Delawares shot three of Sample's best horses and drove off two others, taking their bags, saddles, and blankets—a harbinger of the Delawares' growing disenchantment with the Americans.[8] The day following the altercation, Sample went to Lichtenau seeking Zeisberger's protection. While the trading continued, he remained at the mission until January 30, when he was provided with a safe escort back to Fort Laurens by ten of the Brethren and some of the trusted Delawares from Goschachgunk.[9]

Sample's experience caused Zeisberger to reflect on the new conflict caused by the arrival of the Americans at Fort Laurens. Sample had asked Gibson to send a contingent to escort him back to the fort, but Gibson refused, prompting Zeisberger's entry on January 30, the day Sample was escorted back to the fort by the Brethren. "They [the Americans] made many promises as to how they would protect us, but they would bring the war to our town and we would have to protect them. Mr. Samples [*sic*] stayed here with us most of the time, because he did not believe he was safe in Goschachgunk."[10]

Concerned about the increased Delaware hostility, Zeisberger, on January 8, sent a party of Brethren to Gnadenhutten to guard the vacant village from any further desecration. In early December he received word that the school and Brethren's house had been burned, but he believed that the destruction was from natural causes.[11]

During the first two months of the new year other developments concerning the deteriorating alliance between the Americans and the Delawares were unfolding at Fort Pitt. George Morgan made one more trip to the western theater before he resigned as Indian agent in May. On January 5, he wrote to the Delaware council inviting a delegation of its members to come east and visit his home at Princeton. He thought that while there they could arrange a meeting with General Washington and Congress. It was his last desperate gesture to try to keep the Delawares neutral.[12]

Shortly after the council received Morgan's letter, Zeisberger wrote two letters to the Indian agent, one under his own signature and one for Gelelemend. They dealt with the war belt presented to the Delawares at the treaty conference the previous September. Zeisberger wrote to Morgan "that the War Belt deliver'd to them caused much speculation among the Delaware" and reminded him that the Americans had always instructed the Delawares "to sit still & be quiet, that the United States did not desire them to help fight against the English & this I always observed that they approved of very much." According to Zeisberger, the Delawares were now being told that they should go to war against the other tribes, thus destroying the credibility of the United States and causing confusion in the Delaware council. Gelelemend's letter was more forthright: "After I returned from the treaty, I was looked upon as a warrior, which was the cause of much confusion among my people." He explains his version of the incident at the treaty conference:

> The Tomahawk was handed to me at Fort Pitt, but not in a Warlike manner, we all standing & at no Council Fire, neither did I understand the meaning of it. I neither desired any Implement of War, all that I agreed to was to pilot the Army 'till beyond our bounds, & my great Capt. White Eyes with several others to go before the Army & convey them to the Enemy in order to be of use to both Parties, in case they should desire to speak or treat with one another.[13]

This deception played a large role in destroying the credibility of the United States among the Delawares. It might never have happened had Morgan been present to conduct the proceedings and protect the Indians.

By the middle of February, Morgan returned to his home to await the arrival of the Delaware delegation. This visit to Fort Pitt was George Morgan's "last hurrah." After resigning his commission in May, he never again returned to the western theater as the American Indian agent. His wise counsel would be sorely missed.[14]

The day before Zeisberger wrote to Morgan, he sent an express dispatch to Colonel Gibson at Fort Laurens. He had just received word that Simon Girty and a party of seven men, mostly Mingo and Munsee warriors, were headed toward Fort Laurens. Girty had left the villages on the Upper Sandusky on January 6. Coincidentally, near that same time, Captain John

Clark had left Fort McIntosh with a relief expedition bound for the same destination, carrying desperately needed clothing and miscellaneous supplies, including five kegs of whiskey. Clark arrived on January 21, delivering his precious cargo. He stayed overnight and the next morning headed back to Fort McIntosh. Just three miles beyond the fort, he was ambushed by the Girty party, losing two killed, four wounded, and one missing, but gallantly fought his way back to the fort. Unfortunately, the man carrying dispatches written by Gibson to McIntosh and a copy of Zeisberger's warning was captured by Girty. Girty could not read and carried the incriminating evidence back to Detroit and the British commander.[15]

At the beginning of February, Zeisberger finally decided what action to take regarding the mission at Lichtenau. On February 6, the missionaries consulted the lot for guidance. Edwards and the Mahican Brethren were to return to their old village at Gnadenhutten. A second group, led by Zeisberger, was to establish a new mission near the site of old Schoenbrunn, and the remaining converts, supervised by Heckewelder, were to continue on temporarily at Lichtenau. In several weeks, they began the moves.[16]

On February 20, thirty Wyandot warriors arrived at Goschachgunk. They were the vanguard of some two hundred men approaching Fort Laurens. Led by Pomoacan, the Wyandot chief, and the British captain Henry Bird, the group consisted mostly of Wyandots, augmented by some Mingoes, Munsees, and a sprinkling of Shawnees. Two days later, they had surrounded the fort, undetected by Gibson and his men. On the morning of February 23, unaware that he was besieged, Gibson dispatched a party of sixteen men and horses to gather wood. Just beyond gun range of the fort, the party was attacked by the Indians. Two were taken prisoner and the others were overwhelmed and clubbed to death. Three days later, Zeisberger heard the news at Lichtenau.[17] (See Appendix I for additional details of this massacre.)

From all accounts, the winter of 1778 and 1779 was severe. Snow was two to three feet deep and the temperature hovered near zero most of the winter. The fort buildings provided some protection for the Americans, but the besieging Indians lived in crude shelters. Pomoacan and most of the Wyandots began to return to the Upper Sandusky, leaving a large delegation of Shawnees, Mingoes, and a few Wyandots to continue the siege. On March 7, Zeisberger wrote, "From the Tuscarabi we had word that the Shawanos gave up the siege at Fort Lawrence [*sic*]. The Chiefs in Goschachgunk had sent couriers to them and advised them to stop if they wanted to live and after the couriers had talked to them the second time they agreed."

By the second week in March the Indians were running low on food and began to drift away, heading for Lichtenau, the nearest source, to satisfy their hunger. Beginning on the ninth and continuing through the nineteenth, Lichtenau was filled with more than two hundred starving warriors, Wyandots, Mingoes, Delawares, and mostly Shawnees. "The whole day," Zeisberger wrote, "our town was full of soldiers and even though they were camped at Goschachgunk, most of the time they were here." On March 19, with a sigh of relief, he wrote, "Now that the warriors are gone we thanked the Saviour that he again sent us peace and hope that this will be the worst event for this year. But it cost us for those eight or more days because we had to take care of them alone without the help of the Goschachgunk people."[18]

During the siege the men within the fort were facing starvation with no possible way to alleviate their hunger. By the beginning of the second week in March, meat and flour rations were cut to five ounces a day. Five days later, the storeroom was empty. Not sure of their besieging enemy and tormented by the sight from the bastions of their mutilated comrades killed in the February massacre, they dared not go beyond rifle shot of the fort. Two men, however, slipped out one evening and killed a deer. Within minutes after they returned, the animal was eaten, most of it raw.[19]

Earlier in the month, McIntosh made a gallant but aborted attempt to supply the garrison by the water route. Major Richard Taylor led a party down the Ohio River into the Muskingum. Shortly after they entered the Muskingum, the party was attacked and two men were killed. Several days before the attack, Heckewelder had dispatched a courier to Taylor advising him to turn back. The Indians were waiting for him, and it would have been useless to continue upriver to Fort Laurens. Fortunately, Taylor returned having only lost the two men, but he saved the precious supplies.[20] Gibson, at Fort Laurens, knew of Taylor's repulse from friendly Delaware runners, which only heightened his concern.

The commander and his men now turned to the only resource left to them. They cooked the dried beef hides and some even washed their moccasins and roasted and ate them. Some of the men were so sick they could not forage for themselves. After resorting to eating roots and herbs, two men died from eating poisonous roots. Four others became seriously ill but eventually recovered.[21]

Indian runners and Heckewelder's letters describing the conditions at Fort Laurens had reached McIntosh by the second week in March. On March 19, McIntosh led a relief party of two hundred militia and three hundred regular troops toward the besieged fort. They covered the distance in four days without incident, but as they approached the fort, Gibson's men were so elated they fired their guns in a salute, frightening the packhorses, many of them new to military service. The spooked horses fled into the wilderness, scattering most of the cargo irretrievably in the woods.[22]

McIntosh had planned to push on into the wilderness toward Detroit, but the loss of most of his provisions thwarted that idea. He then proposed to his officers a quick thrust at the Wyandot villages on the Upper Sandusky. To a man they rejected his plan.

Leaving Major Frederick Vernon and 106 men and officers of the Eighth Pennsylvania to replace the tormented Gibson at Fort Laurens, the general returned to Fort McIntosh. Shortly after he arrived, he received his recall. He turned over his command to his arch rival, Colonel Daniel Brodhead.[23]

Near the end of March, Zeisberger approached the long-contemplated moment when he would split the Lichtenau mission. He had purposely delayed announcing the move to the Helpers' Conference until March 7. That day he dispatched Isaac to tell the Delaware council at Goschachgunk. He received a quick response. The following day Gelelemend and the entire council arrived in a huff, requesting that the move be delayed until the following spring. The chiefs planned to go to Philadelphia within a few days, and they suggested that they would talk to Congress about the move. Zeisberger's attempt not to offend his friends was evident in his diary notation for the day: "The answer to this [request] we postponed to a more suitable time." It was becoming clear that he was carefully breaking his close association with the council and going his own way. As a sequel to this incident, on April 5, as the missionaries were preparing to depart from Lichtenau, Zeisberger noted in his diary, "The Goschachgunk people were indeed displeased with our going away, but we paid them no heed."[24]

Dispersal of the Congregations: The Reoccupation of Gnadenhutten and the Building of New Schoenbrunn

By April 6, both parties had pushed away from the banks of the Muskingum at Lichtenau and headed upriver to their new homes. Edwards and one hundred of his Mahican converts were destined for the old location at Gnadenhutten, and Zeisberger, with twenty families, was to continue up the river to the site of old Schoenbrunn. There they planned to build temporary huts until a new village, to be called New Schoenbrunn, could be erected across the river on the west side of the Muskingum. Heckewelder and the rest of the converts remained at Lichtenau. This was probably a final concession to the chiefs not to abandon the Lichtenau site entirely.

Regrettably, Edwards did not keep a diary, but both Heckewelder and Zeisberger wrote complete accounts of life at Lichtenau and New Schoenbrunn. Since Zeisberger frequently visited Gnadenhutten, his account provides a reasonable record of that village. This was Heckewelder's first assignment as a head missionary since he entered mission work in 1771. He had been ordained the previous year in Bethlehem and now assumed the burden of living near the Delaware capital. His detailed diary is most instructive and is the principal source for the events until April 1780, when he and the remaining converts finally left Lichtenau.[25]

On March 26, thirteen of the Delaware chiefs set off for Philadelphia. The convert Israel accompanied the delegation. They would be absent from the valley until late in the summer. In the meantime, Machingue Pushies assumed the duties of head chief.[26]

While Zeisberger and his party continued upriver bound for their new village site, he wrote nostalgically on April 10, "We saw the devastation [at the old village] but at the same time remembered how much blessing and good we had received [here] from our dear Lord." Shortly they came to a pleasant meadow on the western side of the river. Here, on a large, flat, alluvial plain immediately adjacent to the river, they planned to build their new town. Back at Gnadenhutten, Edwards and his people repaired the cabins in the old village and settled down to the regular mission schedule. Zeisberger's first project was to clear the meadow and begin planting crops, followed by fencing the plantations. Temporary Indian huts were constructed at old Schoenbrunn, but on April 17 the weather turned nasty. He wrote, "Today it is sleeting and we are glad to be under roof." It continued to rain, and the river rose at the new site, almost flooding the prospective village.[27]

After Zeisberger left Lichtenau, Heckewelder received several messages warning that a party led by Simon Girty was headed for the frontier. On April 28, Zeisberger received a letter from Heckewelder warning "that my life was sought because I persuaded our Indians to come here to Schoenbrunn." He noted, "It could possibly be so, but we were completely composed and unconcerned and believed the Saviour would care for us." On May 4, the missionaries moved into their new meeting house.[28]

As Zeisberger was toiling to complete his new village, Heckewelder, who had inherited Zeisberger's problems at Lichtenau, was up to his neck

George Rogers Clark, 1752–1818. From Clark's memoirs (Cincinnati: Robert Clark & Co., 1869).

in troublesome inconveniences with the Delaware council. Fortunately, Isaac had remained with him and acted as a buffer between the chief and the Christians. He became Heckewelder's right arm, especially during his first few months as head missionary.

In the middle of April, Heckewelder received a most interesting Indian dispatch. Governor Hamilton had been captured at Vincennes by George

Rogers Clark's valiant little army on February 24, 1779.[29] For a brief period it caused a negative reaction toward the British among the Indians, especially the Wyandots, but life at all three of the missions continued on as usual.

On the last day of the month, Heckewelder received a note from Zeisberger in response to the warning he had sent regarding the Girty party. "If I am in danger," Zeisberger wrote, "I can't change it and leave it up to the Lord I serve as to how he directs my destiny. I am otherwise composed and comforted, but will not willingly put myself in danger." Heckewelder noted, "His answer pleased me."[30]

Sometime during the first week in May, Colonel Brodhead sent a large amount of trade materials to the Delaware Nation—clothing, four hundred matchcoats and a thousand shirts, cloth, twenty rifles, lead, powder, flints, tin and brass kettles, one hundred axes, ribbons, a thousand pounds of nails, shoes, and many miscellaneous articles.[31] Even though the shipment did not contain any liquor, it did eventually contribute to Heckewelder's problem with drunken Indians visiting the mission.

Shortly after the merchandise arrived, Johannes Lange, a white man and the blacksmith at Goschachgunk, whose life had been threatened, fled from the village and came to Lichtenau. He said the Indians had been drinking for fourteen days and were totally beyond the control of the chiefs. Eight days later, Heckewelder noted that a drunken Indian tried to invade his home.[32]

On May 24, Heckewelder mentioned the Americans' gift to the Delawares and explained how the Indians secured their liquor.

> The Goschachgunk people who have finished the twenty-four kegs of brandy are already thinking about how to get more. (A while ago the Commandant in Pittsburgh sent them much gun-powder and lead as a gift, this, along with their bodily clothing they sold to the women for brandy. Now they get back a bit by going hunting, so they [the women traders] have to pay for the hides, so they [the Indians] are again in position to get other drinks. Such trading is done by the women.)[33]

On the same day, Heckewelder received the disturbing news from the Upper Sandusky that a large, mixed party of Wyandots, Mingoes, and Shawnees, led by the British commander Captain Henry Bird, was gathering for an attack on Fort Laurens. Most troubling was the information that they intended to bring cannon, but fate was about to deal Captain Bird a cruel blow in the form of a determined army of Kentuckians.[34] Just as

Captain Bird was preparing to march toward the rendezvous with the Shawnees, news arrived that the Shawnee villages were being attacked by a large body of Kentuckians led by Colonel John Bowman. "The Shawnee town lay in ashes and some of their Captains were taken prisoner," wrote Zeisberger. The Bird contingent dissolved within minutes as the Indians rushed back to protect their villages. The Shawnees arrived home to find their principal town in ashes, some of their leading captains killed, and most of their possessions destroyed or taken as loot. One especially large loss was a quantity of silver the Shawnees had themselves stolen from the settlements. The Bowman attack sealed the allegiance of the Shawnees. From then until sixteen years later, when they were were forced to sign the Treaty of Greenville in 1795, they were firmly in the British camp.[35]

At the end of June, the trader Alexander McCormick arrived at Lichtenau.[36] McCormick was well known by the Moravians and had previously helped the Brethren. Most of his trading career was spent working with the Wyandots, and on this occasion he had just returned from the Upper Sandusky. Heckewelder wrote a letter on June 30 to the commander at Fort Pitt on behalf of the trader, passing along to Brodhead important intelligence. McCormick knew many details about the Wyandots and the conditions at Detroit but demanded that he not be identified as the source of that intelligence. Wyandot pretensions of friendship with the Americans, in McCormick's mind, were a ruse. Since they were so dependent on the British for trade goods, it was only a matter of time until they gave up their feigned overtures of peace toward the Americans. (He was entirely correct in this assumption.)

Heckewelder closed the letter to Brodhead with news that influenced the next few days' events: "I further inform you that Simon Girty with 8 Mingoes is gone to the inhabitants, to fetch a Packet of Letters out of a hollow tree. I understand somewhere about Pittsburgh."[37] (The "Hollow Tree" letters were written by a Loyalist at Pittsburgh passing intelligence on to Detroit.)

Brodhead received Heckewelder's letter, but its content no longer was news to him. He had the information about Girty as early as July 1, one day after Heckewelder wrote McCormick's letter. On the same day, the general dispatched a party led by Captain Samuel Brady and John Montour toward Holiday Cove (across the river from present Steubenville, Ohio), Girty's supposed destination. They were to seize Girty and return him to Fort Pitt.[38] The search proved to be in vain. Girty found his "Hollow Tree" letter and proceeded on toward the Delaware capital.

Zeisberger now became involved in a confused and exaggerated tale. Accompanied by the convert Michael, he had left New Schoenbrunn on June 30 and traveled to Lichtenau, arriving the next day to help Heckewelder with the communion. On July 4, accompanied by Isaac and Michael, he left the mission to return to New Schoenbrunn by way of Gnadenhutten. Before they reached White Eyes's old town, Caleb, an Indian from Goschachgunk, joined the party. A few minutes later they came upon Simon Girty and eight Mingoes with a prisoner moving toward Goschachgunk. It was a fortuitous meeting, and for a moment both groups were bewildered. Zeisberger and Girty had met on previous occasions, but they were not well acquainted. Within minutes of this meeting, a party of Delawares came down the trail following Girty and his Mingoes. Zeisberger's account of what followed is the only eyewitness record of the meeting. He wrote as usual in the third person:

> Here, according to all reasoning something would have happened had Brother David, Michael and Isaac been alone, but everything was decreed before, for as the Mingoes came upon us, a party of Delaware came behind them, but those from Pittsburgh [Girty] came and harassed us until one of them was about to grab Brother David. As this Simon saw David's face he called to his company, "see, there comes the one we have long wanted to see, now do what seems good to you." But the Mingoes Captain was quiet and shook his head. They asked some questions which Brother David answered whereupon they moved on and gave the war whoop.[39]

Many versions of this meeting have been written over the years. Most sources used Heckewelder's description recorded in his *Narrative* in 1820. The aging missionary's memory had faded, and the incident began to take on a histrionic tone. Girty's reputation had grown beyond all reasonable dimensions, thanks to Heckewelder and other writers of this period who erroneously placed Girty at almost every dastardly attack committed on the western frontier. Consul Willshire Butterfield, who conducted exhaustive research, in his *History of the Girtys*, makes the most reasonable assessment of the meeting. First, the encounter was accidental. Girty was not seeking out Zeisberger either to kill him or to take him prisoner, as Heckewelder claims, but had been sent by Detroit to find the "Hollow Tree" letters. If he had taken Zeisberger prisoner, the entire Delaware Nation would have been on his trail in a moment and Girty could not possibly have returned his prisoner to Detroit. Finally, Butterfield wrote, "If he would have killed him, Girty knew too well what effect such a proceeding would have at Detroit. The fear and easy credulity of Heckewelder made it, however, seem certain that the renegade only needed an opportunity, and that then his threats would certainly be carried into execution."[40]

Following its encounter with Zeisberger, the Girty party passed on to Goschachgunk on the afternoon of July 4. Girty hoped to have McCormick translate the letters, but the trader had left the village to return to Upper Sandusky. He then talked briefly to Richard Conner but knew that Conner was a member of the Christian mission and would not be a reliable person to do the translating. Girty told Conner "to tell the Americans, that he did not desire they show him any favors, neither," he said, "would he show them any."[41]

Zeisberger arrived safely back at New Schoenbrunn the day following his encounter with Girty, only to hear rumors of another change of commanders at Fort Laurens. On July 14 he wrote to the new commander, Lieutenant Colonel Richard Campbell of the Thirteenth Virginia Regiment. Campbell had just arrived with seventy-five men to replace Major Vernon, ordered by Brodhead to return with his long-suffering men and most of the supplies. The Fort Pitt commander was preparing to abandon the ill-fated Fort Laurens. Because of the deplorable conditions of the packhorses, Vernon could remove virtually nothing and the packhorses returned to Fort McIntosh with empty bags. For the first time in seven months, the men at Fort Laurens had more than enough to eat. It was Thanksgiving in July.

Campbell wanted to visit New Schoenbrunn, but Zeisberger advised that he "wait a bit for that, since things were very insecure with warriors coming and going." Later, Zeisberger wrote, "We heard that two of his people were killed." These were the last men who gave their lives at Fort Laurens. On August 3, he received a letter, dated August 2, from the fort commander, who was evacuating the post immediately and returning with his men to Fort Pitt. The suffering and dying at Fort Laurens were finally over.[42]

When Zeisberger visited Lichtenau on August 15, the final decision was made to abandon the village the coming spring. Heckewelder wrote, "Since reasons appear daily which make this move necessary (we are as sheep among the wolves) now it is firmly settled."[43]

On September 20, Zeisberger made a fourteen-day trip to Pittsburgh, returning on October 3. The purpose of the trip was not revealed in the diaries. Another treaty conference was taking place in Pittsburgh during this period, attended only by the Delawares and Wyandots. The conference began on September 17 and concluded on September 23, but no formal treaty was signed.[44] Zeisberger probably arrived in Pittsburgh the day the conference closed. The surviving correspondence and the later mission diaries contain no hints as to why Zeisberger made the trip. There is just one tantalizing notation in Heckewelder's entry of October 5: "Isaac delivered a letter from Bro. David, who informed me of his business in Pittsburgh and also a note regarding all sorts of situations."[45] Whatever had been discussed, Zeisberger could not trust to put it in his diary.

Later events seem to confirm that Zeisberger was trying to develop rapport with Brodhead. If that assumption is correct, the visit paid Zeisberger handsome dividends in the coming months. With his return from Pittsburgh, the normal routine returned to the valley.

Several days after Zeisberger returned from Pittsburgh, Gelelemend visited Lichtenau and talked privately with Michael. He explained the alienation of the chiefs toward the Christians. Heckewelder, on October 24, noted part of Gelelemend's conversation: "You Christian Indians would do well to leave Lichtenau and go to your former places. You yourselves see that the people of Goschachgunk don't want to hear about God and don't care about [our] people. In the long run it won't be well with them until you would first be out of the way."[46]

It was now clear that Gelelemend and his friends at the Delaware council were beginning to sever their close relationship with the missionaries and the Christian converts. This is precisely what Zeisberger predicted back in April and was his reason for dispersing the missions, but it put the Christians in a dangerous position because now they had warring factions on each of their flanks.

· 24 ·

The Torch, the Rifle, and the Scalping Knife, 1780–1781

THE WINTER weather of 1779–80 had a strong influence on those who lived on the western frontier.[1] It was perhaps the most severe winter in the annals of the United States. In November, snow began to fill the mountain passes and the temperature dropped below zero. By January the harbor of New York City was frozen solid, permitting the British, who occupied the city, to drive heavily laden wagons over the ice to Staten Island. The snow continued to accumulate, and by February it was four to eight feet deep in the woods and the mountain passes, effectively blocking all supply trains from the East. The garrison at Fort Pitt suffered severely, needing both food and clothing. Because many soldiers lacked shoes, scouting expeditions were out of the question. Some of the Delawares who had visited the fort in the late fall stayed all winter, finding whiskey easier to obtain than bread.[2]

The severe winter had positive effects, too. War parties that normally ranged across the frontier in November and early December were absent. While the hunger and cold were most distressing, they were certainly preferable to the torch, the rifle, and the scalping knife.

But by March 12 attacks on the frontier began again with a vengeance. The first was at Raccoon Creek, not more than thirty miles below

Pittsburgh. At dawn the Wyandots shot and tomahawked a party of five white men and women and carried away their children, two boys and three girls. Brodhead erroneously accused the Delawares of this attack.[3] Several days before he had received a letter from Heckewelder advising him that two war parties, one a combination of Delawares and Munsees, the other led by the sons of Pomoacan, the Wyandot chief, were headed in the direction of Raccoon Creek. It was the Wyandots who made the attack.[4] But Heckewelder's letter is the first indication that some Delawares were now actively working with the British-led Indians. Furthermore, his intelligence was close to the mark. Near the end of the month, the Delaware and Munsee party, led by the Munsee warrior Washnash, attacked a group of whites traveling down the Ohio River, killing three men and taking twenty-one men, women, and children as prisoners. On April 27, Brodhead wrote to President Joseph Reed of Pennsylvania's Supreme Executive Council: "Between 40 and 50 men, women and children have been killed or taken prisoner in Yohogania, Monongalia and Ohio counties." Hostilities continued with heightened regularity throughout the summer and fall.[5]

The Salem Mission

During the second week in February, Zeisberger visited Heckewelder at Lichtenau, and plans were made to move the remaining converts from the forks of the Muskingum upriver to within five miles of the Gnadenhutten mission. The new village was to be called Salem (Peace).[6] On March 28, two days after Easter, the move began. The last meeting at Lichtenau was on April 6, and the meeting house was then destroyed.

The Moravians were now removed from direct access to information originating in the Delaware council. Zeisberger admitted to Brodhead in his letter of April 2, "This place [New Schoenbrunn] is quite out of the way, no Indians which are going to the fort pass by here." This, of course, was Zeisberger's principal objective. It is evident that he believed it was only a matter of time until the Delawares would break their neutrality and officially join the British. Both he and Heckewelder, however, continued their correspondence with Colonel Brodhead, and throughout the year Heckewelder wrote numerous letters for the Delaware chiefs.

For several months following the move from Lichtenau, the converts shuffled about, deciding in which of the three villages they preferred to live. Israel, the Turkey Clan Delaware chief, had moved to Goschachgunk and become an apostate and one of the leading chiefs at the council. As

Captain Johnny he had been baptized by Zeisberger in December 1777 and had maintained a close relationship with the Christians until the previous summer, when he accompanied the chiefs to visit Congress. There he adopted the name of the new French ambassador, Conrad Alexandre Gerard.[7] Following his return to the valley, he had been increasingly immersed in his role as chief at Goschachgunk, neglecting the Moravians.

Meanwhile, Brodhead, like his former commander, Lachlan McIntosh, still hoped to make a strike at Detroit and during the first three months of the year continued plans to raise an army for that purpose. Frustrated and disappointed at each turn, he refused to abandon the project until General Washington finally advised him to drop the idea and confine himself to short local excursions against the hostile tribes.[8] Every scrap of war matériel and supplies, including men, horses, and wagons, was being removed from the western frontier and sent to General Washington, who was desperately trying to keep the Revolution on track, fighting back the British in the southern states.[9]

To keep the Delawares neutral, Brodhead's only recourse was to continue to make vague promises, which were not playing well back at the Delaware capital of Goschachgunk. Captain Johnny (aka Gerard or Israel), now acting as head chief at Goschachgunk, had Heckewelder write to Fort Pitt on April 23. It was a long, rambling, but provocative letter which indicated that the wily chief clearly understood the tacit deception of Brodhead's strategy.

> Brother: You desire me to send some of my Young Men to join Your Army. I therefore now sent six to join You there, but when You once will be on Your March then two of my Capt. shall join You with more Men. . . .
>
> Brother: I see no occasion of sending so many Men to Pittsburgh, as the Enemy we are about to destroy live quite the other Way. . . .
>
> Brother: I am so much mocked at by my Enemy Indians for speaking so long to them for You. Now they laugh at me, and ask me where that great Army of my Brothers, that was to come out against them so long ago, and so often, stays so long. They say to me, did We not tell you that they had no Army and that we were nearly done killing them all, and yet You would believe them?[10]

During the late spring and summer of 1780, Brodhead continued to employ all possible tactics to keep the Delawares neutral. He wrote

Heckewelder on May 4 advising that the "French Major Lanctot [Linctot] will deliver you this letter, he carries a message to the Council at Goschachgunk and I hope the Brethren will show him every mark of respect."[11] Daniel Linctot had been instrumental in assisting Clark during his expedition against the western Indians in 1779 and had gained much respect among the Americans and their Indian allies.

Heckewelder, in his entry of May 26, indicated that the Frenchman passed through Salem on his way to the Delaware capital. After meeting with the Delawares, he proposed to visit the Wyandots. The chiefs quickly dissuaded him from pressing on to the western Indians if he valued his life.

Again on May 30, Heckewelder noted, "The French officer, accompanied by Gelelemend and John Montour, stopped on their way to Pittsburgh." The following day Linctot visited Zeisberger at New Schoenbrunn.[12] He did not proceed to Pittsburgh but returned to the Delaware capital and continued his efforts to forge a peace. He remained in the valley until October and finally returned with a large delegation of Delaware chiefs to Fort Pitt, where they continued their discussion. But they solved none of the desperate problems that confronted the Delaware Nation.

Despite its futility, the Linctot visit is mentioned here because of the proliferation of correspondence to Brodhead from Zeisberger, Heckewelder, and the Delaware chiefs, whose letters were written by Heckewelder. Within a period of less than two months, they wrote more than ten letters in an attempt to assist in the negotiations. Zeisberger wrote three letters to Brodhead in the first twelve days in June.[13] But the effort was to no avail. The vast majority of the Delaware chiefs had gone over to the British camp. Only Gelelemend, Captain Johnny, and a handful of their followers remained to espouse the cause of the Americans among the Delawares, and they were in hiding with the threat of death hanging over their heads from their fellow chiefs, who had joined the British. Those Delaware chiefs were leading war parties against the western frontier under the direction of Major Arent De Peyster, the new British commander at Detroit.

On June 16, Zeisberger received a letter from Pittsburgh announcing the arrival of long-awaited visitors from Bethlehem, led by Bernard Adam Grube. With the Grube party was Gottlob Sensemann, again returning to the mission field. This time he was accompanied by his new wife, Anna Maria. Grube spent the next forty-seven days in the valley, baptizing, preaching, and meeting all of the Indian converts in the three Moravian missions. On July 4, the converts gathered at Salem as he solemnized the wedding of Sara Ohneberg (who had accompanied him from Bethlehem) and John Gottlieb Ernestus Heckewelder. It was the fourth anniversary of the Declaration of Independence. The bride and groom were thirty-four and thirty-seven years old respectively.[14]

During Grube's six-week visit, Zeisberger recorded the final chapter on Fort Laurens: "Several of our Brethren who had been hunting had tracked a strong party of warriors, who were marching toward Fort Pitt, after they had burned down completely all the houses in Fort Lawrence." Thus ended the spurious adventure of the United States into the Ohio Country during the Revolutionary War.[15]

Schebosh, who had taken the Grube party to Bethlehem, returned to Gnadenhutten on November 7, bringing back with him thirty-seven-year-old Michael Jung, who became the new assistant to William Edwards at Gnadenhutten.[16]

As their ninth year in the valley came to a close, all residents of the Christian mission villages had reason to give thanks. It had been their most successful year since 1775. A plentiful harvest filled their storage bins, and a substantial number had been added to the congregation. Relative tranquillity had prevailed throughout most of the year, and all three villages were spared the comings and goings of war parties. The confusing and turbulent atmosphere of the Delaware capital was now removed from their doorstep and only infrequently did the native Indian people left at the village visit the missions. By the end of the year only a semblance of the Delaware Nation's principal council was being held at Goschachgunk. Most of its important chiefs had moved to the Upper Sandusky near Pomoacan and his Wyandots. Gelelemend and a few of his friends retained their close connections with the Americans at Pittsburgh.

As David Zeisberger and his Christian converts gathered on the banks of the Muskingum to celebrate the love feast ushering in the new year, they were cheered by the successes of the previous year. Nearly four hundred converts resided in the three missions, served by a expanded staff of missionaries. Zeisberger and the Sensemanns resided at New Schoenbrunn; William Edwards and Michael Jung were at Gnadenhutten; the Heckewelders managed Salem. They looked forward to many more years of continued growth.[17]

Shortly after the first of the year, Gelelemend again appealed for permission to live at one of the missions. The chief and his handful of friends stood alone among the Delawares who supported the Americans, renegades to be hunted down like animals in the forest and killed. Zeisberger was well aware of Gelelemend's status and how dangerous it would be to accept him and his friends. They would draw the hostile Delaware element to the missions seeking to destroy Gelelemend and his friends.[18] Following the Helpers' Conference's negative decision, Gelelemend disappeared from the mission diaries for the next seven years.[19]

On January 10, Richard Conner and Wilhelm traveled to Fort Pitt. They returned on February 1 with dispatches from Bethlehem. Among those letters was a request from John Frederick Reichel for Zeisberger to attend the synod to be held in Bethlehem during the coming May. He was to leave before Easter.[20] The congregations were informed on March 18, and Zeisberger left New Schoenbrunn with Samuel Moore and Adam as his escorts on March 25.

By April 10, Sam Moore and Adam, Zeisberger's Pittsburgh escorts, returned to the valley. They brought a letter from Zeisberger with disconcerting news: Colonel Brodhead, with some 150 men, was marching to attack the Delaware village of Goschachgunk.[21] They had left Fort Pitt on April 7, stopped at Wheeling, picked up another 134 men, then turned west, crossed the Ohio, and headed straight toward the Delaware capital.[22] On April 19, Heckewelder reported that the army had been sighted at White Eyes's old town on the Muskingum, some six miles from its destination at Goschachgunk.[23]

Brodhead's army attacked the village on the morning of April 20. There was a spirited fight, and the commander noted that he "killed fifteen warriors and took upward of twenty old men, women, and children" who were later released. The Americans burned both villages, Goschachgunk and the former mission of Lichtenau.[24]

The day following the attack, Heckewelder received a letter from Brodhead requesting a meeting. That evening, accompanied by Jung and Schebosh, he met the army four miles south of the Salem mission. The commander proposed that Heckewelder move the Indian congregations nearer to Pittsburgh for greater protection. He also thanked him profusely for his previous help. In discussions the next day, Heckewelder expressed concern for five of his converts who had been held at the Indian village following Brodhead's attack. Fortunately, all of these prisoners were returned safely to the Salem mission within the next few days. Heckewelder noted, "The military Colonels, yes all officers were friendly and look upon our Indians with amazement."[25]

During the first week in July, a small party of converts traveled to Pittsburgh to meet Zeisberger on his return from Bethlehem. They were back in the valley on July 15, much to everyone's relief, but with a surprise that astonished the missionaries and delighted the converts. With him was his new wife, Susan (Lecron).[26]

The Bethlehem visit may be considered a turning point in Zeisberger's life. He had just turned sixty while on the journey to Bethlehem. Never again would he walk those tree-lined streets that he loved so well. Never again would he sit peacefully at the rear of the Gemeinhaus that he helped to build in 1741 and listen to the hymns being sung in the old chapel as they wafted across God's Acre where so many of his friends lay buried. Never again would he walk arm in arm with his old friends Peter Boehler, Nathaniel Seidel, and August Spangenberg. He would never, in the twenty-seven years of his remaining life, return to Bethlehem.

He had been treated well at Bethlehem, where he was considered a distinguished visitor. During his stay he traveled to Philadelphia, where he met and was entertained by President Reed of the Supreme Executive Council, Congress, and the Board of War.[27] He then returned to Bethlehem, where, to his surprise, the elders suggested that he should take a wife, a "helpmeet to protect him in the storm and strife of old age." The more he resisted, the more the elders insisted. In fact, they had just the woman, thirty-seven-year-old Susan Lecron. He finally relented and married Susan as they passed through Litiz on their return trip. The marriage ceremony was conducted by his old friend Bernard Grube on June 4, 1781. She stayed by his side during the tribulations of the next twenty-seven years of his life, faithful to the end.

· 25 ·

There Are Worse Things Waiting for Men Than Death, 1781

WHILE ZEISBERGER was visiting Bethlehem, a new commander had taken over at Fort Pitt. Colonel John Gibson was now temporarily in charge. He was replaced by General William Irwin, who assumed command early in November.[1]

When Zeisberger returned to the mission field, he brought along his old friends Johann and Anna Margareth Jungmann. The Jungmanns had left the valley early in August 1777 at the height of the Indian scare. Their return, more than any other act, indicated Zeisberger's confidence that the missions would weather the remaining months of the Revolution. He would not have continued to increase his staff if he anticipated trouble with the Indians, especially the Delawares and Wyandots.

Events during the first three weeks after Zeisberger's return seemed to confirm his conviction. But on August 7, Heckewelder wrote a devastating entry in his diary: "Had a message: That about 100 men under the leadership of English officers and Half-King were on the way *to take us away*. Immediately, through a courier, I gave this information to Brother David at Schoenbrunn and Edwards at Gnadenhutten."[2]

Heckewelder's diary for the next two days set the stage for the following five weeks of tension and turmoil. It is the only day-to-day record we have

William Irwin, 1741–1804. From C. W. Butterfield, *Washington-Irwin Correspondence* (Madison, Wis.: David Atwood, 1882).

for the first three weeks. Zeisberger undoubtedly was keeping a diary, but he destroyed these papers sometime during the course of the warriors' five-week stay in the valley. In November, he would recreate those events from memory.[3] Heckewelder wrote:

> *9th*. During the night two messengers came from Pomoacan, the Half-King, and were to tell us: That he with 140 men was on the way and had some things to say and request further that we should think about which town he and his men could stay in when he comes to us

> and that his purpose concerns all the Christians who live on the Muskingum. This also I reported [to Zeisberger] and added my own thoughts about it.
>
> *10th*—early through the courier, Gnadenhutten was decided as the meeting place since it is the middle mission. At my request I was sent two Helpers today and in the afternoon at 4 o'clock Captain Elliot, Half-King, Captain Pipe, Wingenund, Abraham Kuhn, the two Snakes (Shawano Chiefs) and other Captains with their people under a big English flag moved in here [Salem]. They camped right at the edge of town on the even land at the River. The Wyandots, Delaware and Shawanos separated themselves from one another. In the middle and right by Half-King's tent the English Captain also stayed, they put the [English] flag on a long pole.[4]

Late in the afternoon of August 10, after the Half-King party had been fed, the Wyandot chief called for a meeting with the missionaries then at Salem. Thus began three weeks of protracted negotiations. At first, the discussion was friendly, with the typical Indian allegorical speeches, Half-King thanking "the great God who lives above who has kept us up to this time that we again see one another," and Heckewelder's appropriate response, "thanking God that he has preserved us for such an occasion." The close of the first meeting was reported as follows: "Here, according to the Indian custom, preparations were made for [the symbolic] painting. Half-King made the eyes of our Indians blue, the ears were cleaned out, the heart set right and the throat cleared out so that they could see well, hear well and understand. Thereupon, after a like greeting and thanks from our Helper's, for this time they left."[5]

That evening Heckewelder met clandestinely with Alexander McCormick, the trader who had helped the missionaries so many times in the past and in the next three months would be crucial to their survival. McCormick was a member of Half-King's party and had sought out Heckewelder in the dead of the night. After pledging Heckewelder to secrecy, with the exception of Zeisberger, whom McCormick trusted, the trader revealed Half-King's plans.

> "These people have come on order of the English to take you away from these three towns. First they will make all kinds of gentle propositions but you can expect nothing less than that you have to leave. The plan is laid, Elliot is the leader. The determination is: Not to let

> anything deter them. The first decision was to seize and kill you as enemies. Now it is: To make your towns a seat of war and thereby make you tired. My advice is that you understand what they propose, for actually you no longer have a choice." After this night I told all this in a letter to Brother David and we decided to meet day after tomorrow in Gnadenhutten.[6]

By August 12, Half-King's party had moved to Gnadenhutten and Pipe's Delawares followed the next day. The discussions continued. Three hundred warriors were gathered in and around the village, including Half-King's Wyandots, Pipe and Wingenund's Delawares, and some Shawnees, Chippewas, and Tawas.[7] On August 14, they formally revealed their plans to remove the Christians, possibly to the Pettquotting River area.[8]

Sometime during the next four days Zeisberger learned that Half-King planned to send some of his party to attack Wheeling, Fort McIntosh, or Fort Pitt.[9] On August 18, Zeisberger wrote to Colonel Brodhead, who had just returned to Fort Pitt. Zeisberger's dispatch was sent by one of his most trusted couriers. Why, with the problems that confronted him in the valley, he chose to jeopardize his position further is difficult to understand. The letter read in part:

> They [Half-King's party] will try to decoy the garrison out where they will lie in ambush. The party is headed by Matthew Elliot and a few English and French. The Indians are Wyandots, Delawares, Monseys, and a small number of Shawnanse [*sic*]. You will be careful not to mention that you had this intelligence from our towns; for it would prove dangerous for us if the Indians should get knowledge of it; which might happen from a prisoner, if they should take one.[10]

That is precisely what happened.

Brodhead received Zeisberger's letter a few days later and promptly warned all of his fort commanders on August 24, enclosing a copy of Zeisberger's correspondence. There was a postscript: "The letters received are from the Rev. Zeisberger, an honest man, and faithful correspondent, but his name must remain a secret less his usefulness may be destroyed."[11] Brodhead might as well have published it in the Pittsburgh newspaper.

In the meantime, Zeisberger continued to negotiate with the Wyandots, but made little progress. He was attempting to delay moving the converts until spring so they could gather their harvest in the fall. On August 19,

Heckewelder's diary noted: "That Half-King and his counsellors were not totally satisfied with our answers to their speech and warned that if we abide by our decision, at the earliest opportunity we would be killed by the Chippewas and Tawas."[12] That was a ruse, and the missionaries knew it.

Zeisberger wrote: "We entertain the Eng. captain [Elliot] and his company the best way we could, and showed them all kindness so far as lay in our power; they likewise behaved in a friendly way toward us, but had secret guile, and we could trust them nought."[13] Beginning on August 20, after all parties had gathered at Gnadenhutten, the negotiations began in earnest, continuing until September 1. Zeisberger seemed to be making progress with Half-King, who acknowledged that there was some wisdom in their remaining until the following spring. To justify his position, Zeisberger called the missionaries together, and they resolved to consult the lot and ask the Lord for guidance. The question was, "Should they compromise further and willingly abide with the Wyandot plan, or stand [firm] by the decision not to move until spring?" Zeisberger recorded the results: "The Lord's answer was we had given enough."[14] It was a serious mistake, and they unfortunately stood by this decision until the very end, when they no longer had any options.

During these ten days of intense negotiations the Brethren at New Schoenbrunn and Salem remained loyal to their Christian vows. But in Gnadenhutten, living with more than two hundred native warriors who were becoming more unruly every day, the converts began to defect. Zeisberger noted, "Yes, it went so far that some of the wicked people spoke and gave us to understand that while they were now at war they could proscribe us the rules, in short, our life depended upon them, and we had reason to be silent."[15]

Despite the tension, Heckewelder noted in his diary that Zeisberger wrote two letters to Brodhead at Fort Pitt on August 26. There appears to be no extant record of this correspondence. With the deteriorating conditions of the command between Brodhead and Gibson at Fort Pitt, they were probably lost.[16]

On August 30, another incident occurred which added to Zeisberger's problems. Anna Sensemann gave birth to a healthy boy. Heckewelder, who baptized him the same day, called the baby Christian David. Any move now or in the near future could jeopardize the lives of Anna and her child.

By September 1, the missionaries were ordered by Half-King to meet again at Gnadenhutten. Zeisberger, Heckewelder, and Sensemann arrived in the afternoon. (Jungmann was left at Schoenbrunn, and Jung, with Sara Heckewelder, remained at Salem.) The missionary party waited there until

September 3. Zeisberger wrote, "We felt the power of darkness, as if the air were filled with evil spirits." Again the question was put to the missionaries: would they give in to the Indians' demands and go with them at once? Zeisberger noted, "We answered them briefly, that we stood by what we had already said, and could not give them any other answer."[17]

This intransigent position may have been one of the greatest mistakes of Zeisberger's life. Alexander McCormick had told Heckewelder the night Half-King arrived in the valley that "you can expect nothing less than you have to leave." Zeisberger's uncompromising stance only added to the already hostile attitude of Half-King, Pipe, and Elliot and possibly led to the suffering and pain later experienced by the converts. Why did he take this stand? It was unlike Zeisberger to be obstinate and not to recognize his precarious position or be willing to compromise his original decision. It appears that the outcome of the lot added to his pertinaciousness.

The negotiations were at a stalemate. Now the humiliation, suffering, and misery would begin. In the afternoon, the three missionaries, Zeisberger, Heckewelder, and Sensemann, went for a walk in the church garden. As they talked, Alexander McCormick passed by the fence and whispered to them, "What is to happen, will be soon."[18] Just after McCormick passed, a party of Wyandots ran into the garden and roughly seized the three men. Shouting the "death hallow," they took them to the Wyandot camp. Here they were stripped and confined to a hut, along with other prisoners who had been taken during raids the warriors had made in the settlements since arriving in the valley. After the three were imprisoned, Indians began looting and plundering the village missionary's house. They did not touch Brother Edwards, so consumed were they in plundering his possessions. Finally, Edwards went out of the house and met McCormick, who took him to join the other prisoners. Edwards had heard shots earlier and presumed that all three men had been killed. He sighed with relief as they pushed him through the door of the prisoners' hut and he saw that they were safe.

Shortly all four men were taken to Elliot's tent. Zeisberger noted, "Here we received compassion and Elliot said, 'it had not been intended that we should be thus treated, although there were express orders from the commander at Detroit to bring us away by force, if it could not be done in a gentler means.'" Elliot provided them with some clothes, but the tragedy came close to a farce when he gave Zeisberger one of Anna Sensemann's old nightgowns. The next day, following their confinement, the other missionaries were also seized and with the death hallow they were brought to Gnadenhutten. Jung was taken from Salem, and Jungmann was brought from Schoenbrunn. The women were permitted to remain at the respective villages for the time being.[19] The looting now began in earnest.

The day after their capture, a young woman, not connected with the mission but accompanying the Wyandot party, became so concerned with how the Wyandots had treated the missionaries that she stole Captain Pipe's horse and set out for Pittsburgh. She was captured but again escaped and made her way to Fort Pitt, where she told the Americans of the events in the valley. Brodhead received her message on September 7 and immediately notified all of his county lieutenants to be on their guard.[20]

After the missionaries had been in captivity for three days, Elliot realized that if he expected to make the move, he must free them so as to organize the converts. Zeisberger knew that he must cooperate and make immediate plans to leave the valley. Packing what little of their possessions and food they could carry, some went in canoes and others traveled by horse and on foot, driving the cattle. On September 8 they began the exodus that moved the Gnadenhutten and New Schoenbrunn people down to Salem. Here they would prepare for their departure.

Later historians have described in detail heavy destruction wrought by the warrior party at the three villages before the Christian Indians departed: the killing of cattle, the destruction of crops and fences, and the burning of houses. In contrast, Zeisberger described the killing of pigs and chickens and also mentioned looting, but not the other incidents. It would appear from the later diaries that the missionaries took most of their cattle with them and that only a small portion of the crops was destroyed. Zeisberger does not mention any destruction of fences or burning of buildings. His later diary is the only eyewitness account of the journey. Heckewelder's diary abruptly ends on September 3, the day of their arrest.

Half-King discovered that Zeisberger had corresponded with Brodhead at Fort Pitt. During the war party's stay in the valley, the chiefs had sent a large contingent against Fort Henry at Wheeling. When they arrived and found the fort prepared for the attack, they quickly gave up the project. Before returning, they captured a young boy, David Glenn, who informed them of the missionary's warning. After giving up their attack against Fort Henry, they moved up Wheeling and Buffalo Creek, where they killed some people and captured additional prisoners. These men also told of the warning and were taken back to Gnadenhutten and confined in the hut with the missionaries.

It is questionable, as some historians claim, that Elliot and Half-King forcefully removed the missionaries because they knew that Zeisberger was working with the Americans. Although it may have intensified their rough treatment, Heckewelder's account up to September 3 and Zeisberger's later diaries do not support the claim that this was Half-King's only reason for removing the Christians.[21]

By September 11, the three contingents were congregated on the banks of the river at Salem. Gathering what was left of their meager possessions after the pillaging, they boarded the canoes and slung their packs on their backs. Most of the converts felt they were living in a nightmare as they pushed away from the banks of the river. A rancid smell from the dead pigs and chickens pervaded the air. Zeisberger wrote, "And thus we turned our backs upon our homesteads and places where we had enjoyed so much that was good and blessed from the hands of the Saviour. Before us we could see nothing wherein to rejoice, nothing but need, misery, and danger."[22]

They traveled slowly. It took them four days to reach the site of old Goschachgunk, where they left the Muskingum and headed into the Walhonding River. Normally this trip by water or on foot could be made in less than a day. Throughout most of the journey, the converts, and especially the missionaries, were followed and closely guarded by a large party of Wyandot warriors who constantly pressed them to move more quickly but offered no assistance.

They stayed in camp at Goschachgunk for two days, then continued upstream on the Walhonding on September 16. Two days later, the journey was interrupted by heavy rains. Two canoes were lost in the high water. Zeisberger noted, "The brethren lost all they had for they sank to the bottom." Many of the Zeisbergers' possessions were in one of those canoes. A two-year-old child died on the seventeenth and was buried the next day.

On September 19, Half-King came to them. His men had just completed plundering Salem, finding numerous things the Brethren had hidden and buried in the woods. On the same day a war party, just returned from the settlement, came with two prisoners, who reported that when the news of the converts' capture reached Pittsburgh, the Americans determined to send an army to rescue the Christians but fortunately gave up the plan. This had been one of Zeisberger's greatest fears. Such an attack would have placed the Christians between two warring factions and would probably have caused the Indians to kill the Christians, at least the ministers. He was relieved to hear that the campaign had been given up. During the next two days, two sisters "were brought to bed with new daughters." After a delay of two days because of rain, they were on the river again. The

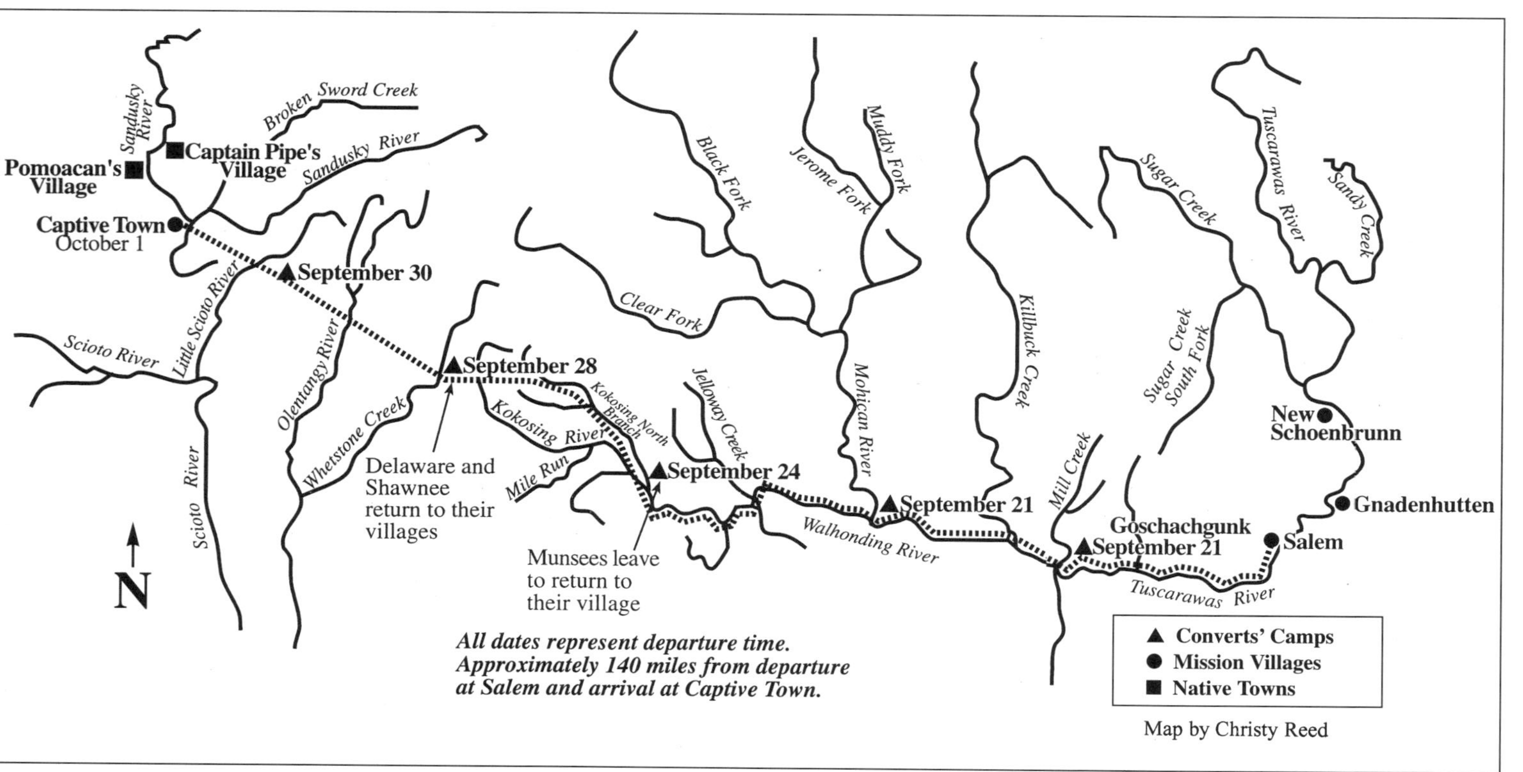

Converts' journey from Salem mission to the Upper Sandusky, September 11 – October 1, 1781.

Munsees, who had followed them throughout the journey, left to go to their villages. Before leaving, their captain spoke with Zeisberger and "showed his displeasure at the conduct of the Wyandot."

On September 24 they entered the mouth of the Kokosing River. Here they passed the old Indian town of Memekasink and continued on to the old Indian village of Gokhosing (the place of the owls) at the headwaters of the Kokosing on September 26. At this point they abandoned their canoes. Throughout the journey both land and water parties stayed together so they could share the evening camp. From now on they all traveled by land. They rested there until September 28 to give the stragglers a chance to catch up to the main party.

At this point the Delawares left to go to their villages as the Shawnees and Munsees had done earlier. The Christian converts were now alone with the Wyandots, who, Zeisberger said, "drove us on like cattle, without having the least compassion for children and sisters, for they left them no time to give the children drink once." The land in this area was covered with many marshes and swamps, and at times the horses' feet stuck fast. Sister Susan fell from her horse twice in quick succession but miraculously was not hurt.

On September 30 they passed out of the swamp and crossed the headwaters of the Scioto River. Now they were on the flat plains in Wyandot country, where, according to Zeisberger, "there is nothing but grass which is so high and long that on horseback a man can hardly see over it, only here and there a little clump of brushes." The next day, October 1, they arrived at the Sandusky River, the end of their journey. It had been twenty days since they left Salem. The journey from the Muskingum to the Wyandot country normally took five or six days. Zeisberger explained their plight: "Here the Wyandot left us and went ten miles to their homes after they had abandoned us in the wilderness, where there was no food to be found and no game to hunt, and many among our brethren had nothing left to eat, but lived only upon what those, who yet had something, divided among them."[23]

At the end of the previous year, 380 converts were living at the three villages on the Muskingum. During their journey, the Wyandots had carefully guarded against any defection from the Christian party. Zeisberger now found himself in hostile Indian country with well over three hundred people to feed, house, and clothe in the middle of a wilderness.

But first he had to decide if they should remain here on the Upper Sandusky or go elsewhere. After consulting the lot, they found that the Lord favored their staying where they were for the remaining months of the winter. In reality, lot or no lot, Half-King would not have permitted him to move beyond his jurisdiction.

With that question settled, they spent the next four days finding a suitable location for the village. After a thorough inspection of the area, they chose a site on the Sandusky River approximately five miles south of the present Upper Sandusky and near an old Wyandot village. On October 7, they moved to that location and began building their new village. Later historians called it Captive Town, but Zeisberger always referred to it as the mission on the Sandusky.[24]

Shortly after they arrived on the Sandusky, Richard Conner and his family, who had accompanied the Christians on the journey, moved to the Lower Sandusky, near present Fremont, Ohio. Before leaving, he told Zeisberger he had heard rumors "that the missionary would be brought to Detroit." Zeisberger had also heard such a rumor but had paid it little notice. Even if he had not been called to Detroit, he had resolved to go on his own to talk with the commander there. On October 14 the summons arrived, carried by Captain Pipe's brother and Wingenund, from Alexander McKee, the British Indian agent at Detroit.[25]

On October 17, seven days before Zeisberger departed for Detroit, Israel, the former convert and chief of the Turkey Clan, arrived at the mission to apply to the Christians for readmission. After a long discussion, Zeisberger relented and finally, in January, permitted him to return.[26]

The stage was now set for one of the most traumatic events in Zeisberger's long and exciting life. On October 25, after receiving the summons from Captain Pipe and Wingenund, he set out for Detroit, accompanied by Heckewelder, Sensemann, and Edwards. The Indian Brethren who went along were William, Tobias, Joshua, and Isaac Eschicanahund, the oldest son of the late Wolf Clan chief, Packanke. Since they were apprehensive about the outcome, Zeisberger's most trusted lieutenant, Isaac Glikhikan, was left behind with Jungmann and Jung to guard the mission. None of the women accompanied the delegation.[27]

They traveled by land around the west end of Lake Erie and reached Detroit on November 2. Immediately after arriving, they asked for and were granted an interview with Major Arent De Peyster, commandant of the fort. It was a stiff, formal, and short conversation. He asked Zeisberger why he had not brought all of the missionaries and their women as he had ordered because he was considering sending them all to Philadelphia. Zeisberger told him that the chiefs had permitted the women to remain behind, and the two missionaries were left to protect the converts and the missionaries' wives. De Peyster said that "the reason why he had removed us from our settlements was that he heard we corresponded with the rebels to the harm of his government for many complaints against us had come to his ears." Zeisberger explained that he had no doubt they had been accused of many things, as demonstrated by the treatment he and his people had received on their trip from the Muskingum. De Peyster also inquired about the Indian converts. Zeisberger responded "that four of the Indians were in his present party" and the remaining converts, "between three and four hundred," were at the mission. He also said, "We could not look upon it as a trifling matter to be apart and separated from our mission, which has been intrusted to us, and if this should happen, would of itself go to destruction, and all of our labor of forty years would have been in vain."

"Think you so?" replied De Peyster. "But if the Indians were harmful to our government?"

Zeisberger quickly replied, "They would not be harmful, but useful, that would be learned, if you were better acquainted with us, for they are an industrious, laborious people."

Finally, the commandant asked if Zeisberger's Indians had gone to war. Zeisberger responded with an emphatic "No."

Although the conversation was short and to the point, little was learned. Zeisberger was pleased with De Peyster's attentiveness, especially the orders he issued to his subalterns for their care. They were quartered together with the Indians by a friendly French couple, the Tybouts. Throughout their stay, the Tybouts were generous with provisions and accommodations.[28]

Twice before their formal hearing, Zeisberger and the Indians tried to contact De Peyster but were rejected on both occasions. In the interim, they had numerous friendly visitors who sympathized with their plight.

On the evening of November 6, Captain Pipe arrived in camp near the village. On the morning of the seventh he entered Detroit with the familiar death hallow, waving scalps borne on sticks and driving prisoners ahead of him.[29]

On Friday, November 9, the formal hearing was held at De Peyster's headquarters within the fort.[30] The commandant and several of his officers sat in the front of the room. Immediately in front of them sat the Pipe delegation and, off to one side, Zeisberger and his party. Pipe appeared in all his Indian finery. He brought with him his counselors, scalps, and the white prisoners. Pipe spoke first, presenting his trophies of war. After these were disposed of and the prisoners removed, Pipe rose to make his presentation.

> Thou hast ordered us to bring the believing Indians with their teachers from the Muskingum. We have done so, and it has been done as ordered us. . . . They are now here before thine eyes, thou cans't now thyself speak with them as thou hast desired, but thou wilt speak good words to them, and I say to thee, speak kindly to them, for they are our friends, and I hold them dear and should not like to see harm befall them;

Pipe repeated the last comment several times and then sat down. Zeisberger and his Indians were stunned—a look of bewilderment passed over their faces. This could not be! This man who was their mortal enemy so recently filled with guile and chicanery! "Speak kindly to them . . . our friends . . . I hold them dear and should not like to see harm befall them." What was he saying? Why was he saying it?

A perplexed commandant sat silently for a moment. Finally, he said, slightly raising his voice, "I brought these people here because of your complaints and those of Half-King and the other chiefs. You have repeatedly told me they were corresponding with the rebels and if this were so they were harmful to our government." He turned to Pipe and said, "I want the exact truth, whether this was so."

Pipe rose and, with downcast eyes, quietly said, "There might be some truth to this thing and I can not say it was all lies, but it will not happen again since they are away from there but now here." But that answer was not satisfactory to De Peyster, and he responded, "So they then have corresponded with the rebels and sent letters to Fort Pitt, for from thine answer I must conclude it is true." Now Pipe became angry and jumped to his feet, almost shouting, "I have told thee that there is something to the matter, now I tell thee straight out, they who are ministers, are innocent, they have not done it of themselves, they had to do it." He struck himself on the breast and shouted: "I am guilty of it and the chiefs who were with me in Goschachgunk; we compelled them to it and forced them; thou must hold us responsible for this." Lowering his voice, he said, "But since we are now here it will not happen again, as I have already told thee."

De Peyster now realized that the principal charge against the missionaries could not be sustained and turned to Pipe with one more question: "What now shall I do with the missionaries? Shall we send them back to the States or permit them to return to their people?" There was a momentary pause as the translation was questioned. Zeisberger detected the error immediately but remained quiet. The error was quickly recognized, and Pipe answered that when they removed the Christians from the Muskingum they promised the converts the missionaries could stay with their people.

For all intents and purposes the trial was over, but De Peyster spent some time questioning Zeisberger before he finally closed the meeting, dismissing the charge of treason. After the meeting he shook hands with all, and as the participants were leaving the meeting, he caught Zeisberger's eye and quietly said, "I wished to speak with you further, at your convenience."

Zeisberger's party spent the next four days in Detroit. De Peyster opened the king's stores to them, showering them with gifts of clothing and food and promising all the help and resources he had. Before leaving, De Peyster and his wife complimented the missionaries on their work among the Indians and assured Zeisberger of his continuing support.[30]

They left Detroit on November 14 and were back on the Sandusky among their own people nine days later. Zeisberger noted: "Many tears of gratitude and joy could be seen running down the cheeks of our brethren."

Most of the remaining five weeks of the year were spent in a frantic search for food. Every possible resource was tapped. Before Zeisberger had left for Detroit, some of the Brethren had traveled to the Muskingum looking for food, after receiving permission from the Half-King. This party straggled into the village, carrying a substantial quantity of corn, the day Zeisberger returned.

It was a long way to haul such a bulky product as corn, but there, on the Muskingum, were hundreds of bushels of their own unharvested crops. It became an alluring lodestar that later drew many of them to their deaths. Schebosh had led this party, but he and his immediate family remained behind to gather more of the crop. A party of militia, led by Captain John Biggs, trailing an Indian war party, arrived at New Schoenbrunn and discovered Schebosh and his family. Captain Biggs took the six members of the family back to Fort Henry and then to Pittsburgh, where they were kindly treated by General Irwin and released, much to the chagrin of the local inhabitants, who would have preferred to see them killed (see Appendix J). (There is a dispute as to who led this party. Some say Lieutenant Colonel David Williamson was in command.)[31]

Shortly after Zeisberger returned from Detroit, their old friend Alexander McCormick and a Mr. Dawson, both traders among the Wyandots, arrived offering their services. They returned again the following month with corn they had purchased from the Indians. During December, Zeisberger sent John Martin and Isaac to the Shawnees for help with some success. They traded one hundred strings of wampum for a quantity of corn and assurances of further help. But it was impossible to alleviate the starvation faced by his people. On December 28, he lamented, "Many of our Brethren suffer hunger, and as no corn can be had, they must subsist upon wild potatoes, which they dig up laboriously and bring from a distance."[32] Zeisberger closed the 1781 diary without the usual year-end statistics. The entire mission was in such a state of flux that it was impossible to determine the population. As he had told De Peyster in November, it was probably between three and four hundred.

The year had begun with optimism and promise because it seemed they would no longer be affected by the dissension and conflict that radiated from the old Delaware capital at Goschachgunk. Most of the Delawares, including their grand council, now resided on the Upper Sandusky. All of the missions were staffed with adequate missionary personnel. Zeisberger's trip back to Bethlehem was crowned with a successful marriage, and the highest officers in the land had applauded his work. Within less than a month after his return, his string of successes had run out. Thirty-six years of struggle and effort came tumbling down around his feet. Most men would have withdrawn and returned to the settlements. But there was a resiliency within the soul of David Zeisberger that came from his deep faith and fervent belief in the wisdom and strength of his Savior. He would now pick up the pieces and put them back together again.

· 26 ·

Gnadenhutten: The Day of Shame, 1782

RESILIENCY AND an abiding faith in the Lord were admirable characteristics, but they did not fill an empty stomach. The desperate plight of those converts remaining at the mission was graphically told in the diaries for the last six weeks of 1781 and the first months of 1782. They are filled with accounts of a frantic search for food. Earlier the Shawnees had provided some assistance. Alexander McCormick and his fellow traders at the Lower Sandusky had given additional temporary relief. Yet this help was wholly inadequate to meet their needs. In a short autobiography written in her later life, Susan Zeisberger captured the pain and suffering during those days on the Sandusky. "Many times," she said, "the Indians shared their last morsel with me, for many times I spent eight days in succession without any food of my own."[1]

As if hanging on the edge of starvation was not sufficient trouble for the missionaries, on January 1, 1782, they received additional unwelcome news. Josy and Abraham, two young converts previously denied permission to leave the village to visit relatives in Pittsburgh, took "French leave," defying Zeisberger's orders. They secretly left the village bound for Fort Pitt. Within hours, Half-King knew of their departure and accused the missionaries of again writing letters to the Americans. It was more than the patient Zeisberger could abide. He scathingly recorded, "Satan rages, and it is as if we were given over to devils to plague us utterly, to torment us and to make trial of fortune with us while we are here, more than ever before not only from without, but also within." Having vented his frustration, he closed the entry with another promise to his Savior: "We are not," he wrote, "cast down nor disheartened, but oppose with might and all of our strength, to destroy and cast out of the church the works of Satan."[2]

Shortly after the first of the year, Zeisberger noted that "evil reports began to circulate" regarding the missionaries and their attempts to open communications with the Americans. In an effort to squelch these rumors, Zeisberger sent Mark, William, and Christian ten miles upstream to Captain Pipe's village to assess what damage might have been done. They arrived back at the mission the following day to report that they had been "well received" by Pipe, who told them "he had also indeed heard these rumors that ten converts had returned to Pittsburgh but had not troubled himself about them." He acknowledged that "there were indisposed persons among the Indians, who took pleasure in spreading lies among us; but we should not be troubled about it, they did no better with him." He cautioned Zeisberger that he "would remain fast and you should remain fast."[3]

But there was additional news from Pipe that could bode possible future problems for Zeisberger. Shortly after the first meeting with De Peyster on November 9 of the previous year, some of Pipe's Delaware captains complained to the commander, vehemently criticizing his decision to release the missionaries and send them back among their converts. They preferred to have them returned to the settlements. De Peyster reminded the captains that he had made his decision based on Captain Pipe's testimony and that during the trial they had adequate opportunity to speak up and disagree with Pipe. Since they had not spoken, his decision would stand, and unless he had "well-founded reasons for calling us away," his decision was sustained.[4] This exchange was the first indication of a clandestine campaign that was carried on over the next two months to separate the missionaries from their converts. But Zeisberger had other pressing matters on his mind.

Throughout January his diary is filled with entries noting the deteriorating condition of the food supply. On the tenth he wrote, "We have sold some of our cattle to a trader for corn, and on this we thought to live for a while, and yet it was little to get." Six days later, another delegation searching for food went to the Shawnees and more went for the same reason to the Muskingum. Jungmann, Michael, John, William, and Adam went to the Lower Sandusky to bring supplies sent by De Peyster from

Detroit. By the twentieth Zeisberger began to despair. "Our brethren," he wrote, "become disheartened and listless, and have no hope of rescue, for always it gets worse, this we can see before our eyes." And then, in a plea to his God, he wrote, "Our Saviour and our dear heavenly Father must know better than we how to bring us through, and how to devise." Near the end of the month he addressed his attention to the desperate condition of one of their greatest assets: "Our cattle generally suffer the greatest want, many die, and it appears that few will live through the winter, so our need increases everywhere." With the beginning of February, as if they had not suffered enough, the weather turned bitterly cold. In the same entry Zeisberger for the first time in his life shows signs of despair. He wrote: "The hunger among our people here at home is so great that for some time already they have had to live upon dead cattle, cows, and horses; never in their lives have they felt such want. . . . Why does the Saviour let all this come upon us?"[5]

The following day, young Joseph Shebosch, along with his sister, arrived at the mission village. In the fall of the previous year he had gone to search for his father, only to be captured with the rest of the family and taken to Pittsburgh. Joseph was the last of the captured party to return to the mission. He brought word that his father had gone on to Bethlehem to deliver the first word of the Christians' removal to the Sandusky. But Joseph brought a far more important piece of information from Pittsburgh. It appeared that the Muskingum Valley was now safe and the converts could return to gather their unharvested crop.

There was a brief respite from the harsh weather during the middle two weeks of February while the village was almost empty. Some of the converts were at their sugar camps, but most had left for the Muskingum. Each of these groups headed for the villages where they formerly lived, some to New Schoenbrunn, others to Gnadenhutten, and the rest to Salem. It was not a mass exodus. Small parties drifted away from the village, a few families at a time, including the men, women, and children. In total, more than 130, and possibly up to 150, had left for the Muskingum. Zeisberger described the situation on February 25: "Our Indian brethren were now partly in the Shawanese towns, but most on the Muskingum and or the bush, scattered about to get the necessaries of life." In the same diary entry, he announced what he had so desperately tried to deny would happen: "So it came about that we, Friday, March 1, through a messenger, were summoned to Pomoacan, who sent word he had something to tell us."[6]

Zeisberger, Heckewelder, and two Indian Brethren left the village the next day. Pomoacan's town was only a short distance down the Sandusky

River from the mission. On arrival, they found the chiefs and their captains gathered in council, expecting them. As he surveyed the room, Zeisberger saw all the principal men of the Wyandot and Delaware Nations: Pomoacan and his captains and all the principal chiefs of the Delaware Nation, Pipe, Wingenund, Buckongahelas, Machingue Pushies. All, except possibly Pipe and Wingenund, were mortal enemies of the Moravians. There was little possibility of justice from that crowd. Near the back of the council Zeisberger saw a familiar face, his old nemesis Simon Girty.

Little time was wasted on formalities. Pomoacan rose and spoke directly to Zeisberger, telling him he had a letter from De Peyster. It was not written to Pomoacan but to Simon Girty. He handed it to Zeisberger, and the missionary read: "You will please present the strings I sent you to the Half-King and tell him I have listened to his demand. I therefore hope he will give you such assistance as you may think necessary to enable you to bring the teachers and their families to this place. I will by no means allow you to suffer them to be punished or in any way plundered or any way ill-treated."[7] Pomoacan had accomplished his objective, to rid himself and his people of what he believed to be the disruptive influence of the Moravian ministers and their families. The most galling part of the bargain was Girty's role as escort.

Zeisberger was devastated but not surprised. The rumors had floated along the Indian grapevine for six weeks. Now they were reality. There was nothing he could do but comply. There would be no equivocating, no ambivalence, this time.

His eyes searched out Girty, and he said, "We have received the commandant's command and will comply. In fifteen days we will be at the Lower Sandusky, however, we beg of you to have a ship there to take us across the lake as our women and children can not make the toilsome journey on foot." That request was quickly granted.[8]

Before he left the Wyandot village, Zeisberger had a conversation with Captain Pipe. Pipe had done his best to convince his people not to insist on such a course, but his pleading was to no avail.[9]

Immediately on their return to the mission, Zeisberger dispatched messengers to the Shawnees and to the Muskingum, asking the converts gathering corn in those areas to return home immediately. He was concerned for these men, women, and children, especially those on the Muskingum, because they were taking far too much time before returning. Within a few weeks the Indian war parties and American troops would be ranging the forest.

By March 7, five days after the messengers were dispatched to the Shawnees, word was received that the converts were on their way back to the mission. Several days later, word arrived from the Muskingum that they were preparing to return. But on March 14, the day before the missionaries planned to leave for Detroit, they received a menacing message from the Indian George, "who brought frightful news that all our brethren who went to the Muskingum had been captured by the Americans and taken to Pittsburgh." But the report carried other disturbing details. Zeisberger explains: "The messenger also related many unpleasant things that occurred, for example that they were bound and some killed."[10] Zeisberger discounted the latter and simply could not believe that the Americans would harm his people.

While awaiting the converts' return, the missionary party prepared to depart for Detroit. A Frenchman, Francis Lavallie, had arrived the previous day and was to be their guide. Half-King was on hand to assure compliance with Girty's orders. Zeisberger was plunged into the depths of despair. Never before in his thirty-eight years among the Indians had he been compelled to leave his post and abandon his flock. It was an excruciating scene. All around the gathering missionary party the converts filled the air with wails of lamentation and moans. Try as he might, Zeisberger could not provide any succor. Finally, he fell to his knees and "thanked the Saviour for all of his goodness and comfort they had enjoyed from him in all of their unhappiness and burdens, in all of our needs and danger from without." He closed, "asking the Lord to be especially watchful to their Indian Church to guard and protect them until we should see each other again."[11]

The departing group on March 15 consisted of Zeisberger and his wife, Susan; John Heckewelder, his wife, Sara, and their one-year-old daughter, Johanna Maria (Polly); Johann Georg Jungmann and his wife, Anna Margaretha; Gottlob Sensemann, his wife, Anna Marie, and their seven-month-old child, Christian David; Michael Jung, who had been Heckewelder's assistant at Salem; and the ever-faithful William Edwards. It took them four days to reach the Lower Sandusky town (present Fremont, Ohio). The women were supplied with horses. Some of the men traveled in a small canoe, and the rest followed on foot. Several of the Indian women converts carried the missionaries' babies on their backs in Indian style. The party took only what they could carry on their backs and left instructions for the men remaining in the village to bring the rest of their supplies later by water. The Lower Sandusky town was almost deserted, but those who remained took the missionary families into their homes and provided them with generous hospitality.

Here they found Richard Conner and his family. From him they discovered why De Peyster had taken them so abruptly from the mission.

Zeisberger wrote: "We learned now what had really been the occasion of our again being called to Detroit. We had in the first place looked upon it as done by the commandant for our own safety, and so indeed it was." Half-King, however, was behind the plot.

> At the instigation of some white people, the Half-King had complained to the commandant that so long as we were in Sandusky we corresponded with the Pittsburghers, and would certainly yet bring [the Americans] here to blot them out [the Wyandots], on which account they besought the commander to take us away. . . . The Half-King said: "His affairs would not be well so long as we [the Moravians] were there, and he feared still another misfortune to fall upon him." Yes, besides this, we heard that if De Peyster had not quickly summoned us, the Wyandot would have put us to death.[12]

Four days after the Zeisberger party arrived at the Lower Sandusky, Joshua and Jacob, Rachel's son, brought their baggage by water from the Sandusky mission. From Jacob they received the first report of the disaster on the Muskingum. Miraculously, he and his friend Thomas had escaped the slaughter of most of the converts who had gone to the valley. What quickly became known as the Gnadenhutten massacre has passed down in American Indian history as one of the most heinous and cold-blooded incidents in the annals of border warfare during the eighteenth century. For sheer butchery, the event has few parallels and can be aptly described as a "day of shame."

The possibility of such an incident had been brewing over the previous seven years since the outbreak of the American Revolution. All along the western frontier, as it borders on the eastern bank of the Ohio River in what is now Pennsylvania and West Virginia, the pioneers had experienced bloody excursions and depredations from Indian war parties. Whites had repeatedly witnessed the killings of their husbands, wives, children, friends, and relations, the burning of their homes and barns, and the killing of their livestock. By the end of 1781, their patience worn thin, they decided to take retribution whenever and wherever they could find an Indian. Rev. Joseph Doddridge later described the mental condition of the victims of this period: "It should seem that the long continuance of the Indian war had debased a considerable portion of our population to the savage state of our nature. Having lost so many of their relatives by the Indians, and witnessed their horrid murders and other depredations upon so extensive a scale, they become subjects of that indiscriminating thirst for revenge."[13]

Site of the Gnadenhutten Massacre, March 8, 1782. Photograph by the author on the two hundredth anniversary of the massacre.

The United States forces stationed at Fort Pitt had long been frustrated by their inability to protect the settlers from Indian raids. By the beginning of 1782, the local militia forces, especially those in Washington County, Pennsylvania, decided to take responsibility for protection into their own hands. That decision was sparked by three separate Indian raids that occurred just after the beginning of the year, long before the Indian killing season began, usually in March and April.

Early in February, while sledding rails on their farm, the Henry Fink family, who lived up the Monongahela River near Buchanan's Fort, was attacked and Fink's grown son John was killed. During the second week in February, the Robert Wallace family, on Raccoon Creek, twenty-five miles west of Pittsburgh, was attacked while the father was absent from the farm. Mary Wallace and her three children, two young boys and an infant girl, were carried off by the Indians. Finally, early in March, near present Wellsburg, West Virginia, John Carpenter was captured by a party of Indians. Fortunately, on the second day after his capture, he escaped from the Indian camp near the mission towns on the Muskingum. Proceeding by way of old Fort Laurens and Fort McIntosh, he arrived safely back in Pittsburgh. But the capture of the Wallace family, well-respected in the county, set off the spark that kindled the flame of action.[14]

Since these raids normally did not begin until late March or early April, organized military retaliation had to be taken to intimidate the Indians against further attacks. Washington County officials targeted the vacant villages on the Muskingum. It was here that the roaming Indian bands rendezvoused, finding shelter and plenty of unharvested corn to satisfy their hunger. The whites agreed that this source of succor must be eliminated.

On March 1, the county lieutenant, James Marshel, called for the county militia to muster and proceed to the Moravian towns and destroy them. About 160 men responded to the muster call. The contingent was commanded by Lieutenant Colonel David Williamson.[15] They assembled on March 4 on the west side of the Ohio River at Mingo Bottoms, three miles below present Steubenville, Ohio. Following the well-traveled Moravian Trail, they arrived in the vicinity of Gnadenhutten on March 6.

Reports of what followed in the next two days contain many contradictions and speculations. Historians received no help from Williamson, who seems not to have filed an official report, or from his troops, who almost to a man refused to discuss their horrible deeds. After arriving home, they faded back into the wilderness, and many of their families did not know they were on the expedition.

Fifteen days after the massacre, Zeisberger interviewed at least one, and possibly both, of the Indian survivors. Jacob, the son of Rachel, and Thomas, who had been scalped, survived. Both were teenagers. Their reports of what happened are, based on written records, generally accurate. Reports were also passed down by word-of-mouth from sketchy frontier sources.[16]

It seems the militia contingent stealthily approached the mission of Gnadenhutten early on the morning of March 7. Zeisberger explained what happened, as reported to him by Jacob and Thomas, the two survivors of the massacre:

> A mile from town they met young Schebosh in the bush, whom they at once killed and scalped, and near by the houses, two friendly In-

> dians, not belonging to us, but who had gone there with our people from Sandusky, among whom there were several other friends who perished likewise. Our Indians were mostly on the plantations and saw the militia come, but no one thought of fleeing, for they suspected no ill. The militia came to them and bade them come into the town, telling them no harm should befall them. They trusted and went, but were all bound, the men being put into one house, the women into another. . . . Then they began to sing hymns and spoke words of encouragement and consolation one to another until they were all slain, and Abraham was the first to be led out, but the others were killed in the house. The sisters also afterwards met the same fate, who also sang hymns together. . . . Two well-grown boys, who saw the whole thing and escaped, gave this information. One of these [Thomas] lay under the heaps of slain and was scalped, but finally came to himself and found opportunity to escape. The same did Jacob, Rachel's son, who was wonderfully rescued. For they came close upon him suddenly outside the town, so that he thought they must have seen him, but he crept into a thicket and escaped their hands. . . . The boy who was scalped and got away, said the blood flowed in streams in the house, which was set on fire. . . . They burned the dead bodies, together with the houses.[17]

Zeisberger indicates that the events took place on March 7. Actually the massacre was on March 8, after the militia had gathered the converts from Salem and brought them to Gnadenhutten. Fortunately, the men and women gathering corn at New Schoenbrunn were spared. The messenger Zeisberger had sent arrived at the village early on March 7, delivering his order that the converts were to return immediately to Sandusky because the missionaries had been called to Detroit. As the runner proceeded on to Gnadenhutten, he passed the scalped body of Joseph Schebosh just north of the village and discovered the tracks of the militia party. He hurriedly returned and warned the Schoenbrunn converts. They departed at once and so were spared the fate that befell those at Gnadenhutten. Zeisberger closed his March 23 entry with these words:

> This news sank deep into our hearts, so that these our brethren, who as martyrs, had all at once gone to the Saviour, were always day and night before our eyes and in our thoughts and we could not forget them, but this in some measure comforted us that they passed to the

> Saviour's arms and bosom in such resigned disposition of heart where they will forever rest, protected from the sins and all the wants of the world.[18]

As the New Schoenbrunn contingent straggled back to the Sandusky, Zeisberger determined that eighty-six members of the flock were killed at Gnadenhutten. Seven days before they left the Lower Sandusky, on April 7, he entered another revealing entry in his diary:

> Warriors came in, bringing a prisoner, from whom we now get certain news that all our Indians in Gnadenhutten and Salem were put to death, and that none were spared; he said the militia had 96 scalps, but our Indians only numbered 86, who went away from us. The rest then must have been friends, who did not belong to us. The prisoner said further that two men alone had accomplished the whole murder after the Indians had been bound, and they killed them one after the other with a wooden mallet.[19]

The final count of converts murdered at Gnadenhutten was ninety: twenty-nine men, twenty-seven women, and thirty-four children. They represented a third of his Christian converts. It was a disastrous blow. But far more devastating was that many of the adult men and women constituted the heart of Zeisberger's mission leaders, the national assistants or the Helpers' Conference members. These men and women had been with him for over thirty years; Isaac Glikhikan and his wife, Anna Benigna; Christian and his wife, Augustina; Philipus, Jr., and his wife, Lorel; Samuel Moore; Johannes Martin; Tobias; and many others were dead. All had been members of the Helpers' Conference at either Gnadenhutten or Salem. Isaac Glikhikan, his most trusted lieutenant, Johannes Martin, who virtually ran Gnadenhutten, and Samuel Moore, the grandson of old Johannes Papunhank, were irreplaceable. It would be years before he could train leaders to take their places.

Zeisberger would never forget the gruesome massacre of March 8, 1782. Some twenty years later, in his old age, and again living on the banks of the Muskingum at Goshen, he frequently lamented to the missionary Benjamin Mortimer the tragic events of that day. Neither did the Indians forget that horrible day in 1782. The natives, enraged, swore revenge. For many years the massacre was the subject of Indian complaints against the whites, and it was repeatedly mentioned in treaty discussions with the United States ambassadors to the Indians.[20]

Sadly, the Williamson expedition did little to reduce the raids against the settlements. The vengeful Wyandots, Delawares, and Shawnees continued their attacks. In fact, many of the men who accompanied Williamson would lose their lives within three months in another attack against the Indians on the Upper Sandusky. What came to be known as the Crawford campaign would cost the lives of more than seventy frontiersmen. Their commander, Colonel William Crawford, would be horribly burned at the stake in retribution for the massacre at Gnadenhutten. Many of Crawford's men were at Gnadenhutten. Williamson was the second in command of the Crawford expedition and barely escaped with his life. The Indians were looking for him, and had they captured him, he surely would have suffered the same fate as Crawford.[21]

As some of Williamson's men returned from the campaign, they attacked the small band of Delawares who had accepted Brodhead's invitation the previous year to move near Fort Pitt for protection. This was the Indian group led by Gelelemend. They were living on Killbuck Island in the Ohio River just opposite Pittsburgh. Two men were killed, including Captain Wilson, an Indian who had been commissioned into service of the United States forces and commended for his valorous services to the nation.[22] The others fled to safety. One of the men to escape was the convert Anton, who had gone to visit his brother who lived on the island. He was the son of Jo Peepe and Hannah. Because of this visit he escaped the massacre at Gnadenhutten. When he arrived back on the Sandusky he called on Zeisberger and told him of the incident. Zeisberger recalled that on several occasions his group had also been invited to move to the Pittsburgh area. On April 8 he angrily recorded in his diary:

> If we had gone there with our Indians, we should have unwittingly, have gone into greater danger. Nowhere is a place to be found to which we can retire with our Indians and be secure. The world is already too narrow. From the white people, or so-called Christians, we can hope for no protection, and among the heathen nations also we have no friends left, such outlaws are we! but praise to God, the Lord our God yet lives, who will not forsake us.[23]

Unknowingly, God's agent, in the shape of Arent De Peyster, the commander at Detroit, was about to answer his plea. Within less than three weeks he would find Zeisberger the haven he desired.

Zeisberger's party left Lower Sandusky on April 15 and arrived in Detroit six days later. De Peyster was full of apologies. Zeisberger wrote: "He had removed us against his will, but for the sake of our own safety . . . he assured us that our lives were in the greatest danger if we had remained longer in Sandusky."[24]

For the next several weeks Zeisberger and De Peyster carried on discussions. De Peyster assured the missionary that he would do all in his power to help him. If he wanted to return to the United States, he would provide a ship for transportation. But if he preferred to remain in the Detroit area, De Peyster would try to find a suitable location for him and his Indians. After consulting the lot, Zeisberger chose the latter. De Peyster promised to send messages to the converts on the Upper Sandusky and among the Shawnees encouraging the Indians to rejoin their missionaries. After a few weeks of negotiations with the Chippewas, De Peyster received permission for a site north of Detroit on the Huron River (now the Clinton) for a mission. Messages were dispatched to the converts, and slowly they began to come.[25]

The Conner family was the first to arrive on June 14. They were fleeing the unrest caused by the defeat of the Crawford expedition on the Upper Sandusky. Samuel Nanticoke and Adam and their families arrived on July 8. They advised Zeisberger that Abraham, Zachary, and Thomas with their families were also on the road.[26]

But on July 11 they received the best news. Zeisberger wrote, "By two ships in from Fort Erie the cheerful news comes that an armistice has been concluded and there is hope for a speedy peace." It would be another year before the plenipotentiaries in Paris would conclude the peace. But happily the fighting was over. The next day Zeisberger noted that fourteen converts had returned.[27]

In the next week they assembled their supplies from the king's stores, courtesy of the commander, and on July 20 they left for the new location.[28] Zeisberger noted it would be called the mission on the Huron. Later historians would call it New Gnadenhutten. Resolutely, he would start to build again.

Epilogue

Zeisberger had twenty-six more years to live. This period of his life is described in my *Blackcoats among the Delaware* (1991). He never again returned to Bethlehem but preferred to spend his time rebuilding his mission and living among his beloved brown brethren. The Christian Indian congregation remained at New Gnadenhutten on the Huron River for the next four years, and in April 1786 they moved back to the United States and founded the mission of Pilgerruh on the Cuyahoga River. They remained there for just a year and then moved west to the Pettquotting River near present Milan, Ohio, arriving in June 1786. By April 1791 Zeisberger counted 212 converts, but again he was threatened by the beginning of the Indian wars of the 1790s and was forced to move back to British territory at the mouth of the Detroit River. He called the mission Die Warte, or a Night Watch, the latter being the Indian term for a stay of one year.

In May 1792 they moved again, to the banks of the Thames River in present Ontario, Canada, and called the mission Fairfield. Today the progeny of those original converts live in the area of the old mission. Zeisberger remained there until 1798.

With the conclusion of the Indian wars and the signing of the Greenville Treaty in 1795, land became available back in his beloved Muskingum Valley. Congress had granted the Indians three four-thousand-acre tracts of land in the valley to be held in trust by the Moravian Church as restitution for the three villages they lost in 1781.

In October 1798 he moved back to the Muskingum and founded his last mission, called Goshen, near present New Philadelphia, Ohio. It was here on November 17, 1808, at the age of eighty-seven, that the door of death opened. Sustained and soothed by an unfailing trust in his beloved Lord, he drew the drapery of his death couch about him and passed over into the arms of his beloved Savior. He lies buried in the tree-lined Indian cemetery, with forty of his converts, on the banks of the Muskingum (now the Tuscarawas River).

· APPENDIXES ·

· APPENDIX A ·

Moravian Missions in North America, 1740–1821

Number	*Name of Mission*	*Location*	*Founded*	*Abandoned*
1	Shekomeko	Dutchess Co., NY	Aug. 1740	Dec. 1744
2	Pachgatgoch	Kent Co., CT	Oct. 1742	Dec. 1762
3	Wechquadnach	Dutchess Co., NY	Oct. 1742	June 1753
4	Friedenshutten I	Bethlehem, PA	Sept. 1745	May 1747
5	Gnadenhutten I	Leighton, PA	June 1746	Nov. 1755
6	Shamokin	Sunbury, PA	June 1747	Dec. 1755
7	Meniologameka	Monroe Co., PA	June 1749	May 1754
8	Nain	Lehigh Co., PA	June 1758	Apr. 1765
9	Wechquetank	Monroe Co., PA	Apr. 1760	Oct. 1763
10	Tuscarawas (Post-Heckewelder)	Bolivar, OH	Apr. 1762	Nov. 1762
11	The Philadelphia Incident	Philadelphia, PA	Oct. 1763	Mar. 1765
12	Friedenshutten II	Bradford Co., PA	May 1765	June 1772
13	Goschgoschunk	Forest Co., PA	June 1768	Apr. 1769
14	Lawunakhannek	Forest Co., PA	Apr. 1769	Apr. 1770
15	Schechschiquanunk	Bradford Co., PA	June 1769	June 1772
16	Friedensstadt (Lagundo Utenunk)	Lawrence Co., PA	Apr. 1770	Apr. 1773

Number	*Name of Mission*	*Location*	*Founded*	*Abandoned*
17	Schoenbrunn (Welhik Thuppeek)	New Philadelphia, OH	May 1772	Apr. 1777
18	Gnadenhutten II	Gnadenhutten, OH	Oct. 1772	Sept. 1781
19	Lichtenau	Coshocton, OH	Apr. 1776	Apr. 1780
20	New Schoenbrunn	New Philadelphia, OH	Apr. 1779	Sept. 1781
21	Salem	Port Washington, OH	Apr. 1780	Sept. 1781
22	Captive Town	Wyandot Co., OH	Oct. 1781	March 1782
23	New Gnadenhutten	Clinton River, MI	July 1782	Apr. 1786
24	Pilgerruh (Pettquotting)	Cuyahoga Co., OH	June 1786	Apr. 1787
25	New Salem	Erie Co., Milan, OH	June 1787	Apr. 1791
26	Warte (Detroit River)	Amhersburg, Ont.	May 1791	Apr. 1792
27	Fairfield	Thames River, Ont.	May 1792	Oct. 1813 Burned
28	Goshen	Goshen, OH (Zeisberger died here Nov. 17, 1808)	Oct. 1798	Nov. 1821
29	White River	Near Anderson, IN	May 1801	Sept. 1806
30	Chippewa	East Sydenham, Ont.	Apr. 1802	Dec. 1806
31	Pettquotting, Second Experience	Milan, OH	June 1804	Apr. 1809
32	New Fairfield	Thames River, Ont.	Aug. 1815	Apr. 1903

Compiled by Earl P. Olmstead, January 2, 1988.

· APPENDIX B ·

Zeisberger's Iroquois Trips

1750 Onondaga Trip with John Frederick Cammerhoff

May 14 Leave Bethlehem		
June 19 Arrive Onondaga	26 days	31 days' residence among Iroquois
Resident in Onondaga	5 days	
June 24 Leave Onondaga, Seneca Country		
July 10 Return to Onondaga	16 days	
Resident in Onondaga	10 days	
July 20 Leave Onondaga		
August 16 Arrive Bethlehem	27 days	

1752 Onondaga Trip with Gottfried Rundt

July 21 Leave Bethlehem		
August 20 Arrive Onondaga	30 days	97 days' residence among Iroquois
Resident in Onondaga	97 days	
November 25 Leave Onondaga		
December 15 Arrive Bethlehem	20 days	

1753 Onondaga Trip with Henry Fry

April 23 Leave Bethlehem		
June 8 Arrive Onondaga	26 days	
Resident in Onondaga	127 days	127 days' residence in Onondaga
October 13 Leave Onondaga		
November 12 Arrive Bethlehem	30 days	

255 Days Spent in Residence in Onondaga at the End of the Third Trip.

1754 Trip with Charles Friedrich

June 9 Leave Bethlehem		
July 21 Arrive Onondaga	42 days	
Resident in Onondaga	309 days	309 days' residence in Onondaga
May 25, 1755 Leave Onondaga		
June 4, 1755 At Bethlehem	11 days	

564 days' residence in Onondaga[a]

[a] The 564 days in Onondaga or among the Iroquois does not include travel time coming from and going to Bethlehem but is actual days in residence. During this period Zeisberger and his companions lived and conversed with each of the tribes in the Six Nations Confederacy (Mohawks, Oneidas, Tuscaroras, Onondagas, Cayugas, and Senecas).

· APPENDIX C ·

Zeisberger's Comments on the Use of Wampum

DURING THIS meeting with Packanke and his council, wampum was given to confirm each of the various points made by the speaker. Being illiterate people with no knowledge of the written word, they needed physical evidence of the conversation. Wampum was used frequently in native diplomacy. Zeisberger has left one of the most succinct yet descriptive explanations of this practice. It was written shortly after a conference with Packanke on July 11, 1770, just before Jacob Gendaskund, a convert and former captain, conferred with Packanke. It also explains why the native chiefs were so opposed to the Christianizing of their people.

> It is common usage among the Indians to support the chiefs and to enable them to negotiate with one another as well as with other nations. For this they need wampum, because in a speech they accompany and confirm each one of their sentences with a string of wampum. Without these, their words do not carry any weight and are not taken any notice of. Now, if for instance they have to send off an important message or to "hold" a treaty with the white people the Indians in all the towns are notified that they will have to contribute Wampum, and sometimes, or rather very seldom, they are asked for furs. There is no law or regulation as to how many they have to give, but

Tilda Marx, trans., "Lagundo Utenunk Diary," July 11, 1770, 116–17.

> every Indian can give as many or as few as he is able to. Everybody contributes willingly as they know that it is of vital importance for their existence. These contributions are only made for important and lengthy negotiations. In every-day affairs the chief takes them from his counsel bay. If this were not done and if the chiefs were not given any support they would have no authority, there would be no government, everybody would do as he pleases and nothing but confusion would result. Yes, they would all be opposed to one another.

Zeisberger explains in the same entry why the "praying Indians" are so "despised and hated" by the native authorities and complains that "those who join us, disregard all the laws and rights of the Indians. They do not pay their dues but despise the chiefs and their government." Zeisberger wisely recognized the chiefs' criticisms, noting, "If the congregations of the Christians become so large the whole Indian constitution would come to an end." At this time the chiefs were notified that the Christian congregation would cooperate and supply their share of the necessary wampum or furs. With one exception, they would not contribute wampum "should they decide to go to war against the white people or against any other Indian nation."

· APPENDIX D ·

*Statutes Agreed upon by the Christian Indians at Lagundo Utenunk and Welhik-Thuppeek in the Month of August 1772**

ZEISBERGER's version recorded on August 29, 1772 (see Chapter 16, page 195).

1. Whosoever wishes to live here must worship God, our creator and Saviour, as the one and only God and must look for everything good, to him alone.

2. Nobody can live with us, who intends to go to heathen feasts and dances held at other places.

3. Nobody who wishes to bring rum here to get drunk, or to make others drunk, or who runs after rum at other places.

4. Nobody who keeps a whore or attemps to seduce the wives of others.

5. Nobody who deserts his wife, nor a wife who runs away from her husband.

6. No son or daughter who, after thorough admonition, wantonly disobeys parents.

7. No thief, nor any person who is in the habit of stealing.

8. Nobody who abuses or strikes his neighbor.

9. Nobody who employes objects of heathen superstition in hunting or in curing diseases, or gives them to others.

10. We will keep the Sunday holy, and will not hunt or work on Sunday, except out of love of neighbor, or from dire necessity.

* Languntoutenunk (Lagunda Utenunk) is Friedensstadt, and Welhik Tuppek (Welhik Thuppeek) is Schoenbrunn. See Appendix A, numbers 16 and 17.

11. Whoever tells stories about others' preparing poison, hunting people at night, and practicing witchcraft, must prove this before the committee, and he of whom such things are proved shall not live with us. If, however, the accuser has been found lying, we will regard him as a tool of the Devil who tries to destroy our love and our peace, and we will not tolerate such a person among us. [See Mahr, trans., "Schoenbrunn Diary," Appendix IV, 185–89.]

On November 24, 1776, Zeisberger and the Helpers' Conference added three additional rules to the original eleven (see Chapter 20, page 256).

12. Noone can live here who wants to be treated (medically) according to the heathen methods.

13. Noone can live here who thinks of going to war, or even to take part in war robbery.

14. Noone who wants to live here should paint himself, nor hang wampum, silver or anything on himself. Who wants to do that cannot be allowed here.

[See Wilde, trans., "Lichtenau Diary," November 24, 1776, original found in box 147, folder 2, Moravian Church Archives.]

The Heckewelder version that follows is found in De Schweinitz, *Zeisberger*, 378–79.

I. We will know no other God but the one only true God, who made us and all creatures, and came into this world in order to save sinners; to Him alone we will pray.

II. We will rest from work on the Lord's day, and attend public service.

III. We will honor father and mother, and when they grow old and needy we will do for them what we can.

IV. No person will get leave to dwell with us until our teachers have given their consent, and the helpers (native assistants) have examined him.

V. We will have nothing to do with thieves, murderers, whoremongers, adulterers, or drunkards.

VI. We will not take part in dances, sacrifices, heathenish festivals, or games.

VII. We will use no tshapiet, or witchcraft, when hunting.

VIII. We renounce and abhor all tricks, lies, and deceits of Satan.

IX. We will be obedient to our teachers and to the helpers who are appointed to preserve order in our meetings in the towns and fields.

X. We will not be idle, nor scold, nor beat one another, nor tell lies.

XI. Whoever injures the property of his neighbor shall make restitution.

XII. A man shall have but one wife—shall love her and provide for her and his children. A woman shall have but one husband, be obedient to him, care for her children, and be cleanly in all things.

XIII. We will not admit rum or any other intoxicating liquor into our town. If strangers or traders bring intoxicating liquor, the helpers shall take it from them and not restore it until the owners are ready to leave the place.

XIV. No one shall contract debts with traders, or receive goods to sell for traders, unless the helpers give their consent.

XV. Whoever goes hunting, or on a journey, shall inform the minister or stewards.

XVI. Young persons shall not marry without the consent of their parents and the minister.

XVII. Whenever the stewards or helpers appoint a time to make fences or to perform other work for the public good, we will assist and do as we are bid.

XVIII. Whenever corn is needed to entertain strangers, or sugar for love-feast, we will contribute from our stores.

XIX. We will not go to war, and will not buy anything of warriors taken in war. [This last statute was adopted during the Revolutionary War.]

· APPENDIX E ·

Population Statistics for Moravian Missions in the Muskingum Valley, 1772–1781

Missions	*1771*	*1772*	*1773*	*1774*	*1775*	*1776*	*1777*	*1778*	*1779*	*1780*	*1781*
Friedenshutten	151						Abandoned June 11, 1772				
Schechschiquanunk	63						Abandoned June 11, 1772				
Lagundo Utenunk (Friedensstadt)	73	115					Abandoned Apr. 13, 1773				
Schoenbrunn		92	184	220	263	204[a]	Abandoned Apr. 20, 1777				
Gnadenhutten		94	108	139	151	136	125[a]	[b]	99	135	[c]
Lichtenau		Founded April 12, 1776				59	232	328	130[a]	Abandoned Apr. 8, 1780	
New Schoenbrunn		Founded April 1779							100	143	[c]
Salem		Founded April 8, 1780								102	[c]
Total	287	301	292	359	414	399	357	328	329	380	

[a] No record, estimate only.
[b] No record available.
[c] Abandoned September 8, 1781.

• APPENDIX F •

Netawatwes's Instruction on Presenting Wampum Belts to the Cherokees

SEVERAL WEEKS after Netawatwes met with Isaac and his delegation of Christian Indians, he called a conference on June 22, 1773, of his subchief and captains. A delegation of Christian Indians from Schoenbrunn and Gnadenhutten was invited to participate in this meeting.

The Cherokees, who at that time were living on the Tennessee River, were threatening to break the peace and go to war against the British. A series of treaties between the Cherokees and the British in 1768, 1770, and 1771 granted parts of the Kentucky territory to Virginia. Although these treaties covered land thought to belong to the Shawnees, the Cherokees had little objection. Now the British were insisting that some of the Cherokee land be surrendered and threatened to go to war. Over the past ten years the Delawares had maintained friendly relations with the Cherokees and encouraged them to settle their differences peacefully.

The conference gives us a rare insight into the operation of Indians' negotiations as the chief instructs his delegation on the words they were to use in speaking to the Cherokees. This diary entry is written by Johannes Roth (Rothe), who was living at Gnadenhutten. He wrote the diary between May 1 and August 13, 1773, until the Schmicks arrived to manage Gnadenhutten. Present during the

See Mahr, trans., "Gnadenhutten Diary," 7b, 8a, 8b, June 22, 1773; Van Dale Every, *Forth to the Wilderness: The First American Frontier, 1754–1774* (New York: Arno Press, 1977), 313–52.

conference were Abraham, Nathaniel, and Samuel from Schoenbrunn and Augustus and Josua, Sr., from Gnadenhutten. They were to accompany the Delaware delegation to the Cherokees and had furnished much of the wampum to be used during the conference.

Roth writes:

> Thereupon the Chief had seven strings of wampum and one especially large peace-belt laid on the blankets spread in a circle; and, likewise, the Brethren's bundle of wampum, which is a beauty far exceeding their own. The Chief's speaker lifted up from one of the blankets the latter one of the Brethren's [belt] before all of the people, and presented it with these words: "Behold the beautiful present," and then he delivered the following address to the young men; "And you, in particular, you will go there as messengers, conduct yourselves well; conduct yourselves as men; be obedient to your superiors (2 captains), and give heed to what they tell you."
>
> Then he made clear to them the meaning of each String, and, likewise, of the belt, in these words:
>
> "This small and first String you shall take when you come near the Cattagu (Cherokee), and some of you who have learned their language, shall step forward and say to them: 'Look in the direction from which we have come. Your grandfather is on the way and approaching you.'"
>
> This second string you shall use after you have entered the land, and you shall say: "Your grandfather sees that your eyes are so dim that you cannot see; he washes them for you and dries them with the cloth" (a piece of fine linen, which, at the same time, is their flag and is to be hoisted wherever they sleep).
>
> To be said with the third string: "I see that your ears are dirty, and that you cannot hear well; hence, I have come to wipe them clean for you; so that you may be able to hear well, and see well. Thereafter, when you will lift up your eyes, you will see that all the dark clouds have passed away, and that all the sky is bright and clean about you."
>
> With the fourth, to which a pipe is attached: "This is the pipe our fathers used to smoke! It is now stuffed with tobacco which our fathers smoked and it is the peace-pipe; this, you, too, shall smoke and pass around among you and when you have drawn in several puffs of the smoke, it will at once make your hearts feel well and you will be able to look cheerfully aloft and see that all looks well about you."
>
> With the fifth: "I see that your house is full of filth; around your beds where you sleep, there is much uncleanliness and I have come to clean up the place, and to move the filth away from you. You look to me like one whose feet will no longer carry him; one who is hanging over to one side, and I have come to set you up again, and to place you firmly on your feet."
>
> With the sixth: "I have looked up high to God, and have there seen and encountered something which I am bringing to you."

> With the seventh small string: "You royal women, we your sons, have come to you and bring you peace and you, too, shall hold on to it with us."
>
> With the eighth: "Pay good attention: The belt (especially large) which you see before you, is the peace-belt; it is from God; you shall lay hold of it in such a manner, as if you wished draw it toward you. [This was the belt furnished by the Christian converts.] And if each of us who at the last peace treaty entered into an agreement will take hold of this belt, as if he wished to draw it over toward himself alone, it will become a strong peace-chain, stretching from the south-west to the north-west, so that strangers will not be able to break through; for they will come to feel well assured thereby, and will gladly return home."

Both Roth's and Zeisberger's diaries are silent as to the results of the peace mission sent to the Cherokees.

· APPENDIX G ·

Johann Schmick's Letter to Matthew Hehl, Gnadenhutten, May 24, 1777

My dearest Brother Matthaeus.

Your last letter, of March 14 of this year, I did receive May 8. It was forewarded from Lichtenau, where it had lain, until there was an opportunity to send it and the list for the Daily Texts for May and June to us. It made us very happy that you, dear Brethren, have so much sympathy with our more or less difficult and often life-threatening circumstances, and that you remember us before the Saviour. This remembrance and the prayers of the congregation and [all] the Brethren has surely helped us a lot. We thank the Saviour from the bottom of our hearts for it and we pray that he may bless them for the future.

I hope that you received my last letter, of Febr. 28, of this year; it was addressed to you and dear Br. Nathanael [Seidel] and contained also the diary for 2 months Nov. and Dec. and the memorabilia of the last year. The good advice and proposal to exchange positions with the Jungmanns last autumn was not followed, since there was no asking the "lot," and at the present it is totally out of the question, because Schoenbrunn was left by all the Brn., and that on request of the Chiefs at Goschachkueng with the consent of the brn. Zeisberger and Jungmann, without thinking and deliberation before the Saviour [i.e., asking the lot in this matter]. The Jungmanns fled immediately at night on account of the rumors which were

The letter also appears in Olmstead, *Blackcoats among the Delaware*, 23–24.

only lies, namely that the Mingoes wanted to kill them and us. They went in a hurry to Lichtenau, in order to keep this station, as agreed upon with Br. David even before one even could think of being so suddenly called away. Now one can see clearly and exactly, why they were not willing last autumn to change places with us. However, it is sad that the congregation of Schoenbrunn got away [i.e., was abandoned] in such a cunning way through the machination of the evil enemy, that the Brethren got dispersed and lost their houses and plantations. They could have as well quietly stayed there, as we did at Gnadenhutten, even though our people had also been requested by the Chiefs to move away. If they had only acted as we did and given the same answer to the chiefs as our Brethren, namely: Friends, we listened well to your words and have thought about it, but it is difficult for us to get up. We want first to wait for the answer of the Delemattonses [i.e., Pomoacan and his Wyandots] and hear what they have to say about the speeches of you and Colonel Morgan. If they had done that, they would still be in Schoenbrunn. However they were not allowed to think and to answer that way, because they were told by Br. David: There is nothing to deliberate about, you just have to get away; there is nothing else to do; you have to move down; it will be war. The chiefs request it and take you from here and leave you near Lichtenau, in order to be close to Goeschachkuenk, to be strong with them when the war will break out. These latter words mean as much as if they had said: If it will be war, you fight together with us. However, Brethren shall not do that because they love peace and want to live with others in peace. Eight of the families moved to us, namely Schebosch, Nathanael Davis, Leonhard, David, A. Johanna, Anton, Joseph and Wilhelmina with three children, also the widow Noah left behind. And Schoenbrunn is now a place where run-aways and partly hermits are living, who took possession of the houses and plantations of the Brethren.

Br. Heckewelder came also to us to live with us; but he is now going for a visit to Bethlehem and can report to you more and even better than I can write it. Br. Heckewelder is in a hurry. Therefore I will finish for this time and send regards to you and your wife, Br. Grube, and the respected Brethren of the Conference. I and my wife greet you very cordially. We recommend us into your prayers. Be respectfully greeted by your humble Br.,

J. J. Schmick.

· APPENDIX H ·

John Heckewelder's Legendary Ride

His Version

From Fort Pitt to Lichtenau

THE FOLLOWING account, written in 1820 some forty-two years after the event, can be found in Heckewelder's *A Narrative of the Mission of the United Brethren among the Delaware and Mohegan Indians; From Its Commencement, in the Year 1740, to the Close of the Year 1808*, 176–82.

The narrative begins with Heckewelder and Schebosh hastily departing from Fort Pitt on April 3, 1778, at the height of the Delaware confrontation with McKee and his fellow conspirators. The Fort Pitt commander and Colonel Morgan were not aware of McKee's visit to Goschachgunk.

Heckewelder wrote:

> Accordingly, in the morning we made our resolution known to cols. Hand and Gibson, whose best wishes for our success, we were assured of; and leaving our baggage behind, and turning a deaf ear to all entreaties of well meaning friends, who considered us lost, if we went, we crossed the Allegheny river, and on the third day, at eleven o'clock at night, reached Gnadenhutten, after having several times narrowly escaped falling in with war parties. . . . We travelled day and night, only leaving our horses time to feed. . . . When arrived within a few miles of Gnadenhutten, we distinctly heard the beat of war drums, and on drawing near, the war songs sung to the beat of the drum, all which being in the direction of the town lay, we natu-

rally concluded that the Christian Indians must have moved off, wherefore we proceeded with caution, less we should fall into the warrior's hands. However, the people being there, informed us, that those warriors we heard, were Wyandots from Sandusky, who arrived that evening, and were encamped on the bluff, two miles below the town, on the opposite side of the river, and who probably would the next morning, travel along the path we had just come.

Fatigued as we were, after our journey, and without one hour of sound sleep, I was now requested by the inhabitants of the place, men and women, not to delay any time, but to proceed on to Gaschochkink (near thirty miles distant) where all was a bustle and confusion, and many were preparing to go off to fight the American people, in consequence of the advice given them by those deserters, before named [the McKee party] who had told them, that the American people were embodying themselves at the time, for the purpose of killing every Indian they should meet with, be such friend or foe, and further we were told, that captain White Eyes had been threatened to be killed if he persisted in vindicating the character of the American people; many believing the stories told them by McKee and his associates, and had in consequence already shaved their heads, ready to lay the plume on, and turn out to war, as soon as the ten days should be expired, and tomorrow being the ninth day, and no message having yet been arrived from their friends at Pittsburgh [McKee's party had arrived at Goschachgunk on April 1; it was now April 6, only six days since Heckewelder's arrival], they now were preparing to go—and further, that this place, Gnadenhutten, was now breaking up for its inhabitants to join the congregation at Lichtenau, those deserters having assured them, that they were not a day safe from an attack by the Americans, while they remained here.

Finding the matter so *very* pressing and not even admitting of a day's delay, I consented, that after a few hours sleep, and furnished with a trusty companion and fresh horse, I would proceed on, when between three and four o'clock in the morning the national assistant, John Morgan, having called on me for the purpose, we set out, swimming our horses across the Muskingum river [Zeisberger wrote that he arrived with Anton, not John Martin], and taking a circuit through the woods in order to avoid the encampment of the war party which was close to our path. Arriving by ten o'clock in the forenoon within sight of the town, a few yells were given by a person who had discovered us, intended to notify the inhabitants, that a white man was coming, and which immediately drew the whole body of Indians into the street; but although I saluted them in passing them, not a single person returned the compliment, which, as my conductor observed, was no good omen. Even Captain White Eyes, and the other chiefs, who always had befriended me, now stepped back when I reached out my hand to them. . . . Yet as no one would reach out his hand to me, I inquired the cause, when captain White Eyes boldy stepping forward, replied; "that by what had been told them by those men (McKee and party) they no longer had a single friend among the American people; if therefore this be so, they must consider every white man who came to them from that side, as an enemy, who only came to them to deceive them, and put them off their guard for the purpose of giving the enemy an opportunity of taking them by surprise." I replied that imputation was unfounded, and that, were I not their friend, they never would have seen me here. "Then (continued captain White Eyes) you will tell us the truth with regard to what I state to you!"—assuring him of this, he in a strong tone asked me: "are the American armies all cut to pieces by English troops? Is General Washington killed? Is there no more congress, and have the English hung some of them, and taken the remainder to England to hang them there? Is the whole country beyond the Mountains in the possession of the English; and are the few thousand Americans who have escaped them, now embodying themselves on this side of the mountains for the purpose of killing all the Indians in this country, even our women and children? Now do not deceive us, but speak the truth" (added he); is all this true what I have said to you?" I declared before the whole assembly, that not one word of what he had just now told me was true, and holding out to him, as I had done before, the friendly speeches sent by me for them, which he however as yet refused to accept. . . . [These were the letters sent by Morgan and forwarded from Gnadenhutten by a special messenger on the morning of April 6. According to Zeisberger's diary, written at the time, Heckewelder and Schebosh did not arrive until later in the evening. Heckewelder continues his account by asking White Eyes to assemble all of the tribe.]

A newspaper, containing the capitulation of general Burgoyne's army, being found enclosed in the packet, captain White Eyes once more rose up, and holding the paper unfolded with both hands, so that all could have a view of it, said "see my friends and relatives, this document containeth great events, not the song of a bird, but the truth!"—Then stepping up to me, he gave me his hand, saying: "you are welcome with us Brother;" when every one present, followed his example; after which I proceeded with my conductor John Martin to Lichtenau, where, to the inexpressible joy of the venerable missionary Zeisberger, and the congregation, we related what had taken place, while they on the other hand assured us, that nothing could have at that time come more seasonable to save the nation, and with it the mission, from utter destruction, than our arrival.

• APPENDIX I •

Analysis of the Skeletons Found in the Mass Grave at Fort Laurens, July–August 1986

AS NOTED in Chapter 23, the massacre at Fort Laurens took place on the morning of Feburary 23, 1779, when a wood-gathering party of colonials was ambushed and brutally murdered within sight of the fort but out of rifle and musket range of the fort defenders. The number of men supposedly involved ranged from eleven to eighteen. Since the fort was under siege at the time, the bodies lay as they were killed probably until the second week in March, when the siege was lifted and the bodies were gathered and buried in one mass grave. According to legend, the hole was dug and the bodies interred. The grave party was interrupted, however, by nightfall and the interment was not completed until the next morning. During the night, wolves invaded the partial grave and some were shot and thrown into the grave the next morning when the work was completed.

Over the intervening years, an elaborate legend has developed surrounding this grisly incident. In an effort to solve some of the mystery surrounding the event, a party of archaeologists, sponsored by the Ohio Historical Society and the Tuscarawas County Historical Society and led by Michael Gramly, excavated the cemetery at Fort Laurens in 1986.

Fourteen bodies were found in the grave. All had been killed with tomahawks or Indian ball clubs. No conclusive evidence was found among the bodies that would support the legend of the wolves. After exhaustive examination at Buffalo, New York, and Columbus, Ohio, the skeletons were returned in July 1991 and reinterred in a crypt in the museum at Fort Laurens. The following information is the result of Gramly's examination of those bodies found in the mass grave.

Skeleton #1 Main Mass No limbs missing, head present; skull marks of iron knife visible plus possible hatchet marks on small, loose skull fragment.

Skeleton #2 Lower legs missing as well as both arms; hatchet chop marks on skull plus scalping marks at crown (on left parietal, rather than on right parietal, which is normal).

Skeleton #3 Lower legs missing and all of arms; mark of pronged ball-headed club on skull plus at least two hatchet cuts; man was scalped.

Skeleton #4 Both arms missing; hardly any skull remains, but cuts from scalping knife are nonetheless in evidence.

Skeleton #5 Both arms missing; at least two hatchet chop marks are present; man was scalped.

Skeleton #6 All limbs are represented; at least three hatchet cut marks are on skull as well as obvious scalping knife cuts.

Skeleton #7 Lower left leg missing; two hatchet cut marks on skull plus marks of scalping knife.

Skeleton #8 Right arm is missing; marks of ball-headed club on skull together with two hatchet chop marks; man was scalped.

Skeleton #9 Both arms missing; fracture caused by club on skull as well as at least one hatchet cut mark; scalping knife cuts present.

Skeleton #10 Lower left leg missing; at least two hatchet cuts on head; man was scalped.

Skeleton #11 Both arms missing; skull badly fragmented but nonetheless three hatchet chops are visible; there are apparently no scalping knife cuts—but person is older (35–45 years) and may have had no hair at crown.

Skeleton #12 Head only, badly fragmented; at least one hatchet chop mark on skull plus scar by ball-headed club; scalping marks are present as well.

Skeleton #13 Head and both arms are missing; no trauma noted on surviving portions of skeleton.

Skeleton #14 Head, both arms, and both lower legs are missing; no trauma noted on surviving portions of skeleton.

The above is taken from page 8 of Michael Gramly's preliminary report of the excavation at Fort Laurens, June 23 to August 5, 1986. The report is entitled "Summary of Archaeological Fieldwork conducted at the Fort Laurens State Memorial, Bolivar, Ohio," and is reproduced with his permission. Gramly is currently completing a definitive account of his three excavations made at Fort Laurens.

· APPENDIX J ·

Letter to Nathaniel Seidel at Bethlehem from Brother Schebosh

SHORTLY AFTER Schebosh and his party were taken to Pittsburgh he wrote this letter to Nathaniel Seidel. It was the first information Bethlehem had received regarding the removal of the Christian congregation from the Muskingum Valley. The sequence of the various incidences connected with the removal are slightly different from Zeisberger's account. The spelling has not been changed from the original.

November 4, 1781

My Dear Brother:

I greet & kiss you & all the Brethren, in Bethlehem, in Litiz. I am glad that I have this opportunity to give you a little account of things of our three Indian congregations. The 4th of August there came a string of Wampum to us from the Half King that he was acoming to us with a great number of Warriors, but don't be affraid, I am your friend & come along. The 6th there came 150 Warriors & made their camp just at the end of the town of Gnadenhutten, the next day was followed by 50 more and so they was comming in by small companies, till the 10th was 220 and more in numbers.

Then they would have all the old men from the three Towns together to a council, where they told us that they would have us to move away with them, for

Box 151, folder 6, item 3, Moravian Church Archives.

we was in their way, when they was going to war. We made them [an] answer, that we could not move at this time & leave our corn, for our children would perish for hunger.

After this they began to kill our Hogges & cattle & destroy every thing that came in their way, & to dance the War Dance all night & make the most dismallist noise that ever they could that we had no rest at night & all the good words we gave them did not move them, but grew every Day worse.

The 15th their Head men had a great council & soon after demanded, that all the head men form the three towns should be there & also their ministers should come with them. So the next day there came allmost all the Indian Brethren & Brother David & John Heckewelder, and their chiefs made the same speech as before & told them that this was the last time that they would speak to them.

Our Indian Brethren desired them, to have a little Patience with them, that they might gather their corn and live this winter in our Towns & in the spring they would be willing to move to them. At this the Half King & their men seemed to be pleased and began to make ready to go over to Wheeling to War, but the English Officers was much displeased & told the Captains that the commanding Officer in Detroit would be much displeased with them; this put a stop to their going off & they began anew to plague us & burn our fences, drove their Horses in the corn, killing Hogges & cattle & destroying what came in their way; this lasted for 5 or 6 days. When they called all the men and ordered that they should bring the white Brethren from the other towns with them. When we was come together, Captain Pipe made a great speech that they would not be contented till they had us along & demanded an answer directly. As soon as our Indian Brethren came together, they made out, that they would answer them as before and desired them to let them alone till spring; this was hardly over before the Wiondots layed hold of the 4 Brethren David Zeisberger, Edwards, John Heckewelder, ane Gotlob Sensemann and all the whole made such dismall cry and dragged them into their camp and then the whole of them ran to the Brethren's House, broke open the door & plundered everything they found and destroyed everything they found and destroyed everything that they did not like. This was no sooner done but there was 2 companies sent to [New] Schoenbrunn and Salem where they took Jungmann & Anna, his wife & Susana, David Zeisberger's wife & Anna Senseman, where they plundered as before in Gnadenhutten. Anna Senseman was sent from Gnadenhutten to Schoenbrunn, where she was delivered of a son 5 days before we was taken prisoners. About midnight the prisoners was brought in with a Death Hollow for every one of them. Michel Young was brought the same time, but Sarah, J. Heckewelder's wife, got leave to stay till morning and was brought in company of some sisters in our care and got liberty to bring them in my house. Soon after we all got orders to make ready to go off without delay or else die. The same day we got liberty for the Brethren to come with their guard & dine with us in my house.

Two days after we with much trouble got the Brethren from under guard in my house and then we was forced to make haste and prepare for the journey. We applied to the English Officers to try to get some of their clothing back, they promised to help what was in their power, they brought them some old clothes, but all the best they kept; all their bedding was riped and destroyed. The 28th of August we left Gnadenhutten and the 1st of September we moved from Salem and from that Day till the last day of September we came to the place where they placed us on the banks of the Sandusky Creek and there we are today, where we have nothing to eat but what we fetched from our old Towns.

When I came away the most part of our people had eat up all their provision they took with them, and the white had nothing left but one bushel of corn among 10 of them. I came the 15th October away and came the 25th with my Daughter and son-in-law & his sister Esther & Henry and a Boy which is not baptized to Schoenbrunn to fetch corn. We had not been about 2 hours there before we was surrouned with 100 militia men who took us all Prisoners and brought us from thence to Weeling and from thence to Fort Pitt where we arrived the 2 Nov. where I soon heard that Brother Weygandt had been there to enquire after us, but had got no intelligence, therefore I would let you know much as I can at present. The Lord knows when I shall get another opportunity. They that took us prisoners did not use us bad but stole two Horses, one saddle, one Kettle, one Asct, 3 Bridles, also 2 blankets, 2 shirts, 2 pairs of leggings, so that what the Wiondots left us, we have lost by them.

Now me dear Brothers I have let you know a little how it went. But there [is] no one can think or tell any thing like as them that have seen it. Besides all this we are in such a great distress for want of provisions, that if our dear Saviour and our heavenly Father does not preserve us, the greatest Part will die for hunger, because in all the Parts where we are, there is nothing to be had. I think the 10th Nov. to set off with my company back again. I greet both you and your Amma Jonana, and all the congregations and desire to be remembered of them.

Schebosh

Notes

1. *That Dusty Road, 1721–1736*

1. Christopher Gist, *Christopher Gist's Journals*, comp. and ed. William M. Darlington (1893; rpt. New York: Argonaut Press, 1966), 36. Gist, on behalf of the Ohio Company, came into this area on December 7, 1750, and recorded the name of the river as Elk's Eye Creek, the Indian meaning for Muskingum.

2. David Zeisberger, "David Zeisberger's History of Northern American Indians," ed. Archer Butler Hulbert and William Nathaniel Schwarze, in *Ohio Archaeological and Historical Quarterly* 19 (April and January 1910): 1–173. This history, written by Zeisberger during the years 1779 and 1780, was never published in its original form until it was translated in 1910 by Hulbert and Schwarze. Bishop George Henry Loskiel used the document in his *History of the Mission of the United Brethren among the Indians in North America* (London: Brethren's Society for the Furtherance of the Gospel, 1794). Loskiel gave the author only one line of credit, despite the fact that one-third of Loskiel's book consists of the Zeisberger material.

3. Ted J. Brasser, "Mahican," in *Handbook of the North American Indians*, ed. Bruce G. Trigger, vol. 15 (Washington, D.C.: Smithsonian Institution, 1978), 198–212; Bert Salwen, "Indians of Southern New England and Long Island," *Handbook of the North American Indians*, ed. Trigger, 15:161–76. The Mahican Indians of the Hudson Valley have been confused in Moravian history with the early Pequot-Mohegans, Indians of the Thames River Valley of eastern Connecticut. A full explanation of these two tribes can be found in the above references.

4. William A. Hunter, "History of the Ohio Valley," in *Handbook of the North American Indians*, ed. Trigger, 15:590. During Zeisberger's time in the valley it was called the Muskingum. I will follow his usage. It later became the Tuscarawas and still carries this name.

Tuscarawas is an English corruption of the Wyandot word *Tuscarabi*, "open mouth of a stream." (It has often been confused, but has no reference, to one of the Six Nation tribes of Indians called the Tuscarora.)

5. Georg Neisser, *A History of the Beginnings of Moravian Work in America*, ed. William N. Schwarze and Samuel H. Gapp (Bethlehem: Archives of the Moravian Church, 1955), 86.

6. J. W. Larned, *The New Larned History*, 12 vols. (Springfield: C. A. Nichols, 1924), 2:1054.

7. Joseph E. Hutton, *A History of the Moravian Church* (London: Fetters Lane, 1909), 193–94.

8. J. Taylor Hamilton and Kenneth G. Hamilton, *History of the Moravian Church, The Renewed Unitas Fratrum, 1722–1957* (Bethlehem, Pa.: Interprovincial Board of Christian Directors, 1967), 16.

9. Ibid., 22.

10. Ibid., 654.

11. Ibid., 24, 654.

12. The German word *Hutberg* means *hill.*

13. John R. Weinlick, *Count Zinzendorf* (New York: Abington Press, 1956), 13–14. Most of the information for this chapter on Zinzendorf's early life comes from this excellent work. The count was a complex man. Paul A. W. Wallace, who wrote extensively of him in his *Conrad Weiser, 1696–1760, Friend of Colonist and Mohawk* (1945; rpt. New York: Russell & Russell, 1971), says, "He was a great-hearted child. . . . [He was] an enigma, proud and passionate, a stickler for his own authority." Saxony was located in what is now the southern part of Germany.

14. Weinlick, *Zinzendorf*, 14.

15. Ibid., 18.

16. Neisser, *History of the Beginnings of Moravian Work*, 144. The English word *choirs* in German is *chor* and was derived from the Greek word *chorus* in Greek drama representing the public. Zinzendorf applied it to the various stages of life and tied it to the life of Christ: for married people, "Christ, the bridegroom of His bride, the church"; for the single Brethren, "the man about thirty"; for the single sister, "the Virgin Mary"; for the children, "the boy in the temple asking the questions." The idea took root and provided over the early years a practical solution to communal living and greatly enhanced the pastoral supervision. By the beginning of the nineteenth century their popularity gradually declined, and by the middle of the century, they were abandoned entirely in most congregations. There were ten different choir divisions: infants in arms, little boys and little girls, larger boys and larger girls, single brethren and single sisters, married people, and widowers and widows. For further information, see Hutton, *History of the Moravian Church*, 221–22.

17. Hutton, *History of the Moravian Church*, 406–7. The lot was a powerful influence in the early history of the Moravian Church. Before 1769 it was haphazardly observed, but at the general synod held at Marienborn in 1769 it was recognized as an important principle of the church's decision-making process. At this synod the Brethren laid down the law that all elections, appointments, and important decisions (including the settlement of church policy) should be ratified by the lot. The weightiest matters were settled in this way. To some critics this practice appeared to be a "symptom of lunacy." It was not regarded so by the Brethren, and those who opposed were quickly referred to the example of the eleven Apostles as recorded in Acts I, verse 26, and also Christ's promise, "Whatsoever ye shall ask in my name, I will do it."

18. *Encyclopaedia Britannica*, 1964 edition, s.v. "Moravian Church."

19. Adelaide Fries, *Some Moravian Heroes* (Bethlehem: Christian Education Board of the Moravian Church, 1936), 74.

20. Weinlick, *Zinzendorf*, 112.

21. Fries, *Some Moravian Heroes*, 75.

22. Hamilton and Hamilton, *History of the Moravian Church*, 76. Ziegenhagen was a curse to the Moravians. Whenever and wherever he touched them there was controversy, principally because of his dislike for Zinzendorf.

23. Neisser, *History of the Beginnings of Moravian Work*, 106–12. The Nitschmann family was one of the largest and most important families of the Renewed Moravian Church in the eighteenth century. We will meet three David Nitschmanns. David, the syndic, a distant cousin of the bishop, was born in Zauchtenthal and was a weaver. The second David, the bishop, also came to Herrnhut in 1724 with his cousin and was the most prominent of the three. He became one of the major influences in the early life of David Zeisberger. David Senior or "Father" Nitschmann, better known as the founder of Bethlehem, was also born in Zauchtenthal. Father Nitschmann was a wheelwright and a carpenter by trade and responsible for most of the early Moravian construction. Other members were Anna, the daughter of Father Nitschmann, who married Zinzendorf shortly before the latter's death. She was the most prominent woman of the family and at fifteen the chief eldress of the church. It is difficult to distinguish one Nitschmann from another. All were related, if only as distant cousins.

24. Hamilton and Hamilton, *History of the Moravian Church*, 62–63. David Nitschmann was consecrated the first bishop in the Renewed Moravian Church by Daniel Ernst Jablonski, the grandson of Amos Comenius, on March 13, 1735.

2. *Branded as a Thief*, 1736–1742

1. Weinlick, *Zinzendorf*, 126.

2. Edmund De Schweinitz, *The Life and Times of David Zeisberger* (Philadelphia: J. B. Lippincott, 1870), 17.

3. Ibid., 18.

4. Neisser, *History of the Beginnings of Moravian Work*, 87.

5. De Schweinitz, *Zeisberger*, 20–21.

6. Anthony Wolff, "Heart of Savannah," *American Heritage* 22 (December 1970): 54. The two-and-one-half-square-mile site was carefully planned by General Oglethorpe in England before coming to America.

7. De Schweinitz, *Zeisberger*, 21.

8. Neisser, *History of the Beginnings of Moravian Work*, 10.

9. Joseph M. Levering, *A History of Bethlehem, Pennsylvania, 1741–1892* (Bethlehem: Times Publishing Co., 1903), 36, n. 4. Seiffert's ordination on March 10, 1736, was the first episcopal function in America.

10. Levin Theodore Reichel, *The Early History of the Church of the United Brethren (Unitas Fratrum) Commonly Called Moravians in North America. A.D. 1734–1748* (Nazareth: Moravian Historical Society, 1888), 67.

11. *Transactions of the Moravian Historical Society*, vol. 2, pt. 3 (Nazareth, 1877–), 208.

12. De Schweinitz, *Zeisberger*, 22.

13. Loskiel, *History of the Mission of the United Brethren*, pt. 2, 5.

14. Neisser, *History of the Beginnings of Moravian Work*, 8.

15. *Encyclopaedia Britannica*, 1964 ed., s.v. "Jenkins, Robert"; Jack Randolph, "Earmarked for War," *American History Illustrated*, February 1985, 34.

16. Reichel, *Early History of the Church of the United Brethren*, 77.

17. *Encyclopaedia Britannica*, 1964 ed., s.v. "Whitefield, George." The trip to America in 1740 was the second of many he made to the North American continent and probably marks the beginning of his ministry, which took him to Scotland, Wales, England, Ireland, and America. His influence on religious life in both the United States and Great Britain was immense.

18. Reichel, *Early History of the Church of the United Brethren*, 78.

19. Neisser, *History of the Beginnings of Moravian Work*, 17–18. This group consisted of Peter Boehler, Anthony Seiffert, Martin Mack, David and Rosina Zeisberger and their son David, Hannah Hummel, and two boys, John Boehner and Matthias Seybold.

20. Levering, *History of Bethlehem*, 52.

21. Ibid., 54.

22. Reichel, *Early History of the Church of the United Brethren*, 80.

23. Joseph E. Illick, *Colonial Pennsylvania* (New York: Charles Scribner's Sons, 1976), 113.

24. Ibid., 126. Illick quotes a passage from "Reise nach Pennsylvanie" (Journey to Pennsylvania), published in 1756 by Gottlieb Mittelberger, a native of Wurttemberg, describing his experiences during the voyage to America in the 1740s.

25. Ibid., 180. William Allen, the man Irish represented, a resident of Philadelphia, was perhaps the richest man in the colony and frequently loaned money to the Penns. He owned thousands of acres in and around the forks, and later Allentown was named for him. By the time Nitschmann made his first contact with Irish, Allen had been elected to the Common Council of Philadelphia, promoted to alderman, chosen for the assembly, and served as the mayor of the city. He later became chief justice of the supreme court. Allen sat at the very pinnacle of power in the colony, and his friendship was worth cultivating. Although his relationship with the Moravians never became intimate, he did on numerous occasions come to their assistance.

26. Neisser, *History of the Beginnings of Moravian Church*, ed. Schwarze and Gapp, 121, 122.

27. William C. Reichel, ed., *Memorials of the Moravian Church* (Philadelphia: J. B. Lippincott, 1870), 167.

28. Ibid., 169. The first house was removed in 1823 to make room for stables of the the new Eagle Hotel. It stood on Rubal's Alley at the rear of the present Hotel Bethlehem.

29. The fifteen-mile area of land, north of the Lehigh to the Blue Mountains, was then known as the "Dry Lands," so named because the limestone rock beneath the soil was so porous few surface streams could be found. Much later it became the center of the Portland cement industry in America.

30. Levering, *History of Bethlehem*, 64. The following is the list of names located in the cornerstone of the Gemeinhaus:

David Nitschmann, Bishop	From Moravia
Anton Seiffert	House Chaplain from Bohemia
Andrew Eschenbach	Itinerate Preacher from Nauenburg
David Nitschmann, Senior	Master Workman from Moravia
David Zeisberger, Senior	Carpenter from Moravia
Rosina Zeisberger	Wife of David, Sr., from Moravia
David Zeisberger, Junior	General Helper from Moravia
Matthew Seybold	Farmer from Wurttemberg
John Boehner	Carpenter from Bohemia
George Neisser	Messenger from Moravia
Christian Frohlich	General Helper from Felsburg in Hesse
John Martin Mack	Assistant Foreman from Wurttemberg
Anna Nitschmann	Daughter of Father Nitschmann
Johanna Hummel	Single sister
Johanna Sophia Molther	

31. Charles H. Glatfelter, *Pastors and People: German Lutheran and Reformed Churches in the Pennsylvania Field, 1717–1793*, 2 vols. (Breinigsville, Pa.: Pennsylvania German Society,

1980–81), 2:80. Conrad Weiser, in his letter to Peter Brunnholtz, February 16, 1747, gives us this sketch of the count: "I take him to be a man who in his youth had the great misfortune never to have had his strong will broken: in his college years, to be sure, he was diligent, and sought the truth, and he was visited in his time by the light of God's grace, for which he, being a high-born count, was much admired and praised. But . . . he never had his fingers properly rapped, instead he was always treated as the high-born count, and in short seems to have come out of the oven with too little baking to make a Reformer of the Church of Christ. He likes to command and dictate. . . . His ideas came in flashes, and were often good, he confirmed them by drawing lots. His flock had to swallow them; They called submission to his dictates 'Giving up one's will.' . . . In attaining his ends, the Count was bound by no law, human or divine. He held that whatever served his flock was right however much falsehood might be involved in it. . . . He is very hot but soon cools again. He holds no grudges. . . . I cannot separate his qualities, I mean the good from the bad. Certainly both are intermixed in him. And I doubt if he by himself, however much he tried, could ever get free from this tangle without the help of God's strong hand: for it is his very life. I hope his enemies, who bombard him without cause, or out of sectarian jealousy, may not read these words."

32. Reichel, *Early History of the Church of the United Brethren*, 119.
33. De Schweinitz, *Zeisberger*, 25.
34. Ibid., 26.

3. *Preventing Mischief, 1743–1745*

1. Reichel, ed., *Memorials of the Moravian Church*, 138–39. John Christopher Pyrlaeus, the Mohawk scholar, was born at Pausa, Voigtland, Saxony, in 1713, the son, grandson, and great-grandson of Lutheran ministers in the village. His father died three months before he was born. The child, along with three brothers and sisters, were raised by his widowed mother, who never remarried. He was educated at the Universities of Leipzig and Jena, where he met the Moravians Martin Dober, John de Watteville, Zinzendorf, and others. He joined the Moravians at Herrnhut on May 30, 1739, and was made an acolyte by Zinzendorf on August 20, 1740, and commissioned to come to America. He attended the first Christmas services in Bethlehem on December 24, 1741, and was ordained a deacon February 22, 1742. He was not only a language scholar but also an accomplished musician with a virtuosic voice. The Bethlehem diary entries for 1742 include numerous entries noting Pyrlaeus's singing performances before the congregation, especially one on December 29, when he sang a complete cantata. During the time he was in America (1741–51), he was among the first to bring the European tradition of Moravian music appreciation to the Pennsylvania settlement.

2. Tiyanoga was the son of a Mahican father and a Mohawk mother and was one of the most powerful chiefs of the Iroquois league. As head chief of the Mohawks he had succeeded to the chieftainship through the matrilineal line. Aside from his own dynamic personality and native ability, his fame came from a visit to London in 1710 when he met Queen Anne and was presented with a huge feathered hat and a lace-fringed coat of royal blue. Although taller than most Indians, he was under six feet but made an imposing picture with his dark bronze skin and slightly hooked nose. A prominent scar ran from the lower left side of his mouth, almost to the left ear, the result of some long-ago battle.

3. De Schweinitz, *Zeisberger*, 123.
4. Ibid., 125.
5. Ibid., 129.
6. Wallace, *Conrad Weiser*, 235.
7. Loskiel, *History of the Mission*, pt. 2, 72–73.

8. George Patterson Donehoo, *A History of the Indian Villages and Place Names in Pennsylvania* (Harrisburg, Pa.: Telegraph Press, 1928), 260–61.

9. Wallace, *Conrad Weiser*, 219.

10. Reichel, ed., *Memorials of the Moravian Church*, 66–68.

11. See Chapter 18 for James Logan's part in the massacre at Baker's cabin during Lord Dunmore's War in 1774.

12. Wallace, *Conrad Weiser*, 220.

13. The word *castle* is used frequently to refer to Indian villages. The word has its origin in early European references to the stockaded Indian villages they encountered on meeting their first natives. By the eighteenth century very few of the villages were protected in this fashion, but the name continued to be used. It generally meant the village of the principal chief of the tribe or nation. It is similar to our word *capital*.

14. Wallace, *Conrad Weiser*, 221.

15. Reichel, ed., *Memorials of the Moravian Church*, 72. Zinzendorf described his first meeting with the Prince in 1742 at Tulpehocken:

> The Black Prince of Onondaga is a terrible savage. On one occasion he broke into a stockaded castle of the enemy, scalped the inhabitants and escaped unhurt. In another incident, while on a visit to a certain Colonel Nicolls, one of his servants poured water on him (the Prince). With the thrust of his knife, the enraged Indian stabbed the man in the stomach so that he fell dead at his feet. Straightway he informed Nicolls of what occurred. "This act," said the latter, "would be regarded as a capital offence in Europe." "With us," retorted the Prince, "trifling with a warrior, is regarded a capital offence, hence I slew your man. If death is decreed me, here I am; do with me, according to your law." The Prince is still living.

16. William M. Beauchamp, ed., *Moravian Journals Relating to Central New York 1745–66* (Syracuse: Dehler Press, 1916), 5–24.

4. *Shamokin: The Stronghold of the Prince of Darkness*, 1746–1749

1. Levering, *History of Bethlehem*, 180.

2. Ibid., 192.

3. During this period the name was spelled Mahoney Valley.

4. Levering, *History of Bethlehem*, 185.

5. *Transactions of the Moravian Historical Society*, vol. 2, 3:175. Cammerhoff was educated at the University of Jena and was a classmate of Zinzendorf's son Christian Renatus. In May 1743, he applied for church membership and a teaching position at the Theological Seminary at Marienborn and was promptly accepted to both. Two years later his work was so outstanding that Zinzendorf appointed him as his secretary, and several months before his departure for America the twenty-five-year-old was consecrated a bishop, the youngest man ever to hold that office in the Renewed Church.

6. De Schweinitz, *Zeisberger*, 182. In those four years he traveled thousands of miles visiting his beloved Indians and baptizing eighty-nine converts, a record probably not excelled by any other Moravian except Zeisberger.

7. Edmund De Schweinitz, "Some Fathers of the American Moravian Church," *Transactions of the Moravian Historical Society*, vol. 2, 3:240.

8. Neisser, *History of the Beginnings of Moravian Work*, 89. John Hagen's place of birth and ancestry are not known, and we have little information on his early life. He came to Georgia on May 18, 1740, and remained there for several years trying to work with the Cherokee Indians. Unsuccessful in this effort, he migrated to Pennsylvania in February 1742

and was one of the eighty people present in Bethlehem at the organization meeting on June 22, 1742. He was unordained.

Joseph Powell was born near White Church, Shropshire, England, in 1710. He was converted to Christianity by Whitefield and Wesley and through them met the Moravians. He and his wife came to America with the First Sea Congregation in 1742. He was ordained a deacon at Bethlehem, May 24, 1756, and was active among the English people and the Indians in Dansbury (now Stroudsburg, Pennsylvania), Staten Island, Long Island, and "The Oblong" (Pachgatgosh and Wechquanach). He died there September 23, 1774, and the grave is marked by the same monument marking David Bruce's grave.

Bruce was a Scottish Presbyterian from Edinburgh, a carpenter, and the first Moravian to come to America whose mother tongue was English. He came to Pennsylvania with Zinzendorf in October 1741.

9. John H. Carter, *Early Events in the Susquehanna Valley: A Collection of the Writings and Addresses as Presented by John H. Carter before the Society* (Millville, Pa.: Precision Printers, 1981), 94–96. Anton Schmidt's home was located at the northwest corner of the Moravian cemetery, "God's Acre," on Market Street in Bethlehem.

10. De Schweinitz, *Zeisberger*, 144.

11. Ibid., 145.

12. Ibid.

13. De Schweinitz, "Some Fathers," 184. John de Watteville was the adopted son of Zinzendorf's old Halle classmate Frederick de Watteville, a rich baron from Switzerland, who had been a lifelong friend of the count and over the years had contributed heavily to Zinzendorf's church work. John, the son of Lutheran clergyman John M. Langguth, was born in 1718 and later adopted by the baron. Shortly after graduating from the University of Jena, he joined the Moravian Church and was consecrated a bishop in 1747. He died on October 7, 1788.

14. Paul A. W. Wallace, *Indian Paths of Pennsylvania* (Harrisburg: Pennsylvania Historical and Museum Commision, 1971), 88. The party could not know, as they passed over Mauch Chunk Mountain, that a village by the same name, one mile to the east, and founded in 1812, would change its name 140 years later in response to twentieth-century bigotry and become the final resting place for one of America's most famous Indian athletes, Jim Thorpe.

15. De Schweinitz, *Zeisberger*, 149. The gift consisted of a knife, fork, and spoon, together with an ivory drinking cup. All were heavily mounted with silver and enclosed in a morocco case attached to a long loop of silk.

16. Wallace, *Conrad Weiser*, 273.

17. Carter, *Early Events in the Susquehanna Valley*, 216. Carter describes the 1850 exhumation by M. L. Hendrick of a grave thought to be Shickellamy's. The skeleton's head was to the east and the feet to the west. From the artifacts discovered, we can presume he was a person of distinction. The grave contained, among other items, four hundred glass, bone, and amber beads (the latter as large as small hickory nuts), three copper finger rings (one decorated on the top side with clasped hands), small bells and dangles for breech pants, six copper bracelets, one iron tobacco box with a small quantity of tobacco, fishing lines, needles, an English copper cent and half cent, a copper medal that was probably struck in England in 1714, a ten-inch scalping knife, and remains of a musket barrel eighteen inches long with the lock attached. With one exception, none of these items survived the 1850 excavations. In 1989, the Northumberland Historical Society recovered the large string of amber beads. They are now displayed at the society's headquarters just a few feet from the original location of Shickellamy's home.

18. Wallace, *Conrad Weiser*, 273. The chief left three sons and a daughter. The first son was Tagheghdoarus, also known as John Shickellamy, who succeeded him. Unfortunately, John would never gain the respect and authority his father held either with the whites or his own people. The second son, Tahgahjute, was renamed James Logan, after the secretary of

Provincial Council of Pennsylvania and a friend of his father for whom he held high regard. He eventually became the famous Logan, chief of the Ohio Mingoes and friend of the whites. The third son, John Petty, was named after a trader who worked at Shamokin and was well respected by Shickellamy. Little is known of the later life of the daughter.

19. Wallace, *Conrad Weiser*, 283.

20. De Schweinitz, *Zeisberger*, 153. At this council de Watteville was adopted into the Turtle Clan of the Onondaga Nation and received the name of Tgarihnotie (A Messenger).

21. Carl John Fliegel, comp., *Index to the Records of the Moravian Mission among the Indians of North America*, 4 vols. (Woodbridge, Conn: Research Publications, 1970), 1:51.

22. J. Max Hark, "Meniologameka: Annals of a Moravian Indian Village an Hundred and Thirty Years Ago," *Transactions of the Moravian Historical Society* 2, pt. 3 (1886): 133.

5. *A Journey into Hell, 1750*

1. Beauchamp, ed., *Moravian Journals Relating to Central New York*, 33–35.

2. Marian E. White, William E. Engelbrecht, and Elisabeth Tooker, "Cayuga," in *Handbook of North American Indians*, ed. Trigger, 15:500–504.

3. Beauchamp, ed., *Moravian Journals Relating to Central New York*, 41, 42.

4. Ibid., 45.

5. Ibid., 110. A bronze tablet on the St. John's Church in Skaneateles, New York, marks the site of the camp called the Pilgrim's Hut at St. John's Beach. I visited this site on October 2, 1985, and made an exhaustive search of the area but found this plaque to be the only modern recognition of the 1750 journey. Cammerhoff and Zeisberger passed through this location four times and camped here June 24 and July 24.

6. De Schweinitz, "Some Fathers," 177.

7. Beauchamp, ed., *Moravian Journals Relating to Central New York*, 66–67.

8. William M. Beauchamp, *Aboriginal Place Names of New York*, New York State Museum Bulletin 108, Archeology 12 (Albany: Grand River Books, 1907), 155–56. I have followed Beauchamp's spelling in most instances. The Moravians generally had their own spelling of most Iroquois proper and place names.

9. Most of Cammerhoff's estimates of distances were highly overstated, often doubling the correct mileage. He judged the length of Cayuga Lake to be sixty-five miles, but it is actually forty miles long. The Indians were equally in error in many of their calculations. They estimated the depth of Cayuga to be 20 to 30 fathoms, or 180 feet. It is, at the deepest point, 455 feet. I have retraced the entire 1750 journey. Considering the terrain, their mode of transportation, and other hazards they encountered, it is little wonder Cammerhoff erred.

10. Beauchamp, *Aboriginal Place Names of New York*, 157. Honeoye means "Finger Lying." The lake received its name from an Indian legend that long ago, a young brave was picking wild strawberries near the lake and was bitten on the finger by a rattlesnake. He took his tomahawk, cut off the offending finger, and left it lying on the ground.

11. Beauchamp, ed., *Moravian Journals Relating to Central New York*, 73, 74. Quotations in the following paragraphs are from this source.

12. Ibid., 79.

6. *You Need Never Fear among Us, 1750–1753*

1. Paul A. W. Wallace, *Indians in Pennsylvania* (Harrisburg: Pennsylvania Historical and Museum Commission, 1961), 182.

2. Anthony F. C. Wallace, *King of the Delawares: Teedyuscung, 1700–1763* (Philadelphia: University of Pennsylvania Press, 1961), 2.

3. A snow was equipped with two masts, resembling the main and foremast of a ship, and a third small mast just abaft the mainsail, carrying a trysail.

4. Levering, *History of Bethlehem*, 259, 260.

5. De Schweinitz, *Zeisberger*, 180–81.

6. Ibid., 185.

7. Ibid. Schmick was the Lutheran pastor at Lavonia, where he became acquainted with the Moravians and joined them in 1748. An accomplished musician and teacher, he had several sharp differences with Zeisberger. Nevertheless, they remained good friends and worked closely on many mission projects.

8. Ibid., 187.

9. Ibid., 188. Charles Godfrey Rundt was born at Konigsberg, May 30, 1713, joined the church at Herrnhut in 1747, emigrated to America in 1751, and became an itinerant missionary among the Indians and white settlers. He died at Bethlehem on August 17, 1764.

10. Beauchamp, ed., *Moravian Journals Relating to Central New York*, 115. A local council had no binding authority on the Six Nation confederacy and served only as a planning session for a particular tribe. Policy and definitive action of the joint confederacy required a grand council meeting at which all tribes were represented.

11. De Schweinitz, *Zeisberger*, 192–94.

12. Ibid., 201. The missionaries carried three passports: from Timothy Horsfield, who had taken Henry Antes's place as the justice of the peace at Bethlehem; from Daniel Schuyler, alderman of Brunswick, New Jersey; and from Edward Holland, mayor of New York City.

13. Loskiel, *History of the Mission of the United Brethren*, 143–44.

14. De Schweinitz, *Zeisberger*, 206. Henry Frey was born in Falkner's Swamp, Pennsylvania, on May 12, 1724. Following his journey with Zeisberger, he served the church in various capacities. He died in Litiz, Pennsylvania, September 25, 1784.

15. Beauchamp, ed., *Moravian Journals Relating to Central New York*, 162.

16. Ibid., 165.

17. Ibid., 169–70.

18. Ibid., 176–77.

19. De Schweinitz, *Zeisberger*, 209.

20. Beauchamp, ed., *Moravian Journals Relating to Central New York*, 180.

21. Ibid., 185.

7. *Prelude to Tragedy, Then Defeat and Disaster, 1754–1755*

1. De Schweinitz, *Zeisberger*, 216. Karl Friedrich was born at Husom, in Holstein, October 4, 1715, and labored among the Indians and Negroes in America and Surinam. He is known principally for this Onondaga visit with Zeisberger. Friedrich died in Surinam on January 24, 1761.

2. Wallace, *King of the Delawares*, 47–49.

3. Ibid., 48.

4. Donehoo, *History of Indian Villages and Place Names in Pennsylvania*, 123.

5. Reichel, ed., *Memorials of the Moravian Church*, 38. Wire Creek was a tributary of Pocopoco Creek.

6. Loskiel, *History of the Mission of the United Brethren*, 151.

7. *Transactions of the Moravian Historical Society*, vol. 2, 3:129.

8. See Chapter 4, p. 43, for details on this purchase.

9. Frequent reference will be made to the word *plantation*, the term used by the Moravians to describe farm acreage where crops such as corn, wheat, and hay were grown for both the village and the farm animals. Small vegetables were usually grown near their houses.

10. Beauchamp, ed., *Moravian Journals Relating to Central New York*, 197–218.

11. Ibid., 199–215.

12. De Schweinitz, *Zeisberger*, 217. De Schweinitz's source was an entry in the Bethlehem diary dated August 1755. He probably misinterpreted the diary entry from Zeisberger's journal noting that the council permitted him to store the wampum in the missionaries' cabin where it would be secure and dry. Zeisberger was not the Iroquois keeper of the wampum.

13. Ibid., 215. Also see James Axtell, *The Invasion Within: The Contest of Cultures in Colonial North America* (New York: Oxford University Press, 1985), 302–27.

14. Beauchamp, ed., *Moravian Journals Relating to Central New York*, 201.

15. Wallace, *King of the Delawares*, 65.

16. Ibid., 66.

17. Levering, *History of Bethlehem*, 297. The message was brought to Bethlehem by Nicholas Scull, who would become the surveyor general of the Pennsylvania colony. He was also the son-in-law of Solomon Jennings, one of the three "walkers" involved in the infamous Walking Purchase Treaty. Scull subsequently became famous as a surveyor and map maker. Many of his maps are still extant and are invaluable sources for eighteenth-century Pennsylvania. The day following Scull's arrival in Bethlehem (July 20), another rider slowly rode into the village bearing news of a far more saddening event. Henry Antes had died at his home in Fredericks. A tower of strength had passed from their midst, and no longer could they call for his wise advice and gentle counseling.

18. Paul E. Kopperman, *Braddock at the Monongehela* (Pittsburgh: University of Pittsburgh Press, 1977), 50–92. Kopperman provides a review of the more than forty eyewitness accounts of the battle.

19. John R. Swanton, *The Indian Tribes of North America* (Washington, D.C.: U.S. Government Printing Office, 1952), 49. Readers may confuse the Munsee and the Mingo tribes of this period. There are generally thought to be two main divisions of the Delaware tribes. The Munsees (sometimes spelled Monsey) were the descendants of the Minisinks, who lived originally in northern New Jersey and the adjacent portions of New York west of the Hudson; and the Unami, who lived in the immediate territory, extending to the western end of Long Island. Mingo (no relation to the Munsee) was a Delaware name loosely assigned to the remnant group of nonleague Senecas and Cayugas of the Six Nations Iroquois who, during the last half of the eighteenth century, migrated into the Ohio Valley near present Steubenville. The nearby town of Mingo Junction, Ohio, reflects their presence in the area. During most of this time they were closely associated with the Shawnees, who lived in southern Ohio along the Scioto River. James Logan, Shickellamy's second son, became the famous Logan, one of their principal chiefs.

20. Reuben Gold Thwaites, *France in America, 1497–1763*, American Nations Series, vol. 7 (New York: Harper & Brothers, 1905), 189–91.

21. C. Hale Sipe, *The Indian Chiefs of Pennsylvania* (Butler: Ziegler Printing, 1927), 232.

22. Ibid., 233.

23. Wallace, *King of the Delawares*, 71.

24. Ibid.

25. Ibid., 72.

26. Ibid., 73.

27. Fliegel, *Index*, 2:664.

28. Levering, *History of Bethlehem*, 310.

29. De Schweinitz, *Zeisberger*, 229. The following is a list of the Brethren living on the west side of the Lehigh on November 24, at the original site of the mission:

Living in the House of the Pilgrims

Joachim Sensemann, overseer of the property
* Anne Sensemann, his wife
* The Sensemann's infant child

* Gottlieb Andres, pastoral supervisor of all the party
* Joanna Andres, his wife
* Martin Nitschmann, cultivator of the land
Susanna Nitschmann, his wife, not killed during the massacre but died later in captivity (see note 31).
George Partsch, cultivator of the land
Susanna Partsch, his wife

Living in the Brethren House
* John Gottermeyer, assistant to Andres and Sensemann
* George Fabricus, student of Delaware language and teacher at the Indian school
* George Schweigert, cultivator of the land
* Martin Presser, supervisor of the carpenter work
* John F. Lesley, instructor of natives in farming techniques
Peter Worbass, cultivator of the land
Joseph Sturgis, cultivator of the land

* Names so marked were killed or died in the massacre.

30. Levering, *History of Bethlehem*, 316. During the third week of April 1756, some five months after the massacre, a company of militia found a man's body lying near the "sand spring" on the west side of the river not far from the site of the massacre. He was lying on his back with the hands folded across his chest and a single bullet hole in his side. From the clothing he was identified as Martin Presser. Since the body had not been scalped, they presumed he had escaped only to crawl to the spot and die.

31. Ibid. Following the massacre, everyone in Bethlehem presumed Susanna Nitschmann had been killed the night of November 24. Some eight months later, Joachin, a baptized Indian, who had fled to the Wyoming Valley after the massacre, visited Bethlehem and explained what had occurred following that fateful evening. Her wound, if any, must have been slight. She was captured and taken to the Wyoming Valley. Sarah, the wife of old Abraham, "threw up her hand in consternation" when she saw her. Another woman of the village, Abigail, the wife of Benjamin, was permitted to care for Susanna in her own hut, but finally her captor dragged her off to Tioga. There she passed her days in weeping and sank into a deep melancholy and died. Her captor was later killed by Teedyuscung in a fit of rage.

32. De Schweinitz, *Zeisberger*, 235.

33. Levering, *History of Bethlehem*, 317–18. The party of twelve Indians was led by Captain Jachebus, a Delaware Munsee from the village of Assinisink, located in present Big Flats, Chemung County, New York, just above the Teedyuscung village at Tioga. Many accounts of the Gnadenhutten-on-the-Mahoney massacre have been written. The Bethlehem diary also records some eyewitness accounts. Accounts by Heckewelder, De Schweinitz, and Loskiel were also consulted. Levering's description combines all of these and seems to be the most balanced of those I have consulted. Joseph Sturgis, whose alertness saved his life, lived to be seventy-nine. Before he died in 1817 he fathered ten children and had thirty-four grandchildren and three great-grandchildren.

8. *The Peacemakers*, 1755–1761

1. Thwaites, *France in America*, 145–46.
2. Levering, *History of Bethlehem*, 329.
3. Ibid., 320–21.

4. Zeisberger, "David Zeisberger's History of North American Indians," 1–173.

5. Carl Van Doren, *Benjamin Franklin* (New York: Viking, 1938), 245.

6. Levering, *History of Bethlehem*, 334.

7. Ibid., 251–52. Of all of the frontier forts built at this time, Fort Allen's physical dimensions were perhaps unique. The traditional configurations were generally square with pentagonal projecting bastions on each of the four corners of the rectangle. Allen was a large rectangular fort, 125 feet long and fifty feet wide with two pointed bastions in the center of each end and two at the center of the width on opposite sides. It took seventy-five axmen just five hours to cut the trees needed. Franklin remarked, "Seeing the trees fall so fast, I had the curiosity to look at my watch when two men began to cut at a pine: in six minutes they had it upon the ground, and I found it of fourteen inches diameter. Each pine made three palisades, each eighteen feet long and pointed at one end."

8. Wallace, *Conrad Weiser*, 434.

9. Ibid., 440.

10. Ibid., 441.

11. William A. Hunter, *Forts on the Pennsylvania Frontier, 1753–1758* (Harrisburg: Pennsylvania Historical and Museum Commission, 1960), 1:217.

12. Wallace, *Conrad Weiser*, 440.

13. Ibid., 459.

14. *Pennsylvania Colonial Records*, 16 vols. (Philadelphia: Jo Severns, 1851–53), 7:320.

15. Wallace, *Conrad Weiser*, 461.

16. Consul Willshire Butterfield, *History of the Girtys* (Cincinnati: R. C. Clarke, 1890), 6–9. The Indian attack against Fort Granville (Lewistown, Pennsylvania) and Armstrong's burning of the Indian village of Kittanning (present Kittanning, Pennsylvania) provides us with an interesting incident. Taken captive at Granville were fifteen-year-old Simon Girty, his younger brothers, James and George, and his stepbrother Thomas, along with his mother and stepfather, Thomas Turner. The stepfather was horribly tortured and killed on their arrival at Kittanning. The stepbrother was freed when Armstrong attacked the village, but the Girty boys were quickly removed from the village at the beginning of the attack. They were adopted into the Indian tribes and lived most of their lives among the Indians. Simon later appeared in David Zeisberger's life.

17. De Schweinitz, *Zeisberger*, 248.

18. Sipe, *Indian Chiefs of Pennsylvania*, 340–41.

19. Reichel, ed., *Memorials of the Moravian Church*, 230.

20. Pennsylvania Indian Forts Commission, *Report of the Commission to Locate the Site of the Frontier Forts of Pennsylvania*, ed. Thomas L. Montgomery, 2d ed., 2 vols. (Harrisburg, Pa.: W. S. Ray, state printer, 1916), 1:219 (hereafter cited as *Frontier Forts*).

21. De Schweinitz, *Zeisberger*, 249.

22. Sipe, *Indian Chiefs of Pennsylvania*, 348–49.

23. Reichel, ed., *Memorials of the Moravian Church*, 343; also Pennsylvania Colonial Records, 7:725.

24. Levering, *History of Bethlehem*, 357; also Reichel, ed., *Memorials of the Moravian Church*, 365.

25. De Schweinitz, *Zeisberger*, 250.

26. Ibid., 251–52.

27. Sipe, *Indian Chiefs of Pennsylvania*, 354.

28. Reuben Gold Thwaites, ed., *Early Western Travels*, 2 vols. (Cleveland: Arthur H. Clarke, 1904–5), 177–291. Post's journals are collected in this volume.

29. Francis A. Jennings, "A Vanishing Indian: Francis Parkman versus His Sources," *Magazine of History and Biography of Pennsylvania* 87 (1963):306–23. Most of the information over the past one hundred years on Post's last two trips into western Indian country has come from Francis Parkman's *Montcalm and Wolfe*, 2 vols. (Boston: Little, Brown, 1902). In

1985, Jennings made a careful study of the extant records and found grave errors in Parkman's accounts. In some cases he accuses Parkman of deliberately altering the truth. Though he does not detract from Post's heroic effort, he makes the point that neither trip would have succeeded without the assistance of Pisquetomen. Pisquetomen would have been the rightful Delaware heir to old Sassoonan's (Allumapees) head chieftainship had it not been for the opposition of the Penn proprietors. The chief had opposed the Walking Purchase Treaty and thus incurred the wrath of the proprietors. Also see Jennings, "The Delaware Interregum," *Pennsylvania Magazine of History and Biography* 89 (1965): 194–98.

30. Wallace, *Conrad Weiser*, 549.

31. Ibid.

32. Loskiel, *History of the Mission of the United Brethren*, 190–91.

33. Sipe, *Indian Chiefs of Pennsylvania*, 301–2.

34. Levering, *History of Bethlehem*, 368–69.

35. Wallace, *Conrad Weiser*, 569.

36. De Schweinitz, *Zeisberger*, 252. Litiz, eight miles north of Lancaster, was an exclusively Moravian town founded in 1757 in Warwick Township, Lancaster County, Pennsylvania. Originally spelled Litiz, it was later changed to Lititz. I use the original spelling throughout this narrative. The name came from the original settlement in Bohemia, where, in 1457, some followers of John Hus formed Unitas Fratrum, now known as the Moravian Church.

37. Levering, *History of Bethlehem*, 371. James Hamilton served two terms as deputy governor of the Pennsylvania colony. The first term was between 1748 and 1754. He was now beginning his second term, having been appointed by the Penns late in 1759 to replace the bumbling Denny. He would continue until 1763, when Thomas Penn (William Penn's grandson) came to America to serve as the governor. On his way home from Easton, Hamilton stopped at the recently opened Rose Inn at Nazareth and was graciously entertained by Peter Worbas and his wife, who were the innkeepers. Worbas's had fully recovered from his harrowing escape at the Gnadenhutten massacre in 1755.

38. John Heckewelder, *A Narrative of the Mission of the United Brethren among the Delaware and Mohegan Indians; From Its Commencement, in the Year 1740 to the Close of the Year 1808* (1820; rpt. New York: Arno Press, 1971), 59–60.

9. *Pontiac and His Indian War, 1761–1763*

1. De Schweinitz, *Zeisberger*, 260. Gottlob Sensemann was the son of Joachim and Anna Catherine Sensemann. His mother was killed at the massacre at Gnadenhutten on the Mahoney in 1755. Young Sensemann remained close to Zeisberger most of his life and became a tireless worker for the missionary program and a frequent assistant to Zeisberger. He died at Fairfield, Canada, on January 4, 1800.

2. Ibid. De Schweinitz erroneously states that Abraham died before Zeisberger and Sensemann arrived in the Wyoming Valley in August 1762. Abraham's death was not reported in Bethlehem until December 2, 1762 (box 125, folder 1, Moravian Church Archives). Zeisberger had returned to Bethlehem several months before this date. See Fliegel, *Index*, 1:10. Abraham is first on the list of the American Indians baptized by the Moravians.

3. Francis Jennings, *The Ambiguous Iroquois Empire* (New York: Norton, 1984), 101.

4. Wallace, *Indians in Pennsylvania*, 173, 181. Shingas, and especially Tamaqua, played significant roles in the western theater during this period. Shingas (Bog Meadow) was the older brother of Tamaqua and a nephew of old Sassoonan, the former "king" or head man of the Delawares, who died in 1747. They were both sons of the sister of Sassoonan, and because the Delawares were matrilineal, he was the logical successor. After an indecisive interregnum of several years, Shingas was appointed the head chief in 1752. He sided with

the French during the war, became known as "Shingas the Terrible," and participated in many bloody massacres, including the defeat of Braddock in 1755. Shingas died in the winter of 1763–64. Tamaqua (the Beaver) replaced his brother as head chief following the French and Indian War and successfully negotiated the peace with Post. James Kenny described him as "a steady, quiet, middle-aged man of cheerful disposition, but low [short] in stature." He became a close friend of Post and died in 1769 at the present site of Gnadenhutten, Ohio, which in 1772 became the location of one of the most successful Moravian missions. Both men were members of the Delaware Turkey Clan.

5. Wallace, *Indian Paths of Pennsylvania,* 62, 142. Post and Heckewelder traveled the Raystown path from present Harrisburg to Fort Pitt and then used the Great Path to the Tuscarawas.

6. Edward Rondthaler, *Life of John Heckewelder,* ed. B. H. Coates (Philadelphia: T. Ward, 1847), 46. I have in my file a copy of the *Tuscarawas Advocate,* published in New Philadelphia, Ohio, dated Friday morning, November 27, 1846. The lead article on the front page describes a visit to the former site of the mission cabin on July 9, 1845. The visitors were Heckewelder's youngest daughter, Susanna, then sixty, her grandson, and Susanna's daughter and son-in-law, Rev. and Mrs. John Christian Luckenbach. They easily located the ruins of the mission house, trader Calhoon's cabin, and Beaver's village. The traces were clearly visible some eighty-five years later. Fort Laurens, the only revolutionary fort in the present state of Ohio, was built near here in 1778.

7. Ibid., 51.

8. Ibid., 51–52, 55–58.

9. De Schweinitz, *Zeisberger,* 261. Following the aborted Muskingum missionary effort, Post left British North America for Central America and many years later returned to Germantown, where he died. He was a brave, fearless, and audacious man, but he was a loner whose erratic and unstable behavior prevented him from conforming to the rigid discipline required by members of the organized church.

10. C. Hale Sipe, *The Indian Wars of Pennsylvania: An Account of the Indian Events in Pennsylvania (of the French and Indian War)* (Harrisburg: Telegraph Press, 1929), 420–38. At the beginning of the Pontiac uprising, at least sixteen traders and eighty-eight of their employees were killed or captured between Fort Pitt and Detroit. The loss of their goods was estimated at £45,000. On June 1, 1763, Calhoon arrived at Fort Pitt from the Tuscarawas. He had been warned by Shingas, the Beaver, and Wingenund at 11:00 the evening of May 27 to leave the village immediately because hostile war parties planned to murder his entire contingent. The chiefs furnished three Indians to guide them. On leaving the Tuscarawas, they were not permitted to take their arms. Shingas and the Beaver assured Calhoon that the guides would protect them from harm. The fourteen men in the Calhoon party left the village several hours later. On May 29, as they were crossing Beaver Creek, they were fired upon by hostile Indians, killing all except Calhoon and two others. On arrival at Fort Pitt, the three shaken men reported to Captain Ecuyer that the guides had disappeared immediately after the firing began, leading them to believe they had been led into a trap.

11. Howard H. Peckham, *Pontiac and the Indian Uprising* (New York: Russell and Russell, 1970), 87.

12. Alexander Henry, *Travels and Adventures in Canada* (1809; rpt. New York: Readex Microprint, 1966), 77–93.

13. Peckham, *Pontiac and the Indian Uprising,* 156–70.

14. De Schweinitz, *Zeisberger,* 264.

15. Wallace, *Indian Paths of Pennsylvania,* 187.

16. Wallace, *King of the Delawares,* 258–59.

17. Ibid., 262.

18. De Schweinitz, *Zeisberger,* 269–70.

19. Ibid., 271–72.
20. Nicholas B. Wainwright, *George Croghan, Wilderness Diplomat* (Chapel Hill: University of North Carolina Press, 1959), 199.
21. Deut. 7:2.
22. De Schweinitz, *Zeisberger*, 276–77.
23. *Frontier Forts*, 1:166.
24. Ibid., 169.
25. De Schweinitz, *Zeisberger*, 279.
26. Levering, *History of Bethlehem*, 399–400.
27. De Schweinitz, *Zeisberger*, 281.
28. Ibid., 282. John Penn was the the grandson of William Penn and the eldest son of Richard and Hannah (Lardner) Penn. Born July 14, 1729, he came to America in 1752 immediately following his graduation from Geneva University in Switzerland and attended the Albany treaty negotiations in 1754. Shortly thereafter, he returned to England. His next trip to America was in 1763, and he stayed until the death of his father in 1771. After returning again to America in 1773 he lived in Pennsylvania for the rest of his life. The last proprietary governor of Pennsylvania, he was universally respected and liked by the colonial Pennsylvanians. He died Feburary 9, 1795.

10. *The Philadelphia Incident, 1763–1765*

1. De Schweinitz, *Zeisberger*, 256. Rev. Frederick von Marschall, the son of Baron G. R. de Marschall, the commandant at the garrison town of Stolpen, Saxony, was born in Stolpen, February 5, 1721. His father supervised a strict military education for his young son, but as an adult the young man transferred to a seminary and eventually became a minister. Later he joined the Moravians. He came to America with Nathaniel Seidel on October 19, 1761. Seidel replaced Spangenberg as head of the Moravian activity in North America, and Marschall became his assistant as the general warden. He served for several years in Bethlehem and was then transferred to Salem, North Carolina. Spending the rest of his life in North Carolina, he served the Moravian congregation with distinction and died there in 1802 at the age of eighty-one.
2. Ibid., 286. Parkman also describes this event in *The Conspiracy of Pontiac and the Indian War after the Conquest of Canada*, 2 vols., 10th ed. (Boston: Little, Brown, 1893), 2:132 132, but states that the converts "reluctantly yielded up their arms." Grube's diary specifically records that they yielded up their arms with "patience and resignation." Parkman was severely criticized by nineteenth-century Moravians for this remark. They correctly believed that he had not done adequate research.
3. De Schweinitz, *Zeisberger*, 388. Johannes Roth, sometimes spelled "Rothe," joined the Moravian missionary work in 1759. He was born in the small Prussian village of Sarmund on February 3, 1726. Educated in the Catholic Church, he learned the trade of a locksmith. In 1748 he joined the Moravian Church at Neusalz, Prussia, and immigrated to America, arriving at Bethlehem in July 1756. He was one of Zeisberger's close associates actively involved in his missionary efforts for the next eleven years. Primarily because of the coming revolution, he left the mission field in 1774 and moved his family back to the settlements, living at York, Pennsylvania, where he died in 1791. See David Luther Roth, *Johann Roth: Missionary* (Greenville, Pa.: Beaver Printing Co., 1922).
4. Martha L. Simonetti, comp., Donald H. Kent and Harry E. Whipkey, eds., *Descriptive List of the Map Collection in the Pennsylvania State Archives* (Harrisburg: Pennsylvania Historical and Museum Commission, 1976), MG-11: 360, map of Philadelphia, Nicholas Scull, 1762.

5. Neisser, *History of the Beginnings of Moravian Work*, 81. Neisser was born in Moravia in 1715 and emigrated to America in 1735. He became the first diarist at Bethlehem and served in a variety of important positions for the church during the Revolutionary period. A strong supporter of the Revolution, he was a chaplain to the Continental Congress at Yorktown, Pennsylvania, and was pastor at Philadelphia at the time of his death in 1784.

6. De Schweinitz, *Zeisberger*, 288.

7. Bernard Adam Grube, "Autobiography," *Transactions of the Moravian Historical Society*, vol. 11, pt. 3 (1931): 205. Grube and Zeisberger remained close friends all of their lives. Grube died in Bethlehem at age ninety-two on March 18, 1808, just eight months before Zeisberger, who was eighty-seven.

8. Donehoo, *Indian Villages and Place Names*, 36–38.

9. Paul A. W. Wallace, *Thirty Thousand Miles with John Heckewelder* (Pittsburgh: University of Pittsburgh Press, 1958), 418; quotation on 77. Judge William Henry, the oldest son of John and Mary Ann (De Vinne) Henry, was born in Chester County, Pennsylvania, on May 29, 1729. He was of Scotch and Huguenot descent. At fifteen, he was sent to Lancaster, Pennsylvania, and apprenticed to Matthew Roesser, a gunsmith. Mechanically inclined, at twenty-one, he became a successful manufacturer of firearms on his own account, furnishing arms for both the Braddock and Forbes campaigns. Henry became a member of Congress in 1784 and a prominent man in Pennsylvanian history. There is a legendary account of his saving the life of a young Indian brave at the battle of the Monongahela in 1755. The Indian, eighteen-year-old Gelelemend, became a major character in the life of David Zeisberger and later took the name of his rescuer, William Henry.

10. *Pennsylvania Colonial Records* 9:102–4. Sheriff John Hays of Lancaster County recorded a list of the Indians killed during the Paxton Boys affair.

11. Ibid., 101.

12. Ibid., 107, 108.

13. Frank J. Cavaioli, "A Profile of the Paxton Boys: Murders of the Conestoga Indians," *Journal of the Lancaster County Historical Society* 87, pt. 3 (1983): 89. This is taken from a declaration made by Lazarus Stewart, one of the Paxton Boys. Although Stewart does not make a frank admission of murder, he says that he was present at the massacre in the Lancaster jail.

14. Wallace, *Thirty Thousand Miles with John Heckewelder*, 78.

15. *Pennsylvania Colonial Records* 9:109–10.

16. De Schweinitz, *Zeisberger*, 294.

17. *Pennsylvania Colonial Records* 9:120.

18. Ibid., 122.

19. Ibid., 132.

20. Illick, *Colonial Pennsylvania*, 242. Benjamin Chew, a Quaker turned Anglican, was a power in colonial politics. He was the attorney general of the province from 1754 to 1774, when he succeeded William Allen as chief justice of the supreme court. During the Revolutionary War, Chew's elegant home, Cliveden, was the focal point of the Battle of Germantown on October 4, 1777. His wavering political affiliations during the war caused him trouble. He was arrested in the summer of 1777 and held until 1778. In 1781, he publicly embraced the Revolution and was returned to favor and appointed again as jurist for the Commonwealth of Pennsylvania.

21. *Pennsylvania Colonial Records* 9:138. A brief synopsis of the nine complaints follows:

> 1. The five frontier counties should be represented in the assembly the same as the three eastern counties, based on the taxable records.
>
> The following table taken from *Votes and Proceedings of the Province of Pennsylvania* (Philadelphia, 1775) 5:8, shows clearly the problem of unequal representation:

	Actual Members	*Taxables*	*Members by Taxables*
Eastern Counties			
Philadelphia City	2	2,634	4
Philadelphia County	8	5,678	8
Chester County	8	4,761	7
Bucks County	8	3,148	4
TOTALS	26	16,221	23
Western Counties			
Lancaster County	4	5,635	8
York County	2	3,302	5
Berk County	1	3,016	4
Northumberland County	1	1,989	3
Cumberland County	2	1,501	2
TOTALS	10	15,443	22

The three eastern counties (Philadelphia, Chester, Bucks) and the city of Philadelphia had 26 representatives when they should have had 23. The five western counties had 10, when they should have had 22. In 1776, when the population rose to 300,000, the western counties successfully altered the situation, and ten new counties were created between 1781 to 1790.

2. All trials for capital offenses had to be tried in the county where the crime was committed.

3. The Moravians were sheltering Christian Indians who participated in attacks against the settlements (a direct reference to the protection of Renatus).

4. Friendly Indians were providing intelligence to their fellow hostile tribes.

5. No protection or succor was given to the white population who had been attacked by hostile Indians.

6. Unlike the French and Indian War, during the Pontiac uprising no scalp bounties had been offered for whites to continue their grisly operation seeking out and killing Indians, which supposedly "reduced them to reason" and discouraged the attacks on the settlements.

7. Trade should be prohibited with all Indians until they returned the white captives taken during the recent raids against the white settlements.

8. Complaints were made against the Quakers, particularly J. P. [James Pemberton], who was dealing directly with the Indians, supposedly unknown to colonial authorities.

9. Fort Augusta, built at a substantial expense to the colonial government, was not being used effectively to protect the frontier settlements.

22. De Schweinitz, *Zeisberger*, 302.

23. *Pennsylvania Colonial Records* 9:142–43.

24. Box 124, folders 1 and 3, Moravian Church Archives, contain Grube's and Schmick's diaries during their stay at Philadelphia. From November 8, 1763, to March 20, 1765, Zeisberger was involved with the Christian converts at Philadelphia. During the time he spent in Bethlehem, he was involved with many details concerning their welfare that could be handled only in Bethlehem. He lived with the Indians in Philadelphia from November 8 to December 21, 1763; January 2–27, 1764; March 7 to May 15, 1764; and September 13–19, 1764. The month before their departure he made a short visit in February 1765.

25. Loskiel, *History of the Mission of the United Brethren*, 228.

26. Ibid., 231.

11. *Indian Missions: A Critical Reappraisal, 1765–1766*

1. Merrill Jensen, *The Founding of a Nation: A History of the American Revolution, 1763–1776* (New York: Oxford University Press, 1968), 34.

2. Louis B. Wright, *The Atlantic Frontier* (New York: Knopf, 1949), 8.

3. Cavaioli, "A Profile of the Paxton Boys," 76.

4. Ibid.

5. Ibid., 78.

6. William C. Reichel, "Wyalusing and the Moravian Mission at Friedenshutten," *Transactions of the Moravian Historical Society*, vol. 1, pt. 5 (1871): 181. Also see Donehoo, *Indian Villages and Place Names*, 257. Heckewelder, in his "Delaware Names of Rivers and Localities in Pennsylvania," regards the word *Wyalusing* a corruption of *M'hwihilusing*, signifying "the place of the hoary veteran." *Mihilusis* signifies in Unami Delaware an old man; and *ing* or *ink* is the usual local suffix of that dialect. The site is two miles below present Wyalusing and one-half mile below Browntown. Sugar Run Creek is just opposite, on the west side of the river.

7. Reichel, "Wyalusing," 194. John Heckewelder visited Friedenshutten five times between May 1765 and September 1771. Otherwise, he had no connection with the mission.

8. George T. Hunt, *The Wars of the Iroquois* (Madison: University of Wisconsin Press, 1940), 137. The Andastes were the early tribes of the Susquehanock who were destroyed by the Iroquois. The remnants were called the Conestogas and were all killed by the Paxton Boys. Also see Beauchamp, ed., *Moravian Journals Relating to Central New York*, 221.

9. Roth, *Johann Roth*, 78. Despite his tribe's burying practices, Nanticoke Sam was admitted to the fellowship of the village. On August 10, 1766, he was baptized by Zeisberger and called Samuel, the first of his nation to join the Moravians. For the next forty years he remained active and involved with the Indian congregation. In the latter part of his life, he drifted away from the missions and was reported to have died near Sandusky in June 1805. See Fliegel, *Index*, 1:368–71.

10. De Schweinitz, *Zeisberger*, 315.

11. Roth, *Johann Roth*, 78; Charles A. Hanna, *The Wilderness Trail* (New York: G. P. Putnam's Sons, 1911), 205–6. Chief Newallike first visited the Wyalusing mission on July 29, 1765. He was the brother-in-law of Anton, the husband of Anton's sister Regina. He was known among the Delawares as a "preacher." From his first contact with the Moravians, Newallike was hostile to their work. Eventually he became a convert and was baptized by Zeisberger at Schoenbrunn on May 12, 1774, and called Augustine. On February 2, 1777, he left the church and became an apostate, creating problems for Zeisberger among the non-Christian Delawares. He was a friend of Captain Pipe. (See Fliegel, *Index*, 1:51, 309–10.) Echgohund, a Munsee chief, cooperated with Newallike and developed a reputation as a troublemaker among the Moravian converts. See Fliegel, *Index*, 1:15. He was married to Queen Esther, the most infamous of all the Montours. After her husband died, she ruled as chieftainess. In 1772, her village was six miles below Tioga Point, at present Ulster, in Bradford County, Pennsylvania. About that time she moved opposite Tioga Point and founded a new village called Queen Esther's Town. During the Pennamite wars and Butler's Wyoming expedition in July 1778 she is said to have led a company of warriors and personally beat to death more than a dozen white prisoners. In the fall of the same year Colonel Thomas Hartly destroyed her village. Afterward she settled near Cayuga Lake, where she died.

12. Fliegel, *Index*, 1:754.

13. Beauchamp, ed., *Moravian Journals Relating to Central New York*, 219.

14. Ibid., 220–21.

15. These meetings were called Helpers' Conferences. Up to this point in the Zeisberger diaries he called the church workers National Helpers or National Leaders. From this point on and throughout his future diaries he refers to them as Native Helpers.

16. Roth, *Johann Roth*, 81.

17. Edmund De Schweinitz, *The Moravian Manual: Containing an Account of the Moravian Church, or Unitas Fratrum* (Bethlehem, Pa.: Moravian Publication Office, 1869), 182.

18. De Schweinitz, *Zeisberger*, 316–17.

19. Roth, *Johann Roth*, 82.

20. Beauchamp, ed., *Moravian Journals Relating to Central New York*, 222. Gottlob Sensemann became a close associate of Zeisberger, accompanying him on his journey over the "Forbidden Path" in 1767 and serving as his assistant at the various missions for the next thirty-four years. He was the son of Joachim Sensemann, who survived the Gnadenhutten massacre in 1755. His mother had been killed at Gnadenhutten. He died at the Fairfield mission in Upper Canada on January 4, 1800 (Fliegel, *Index*, 2:205–7).

21. Beauchamp, *Aboriginal Place Names of New York*, 28–29. Zeniinge, better known as Otseningo, was the early form of Chenango and lay at the junction of the Chenango and Tioughnioga Rivers, now the site of Chenango, New York. Zeisberger came here on May 31, 1753, with the migrating Nanticokes and watched the founding of the village.

22. Beauchamp, ed., *Moravian Journals Relating to Central New York*, 224.

23. Ibid., 229.

24. Ibid., 232.

25. Ibid., 234.

26. Ibid., 236.

27. Ibid., 237.

28. De Schweinitz, *Zeisberger*, 320.

29. Beauchamp, ed., *Moravian Journals Relating to Central New York*, 238. I wish to thank Mr. and Mrs. Harry Schulze, owners of the Friedenshutten mission land, for the pleasant afternoon and evening of May 13, 1987, spent at their home in Wyalusing. They continue to keep alive the memory of the poignant events that occurred at that location so many years ago. Even today, remnants of Indian pottery from the mission period can be found in freshly plowed fields.

12. *Westward to the Delaware Country, 1767*

1. David Zeisberger, "Diary of David Zeisberger's Journal to the Ohio, Called in Delaware the 'Allegene,' From Sept. 20th to Nov. 16th, 1767," trans. Archer Butler Hulbert and William Nathaniel Schwarze, *The Moravian Records*, Ohio Archaeological and Historical Society Publication 21 (1912): 8.

2. Fliegel, *Index*, 4:1295.

3. Zeisberger, "Journal to the Allegene," 8–10. Also see Merle H. Deardorff, "Zeisberger's Allegheny River Indian Towns, 1767–1770," *Pennsylvania Archaeologist* 16 (1969): 1–19. Thanks to the late Merle Deardorff and his antiquarian colleagues at Warren, Pennsylvania, and to my friend Robert Currin, president of the Potter County Historical Society at Coudersport, Pennsylvania, the controversy that has surrounded Zeisberger's route over the Forbidden Path may have been solved. The results of our research lead to the following conclusion. (The names of the present communities are used rather than the complicated Indian names, which in some cases are given in parenthesis.) The Zeisberger party left Bethlehem on September 20, 1767, and arrived at Friedenshutten four days later. After spending six days at the mission village, they began the journey toward the Allegheny on September 30 and the next day crossed to the west side of the Susquehanna, passing the Indian village located just south of present Shesequin, Pennsylvania. The following day they passed Athens, Pennsylvania (Diaogu), crossed to the north side of the Chemung River (Tioga), and camped at a village of Tutelo Indians. On October 3 and 4 they continued up the Chemung, passing over the Great Flats below Painted Post, New York. At noon on the

fourth they reached the junction of the Tioga and Coshocton Rivers. These two rivers form the Chemung at Corning, New York. Turning south, they traveled up the Tioga, arriving on October 5 at the mouth of Cowanesque Creek where it joins the Tioga at Lawrenceville, New York, near the Pennsylvania state line. That evening they camped on the banks of the creek. The next morning they continued their journey westward up the Cowanesque and by noon had reached the Indian village of Pasigachkunk, a deserted Indian town near present Knoxville and Academy Corners, Tioga County, Pennsylvania. It was at this village that Post and Hays were turned back by the Senecas in 1760. There were two Indian towns about a mile apart on the south side of the present villages, one formerly inhabited by Unami Delaware and the other by Mingoes. The location had earlier been the home of Teedyuscung, who was instrumental in arranging the peace with the Indians during the French and Indian War. At this point they were forced to leave the unnavigable Cowanesque and travel on foot for the rest of the journey. Continuing westward on present Route 49 through today's villages of Harrison Valley and Mills in Potter County, Pennsylvania, they turned north, passing North Bingham, where they first encountered the "Big Swamp," a dense wilderness. On October 7, they again crossed the current New York and Pennsylvania state line and kept to the highlands just above Genesee, Pennsylvania, and Shongo, New York, where they forded the Genesee River. On October 8, they con-tinued along the highlands and again crossed the state line into the headwaters of the Eleven Mile Creek to present Shinglehouse, Pennsylvania, at the junction of the Honeyoe and Oswego Creeks. Zeisberger observed correctly, "This was the source of the Ohio." All three creeks are tributaries of the Allegheny River. Here they encountered a deep pine forest, the first Zeisberger had seen in America. (This description through Potter County was furnished by the late historian Floyd Bliss, thanks to Robert Currin, both of Coudersport, Pennsylvania.) On October 9, they reached the Allegheny and continued along the north bank, finally emerging from the dense swamp. Zeisberger noted that it was "incomparably wild." Now traveling on a good road, they reached the first of the three Seneca villages (Tiohuwaquaronta) near present Olean, Cattaraugus County, New York. By noon on the following day they arrived at the second village (Tiozinossungachta). This village was located at the former site of Cold Springs, New York, now covered by the Allegheny Reservoir. Inclement weather delayed the journey for a day. On October 13 they arrived at the third Seneca village (Conewango), now Warren, Pennsylvania. They continued down the Allegheny on October 14 and, after losing the trail for a day, arrived at their destination, Goschgoschunk (The place of the hogs) on October 16 (see Allegheny Region map).

4. M. H. Deardorff, "Zeisberger's Allegheny River Indian Towns," 1–19, n. 10. Zeisberger and Cammerhoff briefly met "Old Mud-eater" (whom they knew as Hagastaes) during their visit to Chenussio in 1750. Most of the villagers, including the chiefs, were "in their cups" during the entire visit. In the Seneca dialect, Hagastaes translates as "he mud eats," "just ordinary road mud, not clay or muck or anything fancy." Later he became a nemesis of Zeisberger (see Chapter 5). Although Hagastaes is a minor figure in recorded white history, he was a major influence among the western Senecas and was well known by the prominent Indians of his day. William Johnson wrote to General Gage on May 25, 1765, describing Hagastaes as "the most influential Indian as far as the Illinois." His anti-English attitude was well known, as was his massacre of most of the British garrisons at Fort Venango and Fort Presque Isle during the Pontiac uprising in 1763. It was through his efforts that the Genesee-Allegheny region was kept as a sanctuary for the Indians until his death in 1768.

5. Fliegel, *Index*, 1:41–46, 191–93, 320. Among the thousands of converts proselytized by the Moravians, Anton and Johannes were two of the most faithful and effective members of the Indian congregation. Neither wavered from the baptismal vows during the many years they lived at mission villages. From his first meeting with the Moravians, Anton lived for twenty-three years among the Christians. The evidence of his activity can be seen in the 431 references to him in the Fliegel *Index*. Baptized on February 8, 1750, he faithfully con-

tributed to the mission program until his death on September 5, 1773. He is buried in the Schoenbrunn Cemetery at New Philadelphia, Ohio.

Much the same can be said of Johannes Papunhank. His first contact with the Moravians came in the summer of 1759 when he and several of his fellow villagers from Wyalusing visited the new mission of Nain. Zeisberger first met him in the spring of 1763. Two months later, he was baptized Johannes. Thus began a friendship that lasted until Papunhank's death on May 15, 1775. He is also buried at Schoenbrunn, near his friend Anton.

6. Zeisberger, "Journal to the Allegene," 20.

7. Deardorff, "Zeisberger's Allegheny River Indian Towns," 6–8. Merle Deardorff has given us the most conclusive pattern of the Zeisberger villages along the Allegheny. The conclusions are based on circumstantial evidence. When Zeisberger arrived, he spoke of three towns. Deardorff places the upper town just north of the present village of West Hickory, Pennsylvania. The middle town was on the West Hickory flats, and the lower town, later called Damascus, was either on the fine flats at the mouth of Jamison Run or over the intervening mountain a mile further down at the mouth of Hunters Run. When Zeisberger returned the next year, the middle village was all but abandoned and most of the villagers were living at the upper town. Both were called Goschgoschunk.

8. Ibid., 7–8. Also Zeisberger, "Journey to the Allegene," 72. Zeisberger noted on August 25, 1768: "It appears that for several years negotiations have been pending for the purchase of all the Indian lands on the east side of the Ohio (Allegheny) from the Six Nations." Because of these rumors, the Allegheny Indians were taking no chances. If the east bank were to go white, they presumed they would be safe on the other side. When the final Treaty of Fort Stanwix was concluded in 1768, the maps were so distorted and the line so imprecise that the actual boundaries were not clarified for some years.

9. Frederick P. Stocker, "F. P. C. Schussele, The Power of the Gospel" (manuscript, Moravian College Library, 1931), 1–13. Christian Schussele's painting *The Power of the Gospel* has probably done more to perpetuate the memory of David Zeisberger than most of the writings about his life. Thousands of copies have been distributed. Commissioned in 1882, some ninety-five years after the incident, the painting erroneously pictures the event taking place in the depth of the Allegheny forest rather than in the council house.

Christian Schussele (1824–79) was born in the French province of Alsace. He came to America and settled in Philadelphia. In 1862, shortly after the picture was painted, he was afflicted with palsy and never painted again. The balance of his life was spent in teaching at the Academy of Fine Arts in Philadelphia. He died at the age of fifty-five. The painting, measuring 6'2" x 9'7", is displayed in the Moravian Church Archives building in Bethlehem, Pennsylvania.

10. Zeisberger, "Journal to the Allegene," 20–22.

11. Ibid., 25.

12. Ibid., 26.

13. Ibid., 23–24. Allemewi, also known as the Blind Chief, was among Zeisberger's first converts in the western theater. Without his assistance the mission on the Allegheny would have undoubtedly failed. His prominent role will be discussed in detail in the next chapter. He was baptized by Zeisberger on December 25, 1779, at the Lawunakhannek mission and died September 27, 1775, at Schoenbrunn, where he is buried.

14. Fliegel, *Index*, 1:20–21.

15. Zeisberger, "Journal to the Allegene," 28–29.

16. Ibid., 29–30.

17. Ibid., 31–32.

13. *Frustration on the Allegheny, 1768–1770*

1. Edwin A. Sawyer, *Christian's Spring: Noble Experiment in Communal Living and First Vocational School in Northampton County* (Nazareth, Pa.: Moravian Hall Square Museum

Craft Shop, 1988), 3–31. Christianbrunn (Christian's Spring) was one of several small communities located a few miles north of Bethlehem. Named after Count Zinzendorf's only son, who died in 1752, it became the home of the single Brethren's choir. Today only one (the single Brethren's house) of the many barns and buildings remains standing near the present Pennsylvania state highway 946.

2. David Zeisberger, "Diary of David Zeisberger and Gottlob Sensemann, Journey to Goschgoschunk on the Ohio and Their Arrival There, 1768," trans. Archer B. Hulbert and William N. Schwarze, The Moravian Records, *Ohio Archaeological and Historical Society Publications* 21 (1912): 42.

3. Ibid., 57.

4. Ibid., 58.

5. Ibid., 59.

6. Ibid., 67.

7. Ibid., 65.

8. Ibid., 65–66.

9. Ibid., 68.

10. Ibid., 71.

11. Ibid., 75. This is Zeisberger's first mention of the warrior chief Gendaskund. For further information see note 20.

12. Ibid., 93–94. Packanke was the principal chief of the Wolfe lineage in Netawatwes's Delaware Nation. The whites more frequently knew him as Custaloga. His first residence was recorded to be on the French Creek, in Pennsylvania, on lands given to him by the Senecas. George Washington had met him in 1753 immediately before the French and Indian War during his expedition to the French at Fort Le Boeuf. He fought with the French in the French and Indian War, but by 1759 he made peace with the English. After Pontiac's uprising in 1763, he moved to Kuskusky on the Beaver River near present New Castle, Pennsylvania. (This was Zeisberger's Kaskaskunk.) He died in 1776 and was succeeded by his nephew, Captain Pipe.

13. Ibid., 94. Beaver (Tamaqua) was the brother of Shingas and Pisquetomen and served as head chief of the Turkey-lineage Delawares in Netawatwes's Delaware Nation. He was the successor to the chieftainship following Shingas's death in the winter of 1763–64. All three brothers were nephews of the Delaware head chief Sassoonan (Allummapees, sons of Sassoonan's sister). Beaver died on August 20, 1769, and was buried near the site where Zeisberger would later found the Gnadenhutten mission on the Muskingum River. He was succeeded by Welapachtachiechen (Captain Johnny), who later became the convert Israel. At the time of Beaver's death, his village was located at Tuscarabi, on the Muskingum. Probably because of his close association with Netawatwes, he became a warm advocate of the Moravians. For the history of both Shingas and Beaver see William A. Hunter, "Documented Subdivisions of the Delaware Indians," paper presented at the annual meeting of the Eastern States Archaeological Federation in Dover, Delaware, 1974.

14. Tilde Marx, trans., "Diaries of the Moravian Missions in Western Pennsylvania, 1769–1772," transcripts in Merle Deardorff Papers, Warren Historical Society, Warren, Pennsylvania, 1–2. I have used the Tilde Marx translations of the mission diaries from January 8, 1769, to April 12, 1772. Marx was commissioned by Merle Deardorff, ethnohistorian and antiquarian from Warren, Pennsylvania. Three diaries contain many of Zeisberger's most profound religious and social comments.

15. Marx, trans., "Diaries," 7.

16. Ibid., 8.

17. Ibid., 18. En route to the new location Zeisberger recorded the following:

> March 30: We went down the creek [Allegheny River] in our canoes, which we had made ourselves, and spent the night near an oil well where, early in the morning,

> March 31, before our departure, the Indians drew 4 quarts of oil in a short time. Where the oil comes to the surface, there is a knee-deep layer of sand and mud, underneath this is—as it seems—a pure rock from where the oil probably comes. There are several places like this along the Creek, and when the latter has not much water, one can see the oil floating everywhere. The traders give about 3 shillings for a quart. It is said to be a good remedy, especially for rheumatism.

Eighty-eight years later almost to the day, Edwin L. Drake founded the Seneca Oil Company. On August 27, 1859, his driller, William A. (Uncle Billy) Smith, struck oil at sixty-nine feet. This became the first well drilled specifically for oil in the world and yielded eight to ten barrels a day. Drake's well was within fifteen miles of the site described in Zeisberger's diary.

18. Ibid., 19. Merle Deardorff places this village three miles north of the Upper Indian Town but on the east side of the Allegheny. It was at the junction of Hickory Creek and the Allegheny River, or near the site of present East Hickory, Forest County, Pennsylvania.

19. Ibid., 22. This is the first mention of the Indian Gatschenis and his wife. He was the brother-in-law of Anna Johanna, the wife of Johannes Papunhank. As Lucas and Pauline, they became faithful converts and remained with the congregation for the rest of their lives. Lucas died on January 31, 1808, at the Fairfield mission in Canada; Pauline had preceded him in death on December 8, 1777, at Lichtenau on the Muskingum.

20. Zeisberger, "Journey to Goschgoschunk, 1768," 75, 114. In December of the next year, Gendaskund was baptized as Jacob; he remained with the Christian congregation for seven years. On March 2, 1777, at the close of the Schoenbrunn mission, he became the leader of a rebellious group of converts and became an apostate.

21. Marx, trans., "Diaries," 36. Few Indians would have as much impact on Zeisberger's life as Glikhikan. He was truly a noble and majestic character. He played an important role in the mission for the next thirteen years until his ignominious death at the hands of Pennsylvania militiamen during the massacre at Gnadenhutten on March 8, 1782.

22. Ibid., 35.

23. Ibid.

24. Ibid., 38. Zeisberger's first contact with the Delaware Unami Chief Netawatwes occurred in July 1766. The chief was living on the Allegheny at Goschgoschunk. A peace message to the Iroquois was sent through Friedenshutten while Zeisberger was serving as head missionary. This message was the second time his name was mentioned in the diaries.

25. Ibid., 36. Gekelemukpechunk was located on a broad alluvial plain between large hills surrounding the valley of the Tuscarawas River, just east of Newcomerstown, Ohio. Netawatwes was called by the whites Chief Newcomer, thus the present name. Tuscarabi was an ancient Indian village just north of present Bolivar, Ohio. The name came from the Ottawa Indian word for "Open mouth of a stream." Sandy Creek joins the Tuscarawas River at the village site. Both villages were in the northeastern part of Ohio in present Tuscarawas County.

26. Ibid., 55–56.

27. Ibid., 56–58.

28. Ibid., 65.

29. Ibid., 68. See note 19 for further information on Lucas and Pauline. The baby Israel grew into manhood among the Christian converts and eventually married Salome, who died at the Goshen mission March 2, 1802. He remarried the convert Ester and remained with the congregation at Fairfield until 1810, then disappeared from the diaries.

30. Ibid., 78. Jeremias (Tschechquoapesch) was the brother of Johannes Papunhank. He stayed with the congregation and became a communicant and valuable native helper. He was with the first contingent to move to Schoenbrunn in April 1772, eventually dying at Lichtenau on December 24, 1778. His wife, Anna Caritas, was also among the first Schoen-

brunn contingent and remained with Zeisberger until she died on March 13, 1789, at the Pettquotting mission. Their son Israel was raised in the Christian missions and eventually appears as an adult convert at Pettquotting on February 15, 1789. He remained a Christian until April 1810, then disappears from the diaries. Beata, the mother of Lucas, lived to be nearly one hundred years old, dying on February 6, 1790, at Pettquotting.

31. Ibid., 78–79.
32. Ibid., 82.
33. Ibid., 77–78, 87–88.
34. Ibid., 86.
35. Ibid., 89–90.
36. Ibid., 90–91; emphasis added.

14. *Lagundo Utenunk on the Beaver, 1770–1771*

1. Marx, trans., "Diaries," 94–97.
2. Ibid., 97–98.
3. Ibid., 98–99.
4. Ibid., 100. Kaskaskunk, the site of Packanke's village, was known in 1770 as the new town. It was located at the junction of the Shenango River and Neshannock Creek. A previous village just south of present New Castle, Pennsylvania, called Old Kaskaskunk, was located at the junction of the Mahoning and Shenango Rivers, a few miles south of the new town. Originally, the old town was the home of the Delaware chiefs Shingas and his brother Beaver. They came there in 1759 as the French and Indian War was coming to a close. When General John Forbes captured Fort Duquesne in November 1758, the Delawares, who were allied with the French, moved north from their village (Sawcunk, or Old Shingas Town) at the mouth of the Beaver and Ohio Rivers to the Old Kaskaskunk location. Shortly after their arrival, Beaver moved over to the old village of Tuscarabi, on the Tuscarawas, now the site of Bolivar, Ohio. Packanke originally lived along the French Creek, but during the French and Indian War he moved to the Muskingum. At the close of the Pontiac uprising (1764), he moved back to the Beaver location and founded the New Kaskaskunk village. It was approximately five miles from Lagundo Utenunk.
5. Ibid.
6. Ibid., 100–101.
7. Ibid., 102–3.
8. Ibid., 103–4. This is just one of many references Zeisberger made regarding the effects of the blackcoat belt. It would plague him for the rest of his life.
9. Ibid., 107.
10. Ibid., 108.
11. Ibid., 111–12.
12. Ibid., 129.
13. Ibid., 135–36. Johann G. Jungmann was born April 19, 1720, at Hockheim, in the Palatinate. In 1731 he immigrated with his father to America and settled near Olney, Pennsylvania. There he became acquainted with the Moravians, whom he joined, to the great indignation of his family. In 1745 he married the widow of Gottlob Buettner and later served the church in various capacities at Falkner's Swamp, Gnadenhutten, Pachgatgoch, Bethlehem, and Friedenshutten until he was called to the Beaver River. His wife, Anna Margaret, was born in Philadelphia, the daughter of John Bechtel, a prominent Philadelphia merchant, also from the Palatinate region in Germany. Gottlob Sensemann first appeared in the mission field in October 1766. That same year he accompanied Zeisberger on a trip to Iroquois Indians at Onondaga. Two years later, he and Zeisberger founded the first mission on the Allegheny at Goschgoschunk. For some reason, Zeisberger never seemed to be com-

fortable with Sensemann during this period. He mentioned several times in his letters to Bethlehem that he could not leave the mission, even for short periods, with Sensemann in charge. Sensemann's principal deficiency, the lack of understanding the Indian dialect, could account for Zeisberger's reticence. He was twenty-six years old and had not been ordained when he left Lagundo Utenunk. Sensemann reappeared in 1780 at New Schoenbrunn and remained with Zeisberger for the next eighteen years. He died at the Fairfield mission on January 4, 1800. During this later period, Zeisberger does not indicate that he had any reservations regarding Sensemann's performance.

14. Ibid., 140, 143.

15. Ibid., 149.

16. Ibid., 124–25.

17. Ibid., 152–53.

18. Ibid., 154. It is believed that Netawatwes moved to the Muskingum sometime around 1764, founding the village of Gekelemukpechunk (New Comers' Town). He was living at this location in November 1764, when Colonel Henry Bouquet and his army arrived at the forks of the Muskingum near present Coshocton, Ohio. Several descriptions of the village other than Zeisberger's are extant. An excellent one was recorded in the diary of David McClure on September 21, 1772, during McClure's travels into the Ohio Country. He wrote: "This town is called New Comers Town by the English, & stands on the West Bank of the Muskingum, containing about 60 houses, some of logs & others the bark of trees, fastened by elm bark to poles stuck in the ground & bent over on the top. There are nearly 100 families. It is the principal town of the Delaware nation, & the resident of the King & the greater part of his councillors. There are several small villages up & down the river. The place is about 60 Miles above the mouth of the Muskingum. Eight or ten acres around the town are cleared. On the opposite side of the river is a large corn field, in rich low ground; it is enclosed within one common fence, & each family has its division to plant. Some houses are well built, with hewed logs, with stone chimnies, chambers & sellers. These, I was told, were built by english captives, in the time of the french wars" (David McClure, *Diary of David McClure, Doctor of Divinity, 1748–1820*, with notes by Franklin B. Dexter [New York: Knickerbocker Press, 1899], 61). The Baptist minister David Jones (1736–1820) visited the village on February 12, 1773. His comments are brief: "This town is situated on the west side of the river Muskingum, which is a pretty large stream. The proper pronunciation in Indian is MOOSKINGUNG, i.e. Elks Eye River. In the language an elk being called moos. This town takes its name from the name of the king, who is called Neetotwhealemon, i.e. New-comer" (David Jones, *A Journey of Two Visits Made to Some Nations on the West Side of the River Ohio, in the Years 1772 and 1773* [1865; rpt. Fairfield, Wash.: Ye Gallion Press, 1973], 90). Both men visited with Zeisberger and his Christian converts, who were living on the Muskingum at the Schoenbrunn and Gnadenhutten missions.

19. Edmund De Schweinitz, in his *Life and Times of David Zeisberger*, states that the missionary delivered the first Protestant sermon preached in Ohio. The statement is erroneous. Actually, it was the fourth "official" or documented sermon by an ordained minister. On December 25, 1750, frontiersman Christopher Frederick Post, not a minister, visited the present site of Coshocton and preached to the Indians. Rev. Charles Beatty, who visited Newcomerstown on September 21, 1766, delivered the "first" sermon. In the afternoon on the same day his associate, a Rev. Duffield, spoke. Two days later, Beatty gave the third sermon, thus Zeisberger's was the fourth.

20. Marx, trans., "Diaries," 156.

21. Ibid.

22. Ibid., 157.

23. Ibid.

24. Ibid., 160.

25. Ibid., 162.

26. Ibid., 163.
27. Ibid., 164.
28. Ibid., 165.
29. Ibid., 195. See also Rondthaler, *Heckewelder*, 3–108. Five years before Heckewelder's death on January 31, 1823, he published the first of three books on his life among the Delaware Indians. It was entitled *History, Manners, and Customs of the Indian Nations Who Once Inhabited Pennsylvania and the Neighboring States*. This publication was followed in 1820 with his *Narrative of the Mission of the United Brethren among the Delaware and Mohegan Indians*. In 1822, one year before his death, he published his final work, *Names, Which the Lenni Lenape, or Delaware Indians Gave to Rivers, Streams, and Localities within the State of Pennsylvania, New Jersey, Maryland and Virginia, with Their Significations*. All were published some forty years after his experience as a missionary. He began his mission work on arrival at Lagundo Utenunk in 1771 and terminated it fifteen years later in 1786 at the Pilgerruh mission in Ohio. Although he was active in the work of the Moravian Church in the years following his experience at Pilgerruh, he never returned as a full-time missionary. These years are explained in detail in my *Blackcoats among the Delaware* (Kent, Ohio: Kent State University Press, 1991). Heckewelder's three volumes became the primary source for historians writing on the Moravian missions. Nineteenth- and early twentieth-century scholars used his material extensively. Almost from the beginning, however, the material met some criticism, especially by historians writing on Delaware Indian history. The first volume, *History, Manners and Customs*, received critical reviews shortly after it was published, but that soon subsided and over the next hundred years it was accepted as a creditable primary source. Beginning in the middle of the twentieth century and continuing up to the present, scholars have questioned the material, particularly Heckewelder's reference to the orthography and ethnography of the Delaware culture. His descriptions of many of the events he witnessed during his fifteen years with the missions, written after a forty-year absence from the mission field, are at variance with the diaries written at the time these events actually occurred. Notwithstanding, we owe a great debt of gratitude to John Heckewelder. Without his writing, much of the marvelous history of this period and the lives of the men and women living in the Moravian missions would have been lost to the generations that followed.
30. Edward Rondthaler, *Life of John Heckewelder*, ed. B. H. Coates (Philadelphia: T. Ward, 1847), 62.
31. Marx, trans., "Diaries," 26. Zeisberger's letter to Nathaniel Seidel, November 2, 1771.
32. Ibid., 201. This is but one of several diary entries expressing the reaction of the Christian Indians on viewing a picture of the Christ.

15. *The Die Is Cast, 1772*

1. Marx, trans., "Diaries," 206.
2. Ibid. Gulpikamen, or Coolpesconain, was baptized by Cammerhoff in Bethlehem and called Ludwig on April 27, 1749. His brothers Johannes and Leonhard and his sister Caritas were baptized the same year. All were members of the mission station at Meniologameka and were friends of George Rex, the native mission leader. He left the mission sometime in 1752 but continued to be friends with the Christian converts, appearing again in the diaries twenty years later at Lagundo Utenunk. In the meantime, he become an important chief in Netwatwes's Delaware council. He appeared again in 1777 at Schoenbrunn as an enemy of the Christians. Later he took the name John Thompson and was one of the Delaware Indians who visited George Washington on May 10, 1779. He appears to have served the Americans during the Revolutionary War.

3. Marx, trans., "Diaries," 207.
4. Ibid., 207–8.
5. Ibid., 208.
6. Ibid.
7. Ibid., 216. Lucas (Gatschenis), baptized on December 3, 1769, was the "first fruit" of Zeisberger's missionary efforts on the Allegheny River in western Pennsylvania. His wife, Pauline, and their infant son, Israel, were baptized the same day. He became a communicant January 1, 1771, thirteen months later, and shortly after appears as a native helper to the congregation. With the exception of a few months in 1787, he remained a faithful convert. He died at the Fairfield mission January 31, 1808. His companion on the trip to the Muskingum, Petrus (Sapen), was baptized at Friedenshutten by Johann Schmick on Christmas Day 1766. Petrus had accompanied Zeisberger on his second trip to western Pennsylvania on May 9, 1768. For some unknown reason he disappears from the diaries after September 1776.
8. Ibid., 218.
9. Ibid., 218–19.
10. Ibid., 220–21.
11. Ibid., 221.
12. Ibid., 222–24.
13. August Carl Mahr, trans., "Zeisberger's Schoenbrunn Diary, 1772–1777," Collection 215, Ohio Historical Society, Columbus, Ohio, 1. Another translation is by William N. Schwarze, "Zeisberger's Schoenbrunn Diary, 1772–1777," box 141, folder 12, item 1, Moravian Church Archives.
14. De Schweinitz, in *Zeisberger*, 372, says there were twenty-eight in the party but does not reveal his source.
15. Schwarze, trans., "Schoenbrunn Diary," 1. The Mingo Town was three miles south of present Steubenville, Ohio, and today bears the name Mingo Junction. The location was an important confluence for both Indian and white traders. It was the eastern terminus of the Mingo Trail that led westward to join the Muskingum Trail near Gnadenhutten, Ohio. It was later called the Moravian Trail.
16. Ibid., 2.
17. Ibid.
18. Fliegel, *Index*, 1:15, 103, 331, Echpalawehund, or Acheodunt, was was one of the captains in the council of Chief Newellike who lived at that time on the Susquehanna just south of the Friedenshutten mission. He first appeared in the Moravian diaries on April 5, 1766, acting as a counselor for Chief Newellike. Between this date and 1772 there are thirty-eight entries in the *Index* listed under Acheodunt. Between 1772 and 1776 he was listed as Chief Echpalawehund and a captain in Netwatwes's council. Forty-three entries cover these four years. During both of these periods he was much involved in native Indian politics, visiting the Moravian missions and carrying dispatches for his chiefs. On February 6, 1774, he was baptized by Johann Schmick and called Petrus at the new mission of Gnadenhutten on the Muskingum. Thirteen months later he died at Massas Town and was buried at Gekelemukpechunk, March 19, 1775. For his short term as a convert there are sixty-seven entries listed under the name Petrus. Many members of his family joined the missions during this period, and most of his time was spent traveling on both mission and native council business trying to assist the missionaries.
19. The men and children in the bass canoe descended the Little Stillwater Creek, passing through the present cities of Dennison and Uhrichsville, Ohio. Just beyond they entered the Big Stillwater Creek and followed it a short distance to arrive at the Muskingum River just below present Midvale, Ohio.
20. Schwarze, trans., "Schoenbrunn Diary," 3.

16. *Chosen by the Lot, 1772*

1. Mahr, trans., "Schoenbrunn Diary," 5b.

2. Ibid., 7b; Kenneth G. Hamilton, "John Ettwein and the Moravian Church during the Revolutionary Period," *Transactions of the Moravian Historical Society*, vol. 12, pts. 3–4 (1940): 85–130. John Ettwein (1721–1802) came to America on the *Irene*, arriving in Bethlehem April 20, 1754. Among his fellow passengers were eleven-year-old John Heckewelder with his family and Christian Frederick Post. Ettwein remained active in church affairs all his life, serving in both Winston-Salem and Bethlehem. At the time he visited Zeisberger he was a member of the Provincial Helper's Council (PHC), Nathaniel Seidel's assistant, and official correspondent for the Moravian Church in America. He became president of the PHC in 1783, serving until his death. He encouraged the establishment of schools for Indian children and urged the missionaries to undertake ethnological studies. Ettwein was one of the most distinguished of all the early American Moravians.

3. Mahr, trans., "Schoenbrunn Diary," Appendix I, 161–73; Roth, *Johann Roth*, 118–52, contains the Ettwein and Roth journals for this trip.

4. Box 137, folder 9, item 1, p. 1, Moravian Church Archives. The three slips read as follows:

a) The Saviour approves.
b) The Saviour does not approve this.
c) –_____________.

The blank slip indicated that no action would be taken on the question at the present time. The secretary recorded the results in the minutes.

5. Ibid.

6. Ibid., 3.

7. Olmstead, *Blackcoats among the Delaware*, 124–51. Subsequent diary entries do not indicate that this provision was later enforced. The only record of communal sharing is found at Zeisberger's last mission at Goshen when the fruit from the orchards was shared by the community.

8. The records of this conference can be found in box 137, folder 9, pp. 1–5, Moravian Church Archives. See also John Ettwein, "Brother Ettwein's Account of His Visit in Lagundo-Utenunk, on the Beaver Cr.," *Transactions of the Moravian Historical Society*, vol. 12, pts. 3–4 (1940): 342–57.

9. With few exceptions, Zeisberger enjoyed good health throughout his life. This bout of sickness may have been a touch of malaria, which was common at Schoenbrunn, especially from July through October.

10. It was important for Zeisberger to bring the members of his Helpers' Conference to Schoenbrunn as quickly as possible. The men and women who accompanied him were among the most important of the conference members. He also wanted them on hand to consult with and be advised by Ettwein during his visit to the village.

11. Ettwein, "Brother Ettwein's Account," 345. Ettwein gives a fine description of the village site: "It has a very beautiful location in a plain, some 10 miles in length and several miles in breadth, near one very large spring and several smaller ones. They, together, give rise to a creek, on which one can paddle during most of the year right up to the settlement, in canoes. Between the settlement itself and the Muskingum river is a stretch of very rich bottom land, more than half a mile wide and probably 5 miles long, suitable for Indian corn; it is covered almost entirely by walnut and locust trees."

12. Ibid., 348.

13. Mahr, trans., "Schoenbrunn Diary," Appendix IV, 185–89. Heckewelder, writing forty-eight years later, records a much different version, which can be found in Appendix D. His version, except for the provision for going to war, was not found in any other archival source I explored or was known by the archivist at Bethlehem. Where Hecke-

welder obtained his highly anglicized version is unknown. The draft originally proposed by the Lagundo-Utenunk conference, though not as sophisticated as the Heckewelder version, sounds far more authentic and would likely be better understood by the Indian converts.

14. Ettwein, "Brother Ettwein's Account," 351–52.

15. McClure, *Diary*, 50–51.

16. Ettwein, "Brother Ettwin's Account," 353–54.

17. Mahr, trans., "Schoenbrunn Diary," 9. This was the second temporary round-log structure to be used as the meeting house. The first was a combination home for Zeisberger and the church meeting house. Later, after the tools were retrieved from Great Island, this structure was replaced by a permanent split-log building.

18. Ibid., 11a.

19. Ibid., 14a and note 14a. Mahr notes, "To many of the Algonquin tribes, especially those who lived in the western plains, bleeding was used as a method of purification. The practice of vomiting was found in the Amazon Basin and in areas around the Gulf of Mexico, where the Shawnee probably borrowed the practice when they resided in Florida."

20. Ibid., 13a.

21. Ibid., 19b.

22. Ibid., 22a, also box 137, folder 3, Moravian Archives.

17. *An Organizational Nightmare, 1773*

1. Mahr, trans., "Schoenbrunn Diary," 31.

2. Box 137, folder 4, April 12, 1773, Moravian Church Archives.

3. Mahr, trans., "Schoenbrunn Diary," 33a, 34a.

4. Box 137, folder 3, December 31, 1772, Moravian Church Archives.

5. "Brother John Heckewelder's Report of Their Travels by Water from Lagundo-Utenunk to Walhik Thuppeek in April," in Mahr, trans., "Schoenbrunn Diary," Appendix II, 174–78.

6. Ibid., 175a, n. 4, and 176a, n. 3.

7. Ibid., 175a–175b.

8. Ibid., 176a, n. 2. This was Captina Island, about two miles downstream from present Dilles Bottom, Ohio.

9. Ibid., 176b, n. 5.

10. Ibid., 177a, n. 3.

11. August Carl Mahr, trans., "Schmick's Gnadenhutten Diary, 1773–1777," Collection 215, Ohio Historical Society, Columbus, Ohio, 1. Roth began the Gnadenhutten diary on May 1, 1773, and continued until the Schmicks arrived in August.

12. August Carl Mahr, "Historical Reasons for the Founding of Schoenbrunn," Collection 215, Ohio Historical Society, Columbus, Ohio, 21–23.

13. Ibid., 23.

14. Ibid., 25–26.

15. Ibid., 26.

16. Mahr, trans., "Schoenbrunn Diary," 125b.

17. Ibid., 35b.

18. Ibid., 35b, 36a, 36b, 37a, for these and the following quotations regarding the conference.

19. Ibid., 41b; Mahr, trans., "Gnadenhutten Diary," 14a. After this point Johann Schmick would be the author of the Gnadenhutten diary.

20. Mahr, "Schoenbrunn Diary," 40b–41a.

21. Levering, *History of Bethlehem*, 261.

22. Lawrence W. Hartzell, *Ohio Moravian Music* (Winston-Salem, N.C.: Moravian Music Foundation Press, 1988), 35.

23. Ibid., 28a.

24. Schmick's diary for this period frequently mentions the schools and their sessions, whereas Zeisberger's diaries seldom carry any information on the schools at Schoenbrunn during this early period. Heckewelder was brought to the missions to be the schoolteacher. Not once from the beginning of Schoenbrunn in 1772 until December 4, 1775, does Zeisberger mention Heckewelder having any connection with the schools.

25. Mahr, trans., "Schoenbrunn Diary," 47b.

26. Jones, *Diary*, 89. David Jones later distinguished himself as the chaplain of Anthony Wayne's army during his campaign against the Indians in 1793–94. He was with Wayne at the signing of the Greenville Treaty in August 1795.

27. Butterfield, *Girtys*, 338. The Quakers noted in their journal, under the date of July 19, 1773, "We had a conference with Captain White Eyes, a Delaware Chief, who was on his return from Philadelphia. He expressed much satisfaction at our arrival, and said he would go with us [to the Delaware capital]."

28. Mahr, trans., "Schoenbrunn Diary," 47b–52.

29. Mahr, trans., "Gnadenhutten Diary," 31b; "Schoenbrunn Diary," 56b. See also Appendix E.

30. Mahr, trans., "Schoenbrunn Diary," 44a, 44b.

18. *Lord Dunmore and His Shawnee Indian War, 1774*

1. Mahr, trans., "Schoenbrunn Diary," 60a.

2. Ibid., 65a.

3. Ibid., 63a.

4. Neville B. Craig, *The History of Pittsburgh* (Pittsburgh: J. R. Weldin, 1917), 98–99. See also *Pennsylvania Archives*, 1st ser., in 12 vols., 4:593.

5. *Frontier Forts*, 2:123. Edmonstone sold all of the pickets, stones, bricks, timber, and iron in the walls and some of the buildings of the fort and redoubts for a sum of £50. The fort was then abandoned. Most of the buildings were not torn down, but the remaining structures were in sad repair.

6. Ibid., 124.

7. Ibid. See also Neville B. Craig, ed., *The Olden Time*, 2 vols. (1846; rpt. Cincinnati: Clarke, 1876), 1:432.

8. Craig, ed., *Olden Time*, 1:437; *Pennsylvania Archives*, 4:477.

9. Craig, ed., *Olden Time*, 439; *Pennsylvania Archives*, 4:484–85.

10. Craig, ed. *Olden Time*, 437–38.

11. Ibid., 442; *Pennsylvania Archives*, 4:493.

12. Reuben Gold Thwaites and Louise Phelps Kellogg, eds., *Documentary History of Dunmore's War, 1774* (Harrisonburg, Va.: C. J. Carrier Company, 1974), 371.

13. Randolph C. Downes, *Council Fires on the Upper Ohio* (Pittsburgh: University of Pittsburgh Press, 1969), 160; Peter Force, ed., *American Archives*, 4th ser., 9 vols. (Washington, D.C., 1837–53), 1:468.

14. Mahr, trans., "Schoenbrunn Diary," 61b, 63a.

15. Force, ed., *American Archives*, 4th ser., 1:468.

16. Ibid.

17. Ibid.; Craig, *Olden Time*, 2:38–39.

18. Mahr, trans., "Schoenbrunn Diary," 63b.

19. Downes, *Council Fires*, 162.

20. Thwaites and Kellogg, eds., *Dunmore's War*, 11. Colonel John Gibson was born in Lancaster, Pennsylvania, in 1740. He received a good education and entered the army in

1758 under General Forbes. At the close of the war he returned to the Indian trade and was captured during the Pontiac uprising by Indians who threatened to burn him at the stake. He was saved after being adopted by an Indian woman and later freed during the Bouquet expedition and continued to trade among the Indians. His wife was killed at the massacre at Yellow Creek. Gibson lived to be eighty-two and died in western Pennsylvania in 1822.

21. Thwaites and Kellogg, eds., *Dunmore's War*, 9–19. Daniel Greathouse died the following year of measles.

22. Mahr, trans., "Schoenbrunn Diary," 63b.

23. Ibid., 64b.

24. *Pennsylvania Archives*, 4:502.

25. Ibid., 513.

26. Ibid.

27. Ibid.

28. Ibid., 525, 533; Mahr, trans., "Gnadenhutten Diary," 59b.

29. Mahr, trans., "Schoenbrunn Diary," 70a, 70b. Sir William Johnson had just over a month to live. He died on July 11, 1774, in the midst of a Indian conference, probably of heart failure.

30. Ibid., 71b; *Pennsylvania Archives*, 4:508.

31. Mahr, trans., "Gnadenhutten Diary," 58a.

32. The Gachnawage Indians (Canawhaga) were former Mohawks who had immigrated to Canada and later were baptized by French missionaries living near St. Regis.

33. Mahr, trans., "Schoenbrunn Diary," 72a.

34. *Pennsylvania Archives*, 4:531–32.

35. Ibid.

36. Mahr, trans., "Schoenbrunn Diary," 77b, 78a.

37. *Pennsylvania Archives*, 4:553.

38. Ibid., 552.

39. Mahr, trans., "Schoenbrunn Diary," 80b.

40. Thwaites and Kellogg, eds., *Dunmore's War*, xvii.

41. Ibid., 302.

42. Ibid., xxi; Force, ed., *American Archives*, 4th ser., 1:1017–18.

43. Matthew Elliot appeared again in Zeisberger's life several times, first, as an enemy of the missions and later, described by Zeisberger as a friend and benefactor of the Christian Indians. In May 1791, he arranged for the Moravians to live on an estate at the mouth of the Detroit River owned by Elliot and his business partner, Alexander McKee.

44. Mahr, trans., "Schoenbrunn Diary," 87b.

45. Thwaites and Kellogg, eds., *Dunmore's War*, 302.

46. Ibid., 303.

47. Ibid., 303–4; *Pennsylvania Archives*, 4:586–87; Mahr, trans., "Schoenbrunn Diary," 90a. When sold, the booty taken by Crawford's men at the Mingo villages amounted to 305 pounds and 15 shillings. The money was divided among his men.

48. Downes, *Council Fires*, 177.

49. Mahr, trans., "Schoenbrunn Diary," 88b; emphasis added.

50. Ibid., 90b.

51. Thwaites and Kellogg, eds. *Dunmore's War*, 384.

52. Mahr, trans., "Schoenbrunn Diary," 92a.

53. Ibid., 93b.

54. Mahr, trans., "Schoenbrunn Diary," 99b.

19. *A Hard, Bloody, and Tragic Business, 1775*

1. John P. McKay, Bennett D. Hill, and John Buckler, *A History of World Societies*, 2d ed. (Boston: Houghton Mifflin, 1988), 773–74.

2. Richard M. Ketchum, ed., *The American Heritage Book of the Revolution* (New York: American Heritage, 1958), 6.
3. Mahr, trans., "Schoenbrunn Diary," 101b.
4. Ibid., 101b, 102a.
5. Ibid., 102a, 102b.
6. Ibid.
7. Ibid.
8. Mahr, trans., "Schoenbrunn Diary," 105a.
9. Ibid., 107a, also Mahr's notes 2, 3, and 4.
10. Zeisberger usually recorded the village name as "Koshachkink," but most historians spell the name as shown here.
11. Ibid., 109a.
12. Ibid., 111a, 111b.
13. Ibid., 113.
14. *Dictionary of American Biography*, s.v. "John Murray, Earl of Dunmore." After trying to incite the slaves to insurrection, Dunmore fought the colonials at the Battle of Great Bridge and was defeated on December 9, 1775. On January 1, 1776, he bombarded and fired the city of Norfolk. He then left Virginia and returned to England. Several years later, he returned as the governor of the Bahamas (1787–96). Though personally brave, Dunmore showed weakness in crisis, and his rash measures brought about his own downfall. He died on March 5, 1809. Dr. John Connolly, "A Narrative of the Transactions, Imprisonment, and Sufferings of John Connolly, an American Loyalist and Lt. Col. in His Majesty's Service," *Pennsylvania Magazine of History and Biography* 12 (1888): 315. Also see Reuben G. Thwaites and Louise P. Kellogg, eds., *The Revolution on the Upper Ohio, 1775–1777* (Port Washington, N.Y.: Kennikat Press, 1970), x, xi.
15. Mahr, trans., "Schoenbrunn Diary," 114a, 114b.
16. Mahr, trans., "Gnadenhutten Diary," 90b, 91a, 91b. This visit marked the first time Cornstalk (Holoqueska) had been in any of the Moravian villages.
17. Thwaites and Kellogg, eds., *Revolution on the Upper Ohio*, 38–40. On July 16, Zeisberger recorded in his diary that seven of the former Mingo prisoners, along with twenty strange Indians carrying six barrels of rum, passed through the villages en route to the Shawnees.
18. Ibid., 34. James Wood's father, with the same name, served with Washington in the French and Indian War. The son was born in 1750 and served as a captain in Dunmore's War. He remained active throughout the Revolution, retiring as a brigader general. He was the governor of Virginia between 1796 and 1799 and died at his home in Winchester in 1813. Also see Force, ed., *American Archives*, 4th ser., 2:1209.
19. *Pennsylvania Archives*, 1st ser., 4:683–84.
20. Connolly, "Narrative," 281–86.
21. Thwaites and Kellogg, eds., *Revolution on the Upper Ohio*, 41. The Shawnee chiefs attending this first meeting were Cornstalk, his brother Nimwha, Wryneck, Blue Jacket, Silver Heels, and about fifteen subchiefs.
22. Ibid., 45–65.
23. Ibid., 64.
24. Ibid., 66–67.
25. Force, ed., *American Archives*, 4th ser., 2:1723.
26. Craig, *Olden Time*, 1:444–45. John Neville (1731–1803) was born in Virginia and served with Washington during Braddock's expedition in 1755. He settled at Winchester, where he served as the sheriff. He had large land interests in the neighborhood of Pittsburgh and later made his home on Chartier's Creek. He was chosen as the delegate of West Augusta County to the Virginia Convention in 1774 but was too sick to attend. He died on Montour's Island in 1803.

27. Mahr, trans., "Schoenbrunn Diary," 119a, 119b.

28. Ibid., 122b; Mahr, trans., "Gnadenhutten Diary," 96a.

29. Mahr, trans., "Schoenbrunn Diary," 122b, 123a.

30. Thwaites and Kellogg, eds., *Revolution on the Upper Ohio*, xii–xiii.

31. Ibid., 20, 33, 77–78, also *Dunmore's War*, 191, 242, 426–27.

Lewis Morris (1726–98), a resident of New York State, graduated from Yale in 1746. During the Revolutionary War he joined the patriot cause and was elected to Congress in 1775 and made commissioner of Indian affairs. He was one of the signers of the Declaration of Independence the following year. He died at Morrisania in 1798.

James Wilson (1742–98) was born in Scotland and settled in Pennsylvania in 1766, later becoming a prominent statesman and a signer of the Declaration in 1776. He supported the patriots and was one of the delegates to the Second Continental Congress. He also became a member of the Constitutional Convention in 1787–89. In 1789 he was appointed by Washington to the Supreme Court of the United States and held that office until his death in 1798.

Colonel John Walker (1744–1809), the son of Dr. Thomas Walker, was born in Albemarle, Virginia. He was captured by the British during the Revolution and after the war served as the United States senator from Virginia by appointment in 1790. He died in 1809.

Dr. Thomas Walker (1715–94) was born in King and Queen County, near the Rappahannock River. He fought as a major in the French and Indian War. An ardent Whig, he served on several Revolutionary committees. Jefferson shared his interest in scientific pursuits and western discovery. Dr. Walker died at his estate of Castle Hill in 1794.

Andrew Lewis (1720–81), born in Ireland as the third son of John Lewis, came with his family to the new settlements of Augusta County. Having been raised on the frontier, his early years fitted him for wilderness life. In 1754, he joined Washington and was wounded at Fort Necessity and in 1758 served as an officer in the Forbes expedition. He was also the commander of the second wing of Dunmore's army that fought the Indians at the Battle of Point Pleasant in 1774. He fought bravely during the Revolutionary War as a brigadier general. He died in 1781.

Adam Stephen was a Scot and educated as a physican. He came early to America and settled in the lower valley. He fought as a major with Washington at the Battle of Fort Necessity. He was severely wounded at Braddock's defeat in 1755. An ardent Whig, he fought in the Revolution at the Battles of Princeton and Trenton and was promoted to major general and served with distinction at the Battle of Brandywine. He died at his home in Martinsburg in 1791. Tall and powerfully built, he was much feared by the Indians.

32. Thwaites and Kellogg, eds., *Revolution on the Upper Ohio*, 126–27.

33. Mahr, trans., "Gnadenhutten Diary," 98a.

34. Mahr, trans., "Schoenbrunn Diary," 124b.

35. Ibid., 125a.

36. Ibid.

20. *The Pasture of Light, 1776*

1. Mahr, trans., "Schoenbrunn Diary," 130a.

2. Ibid., 130b.

3. Ibid., 131b.

4. Ibid., 132a, 132b.

5. Ibid. Both of the Killbucks, Sr. and Jr., were called John. To save confusion, I refer to the son by his Indian name Gelelemend. Also see Wallace, *Indians in Pennsylvania*, 176–77.

6. Mahr, trans., "Schoenbrunn Diary," 133a.

7. Ibid., 137b.

8. Mahr, trans., "Lichtenau Diary," 137b, 138a, 138b. Beginning with this note, the Zeisberger diary is now contained in the translation for Lichtenau. The original German manuscripts are in box 147, Moravian Church Archives. No Schoenbrunn diaries are extant from April 10 to December 31, 1776.

9. Ibid., 138a, 138b.

10. Ibid., 139a.

11. Ibid., 139a, 139b.

12. Ibid., 140a, 140b. Welapachtachiechen, or Captain Johnny, was a member of the Turkey Clan. His village of Assinnink, near present Lancaster, contained approximately ten families and was the former residence of Captain White Eyes. See Mahr, trans., "Lichtenau Diaries," 80a, n. 1, and 129a, n. 1; also C. A. Weslager, *The Delaware Indians: A History* (New Brunswick, N.J.: Rutgers University Press, 1989), 295.

13. Mahr, trans., "Lichenau Diary," 143a.

14. Ibid., 143b.

15. Ibid., 144a.

16. Ibid., 145a.

17. Ibid., 145b. The "further assistance" indicated that white journeyman farmers and craftsmen were to be sent to teach husbandry and other crafts to the natives. The prospect of these additional white people coming into Indian territory did not please the council and dealt the death blow to the project.

18. Ibid. The departure of the individual members of the council indicated silent disapproval of White Eyes's proposal. Also see Gregory Schaaf, *Wampum Belts and Peace Trees* (Golden, Colo.: Fulcrum, 1990), 80–82.

19. Mahr, trans., "Lichtenau Diary," 146a.

20. Ibid., 146b, 147a.

21. Ibid., 147a.

22. Ibid., 149a, 149b. Alexander McKee, a native of Pennsylvania and the son of Thomas McKee, like his father, became a trader among the Indians. Intelligent and literate, McKee became a major character in David Zeisberger's life, playing an early role as his nemesis, then later as his friend and benefactor. He shortly defected to the British and would become their deputy Indian agent at Detroit. He died of lockjaw on January 14, 1799, at Malden, Ontario. See Thwaites and Kellogg, eds., *Revolution on the Upper Ohio*, 74–75. George Morgan, the son of Evan Morgan, was born in Philadelphia in 1742 and as a young man became a trader among the Indians. He later joined the prominent trading firm of Baynton, Wharton, Morgan & Co. Congress appointed him the Indian agent in April 1776 just before this trip. See Thwaites and Kellogg, eds., *Revolution on the Upper Ohio*, 31–32, and Schaaf, *Wampum Belts*, 111–209. Morgan was instrumental in organizing the Indian Treaty of 1776. A fine biography is Max Savelle, *George Morgan, Colony Builder* (New York: Columbia University Press, 1932).

23. Mahr, trans., "Lichtenau Diary," 149a, 149b.

24. Ibid., 150a. August Mahr's English translation of the Muskingum Valley Moravian diaries terminates with the July 1, 1776, entry. With two exceptions, Heckewelder's diary at Schoenbrunn from January 1 to April 21, 1777, and a few pages of the New Schoenbrunn diaries by William Schwarze, no further English translations have been made. In October 1989, I commissioned Margaret Wilde, an assistant at the Moravian Archives in Bethlehem, Pennsylvania, to complete the translation from July 7, 1776, through September 3, 1781. Now, for the first time, we have an English translation of these critical years on the American western frontier. This translation encompasses over three hundred pages of the original diaries written mainly by Zeisberger with a few by John Heckewelder. The following notes will show the box and folder number and the date of the original entry, for example, 147:2, July 13, 1776 (box 147, folder 2, July 13, 1776).

25. Wilde, trans., "Lichtenau Diary," 147:2, July 13, 1776.

26. Ibid., 147:2, July 29, August 11, 1776.

27. Schaaf, *Wampum Belts*, 143–60.

28. Fliegel, *Index*, 3:1025–28.

29. Wilde, trans., "Lichtenau Diary," 147:2, August 27, 1776.

30. Ibid., 147:2, September 14, 1776; Force, ed., *American Archives*, 5th ser., 2:339; Thwaites and Kellogg, eds., *Revolution on the Upper Ohio*, 199–204.

31. Schaaf, *Wampum Belts*, 161–96.

32. Thwaites and Kellogg, eds., *Revolution on the Upper Ohio*, 191. Born in Ireland in 1722, John Montgomery immigrated to America in 1740 and settled at Carlisle, Pennsylvania, becoming a successful merchant. He fought as a captain in the French and Indian War and was appointed by Congress in July 1776 as a commissioner for the treaty conference at Pittsburgh. He later fought as a colonel in the Revolutionary War. He helped to found Dickinson College after the war and died in 1808. Jasper Yeats was a member of a prominent Philadelphia family and was born in that city in 1745. He became a lawyer and an eminent jurist, later becoming a member of the supreme court of Pennsylvania (1791–1817). He was a member of the Pennsylvania delegation that ratified the Constitution. He died at his home in Lancaster in 1817.

33. Schaaf, *Wampum Belts*, 186.

34. Ibid., 191.

35. Wilde, trans., "Lichtenau Diary," 147:2, November 5, 1776.

36. Delaware Tribe of Western Oklahoma, *Turtle Children*, Indian Child Welfare Program, title 2 (Andarko, Okla.: Bureau of Indian Affairs, 1985), 32–33.

37. Wilde, trans., "Lichtenau Diary," 147:2, November 5, December 11, 1776. William Edwards would remain at Zeisberger's side for the next twenty-five years. See Olmstead, *Blackcoats among the Delaware*, 191–92.

38. Wilde, trans., "Lichtenau Diary," November 16, 1776.

39. Ibid., 147:2, November 20, December 23, 1776.

40. Ibid., 147:2, November 24, 1776.

41. Ibid., 147:2, December 31, 1776.

21. *A Conspiracy on the Muskingum, 1777*

1. Ketchum, ed., *American Heritage Book of the Revolution*, 129–31.

2. Jack M. Sosin, *The Revolutionary Frontier, 1763–1783* (New York: Holt, Rinehart and Winston, 1967), 108; Downes, *Council Fires*, 182; Force, ed., *American Archives*, 4th ser., 1:1347–49.

3. Wilde, trans., "Lichtenau Diary," 147:2, January 20, 1777; Thwaites and Kellogg, eds., *Revolution on the Upper Ohio*, 206, n. 47.

4. Mahr, trans., "Schoenbrunn Diary," 147a, n. 1. Killbuckink or Killbuck Town was located on the upper extremities of Killbuck Creek in Killbuck Township, Holmes County, at present Killbuck, Ohio, and was shown on the Hutchins map dated 1764. Heckewelder, in his entry for January 24, page 146b, advises that Killbuck, Sr., had just returned from Philadelphia "and is now totally blind."

5. Ibid., 150b.

6. Ibid., 149a. Walhondink means a "place where there is a ditch or trench." It was seventeen miles up the Walhonding River from present Coshocton, Ohio, at a point where the confluence of the Mohican and the Kokosing Rivers forms the Walhonding.

7. Ibid., 150b.

8. William N. Schwarze, trans., "Schmick's Gnadenhutten Diary," box 144, folder 12, item 2, March 6, 1777, Moravian Church Archives, Bethlehem, Pa.

9. Wilde, trans., "Lichtenau Diary," 147:2, March 2, 1777.

10. Ibid., 147:2, March 11, 1777.
11. Ibid.
12. Ibid., 147:2, March 14, 1777.
13. Ibid., 147:2, March 18, 1777.
14. Schwarze, trans., "Gnadenhutten Diary," 144:13, March 19, 1777. Schmick is the only diarist who mentions the name of the courier who carried this message from Morgan. Under his entry of March 19, he wrote: "From Pittsburgh there came Mr. O'Hare with the uncle of White Eyes with some pleasant speeches addressed to the Delaw. Shawnee, and Delemattenoes [Wyandot], and went with them to Goschachgunk on March 20." James O'Hare was an Irishman who entered the Indian trade at Fort Pitt sometime before 1773. He was the quartermaster of the Ninth Virginia Regiment during the Revolution. He filled a similar office under General Anthony Wayne in 1794. After the Revolution he became a businessman at Pittsburgh and established the first glass manufacture west of the Alleghenies. He died in 1810, leaving a large estate mainly in land. His daughter married William Croghan, Jr., nephew of George Rogers Clark. See Thwaites and Kellogg, eds., *Revolution on the Upper Ohio*, 253–54, n. 1.
15. Wilde, trans., "Lichtenau Diary," 147:2, March 21, 1777.
16. Schwarze, trans., "Gnadenhutten Diary," 144:13, March 22, 1777.
17. Mahr, trans., "Schoenbrunn Diary," 153b.
18. Ibid., 154a; emphasis added.
19. Schwarze, trans., "Gnadenhutten Diary," 144:13, March 24, 1777.
20. Mahr, trans., "Schoenbrunn Diary," 154b.
21. Ibid., 155a.
22. Ibid.
23. Schwarze, trans., "Gnadenhutten Diary," 144:13, April 2, 1777; Mahr, trans., "Schoenbrunn Diary," 155a, 155b.
24. Ibid.
25. Mary C. Darlington, ed., *Fort Pitt and Letters from the Frontier* (Pittsburgh: J. R. Weldin, 1892), 203–4; emphasis added. This letter confirms Schmick's versions of the events of April 1 and 2 and reveals the incident that provoked the abandonment of Schoenbrunn. This is the first time O'Hare's letter has been published in connection with this episode. He erred by one day. The events occurred on April 1, rather than April 2, 1777.
26. Mahr, trans., "Schoenbrunn Diary," 155b.
27. Ibid., 156b, 157a.
28. Ibid., 158b–59b.
29. Reuben Gold Thwaites and Louise Phelps Kellogg, eds., *Frontier Defense on the Upper Ohio, 1777–1778* (Madison: Wisconsin Historical Society, 1912), x; Thwaites and Kellogg, eds., *Revolution on the Upper Ohio*, 96, n. 17. Guy Carleton (1724–1808), the governor of Canada, resigned shortly after and was replaced in 1778 by Sir Frederick Haldimand. In 1782, Carleton was appointed commander in chief of all British forces in America and carried out a policy of clemency and conciliation.
30. Thwaites and Kellogg, eds., *Revolution on the Upper Ohio*, 256, n. 5. Edward Hand was born in Ireland December 31, 1744. Educated as a physician, he was appointed as a surgeon's mate and came to America with the Eighteenth Royal Irish Guard in 1767. He was assigned to Fort Pitt, where he became popular with all classes. At the outbreak of the Revolution, he was living in Lancaster, Pennsylvania, and joined Washington as a lieutenant colonel of the First Pennsylvania Regiment. In April 1777, he was appointed brigader general and sent west to be commander at Fort Pitt. At his request, he was recalled in 1778 and served for the balance of the war with General Washington's army. He was with the army at Yorktown. At the end of the war he retired to his estate at Lancaster and died in 1802. He was of a genial disposition, popular with both his superiors and his subordinates.
31. Thwaites and Kellogg, eds., *Frontier Defense*, xi.
32. Fleigel, *Index*, 3:1026–27.

33. Thwaites and Kellogg, eds., *Frontier Defense*, 18–19.
34. Wilde, trans., "Lichtenau Diary," 147:3, July 7, 1777.
35. Ibid., 147:3, July 21, 22, 23, 1777.
36. Thwaites and Kellogg, eds., *Frontier Defense*, 27–29. A complete copy of this letter of July 9, 1777, can be found in this reference.
37. Wilde, trans., "Lichtenau Diary," 147:3, August 5, 1777.
38. Ibid., 147:4, August 7, 1777.
39. Ibid., August 8, 1777.
40. Ibid.
41. Ibid., August 10, 1777.
42. Ibid., August 20, 21, 22, 1777.
43. Ibid., September 5, 7, 1777.
44. Ibid., 147:4, September 12, 1777; emphasis added.
45. Ibid. Also see Savelle, *George Morgan*, 146–47.
46. Wilde, trans., "Lichtenau Diary," 147:4, September 15, 1777.
47. Ibid.
48. Ibid., September 17, 1777; Thwaites and Kellogg, eds., *Frontier Defense*, 86–87, 91–92. Both letters were written at Fort Pitt, Hand's on September 17 and Morgan's on September 18.
49. Wilde, trans., "Lichtenau Diary," 147:5, September 22, 23, 1777. Zeisberger's letter of September 22 can be found in Thwaites and Kellogg, eds., *Frontier Defense*, 93–97; for the other entries see ibid., 100–104.
50. Wilde, trans., "Lichtenau Diary," 147:5, September 27, 1777.
51. Ibid., October 2, 6, 1777; Thwaites and Kellogg, eds., *Frontier Defense*, 106–7. The Foreman massacre took place near Captina Creek eighteen miles below Wheeling (Fort Henry). Of the forty-six men in Foreman's party, twenty were killed in the ambush.
52. Wilde, trans., "Lichtenau Diary," October 9, 1777; Thwaites and Kellogg, eds., *Frontier Defense*, 112–18. All three of these letters were written on October 1, 1777. Hand and Morgan each wrote one letter to the Delaware council, and Morgan wrote a separate personal letter to White Eyes and Gelelemend (Killbuck).
53. Wilde, trans., "Lichtenau Diary," 147:5, October 22, 1777.
54. Thwaites and Kellogg, eds., *Frontier Defense*, 149, n. 13. Accompanying Cornstalk was a fellow chief, Redhawk, and a chief who had lost one eye and was better known as "Old Yie." His Indian name was Petalla; ibid., 157–63; Downes, *Council Fires*, 206–7.
55. Wilde, trans., "Lichtenau Diary," 147:5, December 31, 1777.

22. *Grasping at Straws, 1778*

1. Wilde, trans., "Lichtenau Diary," 147:5 and 6, January 1–28, 1778.
2. Ibid., February 1, 7, 1778.
3. Ibid., February 11, 1778.
4. Ketchen, ed., *American Heritage Book of the Revolution*, 254.
5. Thwaites and Kellogg, eds., *Frontier Defense*, 201–2.
6. Ibid., 215–16.
7. Ibid., 216–23.
8. Butterfield, *Girtys*, 43–46.
9. Reginald Horsman, *Matthew Elliot, British Indian Agent* (Detroit: Wayne State University Press, 1964), 18–24; Butterfield, *Girtys*, 50–52.
10. Butterfield, *Girtys*, iv, 50–56. Girty and Elliot finally settled on the Canadian side at the mouth of the Detroit River. Girty died and is buried there. In October 1990, I visited the site and was given a description of Simon Girty that is totally different from the way American historians have pictured him. To Canadians, he is a hero.

11. Thwaites and Kellogg, eds., *Frontier Defense*, 250–52.

12. Wilde, trans., "Lichtenau Diary," 147:6, April 1, 1778.

13. Heckewelder, *Narrative*, 180. Heckewelder is the only source of these wild rumors spread by the McKee party. Heckewelder was not a witness to these meetings. He was returning from Bethlehem and did not arrive until April 6, 1778, two days after the Delaware council made a decision. Butterfield in his *Girtys*, 58, states that the rumors were "doubtless an exaggertion to some extent." See also Olmstead, *Blackcoats among the Delaware*, 29.

14. Wilde, trans., "Lichtenau Diary," 147:6, April 4, 1778.

15. Thwaites and Kellogg, eds., *Frontier Defense*, 241–44.

16. Wilde, trans., "Lichtenau Diary," 147:6, April 6, 1778; *Pennsylvania Archives*, 1st ser., 6:714.

17. Thwaites and Kellogg, eds., *Frontier Defense*, 269–70.

18. Heckewelder, *Narrative*, 175–82; see Appendix H. Butterfield, in his *Girtys*, points out numerous examples of occasions when Heckewelder exaggerated events during this period. Undoubtably, Heckewelder, in his advanced age, had forgotten many of the details that took place during this time.

19. Wilde, trans., "Lichtenau Diary," 147:6, April 27, 1778.

20. Ibid., April 30, 1778.

21. Wilde, trans., "Lichtenau Diary," May 2, 1778.

22. Ibid., May 5, 1778.

23. Ibid., June 9, 16, 1778.

24. General Lachlan McIntosh was born in the Scottish Highlands in 1725. He came to America as an eleven-year-old boy. As a youth he went to Charleston as a protégé of Henry Laurens, who developed a warm friendship with the young man. During the Revolutionary War he was appointed to head the Georgia colony's troops. His success in several engagements brought him to the attention of General Washington, who appointed him a brigadier general in 1776. He then returned to Georgia to head the colonial troops. Button Gwinnett, signer of the Declaration of Independence, was killed in a duel with McIntosh over a personal matter. Shortly thereafter, at the request of Henry Laurens, he returned to the main army. He spent the winter of 1777 at Valley Forge. The following spring, Washington sent him to Fort Pitt. After his unsuccessful experience in the western theater, in May 1779 he returned to Georgia for the remaining years of the war. He died at Savannah on February 20, 1806.

25. Wilde, trans., "Lichtenau Diary," 146:6, July 16, 1778.

26. Louise P. Kellogg, *Frontier Advance on the Upper Ohio, 1778–1779* (Madison: Wisconsin Historical Society, 1916), 131–32; Morgan Papers, Reel 247, p. 239, National Archives.

27. Wilde, trans., "Lichtenau Diary," 147:6, July 27, 1778; Butterfield, *Girtys*, 68–69. The destruction and havoc are evident in a letter from Governor Hamilton to General Haldimand on September 17, 1778. He wrote that since May the Indians in his district had taken thirty-four prisoners and eighty-one scalps.

28. Kellogg, *Frontier Advance*, 132–33.

29. Charles J. Kappler, *Indian Affairs: Laws and Treaties*, 7 vols. (Washington, D.C.: U. S. Goverment Printing Office, 1904–41), 2:3–6; Downes, *Council Fires*, 216.

30. Kellogg, *Frontier Advance*, 277.

31. Wilde, trans., "Lichtenau Diary," 147:8, October 2, 1778.

32. Ibid., 147:6, October 5, 1778.

33. Ibid., October 28, 1778.

34. Ibid., November 7, 1778.

35. Ibid., November 20, 1778.

36. Morgan to Thomas Mifflin, May 12, 1784, Morgan Papers, M247, roll 180, p. 365, National Archives.

37. Morgan to Treasury Dept., September 25, 1788, ibid., M247, roll 104, p. 619.

38. That White Eyes was murdered is stated in Downes, *Council Fires*, 217; C. A. Weslager, *The Delaware Indian Westward Migration* (Wallingford, Pa.: Middle Atlantic Press, 1978), 41; Dale Van Every, *A Company of Heroes: The American Frontier, 1775–1783* (New York: Morrow, 1962), 289; and a host of others. Herbert C. Kraft, however, in his *The Lenape: Archaeology, History, and Ethnography* (Newark: New Jersey Historical Society, 1986), 235, acknowledges that White Eyes's death by murder "remains unproven." I agree with Kraft.

39. Kellogg, *Frontier Advance*, 157.

40. Ibid., 200–201.

41. *Pennsylvania Archives*, 1st ser., 12:146, Brodhead to Gen. Greene, August 2, 1779. Daniel Brodhead was born in Ulster County, New York, in 1736. While he was an infant, his family moved to Monroe County, Pennsylvania, near Stroudsburg. When he was in his twenties, this area was frequently attacked by Indian war parties during the French and Indian War. In 1777, Brodhead moved to Reading, Pennsylvania, where he became a deputy surveyor. At the outbreak of the Revolution he was chosen as a delegate to the Pennsylvania Convention and raised a company of riflemen who joined Washington's army. In March 1777 he was promoted to lieutenant colonel and assigned to the Eighth Pennsylvania regiment. He participated in the campaigns of 1777–78 and passed the winter at Valley Forge. That summer his regiment was assigned to the western theater. After the recall of General McIntosh in the spring of 1779, he was appointed theater commander until recalled in a dispute with John Gibson in September 1781. Gibson succeeded him in command at Fort Pitt. In 1789, Brodhead was appointed surveyor-general of the state of Pennsylvania. His latter years were spent at Milford, Pike County, Pennsylvania, where he died on November 15, 1809.

42. Thomas I. Pieper and James Gidney, *Fort Laurens, 1778–1779* (Kent, Ohio: Kent State University Press, 1976), 32–38.

43. *Pennsylvania Archives*, 1st ser., 12:110.

44. Kellogg, *Frontier Advance*, December 7, 1778, 183–84, also see note 3; Pieper and Gidney, *Fort Laurens*, 45–46. Fort Laurens was on the west side of the Muskingum (now the Tuscarawas), a half mile below the mouth of the Sandy Creek at the present town of Bolivar, Ohio. It was a square, stockaded fort with two gates, one next to the river and one to the west on the opposite end of the fort. The palisade walls were twelve to fourteen feet high with extended bastions on each of the four corners. The fort was surrounded by a ditch four feet wide and three feet deep, which covered three sides of the fort with the river on the other side. On each side of the river gate, rows of pickets extended to the river for the protection of the soldiers going for water. The fort covered approximately one acre. Barracks for the men and officers covered the inside walls, and the western gate was guarded by a blockhouse, which extended above the palisade wall to guard against any enemy approaching the western gate. The fort was built by the French engineer Louis Antoine Jean-Baptiste, chevalier de Cambray-Digny.

45. Downes, *Council Fires*, 220.

46. Kellogg, *Frontier Advance*, 178–79.

47. Wilde, trans., "Lichtenau Diary," 147:8, November 27, 1778.

48. Ibid., December 14, 1778. Zeisberger consistently spelled the name of the fort as Fort Lawrence.

49. Ibid., December 31, 1778.

23. *Estrangement among the Delawares, 1779*

1. The principal sources for this chapter, other than the mission diaries, can be found in the Pennsylvania Archives, 1st ser., vols. 7 and 12; "The Haldimand Papers," *Michigan*

Pioneer and Historical Collection, vols. 10 and 19; the Draper manuscripts found in Kellogg, *Frontier Advance*, and *Frontier Retreat on the Upper Ohio, 1778–1779* (Madison: Wisconsin Historical Society, 1917), and the George Morgan Letter Books, vols. 1, 2, and 3, Carnegie Library of Pittsburgh.

2. Wilde, trans., "Lichtenau Diary," October 23, November 24, 1778.

3. De Schweinitz, *Zeisberger*, 446, 470.

4. Pieper and Gidney, *Fort Laurens*, 48.

5. Ibid., 38; Consul Willshire Butterfield, *Washington-Irvine Correspondence* (Madison, Wisc.: D. Atwood, 1882), 28, n. 5.

6. Pieper and Gidney, *Fort Laurens*, 49; Butterfield, *Washington-Irvine Correspondence*, 29.

7. Wilde, trans., "Lichtenau Diary," 147:8, December 28, 1778.

8. Pieper and Gidney, *Fort Laurens*, 49; Kellogg, *Frontier Advance*, 224–25. The man killed was John Nash.

9. Wilde, trans., "Lichtenau Diary," 147:9, January 30, 1779. Zeisberger closed this entry indicating that the support party responsible for returning the men to the fort had "then brought the wounded to water." He frequently used this term to indicate that disabled men who had been sick and wounded in a skirmish were returned to their home base or to someplace where they could be adequately treated.

10. Ibid.

11. Ibid., 147:8, January 8, 1779.

12. Kellogg, *Frontier Advance*, 193.

13. Ibid., 201–5.

14. Savelle, *George Morgan*, 161.

15. Kellogg, *Frontier Advance*, 240–42. See also Pieper and Gidney, *Fort Laurens*, 58–59; Butterfield, *Washington-Irvine Correspondence*, 31–32. Between June and August 1986, Michael Gramly and his staff of archaeologists excavated the cemetery at Fort Laurens. Fourteen skeletons were retrieved from the mass grave where they had been buried in March 1779, along with the other men killed and buried at the fort. Gramly has permitted us to include in this volume the results of his preliminary examination of these bodies. His report can be found in Appendix I.

16. Wilde, trans., "Lichtenau Diary," 147:9, February 6, 10, 1779.

17. Ibid., February 20, 26, 1779; Pieper and Gidney, *Fort Laurens*, 59.

18. Wilde, trans., "Lichtenau Diary," 147:9, March 9–19, 1779.

19. Pieper and Gidney, *Fort Laurens*, 60.

20. Ibid., 62–63; Kellogg, *Frontier Advance*, 242–47, 249–51; see also Downes, *Council Fires*, 222.

21. Pieper and Gidney, *Fort Laurens*, 60.

22. Kellogg, *Frontier Advance*, 256–58.

23. Pieper and Gidney, *Fort Laurens*, 63–64; Kellogg, *Frontier Advance*, 271–74.

24. Wilde, trans., "Lichtenau Diary," 147:9, March 7, April 5, 1779.

25. Ibid. At this point Zeisberger began to write the New Schoenbrunn diary, found in the Moravian Church Archives, box 147, folder 9, and Heckewelder continued to write the "Lichtenau Diary," found in box 147, folder 10.

26. Delaware Tribe of Western Oklahoma, *Turtle Children*, 33.

27. Margaret Wilde, trans., "Zeisberger's New Schoenbrunn Diary, 1779–1781," 149:9, April 10, 17, 1779. The location chosen for New Schoenbrunn was unusual. With few exceptions, Zeisberger built near rivers but seldom in floodplains. William Rufus Putman's survey map drawn in 1797, eighteen years after the mission's founding, locates the site near the river. Remnants of the village were extant at the time the map was made. Most historians have believed the village was located on a high bank approximately nine hundred yards from the river, beyond the floodplain. The site of the village next to the river was approximately twenty feet above the normal river level and certainly within the floodplain. Zeisberger's

diary entry of May 15, 1779, confirms that it was indeed near the river and susceptible to flooding. "Much rainy weather for several days caused the Muskingum to so overflow that we were in danger of being flooded. We were already surrounded and if the water had risen one more foot we would have had to flee, but it cleared and the water receded." Zeisberger, in his diaries, always referred to this site as "Schoenbrunn." De Schweinitz, in his *Zeisberger*, called it New Schoenbrunn to distinguish it from the former village. To avoid confusion, I follow De Schweinitz. On April 10, 1993, the Tuscarawas County Historical Society erected a plaque marking the long-forgotten site.

28. Wilde, trans., "New Schoenbrunn Diary," 147:9, April 28, May 4, 1779.

29. Wilde, trans., "Lichtenau Diary," 147:10, April 16, 1779; Kellogg, *Frontier Advance*, 295; also Olmstead, *Blackcoats among the Delaware*, 31, 32.

30. Wilde, trans., "Lichtenau Diary," 147:10, April 30, 1779.

31. Kellogg, *Frontier Advance*, 412–14. There were eighty-six different items on this list of materials.

32. Wilde, trans., "Lichtenau Diary," 147:10, May 7, April 15, 1779.

33. Ibid., May 24, 1779.

34. Ibid., May 25, 1779.

35. Ibid.; "Bowman Expedition against Chillicothe, May–June 1779," *Ohio Archaeological and Historical Publication* 19 (1910): 446–59. This article is based on the Draper Manuscripts at the Wisconsin Historical Society, Madison, Wisconsin. Bowman attacked the village of Chief Black Fish, one of the head chiefs of the Shawnee Nation. Black Fish was killed. Bowman lost eight men. This booty captured by Bowman was eventually sold by the Kentuckians for £32,000. The money was divided among the men, each one receiving £110, a tidy sum in those days.

36. Wilde, trans., "Lichtenau Diary," 147:10, June 28, 1779; Kellogg, *Frontier Advance*, 246. Alexander McCormick was an Irishman and had been trading at Fort Pitt and in Indian country before the Revolution. In 1777 he was living at Pomoacan's Wyandot village at Upper Sandusky. He was always very friendly to the Moravians. On several occasions he protected them from insult and injury from their critics at the time they were moved from the Muskingum in 1781. In 1785 he married Elizabeth Turner, an Indian captive, and settled at the foot of the Maumee River rapids on the grounds where Anthony Wayne's Battle of Fallen Timbers was fought in 1794. After that battle he moved to western Ontario and died in 1803. See Olmstead, *Blackcoats among the Delaware*, 47.

37. Kellogg, *Frontier Advance*, 382–83; *Pennsylvania Archives*, 1st ser., 7:524–26.

38. *Pennsylvania Archives*, 1st ser., 133–34.

39. Wilde, trans., "New Schoenbrunn Diary," July 4, 1779.

40. Butterfield, *Girtys*, 98–104.

41. *Pennsylvania Archives*, 1st ser., 7:541–42. In his letter to Brodhead, Heckewelder blamed Big Cat for not seizing Girty if he visited the capital as Brodhead had instructed the chiefs to do.

42. Wilde, trans., "New Schoenbrunn Diary," July 14, 1779; Pieper and Gidney, *Fort Laurens*, 78.

43. Wilde, trans., "Lichtenau Diary," August 15, 1779.

44. Downes, *Council Fires*, 255; Kellogg, *Frontier Retreat*, 66–76; Craig, *Olden Time*, 2:311–17.

45. Wilde, trans., "Lichtenau Diary," October 5, 1779.

46. Ibid., October 24, 1779.

24. *The Torch, the Rifle, and the Scalping Knife, 1780–1781*

1. Edgar Hassler, *Old Westmoreland: A History of Western Pennsylvania during the Revolution* (Pittsburgh: J. R. Weldin, 1900), 102.

2. Ibid., 103; Kellogg, *Frontier Retreat*, 20.

3. *Pennsylvania Archives*, 1st ser., 8:140.

4. Ibid., 8:152.

5. Ibid., 8:210; Kellogg, *Frontier Retreat*, 163. The Ohio River party consisted of Joseph Mallot, his family, and a few friends, who were immigrating from Maryland to Kentucky. Mallot, the cattle, horses, and family belongings were in one boat. Mallot's family and friends were in the second boat manned by a Mr. Reynolds. They were captured by the Indians, but Mallot escaped in his boat. Among those captured was fourteen-year-old Catherine Mallot, who later married Simon Girty.

6. Wilde, trans., "Lichtenau Diary," 147:11, March 26 through August 20, 1798. The Salem mission was located on a large alluvial plain approximately one and one-half miles south of the present village of Port Washington on the west side of the Tuscarawas River. In the summer of 1993, the Tuscarawas County Historical Society erected a plaque marking the site of this mission. De Schweinitz, in his *Zeisberger*, 477, n. 1, records this comment: "On the Twentieth of June, 1863, Mr. Blickensderfer and I discovered the site of Salem. The plain in which it stood was well known; but we succeeded in identifying the very spot which it once occupied, and clearly traced the line of the houses by the discoloration of the soil, at regular intervals, in a field of young corn, and numerous relics which we dug up."

7. Kellogg, *Frontier Retreat*, 44.

8. Ibid., 147–48.

9. Downes, *Council Fires*, 258–59.

10. Kellogg, *Frontier Retreat*, 172–73.

11. *Pennsylvania Archives*, 1st ser., 12:227–28. Heckewelder signed all of his letters during these years as John Hackenwelder. Later he corrected the spelling to Heckewelder. Daniel Maurice Godefroy de Linctot was one of two sons of a French officer who had been active during the French and Indian War. During this conflict he obtained the rank of ensign. Following the war the two brothers became fur traders on the Mississippi. Daniel entered the American service in May 1779, serving under George Rogers Clark and distinguishing himself during Clark's and his Indian allies' exploits.

12. Margaret Wilde, trans., "Heckewelder's Salem Diary, 1780–1781," Moravian Church Archives, 147:11, May 30, 1780.

13. Kellogg, *Frontier Retreat*, 189–93.

14. Schwarze, trans., "New Schoenbrunn Diary," 141:17, June 30, 1780; Wilde, trans., "Salem Diary," 147:11, July 1, 3, 1780.

15. Schwarze, trans., "New Schoenbrunn Diary," 141:17, July 24, 1780.

16. Ibid., 141:17, November 7, 1780. Michael Jung was born in Alsace, Germany, on January 5, 1743. He immigrated with his parents to Broadbay, Maine, in 1751, where he joined the Moravian Church. In 1767, he moved to Bethlehem and served there until he was called to mission service in 1780. He was a faithful missionary for the next thirty-three years, retiring to Litiz, Pennsylvania, in 1813. He died December 13, 1826. He apparently never married.

17. This buildup of the missionary staff in the previous year indicated that Zeisberger had full confidence that his troubles with the Delawares were over and the future of his work in the valley looked secure.

18. Schwarze, trans., "Schoenbrunn Diary," January 8, 1781.

19. Olmstead, *Blackcoats among the Delaware*, 76, 77. Gelelemend, or William Henry, would later become probably the most distinguished convert Zeisberger ever baptized. He lies buried in the Goshen, Ohio, cemetery beside David Zeisberger. He died February 17, 1811, outliving Zeisberger by three years.

20. Schwarze, trans., "Schoenbrunn Diary," March 5, 1781.

21. Wilde, trans., "Salem Diary," April 10, 1781.

22. Butterfield, *Washington-Irvine Correspondence*, 51–52.

23. Wilde, trans., "Salem Diary," April 19, 1781.

24. *Pennsylvania Archives*, 1st ser., 9:160–61; Joseph Doddridge, *Notes on the Settlement and Indian Wars* (1912; rpt. Parsons, W. Va.: McClain Printing Co., 1960), 224–26; Butterfield, *Girtys*, 128–30. Butterfield correctly questions many of the events recorded by Doddridge. The subsequent account of a massacre of eleven Indians, not mentioned in the text, seems erroneous. Heckewelder, in his diary, makes no reference to this event, and if it occurred, he surely would have known. Until recently the translation of Heckewelder's diaries has not been available to historians. Doddridge's description of this massacre is the only source. This event has come down in historical legend as "the Brodhead Massacre."

25. Wilde, trans., "Salem Diary," April 21, 22, 1781.

26. Susan (Lecron) Zeisberger was born at Lancaster, Pennsylvania, February 17, 1744. Her parents, who were Lutherans, moved to the neighborhood of Litiz in 1758, where she joined the Moravian Church. She may have met Zeisberger at age sixteen when he spent the year of 1760 as the superintendent of the single Brethren house at Litiz. After Zeisberger's death at Goshen in 1808, she returned to Bethlehem the following year, where she died on September 8, 1824.

27. *Pennsylvania Archives*, 1st ser., 9:57.

25. *There Are Worse Things Waiting for Men Than Death, 1781*

1. *Pennsylvania Archives*, 1st ser., 9:395.

2. Wilde, trans., "Salem Diary," August 7, 1781.

3. David Zeisberger, *Diary of David Zeisberger, a Moravian Missionary among the Indians of Ohio*, trans. and ed. Eugene F. Bliss, 2 vols. (Cincinnati: R. Clarke,, 1885), 1:1–2. Unlike Heckewelder's diary, which goes to September 3, when the missionaries were seized, Zeisberger apparently destroyed all of his diaries from July 15 until September 3. Following their capture on September 3, none of the missionaries were permitted to keep diaries or even to have pen in hand. When they returned from Detroit on November 22, Zeisberger wrote his first entry: "We have since our captivity, on 3rd September, until now had, no pen in our hand, and have strictly kept our promise." He now filled in the diary from September 3 to November 22 with the help of the other missionaries.

4. Wilde, trans., "Salem Diary," June 9, 10, 1781.

5. Ibid., August 10, 1781.

6. Ibid.

7. Ibid., August 12, 1781.

8. Ibid., August 14, 1781.

9. Zeisberger, *Diary*, trans. Bliss, 1:4.

10. Butterfield, *Washington-Irvine Correspondence*, 58.

11. Craig, *Olden Time*, 2:396.

12. Wilde, trans., "Salem Diary," August 19, 1781.

13. Zeisberger, *Diary*, trans. Bliss, 1:4.

14. Ibid., 6.

15. Ibid., 7.

16. Wilde, trans., "Salem Diary," August 26, 1781.

17. Zeisberger, *Diary*, trans. Bliss, 1:9–10.

18. Wilde, trans., "Salem Diary," September 3, 1781. This was the last entry in Heckewelder's Salem diary. It ended abruptly with garbled words.

19. Zeisberger, *Diary*, trans. Bliss, 1:10–12. The "death hallow" was an eerie shout or cry made by a party of Indians as they arrived at the village announcing they had prisoners or scalps of the enemy.

20. Butterfield, *Washington-Irvine Correspondence*, 60; Craig, *Olden Time*, 2:399.

21. Butterfield, *Washington-Irvine Correspondence*, 59–60. Butterfield contends that Zeisberger's correspondence to Fort Pitt caused the Half-King to change his mind and arrest the missionaries, and this led to their removal. But when he wrote this volume, neither Zeisberger's nor Heckewelder's diaries were available to him. Those diaries prove rather conclusively that this was not the reason for the removal. When Half-King and Elliot first came to the valley, they were under strict orders from the British commander, Major De Peyster, to remove the Moravians either peacefully or by force.

22. Zeisberger, *Diary*, trans. Bliss, 1:16–20. The diary for the days between September 11, when they left Salem, until October 1, on arrival at the Sandusky, can be found in these pages.

23. Ibid., 17–20.

24. Ibid., 21.

25. Ibid., 21–24.

26. Ibid., 24–25.

27. Ibid., 29.

28. Ibid., 29–34.

29. Ibid., 35–37.

30. Ibid., 37–43. The full text of the trial can be found in these pages, and they are the source of the following quotations. Also see Olmstead, *Blackcoats among the Delaware*, 41–46.

31. Butterfield, *Washington-Irvine Correspondence*, 342–43. Heckewelder, in his *Narrative*, says Captain Biggs was the leader of this expedition. Other sources insist that Colonel Williamson was the leader. He would lead the Pennsylvania militia against the Christians the following year and participate in the Gnadenhutten massacre.

32. Zeisberger, *Diary*, trans. Bliss, 1:54.

26. *Gnadenhutten: The Day of Shame*, 1782

1. Susan Zeisberger's Lebenslauf (Memoir), Moravian Church Archives, Bethlehem, Pa. Very little is to be found regarding Susan Zeisberger in the missionary diaries. Seldom did Zeisberger mention the role of the missionary women in his writing.

2. Zeisberger, *Diary*, trans. Bliss, 1:56.

3. Ibid., 57. Pipe remained a good friend of Zeisberger's throughout the rest of his life and was especially helpful when he moved to the Pettquotting River mission in 1786.

4. Ibid., 58.

5. Ibid., 63–64

6. Ibid., 64–67.

7. Ibid., 68.

8. Ibid., 69.

9. Ibid., 70–71.

10. Ibid., 72–73.

11. Ibid., 74.

12. Ibid., 76–77.

13. Ibid., 78. See also Doddridge, *Notes on the Settlement*, 188–203. See also Consul W. Butterfield, *An Historical Account of the Expedition against the Sandusky under Col. William Crawford in 1782* (Cincinnati: R. Clarke, 1873). 41. Butterfield comments, "Perhaps Doddridge was a bit harsh on the Washington County settlers."

14. Butterfield, *Washington-Irvine Correspondence*, 99, 100, 243; Alexander S. Withers, *Chronicles of Border Warfare*, ed. Reuben G. Thwaites (Cincinnati: Stewart & Lidd, 1895), 318–20.

15. Louise Martin Mohler, *The Gnadenhutten Massacre of 1782* (Washington, Pa.: Privately printed, 1984), 6, 11–16; William H. Egle, ed., *Pennsylvania in the War of the Revolution*

(Harrisburg: E. K. Myers, State Printer, 1888), 2:753–54. These works contain a partial list of the men who accompanied the Williamson expedition. See also Butterfield, *Washington-Irvine Correspondence*, 366. David Williamson was a well-respected officer of the Washington County militia. He was born the son of John Williamson near Carlisle, Pennsylvania, in 1752. When he was a boy, the family settled on Buffalo Creek in what subsequently became Washington County, approximately twenty-five miles from the Ohio River. He was active during the Revolution and wanted to defend his area, having previously held a captain's commission during Dunmore's War. After the Revolution he was popular with the people. In 1785 he was elected sheriff—the first county lieutenant to serve that position—and in 1789 was reelected. He was unsuccessful in business and died in poverty in 1814. His body was interred in the old burial grounds on North Main Street, Washington, Pennsylvania, but no stone marks the spot.

16. Doddridge, *Notes on the Settlement*, 188–203; Boyd Crumrine, *History of Washington County, Pennsylvania, with Biographical Sketches of Many of Its Pioneers and Prominent Men* (Philadelphia: L. H. Everts, 1882), 102–10; *Pennsylvania Archives*, 1st ser., 9:524–25. Numerous authors of monographs and many historians over the years have written accounts of the Gnadenhutten massacre. Zeisberger in his diary provides an account from the Moravian perspective. Most of the other reliable information from the border settlers' viewpoint comes from the three sources given above.

17. Zeisberger, *Diary*, ed. Bliss, 1:79–81.

18. Ibid., 81.

19. Ibid., 85.

20. Olmstead, *Blackcoats among the Delaware*, 55. This is the first time Zeisberger's full account of the massacre, as taken from his diaries, has been published.

21. Ibid., 57–58, provides a short account of the Crawford expedition in 1782. A full discussion of the expedition can be found in Butterfield's *Expedition against the Sandusky;* also see Parker B. Brown, "The Battle of Sandusky," *Western Pennsylvania Historical Magazine* 65, no. 2 (1982): 115–51.

22. Butterfield, *Washington-Irvine Correspondence*, 102–3.

23. Zeisberger, *Diary*, ed. Bliss, 1:85–86.

24. Ibid., 88.

25. Ibid., 90–91.

26. Ibid., 96–98.

27. Ibid., 100.

28. Ibid., 102.

Selected Bibliography

Allen, Walser H. *Who Are the Moravians: The Story of the Moravian Church, a World-Wide Fellowship*. Bethlehem, Pa.: Allen, 1966.

Axtell, James. *The European and the Indian: Essays in the Ethnohistory of Colonial North America*. New York: Oxford University Press, 1981.

———. *The Invasion Within: The Contest of Cultures in Colonial North America*. New York: Oxford University Press, 1985.

Beauchamp, Rev. William M. *Aboriginal Place Names of New York*. Albany: New York State Educational Department, 1907.

———. "A History of the New York Iroquois." University of the State of New York, Bulletin 329 (1905).

———, ed. *Moravian Journals Relating to Central New York, 1745–66*. Syracuse: Dehler Press, 1916.

Booth, Russell H., Jr. *The Tuscarawas Valley in Indian Days, 1750–1797*. Cambridge, Ohio: Gomber House Press, 1994.

Brasser, Ted J. "Mahican." In *Handbook of the North American Indians*, ed. Bruce G. Trigger, 15:198–212. Washington, D.C.: Smithsonian Institution, 1978.

Butterfield, Consul Willshire. *An Historical Account of the Expedition against the Sandusky under Col. William Crawford in 1782*. Cincinnati: R. Clarke, 1873.

———. *History of the Girtys*. Cincinnati: R. Clarke, 1890.

———. *Washington-Irvine Correspondence*. Madison, Wisc.: D. Atwood, 1882.

Carter, John H. "The Moravians at Shamokin, Early Events in the Susquehanna Valley." In *Early Events in the Susquehanna Valley: A Collection of the Writings and Addresses as Presented by John H. Carter before the Society*. The Northumberland Historical Society. Millville, Pa.: Precision Printing, 1981.

Cavaioli, Frank J. "A Profile of the Paxton Boys: Murder of the Conestoga." *Journal of the Lancaster County Historical Society* 87, part 3 (1983): 74–96.

Connolly, Dr. John. "A Narrative of the Transactions, Imprisonment, and Suffering of John Connolly, an American Loyalist and Lt. Col. in His Majesty's Service." *Pennsylvania Magazine of History and Biography* 12 (1888): 310–91.

Craig, Neville B. *The History of Pittsburgh*. Pittsburgh: J. R. Weldin, 1917.

———, ed. *The Olden Time*. 2 vols. 1846. Reprint. Cincinnati: Clarke, 1876.

Crumrine, Boyd. *History of Washington County, Pennsylvania, with Biographical Sketches of Many of Its Pioneers and Prominent Men*. Philadelphia: L. H. Everts, 1882.

Darlington, Mary C. *History of Col. Henry Bouquet and the Western Frontiers of Pennsylvania, 1747–1764*. 1920. Reprint. New York: Arno Press, 1971.

———, ed. *Fort Pitt and Letters from the Frontier*. Pittsburgh: J. R. Weldin, 1892.

Deardorff, Merle H. "Zeisberger's Allegheny River Indian Towns, 1767–1770." *Pennsylvania Archaeologist* 16, no. 1 (1969): 1–19.

Delaware Tribe of Western Oklahoma. *Turtle Children*. Delaware Indian Child Welfare, title 2. Andarko, Okla.: Bureau of Indian Affairs, 1985.

De Schweinitz, Edmund. *The Life and Times of David Zeisberger*. Philadelphia: J. B. Lippincott, 1870.

———. *The Moravian Manual: Containing an Account of the Moravian Church, or Unitas Fratrum*. Bethlehem, Pa.: Moravian Publication Office, 1869.

———. "Some Fathers of the American Moravian Church," *Transactions of the Moravian Historical Society* 2, parts 4–5 (1886): 145–269.

Doddridge, Joseph. *Notes on the Settlement and Indian Wars*. 1912. Reprint. Parsons, W. Va.: McClain Printing Co., 1960.

Donehoo, George Patterson. *A History of the Indian Villages and Place Names in Pennsylvania*. Harrisburg, Pa.: Telegraph Press, 1928.

Downes, Randolph C. *Council Fires on the Upper Ohio*. Pittsburgh: University of Pittsburgh Press, 1969.

Dunbar, John R. *The Paxton Papers*. The Hague: Martinus Nijhoff, 1957.

Fenton, William N., and Elisabeth Tooker. "Mohawk." In *Handbook of North American Indians*, ed. Bruce G. Trigger, 15:466–80. Washington, D.C.: Smithsonian Institution, 1978.

Fliegel, Carl John, comp. *Index to the Records of the Moravian Mission among the Indians of North America*. 4 vols. Woodbridge, Conn.: Research Publications, 1970.

Force, Peter, ed. *American Archives*. 9 vols. Washington, D.C., 1837–53.

Fries, Adelaide. *Some Moravian Heroes*. Bethlehem, Pa.: Christian Education Board of the Moravian Church, 1936.

Gist, Christopher. *Christopher Gist's Journals*. Comp. and ed. William M. Darlington. 1893. Reprint. New York: Argonaut Press, 1966.

Glatfelter, Charles H. *Pastors and People: German Lutheran and Reformed Churches in the Pennsylvania Field, 1717–1793*. 2 vols. Breinigsville, Pa.: Pennsylvania German Society, 1980–81.

Goddard, Ives. "Delaware." In *Handbook of North American Indians*, ed. Bruce G. Trigger, 15:213–39. Washington, D.C.: Smithsonian Institution, 1978.

Haldimand Papers. Michigan Pioneers and Historical Collection, vols. 10 and 19. Lansing, Michigan.

Hale, Horatio. *The Iroquois Book of Rites*. Philadelphia: D. G. Brinton, 1883.

Hamilton, J. Taylor. *A History of the Church Known as the Moravian Church, or the Unitas Fratrum, or the Unity of the Brethren, during the Eighteenth and Nineteenth Centuries*. 1900. Reprint. New York: AMS Press, 1971.

Hamilton, Kenneth G. "John Ettwein and the Moravian Church during the Revolutionary Period." *Transactions of the Moravian Historical Society* 12, nos. 3–4 (1941): 85–130.

Hamilton, Milton W. "Sir William Johnson and Pennsylvania." *Pennsylvania History, Quarterly Journal of the Pennsylvania Historical Association* 19, no. 1 (January 1952): 1–24.

Hanna, Charles A. *The Wilderness Trail*. New York: G. P. Putnam's Sons, 1911.

Hark, Joseph Maximilian. "Meniologameka: Annals of a Moravian Indian Village an Hundred and Thirty Years Ago." *Transactions of the Moravian Historical Society* 2, part 3 (1886): 129–44.

Harrington, J. C. *New Light on Washington's Fort Necessity*. Richmond: Eastern National Park & Monument Association, 1957.

Hartzell, Lawrence W. *Ohio Moravian Music*. Winston-Salem, N.C.: Moravian Music Foundation Press, 1988.

Hassler, Edgar. *Old Westmoreland: A History of Western Pennsylvania during the Revolution*. Pittsburgh: J. R. Weldin, 1900.

Heckewelder, John. *History, Manners, and Customs of the Indian Nations Who Once Inhabited Pennsylvania and the Neighboring States*. 1876. Reprint. New York: Arno Press, 1971.

———. *A Narrative of the Mission of the United Brethren among the Delaware and Mohegan Indians; From Its Commencement, in the Year 1740 to the Close of the Year 1808*. 1820. Reprint. New York: Arno Press, 1971.

Henry, Alexander. *Travels and Adventures in Canada*. 1809. Reprint. New York: Readex Microprint, 1966.

Hindle, Brooke. "The March of the Paxton Boys." *William and Mary Quarterly* 3d ser., 3 (Oct. 1946): 467.

Horsman, Reginald. *Matthew Elliot, British Indian Agent*. Detroit: Wayne State University Press, 1964.

Hubbard, Jake T. "Americans as Guerrilla Fighters: Robert Rogers and His Rangers." *American Heritage* 22 (August 1971): 81–86.

Hunt, George T. *The Wars of the Iroquois*. Madison: University of Wisconsin Press, 1940.

Hunter, William A. *Forts on the Pennsylvania Frontier, 1753–1758*. Harrisburg: Pennsylvania Historical and Museum Commission, 1960.

———. "History of the Ohio Valley." In *Handbook of the North American Indians*, ed. Bruce G. Trigger, 15:588–93. Washington, D.C.: Smithsonian Institution, 1978.

Hutton, Joseph E. *A History of the Moravian Church*. London: Fetters Lane, 1909.

Illick, Joseph E. *Colonial Pennsylvania*. New York: Charles Scribner's Sons, 1976.

Jacobs, Wilbur R. *Diplomacy and Indian Gifts: The Northern Colonial Frontier, 1748–1763*. Lincoln: University of Nebraska Press, 1950.

James, Alton. *John Papunhank: A Christian Indian of North America*. Dublin: C. Benton, 1820.

Jennings, Francis. *The Ambiguous Iroquois Empire*. New York: Norton, 1984.

———. "The Delaware Interregum." *Pennsylvania Magazine of History and Biography* 89 (1985): 175–98.

———. *Empire of Fortune: Crowns, Colonies, and Tribes in the Seven Years War in America*. New York: Norton, 1988.

———. *The History and Culture of Iroquois Diplomacy*. Syracuse: Syracuse University Press, 1985.

———. *The Invasion of America: Indians, Colonialism and Cant of Conquest*. New York: Norton, 1976.

Jensen, Merrill. *The Founding of a Nation: A History of the American Revolution, 1763–1776*. New York: Oxford University Press, 1968.

Johnson, Frederick. "Count Zinzendorf and the Moravians and Indians Occupancy of the Wyoming Valley, 1742–1763." *Proceedings and Collection of the Wyoming Historical and Geological Society* 8 (1902–3): 119–82.

Jones, David. *A Journey of Two Visits Made to Some Nations on the West Side of the River Ohio, in the Years 1772 and 1773*. 1865. Reprint. Fairfield, Wash.: Ye Galleon Press, 1973.

Kappler, Charles J., comp. and ed. *Indian Treaties, 1778–1883*. New York: Interland, 1972.

Kent, Donald H. *The French Invasion of Western Pennsylvania, 1753*. Harrisburg: Pennsylvania Historical and Museum Commission, 1954.

Kellogg, Louise P. *Frontier Advance on the Upper Ohio, 1778–1779*. Madison: Wisconsin Historical Society, 1916.

———. *Frontier Retreat on the Upper Ohio, 1778–1779*. Madison: Wisconsin Historical Society, 1917.

Ketchum, Richard M., ed. *The American Heritage Book of the Revolution*. New York: American Heritage, 1958.

Kopperman, Paul E. *Braddock at the Monongahela*. Pittsburgh: University of Pittsburgh Press, 1977.

Kraft, Herbert C. *The Lenape: Archaeology, History, and Ethnography*. Newark: New Jersey Historical Society, 1986.

Larned, J. W. *The New Larned History*. 12 vols. Springfield, Conn.: C. A. Nichols, 1924.

Levering, Joseph M. *A History of Bethlehem, Pennsylvania, 1741–1892*. Bethlehem: Times Publishing Company, 1903.

Loskiel, George Henry. *History of the Mission of the United Brethren among the Indians in North America*. London: Brethren's Society for the Furtherance of the Gospel, 1794.

Lowdermilk, William Harrison. *History of Cumberland*. Washington, D.C.: J. Anglim, 1878.

McKay, John P., Bennett D. Hill, and John Buckler. *A History of World Societies*. 2d ed. Boston: Houghton Mifflin, 1988.

Mahr, August Carl. "Health Conditions in the Moravian Indian Missions of Schoenbrunn in the 1770's." *Ohio Journal of Science* 50 (1950): 121–31.

———. "Historical Reasons for the Founding of Schoenbrunn." Manuscript. Collection 215, Ohio Historical Society, Columbus, Ohio.

———. "How to Locate Indian Place Names on Modern Maps." *Ohio Journal of Science* 53 (May 1953): 129–37.

———, trans. "Schmick's Gnadenhutten Diary, 1773–1777." Manuscript. Collection 215, Ohio Historical Society, Columbus, Ohio.

———. "Zeisberger's Lichtenau Diary, 1776—April 10 to July 7." Manuscript. Box 147, Moravian Church Archives, Bethlehem, Pennsylvania.

———. "Zeisberger's Schoenbrunn Diary, 1772–1777." Manuscript. Collection 215, Ohio Historical Society, Columbus, Ohio.

Marx, Tilda, trans. "Diaries of the Moravian Missions in Western Pennsylvania, 1769–1772." Unpublished manuscript commissioned by Merle Deardorff. Warren Historical Society, Warren, Pa.

McClure, David. *Diary of David McClure, Doctor of Divinity, 1748–1820*. Notes by Franklin B. Dexter. New York: Knickerbocker Press, 1899.

Mohler, Louise Martin. *The Gnadenhutten Massacre of 1882*. Washington, Pa.: Privately printed, 1984.

Moravian Historical Society. *A Memorial of the Dedication of Monuments Erected by the Moravian Historical Society, to Mark the Sites of Ancient Missionary Stations in New York and Connecticut*. New York: C. B. Richardson, 1860.

Morgan, George. Letter Books. Carnegie Library of Pittsburgh, vols. 1, 2, and 3.

Morgan, Lewis Henry. *League of the Iroquois*. 1851. Reprint. Secaucus, N.J.: Citadel Press, 1962.

Morgan Papers, Reel M247, National Archives Microfilms, Washington, D.C.

Neisser, Georg. *A History of the Beginnings of Moravian Work in America*. Ed. Willam N. Schwarze and Samuel H. Gapp. Bethlehem, Pa.: Archives of the Moravian Church, 1955.

Olmstead, Earl P. *Blackcoats among the Delaware: David Zeisberger on the Ohio Frontier*. Kent, Ohio: Kent State University Press, 1991.

O'Meara, Walter. *Guns at the Forks*. Englewood Cliffs, N.J.: Prentice-Hall, 1965.

Parkman, Francis. *The Conspiracy of Pontiac and the Indian War after the Conquest of Canada*. 2 vols. 10th ed. Boston: Little, Brown, 1893.

———. *Montcalm and Wolfe*. 2 vols. Boston: Little, Brown, 1912.

Peckham, Howard H. *Pontiac and the Indian Uprising*. New York: Russell & Russell, 1970.

Pennsylvania Archives. 1st ser., 1664–1790. 12 vols. Philadelphia: Joseph Severns, 1860.

Pennsylvania Colonial Records. 16 vols. Harrisburg: J. Severns, 1851–53.

Pennsylvania Indian Forts Commission. *Report of the Commission to Locate the Site of the Frontier Forts of Pennsylvania*. 2 vols. Harrisburg: C. M. Busch, State Printer, 1896.

Pieper, Thomas I., and James Gidney. *Fort Laurens, 1778–1779*. Kent, Ohio: Kent State University Press, 1976.

Pyrlaeus, Johann Christopher, "Autobiography." *Transactions of the Moravian Historical Society* 12, part 1 (1938): 18–25.

Reeves, J. C. "Henry Bouquet: His Indian Campaigns." *Ohio Archaeological and Historical Society* 26 (1918): 489–506.

Reichel, Levin Theodore. *The Early History of the Church of the United Brethren (Unitas Fratrum) Commonly Called Moravians in North America. A.D. 1734–1748*. Nazareth, Pa.: Moravian Historical Society, 1888.

Reichel, William C., ed. *Memorials of the Moravian Church*. Philadelphia: J. B. Lippincott, 1870.

———. "Wyalusing and the Moravian Mission at Friedenshutten." *Transactions of the Moravian Historical Society* 1, no. 5 (1871): 178–224.

Rishel, Dr. Jonas. *The Indian Physician*. 1828. Reprint. Columbus: Ohio State University Libraries Publications, 1980.

Rondthaler, Edward. *Life of John Heckewelder*. Ed. B. H. Coates. Philadelphia: T. Ward, 1847.

Rosebroom, Eugene H., and Francis P. Weisenburger. *A History of Ohio*. Columbus: Ohio Historical Society. 1953.

Roth, David Luther. *Johann Roth: Missionary*. Greenville, Pa.: Beaver Printing Co., 1922.

Salwen, Bert. "Indians of Southern New England and Long Island: Early Period." In *Handbook of the North American Indians*, ed. Bruce G. Trigger 15:160–76. Washington, D.C.: Smithsonian Institution, 1978.

Savelle, Max. *George Morgan, Colony Builder*. New York: Columbia University Press, 1932.

Sawyer, Edwin A. *Christian Spring: Noble Experiment in Communal Living and First Vocational School in Northampton County*. Nazareth, Pa.: Moravian Hall Square Museum Craft Shop, 1988.

———. "John Amos Comenius: An Outline of His Life, Career and Major Writings." M.A. thesis, Union Theological Seminary, 1953.

———. "The Religious Experience of the Colonial American Moravians." *Transactions of the Moravian Historical Society* 18, part 1 (1961): 1–227.

Schaaf, Gregory. *Wampum Belts and Peace Trees*. Golden, Colo.: Fulcrum, 1990.

Schwarze, William N., trans. "Schmick's Gnadenhutten Diary, 1773–1777." Box 144, Folders 1–13, Moravian Church Archives, Bethlehem, Pa.

———. "Zeisberger's New Schoenbrunn Diary, 1779–1781." Box 141, Folder 17, Moravian Church Archives, Bethlehem, Pa.

———. "Zeisberger's Schoenbrunn Diary, 1772–1777." Box 141, Folders 12–16, Moravian Church Archives, Bethlehem, Pa.

Sessler, Jacob John. *Communal Pietism among Early American Moravians*. New York: Henry Holt, 1933.

Sherman, C. E. *Original Ohio Land Subdivisions*. Vol. 3. Columbus: Press of the Ohio State Reformatory, 1925.

Simonetti, Martha L., comp. *Descriptive List of the Map Collection in the Pennsylvania State Archives*. Harrisburg: Pennsylvania Historical and Museum Commission, 1976.

Sipe, C. Hale. *The Indian Chiefs of Pennsylvania*. Butler, Pa.: Ziegler Printing, 1927.

———. *The Indian Wars of Pennsylvania: An Account of the Indian Events in Pennsylvania of the French and Indian War*. Harrisburg: Telegraph Press, 1929.

Smith, De Cost. *Martyrs of the Oblong and the Little Nine*. Caldwell, Ida.: Caxton Printers, 1948.

Smith, Kenneth L. *A Practical Guide to Dating Systems for Genealogists*. Columbus, Ohio: K. L. Smith, 1983.

Sosin, Jack M. *The Revolutionary Frontier, 1763–1783*. New York: Holt, Rinehart and Winston, 1967.

Swanton, John R. *The Indian Tribes of North America*. Bureau of American Ethnology, Bulletin 145. Washington, D.C., 1982.

Thwaites, Reuben Gold. *France in America, 1497–1763*. American Nations Series, vol. 7. New York: Harper & Brothers, 1905.

———, ed. *Early Western Travels*. 2 vols. Cleveland: Arthur H. Clarke, 1904–5.

Thwaites, Reuben Gold, and Louise Phelps Kellogg, eds. *Documentary History of Dunmore's War, 1774*. Harrisonburg, Va.: C. J. Carrier Co., 1974.

———. *Frontier Defense on the Upper Ohio, 1777–1778*. Madison: Wisconsin Historical Society, 1912.

———. *The Revolution on the Upper Ohio, 1775–1777*. Port Washington, N.Y.: Kennikat Press, 1970.

Van Doren, Carl. *Benjamin Franklin*. New York: Viking, 1938.

Van Every, Dale. *Ark of Empire: The American Frontier, 1784–1803*. New York: Morrow, 1963.

———. *A Company of Heroes: The American Frontier, 1775–1783*. New York: Morrow, 1962.

———. *The Final Challenge: The American Frontier, 1804–1845*. New York: Morrow, 1974.

Wainwright, Nicholas B. *George Croghan, Wilderness Diplomat*. Chapel Hill: University of North Carolina Press, 1959.

Wallace, Anthony F. C. *King of the Delawares: Teedyuscung, 1700–1763*. Philadelphia: University of Pennsylvania Press, 1961.

———. "Women, Land and Society: Three Aspects of Aboriginal Delaware Life." *Pennsylvania Archaeologist* 17, nos. 1–4 (1947): 1–35.

Wallace, Paul A. W. *Conrad Weiser, 1696–1760: Friend of Colonist and Mohawk*. 1945. Reprint. New York: Russell & Russell, 1971.

———. *Indian Paths of Pennsylvania*. Harrisburg: Pennsylvania Historical and Museum Commission, 1971.

———. *Indians in Pennsylvania*. Harrisburg: Pennsylvania Historical and Museum Commission, 1961.

———. *The Muhlenbergs of Pennsylvania*. Philadelphia: University of Pennsylvania Press, 1950.

———. *Thirty Thousand Miles with John Heckewelder*. Pittsburgh: University of Pittsburgh Press, 1958.

Washburn, Wilcomb E. "Seventeenth-Century Indian Wars." In *Handbook of the North American Indians*, ed. Bruce G. Trigger. 15:89–100. Washington, D.C.: Smithsonian Institution, 1978.

Washington, George. *The Journal of Major George Washington*. 1754. Reprint. New York: Readex Microprint, 1966.

Weinland, Joseph E. *The Romantic Story of Schoenbrunn: The First Town in Ohio*. Dover, Ohio: Seibert Printing Company, 1930.

Weinlick, John R. *Count Zinzendorf*. New York: Abingdon Press, 1956.

Weslager, C. A. *The Delaware Indian Westward Migration*. Wallingford, Pa.: Middle Atlantic Press, 1978.

———. *The Delaware Indians: A History*. New Brunswick, N.J.: Rutgers University Press, 1989.

Wilcox, Frank N. *Ohio Indian Trails*. 2d ed. Cleveland: Gates Press, 1933.

Wilde, Margaret, trans. "Heckewelder's Salem Diary, 1779–1781." Commissioned by Earl P. Olmstead. Moravian Archives, Bethlehem, Pa.

———. "Zeisberger's Lichtenau Diary, 1776–1780." Commissioned by Earl P. Olmstead. Moravian Archives, Bethlehem, Pa.

———. "Zeisberger's New Schoenbrunn Diary, 1779–1781." Commissioned by Earl P. Olmstead. Moravian Archives, Bethlehem, Pa.

Withers, Alexander S. *Chronicles of Border Warfare*. Ed. Reuben G. Thwaites. Cincinnati: Stewart & Lidd, 1920.

Wolff, Anthony. "The Heart of Savannah." *American Heritage* 22 (December 1970): 54–61.

Wright, Louis B. *The Atlantic Frontier*. New York: Alfred A. Knopf, 1947.

Zeisberger, David. "David Zeisberger's History of Northern American Indians." Ed. Archer Butler Hulbert and William Nathaniel Schwarze. In *Ohio Archaeological and Historical Quarterly* 19 (April and January 1910): 1–173.

———. *Diary of David Zeisberger, a Moravian Missionary among the Indians of Ohio*. Trans. and ed. Eugene F. Bliss. 2 vols. Cincinnati: R. Clarke, 1885. Reprint. St. Clair Shores, Mich.: Scholarly Press, 1972.

———. "Diary of David Zeisberger and Gottlob Sensemann, Journey to Goschgoschunk on the Ohio and Their Arrival There, 1768." Trans. Archer B. Hulbert and William N. Schwarze. *The Moravian Record,* Ohio Archaeological and Historical Society Publication 21 (1912): 42–69.

———. "Diary of David Zeisberger's Journey to the Ohio, Called the 'Allegene,' from September 20th to November 16th, 1767," trans. Archer Butler Hulbert and William Nathaniel Schwarze. *The Moravian Records*, Ohio Archaeological and Historical Society Publication 21 (1912): 42–69.

Index